W9-CTC-137

The New Meaning

of Treason

OTHER BOOKS BY REBECCA WEST

REBECCA WEST

The New Meaning of Treason

THE VIKING PRESS: NEW YORK

M B G

Grateful acknowledgment is made to The New Yorker, *in which portions of* Parts I *and* II *originally appeared, in somewhat different form; and to* Esquire, *in which a chapter from Part III was first published.*

The lines from "If" and "Recessional" by Rudyard Kipling, quoted on pages 136 and 139, are from Rewards and Fairies, *Copyright 1910 by Rudyard Kipling, and are reprinted by permission of Mrs. George Bambridge, Double-day & Company, Inc., and The Macmillan Company of Canada Ltd.*

Library of Congress catalog card number: 64-25703
Set in Baskerville and Bulmer types by The Colonial Press, Inc.
Printed in U.S.A.

TO THE MEMORY OF HAROLD ROSS,

FIRST EDITOR OF *THE NEW YORKER*

FOREWORD

THROUGHOUT this book, when I write of con-
victed persons whose trials received no great publicity and who
are likely to return to the outer world after a short period, I
allude to them by names other than their own. The reader should
be warned that these persons and all others mentioned in these
pages must not be regarded as holding the same opinions and
performing the same sorts of action as they did when they broke
the law. A number of them have not changed, but there are those
who can hardly be considered as the same persons. This is either
because they committed their offences under pressure, or because
they went on growing. For two of those who have made other
lives, I have come to feel great respect and admiration.

The first version of *The Meaning of Treason* was written because I had reported the trials of William Joyce and John Amery
for *The New Yorker,* and my interest in these two men made me
attend the trials of some other pro-Nazis who had been involved
with disloyalty of one kind or another. I was encouraged to make
a book about these people by an eminent lawyer who was concerned because the shortage of newsprint due to the war meant
that these trials were either not reported or were reported too
briefly for the public to gain any real information regarding a
significant tendency. When I began my book I was under the
impression that I was dealing with a spent force only interesting
as part of the past, but when I was halfway through it Alan Nunn
May followed William Joyce into the dock of the Old Bailey, and
I became aware that the force still lived, and that its significance
was even more grave than had been supposed.

Since then I have attempted to keep abreast with the story of
disloyalty as it has unfolded, and the present version of this book
carries it on to the end of 1963. The subject is now so large that
I have been obliged to leave unanswered many questions which
will occur to the reader. For this reason I would like to recom-

mend Mr. Sanche de Gramont's *The Secret War* (Putnam, 1962), which gives much information about the espionage and counter-espionage organizations of the world, as does Mr. Allen Dulles's *The Craft of Intelligence* (Harper and Row, 1963); the report of the Royal Commission appointed by the Canadian Government to investigate the Atom Spy Ring (1946) and the United States Government publication, *Soviet Atomic Espionage* (1951), which gives a concise and accurate account of transactions often misrepresented; Mr. James B. Donovan's *Strangers on a Bridge: The Case of Colonel Abel* (Atheneum, 1964), which thoroughly explores a modern case of espionage; and the Report of the Royal Commission appointed by the Australian Government to investigate matters arising out of the defection of the Soviet diplomat Petrov (1955), which gives a vivid picture of unfamiliar aspects of the problem.

CONTENTS

⇛ I ⇚

The Revolutionary

1

THE IDEA of a traitor first became real to the British of our time when they heard the voice of William Joyce on the radio during the war. The conception of treachery first became real to them when he was brought to trial as a radio traitor. For he was something new in the history of the world. Never before have people known the voice of one they had never seen as well as if he had been a husband or a brother or a close friend; and had they foreseen such a miracle they could not have imagined that this familiar unknown would speak to them only to prophesy their death and ruin. A great many people had experienced this hideous novelty, for it was easy to chance on Joyce's wave length when one was tuning in on the English stations, and there was a rasping yet rich quality about his voice which made it difficult not to go on listening; and he was nearly convincing in his assurance. It seemed as if one had better hearken and take warning when he suggested that the destiny of the people he had left in England was death, and the destiny of his new masters in Germany life and conquest, and that, therefore, his listeners had better change sides and submit; and he had the advantage that the news in the papers confirmed what he said. He was not only alarming, he was ugly. He opened a vista into a mean life. He always spoke as if he was better fed and better clothed than we were, and so, we now know, he was. He went farther than that mockery of his own people's plight. He sinned that sin which travesties legitimate hatred because it is felt for kindred, as incest is the travesty of legitimate love. When the U-boats were sinking so many of our ships that to open the newspapers was to see the faces of drowned sailors, he rolled the figures of our lost tonnage on his tongue. When we were facing the hazard of D-day, he rejoiced in the thought of the English dead which would soon lie under the West Wall.

So all the curious went off to the Central Criminal Court on September 17, 1945, when he came up for trial. The Old Bailey

3

was as it had not been before the war and is not now. Because of
the blitz it stood in a beautiful desert of charred stone. Churches
stood blackened but apparently intact; birds, however, flew
through the empty sockets of the windows, and long grass grew
around their altars. A red brick Georgian mansion, hidden for a
century by sordid warehouses, looked at the dome of Saint
Paul's, now astonishingly great, across acres where willow-herb,
its last purple flowers passing into silver clouds of seed dust, and
yellow ragwort grew from the ground plan of a city drawn in
rubble. The grey stone of the Old Bailey itself had been gashed
by a bomb. Its solidarity had been sliced as if it were a cake, and
the walls of the slice were crude new red brick. Inside the
building, because there was not yet the labour to take down the
heavy black-out, the halls and passages and stairs were in perpetual dusk. The courtroom—the Court No. 1, where all the most
famous criminal trials of modern times have taken place—was lit
by electric light, for the shattered glass dome had not yet been
rebuilt. Bare boards filled it in, giving an odd-come-short look to
what had been a fine room in its austere way.

The strong light was merciless to William Joyce, whose appearance was a shock to all of us who knew him only over the air.
His voice had suggested a large and flashy handsomeness, but
he was a tiny little creature and not handsome at all. His hair
was mouse-coloured and sparse, particularly above his ears, and
his pinched and misshapen nose was joined to his face at an odd
angle. His eyes were hard and shiny, and above them his thick
eyebrows were pale and irregular. His neck was long, his shoulders narrow and sloping, his arms very short and thick. His body
looked flimsy and coarse. There was nothing individual about
him except a deep scar running across his right cheek from his
ear to the corner of his mouth. But this did not create the savage
and marred distinction that it might suggest, for it gave a mincing immobility to his small mouth. He was dressed with a
dandyish preciosity which gave no impression of well-being, only
of nervousness. He was like an ugly version of Scott Fitzgerald,
but more nervous. He moved with a jerky formality and, when
he bowed to the judge, his bow seemed sincerely respectful but
entirely inappropriate to the occasion, and it was difficult to
think of any occasion to which it would have been appropriate.

He had been defying us all. Yet there was nobody in the

court who did not look superior to him. The men and women in the jury box were all middle-aged, since the armies had not yet come home, and, like everybody else in England at that date, they were puffy and haggard. But they were all more pleasant to look at and more obviously trustworthy than the homely and eccentric little man in the dock; and compared with the judicial bench which he faced he was, of course, at an immense disadvantage, as we all should be, for its dignity is authentic. The judge sat in a high-backed chair, the sword of justice in its jewelled scabbard affixed to the oak panel behind him, splendid in his scarlet robe, with its neckband of fine white linen and its deep cuffs and sash of purplish-black taffeta. Beside him, their chairs set farther back as a sign of their inferiority to him, sat the Lord Mayor of London and two aldermen, wearing antique robes of black silk with flowing white cravats and gold chains with pendant badges of office worked in precious metals and enamel. It sometimes happens, and it happened then, that these pompous trappings are given real significance by the faces of men who wear them. Judges are chosen for intellect and character, and city honours must be won by intellect combined with competence at the least, and men in both positions must have the patience to carry out tedious routines over decades, and the story is often written on their features.

Looking from the bench to the dock, it could be seen that not in any sane community would William Joyce have had the ghost of a chance of holding such offices as these. This was tragic, as appeared when he was asked to plead and he said, "Not guilty." Those two words were the most impressive uttered during the trial. The famous voice was let loose. For a fraction of a second we heard its familiar quality. It was as it had sounded for six years, reverberating with the desire for power. Never was there a more perfect voice for a demagogue, for its reverberations were certain to awake echoes in every heart tumid with the same desire. Given this passionate ambition to exercise authority, which as this scene showed could not be gratified, what could he ever have done but use his trick of gathering together other poor fellows luckless in the same way, so that they might overturn the sane community that was bound to reject them, and substitute a mad one that would regard them kindly?

That was the reason why he was in the dock; that, and Irish

history. For it was at once apparent that this trial, like the great treason trial of the First World War, which sent Sir Roger Casement to the gallows, had started on the other side of the Saint George's Channel. There had been rumours that Joyce was Irish, but they had never been officially confirmed, and his accent was difficult to identify. But there was no doubt about it when one saw him in the dock. He had the real Donnybrook air. He was a not very fortunate example of the small, nippy, jig-dancing kind of Irish peasant, and the appearance of his brother, who attended the court every day in a state of great suffering, proved the family's origin. Quentin Joyce, who was then twenty-eight, was eleven years William's junior. He was the better-looking of the two, with a sturdy body, a fresh colour, thick lustrous brown hair, and the soft eyes of a cow. Nobody could mistake him for anything but a country-bred Irishman, and there were as clear traces of Irish origins in many of the followers of Joyce who watched the trial. True, his best friend was visibly a Scot: a black Highlander, with fierce black eyes blazing behind thick glasses, a tiny fuzz of black hair fancifully arranged on his prematurely bald head, and wrists and ankles as thin as lead piping. He was Angus MacNab, the editor of a Fascist paper. He was plainly foredoomed to follow odd bypaths, and a variation in circumstances might have found him just as happily a spirit-ualist medium or a believer in the lost ten tribes of Israel. As it was, he was wholly committed to Joyce. So too were the rank and file of the faithful, who were for the most part men of violent and unhappy appearance, with a look of animal shyness and ferocity, and, in some cases, a measure of animal beauty. They were on the whole rather darker than one would expect in subscribers to the Aryan theory. One, especially, looked like a true gipsy. Many of them had an Irish cast of feature, and some bore Irish names. It was to be remembered that Joyce had seceded from Mosley's movement some years before the war and had started his own. These were not at all like Mosleyites, who were as a rule of a more varied and more cheerfully brutal type.

The case was tinged with irony from the start because the prosecuting counsel for the Crown was Sir Hartley Shawcross, the Attorney-General appointed by the new Labour Government. People in court were anxious to see what he was like, for when the Labour Party had previously held office it had experienced some difficulty in getting law officers of the quality the Tories could provide; and it was a relief to find that he was a winning personality with a gift for setting out a lucid argument in the manner of a great advocate. He was, in fact, certain to enjoy just that success which the man he was prosecuting had desired so much as to put himself in danger of a capital charge; a capital charge of which he was sure, it seemed in the earlier parts of the case, to be convicted.

There were three counts in the indictment brought against him. He had offended, it seemed, against the root of the law against treason: a statute in which Edward III, in the year 1351, "at the request of the lords and commons" declared that "if a man do levy war against our Lord the King in his realm or be adherent to the King's enemies in his realm, giving them aid and comfort in the realm or elsewhere," he was guilty of treason. So the Clerk of the Court, Sir Wilfred Knops, said: "William Joyce, you are charged in an indictment containing three counts with high treason. The particulars in the first count are that on the 18th September, 1939 and on other days between that day and the 29th May, 1945, you, being a person owing allegiance to our Lord the King, and when a war was being carried on by the German realm against our King, did traitorously adhere to the King's enemies, in parts beyond the seas, that is to say in Germany, by broadcasting propaganda. In a second count of the same indictment, it is charged that you, on the 26th September, 1940, being a person owing allegiance as in the other count, adhered to the King's enemies by purporting to become naturalized as a subject of Germany. And in the third count, the particulars are the same as in the first count, that is to say, you are charged with broadcasting propaganda, but the dates are different, and the dates in this case are the eighteenth day of September, 1939, and on days between that day and the second day of July, 1940, being then to wit, on the said several days, a person owing allegiance to our Lord the King." Later the first two counts were amended, for reasons emerging during the trial, and he was described in them as "a British subject," but, significantly, no such change was made in the third.

It seemed as if William Joyce must be found guilty on the first two of these counts. What was first told of his life in court showed it as an open-and-shut case. William Joyce's dead father had been a Galway man named Michael Joyce, who had worked as a builder and contractor in America during the nineties; he married in May 1902 a Lancashire girl named Gertrude Emily Brooke in New York at the Roman Catholic Church of All Saints on Madison Avenue and 129th Street, and had settled down with her in Brooklyn, where William had been born in 1906. Later inquiry into the story behind the evidence showed their life to have been very pleasant. The Joyces must have been quite prosperous. They lived in a very agreeable house, now a realtor's office, on a corner lot in a broad street planted with trees, charming with the square, substantial, moderate charm of old Brooklyn. Now that street is occupied at one end by Negroes and at the other by Italians, but then it was a centre of the staider Irish, and the solid petty-bourgeois German quarter was not far off.

In 1909 he took his family back to Ireland, a decision he must often have regretted. But at the time he must still have been very happy. By the time the First World War broke out he was the owner of considerable house property in County Mayo and County Galway, and he was manager of the horse-tramway system in Galway.

In 1922 he left Ireland, because it had become Eire. He was one of those native Irish who were against their own kind and on the side of the English oppressor. Nowadays we recognize the existence of such people, but fancy them quislings, which is quite often unjust. Doubtless some of them were seduced by bribery dispensed by Dublin Castle, but many, and amongst those we must include Michael Joyce, were people who honestly loved law and order and preferred the smart uniforms and soldierly bearing of the English garrisons and the Royal Irish Constabulary to the furtive slouching of a peasantry distracted by poverty and revolutionary fever. The error of such people was insufficient inquiry into first causes, but for simple natures who went by surface indications the choice was natural enough.

In any case Michael Joyce paid the price of his convictions, and it was not light. He came to England for three very good reasons. The first was that the horse-tramways in Galway were abolished. One may deduce that he was a man of courage because he apparently ranked that reason as equal in importance to the other two, which were that his neighbours had been so revolted by his British sympathies that they burned down his house, and that he had been confused in many people's minds with an informer, also called Michael Joyce, who had denounced a priest to the Black and Tans. (It must be noted that William Joyce's father was indeed innocent of this crime, and, so far as is known, of any other; the identity of the other Michael Joyce was well established.)

On arriving in England the Joyces settled in Lancashire, and William alone made his way down to London, where he enrolled as a science student at Battersea Polytechnic. In August 1922 he, being sixteen years of age, sent a letter of application to the London University Officers' Training Corps, in which he said he wanted to study with a view to being nominated by the university for a commission in the Regular Army. This letter was read in court, and it is very touching. It must have startled the recipient. It would not (nor would the note Joyce's father wrote later in support of the application) have convinced him that by the still snobbish standards of 1922 this was a likely candidate for the officers' mess, but it had another point of interest. "I have served with the irregular forces of the Crown in an Intelligence capacity, against the Irish guerrillas. In command of a squad of sub-agents I was subordinate to the late Captain P. W. Keating, 2nd RUR, who was drowned in the *Egypt* accident. I have a knowledge of the rudiments of Musketry, Bayonet Fighting, and Squad Drill." The *Egypt* was sunk off Ushant in May 1922; which meant that, if this story was true, the boy was engaged in guerrilla fighting with the Black and Tans when he was fifteen years old. The story was true. A photograph of him taken at that time shows him in a battle dress, and a number of people remembered this phase of his life. Later, on an official form, he gave the duration of his service as four months, named the regiment with which he had been associated as the Worcestershires. Further confirmation was given during his trial by an old man from County Galway who stood in the crowd outside and expressed to bystanders his hearty desire that William Joyce should be hanged for treason against the King of England, on the ground that he had worked with the Black and Tans in persecuting the Irish when they were revolting against the English. The crowd, with that toleration which foreigners possibly correctly suspect of being a form of smugness, was amused by the inconsistency.

But there was something in the letter more relevant to his trial. "I must now," wrote Joyce, "mention a point which I hope will not give rise to difficulties. I was born in America, but of British parents. I left America when two years of age, have not returned since, and do not propose to return. I was informed, at the brigade headquarters of the district in which I was stationed in Ireland, that I possessed the same rights and privileges as I would if of natural British birth. I can obtain testimonials as to my loyalty to the Crown. I am in no way connected with the United States of America, against which, as against all other nations, I am prepared to draw the sword in British interests. As a young man of pure British descent, some of whose forefathers have held high position in the British army, I have always been desirous of devoting what little capability and energy I may possess to the country which I love so dearly. I ask that you may inform me if the accident of my birth, to which I refer above, will affect my position. I shall be in London for the September Matriculation Examination and I hope to commence studies at the London University at the beginning of the next academic year. I trust that you will reply as soon as possible, and that your reply will be favourable to my aspirations." At an interview with an official of the OTC he conveyed that he was "in doubt as to whether he was a 'British subject of pure European descent,'" a doubt which must have been honest if he expressed it at all in view of the ardent hope expressed in his letter; but he asserted that his father had never been naturalized. This the father confirmed when the official wrote to him for further particulars. "Dear Sir, your letter of the 23rd October received. Would have replied sooner, but have been away from home. With regard to my son William. He was born in America, I was born in Ireland. His mother was born in England. We are all British and not American citizens."

Now, there was some doubt in William Joyce's mind about his status. Throughout his life when he was filling in official forms he was apt to give his birthplace as Ireland or England, although he had a birth certificate which gave it as Brooklyn. But his disquiet was vague. In the statement he made to the

Intelligence officers on his arrest he expressed himself un-certainly. "I understand, though I have no documents to prove my statement, that my father was American by naturaliza-tion at the time of my birth, and I believe he lost his American citizenship later through failing to renew it, because we left America in 1909 when I was three years old. We were generally treated as British subjects during our stay in Ireland and Eng-land. I was in Ireland from 1909 till 1921 when I came to England. We were always treated as British during the period of my stay in England whether we were or not." But when his defence counsel began to outline his case, there was not the faintest doubt about it: William Joyce had not been born a British subject. Documents were brought into court which showed that Michael Joyce had become an American citizen in 1894, twelve years before the birth of William at 1377 Herkimer Street, Brooklyn. In 1909 he had travelled back to England on an American passport. When he and his wife had oscillated between Lancashire and Galway during the First World War they had had to register under the Aliens Act 1915. An old man gave evidence, who had known Michael Joyce all his life. On Joyce's advice this witness had gone to America, worked as a civil engineer, and taken American citizenship, but he had re-turned to Great Britain during the First World War and had been greatly inconvenienced by his alien status. He spoke of a visit to Mrs. Joyce, who was known as Queenie, and who seems to have been very well liked, at her house in a Lancashire town. They had exchanged commiserations because they both had to report all their movements to the police. His cracked old voice evoked a picture of two people cosily grumbling together over their cups of good strong tea thirty years ago.

William's brother Quentin went into the witness box. There passed between him and the man in the dock a nod and a smile of pure love. One realized that life in this strange family must sometimes have been great fun. But it evidently had not been fun lately. Quentin told the court that his father had died in 1941, shortly after the house in which he had lived for eight-een years had been destroyed by a bomb, and his mother had died in 1944. Out of the wreckage of the house there had been recovered a few boxes full of papers, but none had any bearing on the question of the family's nationality, and there was a reason for that. Michael Joyce had told young Quentin, when he was ten years old, that he and all the family were American citizens but had bade him never to speak of it, and had in later years often reiterated this warning. Finally, in 1934, the boy, who was then sixteen, had seen him burn a number of papers, including what appeared to be an American passport. He had given a reason for what he was doing, but the witness was not required to repeat it. The date suggests what that reason may have been. By that time the police knew William Joyce as a troublesome instigator of street fighting and attacks on Communists and Jews, and in November 1934 Joyce was prosecuted, together with Sir Oswald Mosley and two other Fascists, on a charge of riotous assembly at Worthing; and though this prosecution failed, it indicated a serious attempt by the authorities to rid themselves of the nuisance of Fascist-planned disorder. Michael Joyce had every reason to fear that, if the police ever got an inkling of his secret, they would deport his son and, not improbably, the whole family.

Now it seemed as impossible to convict William Joyce as it had been, when the prosecution was opening its case, to imagine his acquittal. The child of a naturalized American citizen, born after his father's naturalization, is an American citizen by birth. Therefore William Joyce owed the King of England no allegiance such as arises out of British nationality. It seemed he must go scot free. He had committed no offence whatsoever in becoming a naturalized German subject on September 26, 1940. That would have been high treason had he been a British subject, for a British subject is forbidden by law to become the naturalized subject of an enemy country in wartime. But when he took out his naturalization papers in Germany he was an American citizen, and even the American government could not have questioned his action, being then at peace with Germany, which did not declare war on the United States until December 11, 1941. It followed, then, that his broadcasting was, if only his nationality had to be considered, an offence against nobody. After September 26, 1940, he had been a good German working for the fatherland. But our law is not really as arbitrary as all that. Allegiance is not exacted by the Crown from a subject simply because the Crown is the Crown. The idea of the divine right of kings is a comparatively modern vulgarity. According to tradition and logic, the state gives protection to all men within its confines, and in return exacts their obedience to its laws; and the process is reciprocal. When men within the confines of the state are obedient to its laws they have a right to claim its protection. It is a maxim of the law, quoted by Coke in the sixteenth century, that "protection draws allegiance, and allegiance draws protection" (*protectio trahit subjectionem, et subjectio protectionem*). It was laid down in 1608, by reference to the case of Sherley, a Frenchman who had come to England and joined in a conspiracy against the King and Queen, that such a man "owed to the King obedience, that is, so long as he was within the King's protection." That is fair enough; and indeed very fair, if the limitations which were applied to this proposition are considered. For in Hale's *History of the Pleas of the Crown,* in the seventeenth century, it was written: "Because as the subject hath his protection from the King and his laws, so on the other side the subject is bound by his allegiance to be true and faithful to the King. And hence it is, that if an alien enemy come into this kingdom hostilely to invade it, if he be taken, he shall be dealt with as an enemy, but not as a traitor, because he violates no trust nor allegiance. But if an alien, the subject of a foreign prince in amity with the King, live here, and enjoy the benefit of the King's protection, and commit a treason, he shall be judged and executed, as a traitor, for he owes a local allegiance."

There could be no doubt whatsoever that William Joyce owed that kind of allegiance. He had certainly enjoyed the protection of the English law for some thirty years preceding his departure to Germany. The lawyers for the defence, in proving that he did not owe the natural kind of allegiance which springs from British birth, had found themselves under the necessity of disproving beyond all doubt that he owed this other acquired kind; and there were the two damning sentences in his statement: "We were generally counted as British subjects during our stay in Ireland and England. . . . We were always treated as British during the period of my stay in England whether we were or not." Thus, though an alien, William Joyce owed the Crown allegiance and was capable of committing treason against it. Again he was heading for conviction. But not for certain. There was a definition of the law which was likely to help him.

In 1707 an assembly of judges laid it down that "if such

alien seeking the Protection of the Crown having a Family and Effects here should during a War with his Native Country go thither and there Adhere to the King's Enemies for the purpose of Hostility, He might be dealt with as a Traitor. For he came and settled here under the Protection of the Crown. And though his Person was removed for a time, his Effects and Family continued still under the same Protection."

Now, the letter of this judgment did not apply to William Joyce. He had taken his wife with him to Germany, and by that marriage he was childless. He had two children by a former marriage, but they were in the care of their mother and did not enter into this case. The effects he possessed when he quitted England were of such a trifling nature that it would be fairer to regard them as abandoned rather than as left under the protection of the Crown. Had he retained any substantial property in the country he would not have had to avail himself of the provisions of the Poor Prisoners' Defence Act. But he was within the sphere of the spirit of the judgment. Joyce disappeared from England at some time between August 29, 1939—when he issued an order dissolving the National Socialist League, the Fascist organization of which he was the head—and September 18, when he entered the service of the German radio. He was the holder of a British passport; it was part of his lifelong masquerade as a British subject. He had declared on the application papers that he had been born in Galway and had not "lost the status of British subject thus acquired." He obtained his passport on July 6, 1933, and there is perhaps some significance in that date. He had become a member of the British Fascists in 1923, when he was seventeen, but had left this organization after two years, to become later an active member of the Conservative Party. In January 1933 Hitler seized power, and later in the year Mosley formed the British Union of Fascists, which William Joyce joined. This passport was, like all British passports, valid for five years. When July 1938 came round he let it lapse, but applied on September 24, 1938, for a renewal for the customary period of one year; and there is, perhaps, some significance in that date also, for the Munich Agreement was signed on September 29. The next year he was careful not to let it lapse. He made an application for renewal over a month before its expiry, on August 24, 1939, and there was certainly some significance in that date, for war broke out on September 3. Each of these renewals was dated as if the application had been made when the passport expired. So when William Joyce went to Germany he was the holder of a British passport which was valid until the beginning of July 1940. That was why the third count of the indictment charged him with committing high treason by broadcasting between "the eighteenth day of September, 1939, and on divers other days thereafter, and between that day and the second day of July, 1940, being then to wit, on the said several days, a person owing allegiance to our Lord the King." It was, in fact, the case for the prosecution that a person obtaining a passport placed himself thereby under the protection of the Crown and owed it allegiance until the passport expired.

No ruling on the point existed, because no case of treason involving temporary allegiance had been tried during the comparatively recent period when passports, in their modern sense, have been in use, so the judge had to make a new ruling; and for one sultry afternoon and a sultrier morning the prosecuting and defending counsel bobbed up and down in front of the bench, putting the arguments for and against the broadening of the law by inclusion of this modern circumstance. People with legal minds were entranced, and others slept. Joyce enjoyed this part of the trial very much, and frequently passed down to his counsel notes that were characteristically odd. Like all prisoners in the dock, he had been given octavo sheets to write on, and could certainly have had as many as he wanted. But when he wrote a note he tore off irregularly shaped pieces and covered them with grotesquely large handwriting; so large that it could be read by people sitting in the gallery. One ended with the words, "but it is not important." His enjoyment of the argument was not unnatural in one who loved complications, for no stage of it was simple. Much depended on the nature of a passport, and this had never been defined by the law, for a passport has been different things at different times and has never been merely one thing at a time. It was originally a licence given by the Crown to a subject who wished to leave the realm, an act as a rule prohibited because it deprived the King of a man's military services; but it was also a licence given to an alien to travel through the realm; and it was a pass given to soldiers going home on leave, or paupers discharged from a hospital. Through the ages it changed its character to a demand by the issuing state that the person and property of one of its subjects shall be respected by other states when he travels in their realms; a voucher of his respectability, demanded by the states he intends to visit, as a precaution against crime and political conspiracy; and a source of revenue to the states, which charged heavily for such permits. Of its protective nature in our day there can be little doubt, since the preamable on every British passport announces that "we," the Foreign Secretary of the day, "request and require in the Name of His Majesty all those whom it may concern to allow the bearer to pass freely without let or hindrance, and to afford him or her every assistance and protection of which he or she may stand in need." In 1905 the Lord Chief Justice of that day, Lord Alverstone, defined a passport as "a document issued in the name of a Sovereign, on the responsibility of a Minister of the Crown, to a named individual, intended to be presented to the governments of foreign nations and to be used for that individual's protection as a British subject in foreign countries."

It is a strange thing that many people found something distasteful in this argument that William Joyce, alien by birth, who had acquired a temporary and local allegiance, did not lose it when he left England to take service with the Nazis because he took his British passport with him. They did not reflect on what would have followed from the rejection of this argument. If it had been established that a temporary allegiance could not be carried over by an alien to the Continent, that he divested himself of it by the mere act of passing beyond the three-mile territorial limits, then an alien who was resident in England and for some reason had been given a British passport (as sometimes happens in the case of one who has rendered special services to England) could pop across the Channel, conspire with an enemy of England at Calais, and pop back again, not only once but hundreds of times, and never be tried for treason, because at three miles from Dover he lost his duty of allegiance.

Joyce's counsel also argued that his client's passport could give him no protection because he had acquired it by a false statement; yet it was hard to see how it could fail to protect him until the fraud was discovered and the passport was withdrawn. Supposing that William Joyce had fallen out with the Germans during 1940 and had become a civil internee; he could have called on the assistance of the Swiss Embassy in Berlin, as Switzerland was "the protective power" appointed to safeguard the interests of Britons in hostile territory during wartime.

All this filigree work delighted the little man in the dock, who watched his lawyers with a cynical brightness, as if he were interested in seeing whether they could get away with all this nonsense but had no warmer concern with the proceedings. He showed no special excitement, only a continuance of amused curiosity, when on the third day of the trial, at the end of the morning, the judge announced that he would give his ruling on these legal submissions after the luncheon interval; and at two o'clock he returned to the dock with his usual eccentric excess of military smartness and his sustained tight-lipped derisiveness. The judge announced that "beyond a shadow of doubt" William Joyce had owed allegiance to the Crown of this country when he applied for his passport, and that nothing had happened to put an end to that allegiance during the period when the passpport was valid. In other words, he ruled that a person holding a British passport owed allegiance to the Crown even when he was outside the realm. This ruling made it quite certain that William Joyce was going to be sentenced to death.

If the sentence was carried out he would die the most completely unnecessary death that any criminal has ever died on the gallows. He was the victim of his own and his father's lifelong determination to lie about their nationality. For had he not renewed his English passport, and had he left England for Germany on the American passport which was rightfully his, no power on earth could have touched him. As he became a German citizen by naturalization before America came into the war, he could never have been the subject of prosecution under the American laws of treason.

It is not easy to understand why the family practised this imposture; Michael Joyce is an enigmatic figure. Since he loved England it would have been more natural for him to emigrate to England than to America. There were, of course, some pro-English Irish who went to America to act as informers on the anti-English Irish, who were at that time fomenting the Fenian and other separatist movements. It is said that Michael Joyce was a candid and honourable man, but even such could, even against their own wish, be entangled in the fierce intrigues and counter-intrigues of those days. It is very difficult to see why, when Michael Joyce returned to England and found his American citizenship such a burden that he warned his children to keep it a deadly secret, he never took the simple steps which would have readmitted him to British nationality. It would have cost him only a few pounds, and he was in those years well-to-do. It cannot have been the legal technicalities which baffled him; his wife's brother was a solicitor. The official resistance to the process was not great. Can Michael Joyce have feared to remind either the British or the American government of his existence? Had he once been involved in some imbroglio and got a black mark against his name? Was he working his passage home when he gained the good opinion of the Royal Irish Constabulary? There is probably nobody alive now who knows. All that we can be sure of is that the story was probably incredibly complicated. Nothing was simple in that world of espionage and counterespionage.

William Joyce was being sentenced to death because his father had tried to save him from what must have been a lesser danger; and sentence was passed on him in a terrible way, because nobody in court felt any emotion at all. People wanted Joyce to pay the proper legal penalty for his treason, but not because they felt any personal hatred against him. They wanted to be sure that in any other war this peculiarly odious form of treachery, which invaded the ears of frightened people, would be discouraged before it began, and that was about the limit of their interest in the matter. At no other such trial have the spectators, as soon as the jury went out to consider their verdict and the judge retired from the bench and the prisoner was taken down to the cells, got up from their seats and strolled about and chattered as if they were at a theatre between the acts. At no other such trial have the jury come back from considering the verdict looking as if they had been out for a cup of tea. And at no other such trial has the judge assumed the black cap—which is not a cap at all but a piece of black cloth that an attendant lays across his wig—as if it were in fact just a piece of black cloth laid across his wig. He spoke the words of the sentence of death reverently, and they were awful, as they always must be: "William Joyce, the sentence of the Court upon you is, that you be taken from this place to a lawful prison, and thence to a place of execution, and that you be there hanged by the neck until you are dead; and that your body be afterwards buried within the precincts of the prison in which you shall have been confined before your execution. And may the Lord have mercy on your soul."

But the effect of these words was, on this uniquely shallow occasion, soon dissipated. It was indeed pitiful when Joyce was asked if he wanted to make a statement before sentence was passed on him, and he shook his head, the hungry and inordinate voice in him at last defeated. He had been even more pitiful earlier in the trial, when the judge had warned the jury to consider very carefully their verdict because a person found guilty must be sentenced to death, for he had put up his hand and touched his neck with a look of wonder. That he deserved pity was noted by the intellect; pity was not felt. Nor was anybody in the court very much moved by the extreme courage with which he bore himself, though that was remarkable. He listened to the sentence with his head high, gave one of his absurd stiff bows, and ran down to the cells, smiling and waving to his brother and his friends, acting gaiety without a flaw. Such a performance would once have moved us, but not then. All had changed. Even a trial for a capital offence was then quite different from what it had been before the war, when the spectators were living in a state of security, and the prisoner was an exceptionally unfortunate person who had strayed into a district not generally visited, perhaps for lack of boldness. But every man and woman who attended Joyce's trial had at some time during the last six years been in danger of undeserved death or pain, and had shown, or seen others showing, great courage. William Joyce could not make any claim on them by being pitiful and brave. He could not arouse their interest because it was exceptional to meet violent death, since he was in the dock by reason of failure to acquit himself well when that had been their common destiny. So they turned away from him and left the court as if it had been a cinema or concert. But in the dark corridor a woman said, "I am glad his mother's dead. She lived near us in Dulwich. She was a sweet little lady, a tiny little woman. I often used to stand with her in the fish queue. In fact, that's how I met her. One day after the blitz had been very bad I said something about that blasted Lord Haw-Haw, and someone said, 'Hush, that's his mother right beside you,' and I felt dreadful. But she only said—but she was ever so Irish, and I can't speak like she did—'Never mind, my dear, I'm sure you didn't mean it unkindly.' " This story recalled the lilt of affection of the old man in the witness box when he had spoken of having tea with Queenie.

The dark corridor passed to a twilit landing. Down a shadowed staircase the band of Fascists were descending, tears shining on their astonished faces. Joyce's brother walked slowly, his eyes that were soft and brown like a cow's now narrowed and wet, and the slight blond solicitor just behind him. There was a block, and for a minute the crowd all stood still. The solicitor plucked at Quentin Joyce's jacket and said kindly, "This is just what he expected, you know." "Yes," said his brother, "I know it's just what he expected." The crowd moved on, but after it had gone down a few steps the solicitor plucked at the young man's jacket again and said, "It's the appeal that matters, you know," and Quentin said, "Yes, I know. The appeal's everything."

At the counter where the spectators had to collect their umbrellas and coats, a jurywoman was saying good-bye to one of her colleagues. They were shaking hands warmly and expressing hopes that they would meet again. They might have been people parting at the end of a cruise. Jostling them were the Fascists, waiting for their raincoats, garments which those of their kind affect in all weathers, in imitation of Hitler. The young man who looked like a gipsy held his head down. Heavy tears were hanging on his long black lashes. He and his friends still looked amazed. They had wanted people to die by violence, but they had not expected the lot to fall on any of their own number. Another dark and passionate young man was accosted by a reporter, and he cried out in rage that he had been four years in Brixton Jail under Security Regulation 18B, all for patriotism, and he had come out to see the persecution of the finest patriot of all. His black eyes rolled and blazed about him. It did not do. About him were standing people who had been in the Dieppe expedition, at Arnhem, in submarines, in prison camps; even the women knew about fear, had been, perhaps, on the Gestapo list of persons to be arrested immediately after the Germans conquered England. There was this new universality of horrible

experience, this vast common martyrdom, which made it no use
to play execution as if it were a trump card.

The little band of Fascists gathered together in a knot by
the door, and after they had wiped their faces, and composed
themselves, they went into the street. In the open space in front
of the building was a line of parked cars, and behind them stood
a crowd of silent people. The Fascists walked away from this
crowd, down a street that narrowed and lost itself in a network
of alleys. Nobody followed them, but they began to hurry. By
the time they got into the shelter of the alleys, they were almost
running.

2

THE fight between the Crown and William Joyce was
waged throughout four months and all across London. It began
in a golden September in the Old Bailey, came up again during
bright November in another damaged building, the Royal
Courts of Justice, usually called the Law Courts, and then went
to the House of Lords, where he made his last stand in the
precincts of Westminster Palace, which, still hugger-mugger
within from bomb damage, looked across the river through
December mists at one of the most moving memorials of the
blitz, Saint Thomas's Hospital, still treating the sick, but itself
architecturally sick after much bombing.

For a week the trial imposed its routine on Westminster Palace.
In the morning the spectators, either journalists or the faithful
in their Hitler raincoats with their look of Irishry and their wild
unhappiness, went up the stone staircase to a lobby full of
gossiping lawyers, outside the chamber where the Lords were
meeting temporarily because they had given their chamber over
to the Commons, whose home had been damaged by a bomb.
They were then taken in hand by the attendants of the House of
Lords, a body of spare and anonymous-looking men in ordinary
white-tie evening dress, with the silver-gilt badge of the Royal

Arms at their waists, under the supervision of a most elegant retired general, whose appearance and manners would have delighted Ouida. They shepherded all the pressmen and the prisoner's friends into the Royal Gallery, a hall conceived and executed in the brownest style of Victorian interior decoration, which held that everything rich, and not just plum cake, should be dark. On the wall strips of mulberry and gold brocade divide vast blackish frescoes in which a welter of arms and legs set at every angle round a few war horses suggests military effort; dingy gilded figures of kings and queens guard the doors; and in an alcove two togaed figures, quite black, though obviously they represent persons belonging to the white race, make expansive political gestures of a meliorist type. Brightness comes only from one object. In a corner there is a glass-covered display table lit from within, in which there lies a book inscribed with the names of peers and their sons who were killed in war, but not the last war, the one before that, of 1914 to 1918. Each day a fresh page is turned.

Every morning, while we waited, a bishop in black robes and huge white lawn sleeves hovered at the door of the chamber in which the Lords sat, ready to go in and say the prayers which open the day's session, until an attendant cried, "Make way for the Mace!" and we were all ordered off the strip of oatmeal matting which runs across the tiled floor. Then a procession came in, never quite at ease, it was so small and had never had enough start to get up the processional spirit. The Sergeant-at-Arms came first, carrying the great golden pepper-pot on a stalk which is the Mace. Another attendant followed, carrying a purse embroidered with the Royal Arms, representing the Great Seal. Then came the Lord Chancellor, Lord Jowitt, superb in his white full-bottomed wig, its curls lying in rows on his shoulders, and wearing a long black silk gown with a train carried by an attendant. He carried between the forefinger and thumb of each hand his black velvet cap. The ritual is not mere foolishness. The procession and the symbols are a mnemonic guide to the constitutional functions of the House of Lords, and are part of a complicated convention into which most of the legislative and judicial activities of Parliament fit conveniently enough, and which nobody would much care to rewrite, in view of the trickiness of procedure.

While prayers were said by the Lords we stood and waited. Around the room ran a shiny quilted red leather bench, but nobody ever sat on it except Joyce's solicitor, a slight and pensive dwarf with blond hair. This man, who was much respected in his profession, looked much older than he had at the first trial, and indeed he shortly afterwards became ill and died. It is not easy to estimate what it must have cost him to have conducted for four months, with an efficiency remarked on by all the lawyers who followed the case, the defence of one whose opinions were unattractive to him and whom he had not chosen to defend, simply having been allotted to him under the Poor Prisoners' Defence Act. He conferred, his appearance of fatigue daily increasing, with William Joyce's brother Quentin, who also looked much older. At the Old Bailey he had been a fresh-faced boy but now he might have been getting on for forty. Deep furrows were grooving his forehead, and his eyes were small and sunken and, in the mornings, red with weeping. With him were always two friends: one was tall Angus MacNab, who was plainly the cranky gentleman so often (as the great American Henry Adams so memorably complained) produced by the British people. The other was a young Fascist of Scottish origin, whose remote blue-grey eyes showed that he had escaped from the world into dreams, not vaguer and kinder than the existence round us, as the dreams of most people are, but harsher and more troubled. All three were lifted to the heights of dignity by their grief for William, whom assuredly they were mourning as early Christians might have mourned a brother about to go into the arena.

There was a real cult around the little man. Some rumour of it had been spreading abroad since the trial began. The City of London greatly respected a certain aged stockbroker, belonging to a solid Scottish family, who conducted a large business with the strictest probity and was known to his friends as a collector of silver and glass and a connoisseur of wine. He had a beautiful house, kept for him by his sister, a tall and handsome maiden lady given to piety and good works, whose appearance was made remarkable by an immense knot of hair twisted on the nape of her neck in the mid-Victorian way. The old man's last years were afflicted by a depressing illness, during which he formed a panic dread of socialism, and for this reason he fell under the influence of Sir Oswald Mosley, to whom he gave a considerable amount of money and whose followers he often entertained. This is a sad thought when it is remembered that many of those followers were very ugly scoundrels; one was prosecuted for living on the earnings of a prostitute. The old man had a special fondness for William Joyce, who, being a lively, wisecracking, practical-joking little creature, as well as intelligent, was able to cheer up an invalid; and after his death his sister, who carried on all his enthusiasms, treated Joyce like a son. She let him use her country house as a meeting-place for the heads of his organization and entertained him there so often that it was one of the first places searched by the police at the outbreak of war when they found that Joyce had left his home.

This woman, then over eighty and crippled by a painful disease, rose from her bed to travel up to London, an apocalyptic figure, tall and bowed, the immense knot of hair behind her head shining snow-white, and went to see William Joyce in prison. She returned weeping but uplifted by his courage and humility and his forgiveness of all his enemies and his faith in the righteousness of his cause. To all those whom she specially loved she sat down and wrote letters describing her visit to this holy and persecuted man which truly might have wrung the heart, and she followed them with copies of the letters that he wrote to her from prison, in which he said that he knew well that the issue of his trial might be against him but was not dismayed, since he could think of no better death than dying for his faith. These pretensions on behalf of a man who worked to enable Hitler and Göring to set up Nazism in England were obviously fantastic, and there was only a minute and crazed fraction of the population which would have accepted them at that time. His luck at other times would have been variable. There is always a market for Messiahs, but some (and surely he was one and that was his tragedy) are never quoted very high.

Presently we were let into the room where Joyce was tried. We found ourselves in a twilit space under a gallery, quite close to the barristers, sitting in their wigs and gowns, who were silhouetted against the brightness of the lit chamber beyond. Their faces turned to one of their number who stood speaking to the Lord Chancellor, who, dressed in his robes, was sitting at a table in the broad aisle which ran down the middle of the chamber, together with four old judges who were dressed in lounge suits and swathed in steamer rugs. There was, of course, not enough fuel available at that time to heat the place, and it was bitterly cold. In the farthest corner of the darkness under the gallery, with four warders to guard him, was William Joyce, his face altered by new wisdom and yellowish prison pallor. Like his brother, he had changed greatly since the trial at the Old Bailey. There he had seemed meanly and repulsively ugly, but at the Law Courts, where his first appeal was heard, he was not so. He was puny and colourless, but his face had an amusing, pleasant, even prettyish character. It was not good-looking, but it could be imagined that people who knew him well would find it easy to believe him far better-looking than he was. This alteration was due in part to improvement in his health. He had arrived in England from Germany shabby and tousled and sickly, pulled down by the hardships he had endured when he was on the run between his last broadcast and his capture by English troops, and by the wound in his leg he had sustained when he was arrested. During his imprisonment he had eaten and slept well and was among those prisoners who had put on weight while under sentence of death. But he looked better because he had sat at the Old Bailey with the right side of his face turned towards spectators, while at the Law Courts it was the left side we saw; and a deep scar ran from the lobe of his right ear to the right corner of his mouth, destroying the contour of the cheek.

There was a certain mystery about this scar. His friends were reticent about it. At the time he received it he was a student at Battersea Polytechnic, and it was then believed by his fellow students and at least one of the staff that he had either been slashed with a razor or mauled with the leg of a chair by a Communist in a street fight arising from a British Fascist meeting. But he had sustained the wound in the General Election of 1924 when defending the platform at a Tory meeting in Lambeth from an ugly rush; and it was perhaps embarrassing to the anti-Semitic Joyce that the Tory candidate he had defended was Jewish: a Mr. Jack Lazarus. In any case it added to the handicaps already laid on him by his smallness and oddity.

In the Law Courts one saw what he would have been like had he not been, on some occasion, cut to the bone; and one saw the humour nothing had taken from him. Prisoners in the dock laugh more freely than is generally imagined; judicial jokes which so often annoy the newspaper reader are to them an opportunity for relaxation. But Joyce's amusement at his own appeal was more subtle than that. One of the judges on the bench was most picturesquely comic in appearance and might have come straight out of the *commedia dell' arte*. William Joyce watched him with delight; and he followed the legal arguments with an unusual detachment, once nodding in approval when a point was decided against him.

But here at the House of Lords he had endured a further change. He still followed the legal argument with a bright eye. But the long contemplation of death had given him a dignity and refinement that he had lacked before. It could be recognized when he turned his eyes on the spectators who paused to look at him before they went up to their seats in the gallery. At the Old Bailey he had soon come to recognize those who were sitting through the whole trial, and it had entertained him to catch their eyes and stare them out. At the Court of Appeal he gave the spectators an inquisitive and gentler eye. That he was a civilized man, however aberrant, was somehow clear before our eyes, and mournful. At the House of Lords he had gone past comparison, looking at us from a territory whose clocks kept another time, and listening to the striking of an hour that had not yet struck for us. A steep staircase led up to the gallery, where one sat under the huge shapes of Edwardian frescoes dedicated to the obsessive devotion felt by the British aristocracy for the horse. That had been traceable outside in the Royal Gallery, for in the blackish frescoes the horses had been the only living creatures which in a scene of catastrophe had remained the right way up. Within, the tribute was even more ardent. The fresco beside the gallery had the word "Hospitality" written underneath it, and showed a lot of people in old Covent Garden Wagnerian costumes on a Covent Garden abbey set, all of them welcoming a man who, oddly enough, was riding in on a horse. But that was not really hospitality. They were plainly glad to see him because he was riding a horse. Behind the gallery the word "Generosity" was written under a fresco showing a horseman refraining from killing a man lying on the ground, on the advice of his horse, who was turning an elder-statesman muzzle toward him. There was a horse in every fresco except one, in which there was a divine person instead.

At the end of the chamber were the two royal thrones—the Queen's carefully built a little lower than the King's—raised on a dais with two steps. In front of the thrones, on the floor of the house, was the Woolsack, a red stuffed pouf on which the Mace was lying; during normal sessions of the House the Lord Chancellor sits on it. On the floor of the House there was also a table covered with very new and bright red leather, at which a clerk in wig and gown sat throughout the trial, doing some official task not to be comprehended by the uninitiated, cutting up paper with scissors as if he were preparing to amuse an infinite number of children. Running lengthwise on each side of the floor were the three rows of benches on which the peers sat, and there some were sitting. But they were no part of Joyce's trial; they were spectators like the rest of us. For though a prisoner appeals to the whole House of Lords for judgment on his case, the House refers the matter to a small committee of judges, drawn from a panel of law lords. In Joyce's case these judges numbered four, with the Lord Chancellor as a fifth. The counsel address this committee not on the floor of the House but from the bar of the House, which was just under the gallery where we were all sitting. To follow the case we had to listen to a thin thread of sound emitted by invisible speakers under our feet. Quentin Joyce had to partake in this general inconvenience, and surely Hell could provide no greater torture than to follow a brother's destiny in these conditions.

The lawyers swung their argument back and forth for four days. Midmornings a stately attendant glided across the scene of baronial pomp, bearing a very common little teatray for the comfort of the shivering judges. Peers dropped in to listen and sat about on the red rep benches; some of their eldest sons exercised their curious right to sit on the steps of the dais beneath the thrones. One peer lived through a most painful moment of his life during the trial. Following an intricate point, he ran his finger thoughtfully up and down behind the lapel of his coat, but suddenly stopped. A look of agony passed over his face, and he turned back the lapel. He had found a moth hole and for a long time was unable to think about William Joyce. These were the days of clothes coupons.

The story became more ironical each time it was restated: here was a man who was being strangled by the sheer tortuousness of his family destiny. He was an American by birth who, by his father's wish, had pretended all his life to be British. Why? In the third trial, as in the first and the second, that question was never answered. It had become more perplexing as more knowledge about William Joyce had come into currency. He had stood as a candidate at a London County Council election and had at that time had to declare that he was a British subject; and that false declaration might have brought on him, had he been elected, a fine of £50 for every occasion on which he had sat on the council. Why did the father—who had by all accounts loved his eldest son very dearly, and must have acquired a reasonable notion of the law's view of such ongoings in the course of his life as a close friend of the British Police Government of Ireland—keep his own and his family's status a close secret as if their lives depended on it? Perhaps they did, but it is not likely. This mysterious imposture was bringing Joyce closer and closer to the gallows as we listened to the thread of sound beneath our feet.

The legal content of each of Joyce's trials was slightly different; different as, say, three performances of the same concerto by the same conductor and the same soloist but by three different orchestras. At the Old Bailey the fantastic novelty of the case, and the disturbing presence of the Judas whose voice we all knew so well, had overwhelmed the court, and the proceedings were rough-hewn. In the Court of Appeal the performance was more delicate. The contentions on which Joyce's counsel asked the Court of Appeal to reverse the verdict returned at the Old Bailey were four, and they were by that time strictly lawyers' meat. The argument which impressed the public most was in fact the least respectable: that a man who obtained a passport by fraud as Joyce had done could not owe allegiance in return for the protection he derived from it. This is not horse sense, for it means that a man who fraudulently obtained a British passport would be better off than a man who obtained it legally. He would get protection without having to give allegiance. It is not easy to imagine why the public conceived tenderness for this argument, and perhaps less would have been felt had it been realized on what grounds Joyce's counsel justified it. First, he claimed, that protection which attracted allegiance was not protection *de facto* but protection *de jure*, not actual protection but the legal right to it, and therefore a man who obtained a passport by fraud and was not getting its protection lawfully could use it to what benefit was possible and then walk off whistling. The other argument was that the moment the holder of a passport committed treason the power which granted the passport withdrew its protection, so the whole transaction regarding the document was null and void. One of the three judges at the Court of Appeal, the one who looked like a character in the *commedia dell' arte*, thought little of this point and showed it, puffed out his cheeks and spouted out air through his leathery old lips dolphin-wise, while William Joyce watched him with amusement.

Here in the House of Lords the performance became even quicker, finer, subtler, and Joyce enjoyed himself thoroughly. When the four old judges had a passage with counsel, it was not only, presumably, great law; it was also as good entertainment as first-class tennis. All of them had supremely good minds, as well as the physiological luck that makes a man able to go on through the seventies into the eighties doing what he has done all his life better and better, even though he may not be able to address himself to new tasks or work continuously. The voice of each old man was characteristic enough to be easily identifiable, and often, in the quieter moments, recalled what was generally known about him. One amongst them had a small manor-house set in a forest lying under the Wiltshire Downs. He lived there with a wife much younger than himself, who was perhaps the most celebrated professional horsewoman in England. At night he sat at his end of the table, surrounded by his pupils, who had come to learn from him the subtlest mysteries of the law, and she sat at her end, surrounded by her pupils, who had come to learn from her the subtlest mysteries of fox-hunting and horse-breaking. The two groups were hardly able to communicate with each other, owing to the extreme specialization of each, but, as there is nothing so civilizing as scholarship and craftsmanship which have not lost touch with life, the judge and his wife lived together in the most agreeable amity.

It was not fair. Here were these old men, full of honours because of an intellectual distinction which Joyce shared with them to a considerable degree; otherwise he would not have felt the admiration for them he expressed to those who visited him in prison. Here was the Palace of Westminster, built to house and glorify a system which he would have liked to adorn. Every morning he was taken into court by his guard while the public was still waiting for admission, and on all four days he owned to his warders, laughing at himself yet quite in earnest, how much he enjoyed making this ceremonial entrance into the Mother of Parliaments. Had he been able to range freely round the pompous halls and corridors, he would have seen the reason for the pomp far better than most visitors. With real reverence he would have bent over the glass-covered display table and looked at the book inscribed with the names of the peers and their sons who had fallen in the First World War; the procession of the Mace into the House of Lords would have been recognized by him as having a meaning. His relationship with the state might have been perfect, had it not been that he had made one stipulation which could not be fulfilled. He wanted to govern, not to be governed; and that, for reasons which were not fair, was quite impossible.

That became visible as the trial came to its conclusion, which was painfully protracted. This third trial began on a Monday, and it looked as if the verdict would be given on Thursday afternoon. At one o'clock on Thursday counsel had finished their arguments, and the Lord Chancellor dismissed the court and bade it reassemble at three. Joyce's brother Quentin and his friend the Scottish Fascist rose miserably and went off to look for some lunch. This would be difficult to get, for in those days, just after the war, people lunched early, and in few restaurants would there be tables free or much food left. Outside the House of Parliament everyone knew who they were and eyed them with wonder, aware of their peculiar grief, their terrifying sympathies. They crossed the street and passed into the crowds of Whitehall, and there they became two young men in raincoats among ten thousand such.

When everyone had reassembled, the Lord Chancellor announced that the judges required more time to consider their verdict and dismissed the court again until Tuesday morning.

Tears stood in Quentin Joyce's eyes, and he and his friends pressed forward to get out of the hated place as soon as might be. But the attendants held all of us back, and we stood together at the head of the steep stairs, looking down on William Joyce as he was marched out among the four policemen on his way back to jail. Now his courage was impressive. At the Old Bailey he had behaved well, but under a simple though supreme danger of which most of those present had some experience. But now he was doing something more difficult. He had lived four months under the threat of death, and now he had not heard the decisive sentence he had been braced to hear, and after this disabling moment had had to walk through a crowd of his enemies, a little ill-made man surrounded by four drilled giants. He held his chin high and picked his feet up, as the sergeant majors say, and though he held his chin so very high that his face was where the top of his head ought to have been and though his feet flapped on his weak ankles, his dignity was not destroyed, but was made idiosyncratic, his very own. It appeared that there could be such a thing as undignified dignity. Yet in that moment when he compelled respect, it became quite clear that he could never have been one of our governors. Even if he had not been a Fascist, if he had been sponsored by the Tory or the Labour or the Liberal Party, he would never have been given power.

There was a bar between Joyce and advancement, no matter what he made of himself. He had taken a good degree in English at London University; but that could not be guessed from any of his writings or his speeches, and it is said that he became a coach because his application for posts in schools and colleges met with embarrassed discouragement. Though he had developed his gifts for public speaking in the service of the Conservative Party, there had never been any question of any local committee's nominating him as Parliamentary candidate. There was some element in him that resisted the cultivation of all his merits. It was even manifest in his body. He was a good rider, a still better swimmer and diver, he fenced and had tried hard as a feather-weight boxer; but his little body looked as if he never cared to exercise it. He seemed mediocre when he was not, perhaps because of some contrary quality, which put people off, an exaggeration amounting to clownishness. For example, he always retained the love of England which he expressed in his boyish

letters to the London University Committee for Military Education; but in after life it led him to make a demand, which struck
many of his English acquaintances as a sign of insanity, that any
social evening he spent with his friends, even the quietest, should
end with the singing of the National Anthem.

When Tuesday came, the press and the Fascists no longer
had the Royal Gallery to themselves. It was thronged with Members of Parliament, a comradely and self-assured crowd, happily gossiping on their own stamping-ground and much less
respectful to the ceremonies of the place than the press and the
Fascists had been. They had to be pushed off the carpet by the
attendants when the Mace and the Lord Chancellor went by, so
busy were they exchanging comments on Joyce which were not
meant inhumanly but sounded so, because they themselves were
in such good health and so unlikely, if things went on as they
were going, to be hanged: "They say he isn't here today." "No,
if he were acquitted, it would be awkward. They'd want to
arrest him immediately on defence-regulation charges, and nobody can be arrested within the Palace of Westminster. They'd
have to let him go down the street, and he might get away."
"Perhaps he's chosen not to come today. Shouldn't blame
him." "He's very plucky. I saw him at the Old Bailey." "So
did I. What a queer little fish!" Joyce's brother was standing
beside the last speaker, but he seemed not to hear. Both the
Fascists and the pressmen were all preoccupied with the need to
dash up into the gallery the minute the signal was given, because
the announcement of the verdict would take only a few seconds
and might be over before they had climbed the stairs.

The Lord Chancellor and the four judges were sitting
around the table at the bar of the House, as they had done every
day, but now the red benches were fully occupied, the House was
crowded with peers; there seemed so many it was remarkable
that nobility had kept its distinction. As the press and the public
took their seats in the gallery, the Lord Chancellor rose and
stood until there was silence, and then said, "I have come to the
conclusion that the appeal should be dismissed. In common with
the rest of your Lordships, I should propose to deliver my
reasons at a later date." Then the four old judges rose in turn
and gave their opinions. While the first was saying, "I agree,"
Joyce's brother and his friends got up from their seats beside

mine in the second row and clambered down to some seats in the front row which had been assigned to newspaper agencies and were not now occupied. Suddenly one of the suave attendants was standing behind them and was saying, in a tone of savagery the more terrifying because it was disciplined and was kept low so that the proceedings should not be disturbed, "You get out of there and go back to the seats where you belong." This seemed a most brutal way of behaving to men who were listening to a judgment that doomed one whom they loved; for all the judges except one were saying, "I agree," and that meant that Joyce must hang. But on the face of the attendant, and of others who had joined him, there was real fear. Innocent though Quentin Joyce and his friends were, they had become associated with the idea of violence, and from the front of the gallery a violent man could have thrown grenades into the court.

Meanwhile the ceremony went on, affecting in its beauty and its swiftness. The Lord Chancellor moved backward down the floor of the House, in his black robe and curled white wig, the only figure in a historic dress in the assembly, the symbol of the continuing rule of law. He halted at the Woolsack. He stretched out his hands to the peers on each side of the chamber and bade those vote who were content with the judgment. This was the last sad stage of the outnumbering of Joyce by the law. Now scores of judges faced the dock, and he was gone from it. The peers nodded and murmured and raised their hands. At this point a young man with hollow eyes and pinched nose and a muffler round his scrawny neck, who was sitting on the public bench of the gallery among the Negroes and the Hindus, cried out some words which some among us could recognize as Scottish Gaelic, and then proclaimed in English but with a strong northern accent that William Joyce was innocent. Attendants formed a wall around him, but did no more, for fear of interrupting the proceedings. The Negroes beside him expressed horror with rolling eyes; the Hindus looked prim. Joyce's friends threw a glance at him which was at first startled and then snobbish. The interrupter was not one of their sort of Fascist. Meanwhile the Lord Chancellor bade those peers who were not content with the judgment to vote and there was silence. He declared, "The contents have it," and strode from the chamber. The peers streamed after him. The place was empty in a moment.

Quentin Joyce and his friends ran down the stone staircase into the street. They did not look so upset as might have been expected. The man who had shouted made his way out of the gallery without being touched by the attendants, who looked away from him, having taken his measure. In the lobby outside, crowds of pressmen gathered round him and questioned him and took down his answers, which he delivered with the gasping haste of the evangelist who knows he never keeps his audience long. The elegant general who was in charge of the attendants murmured to the Superintendent of Police, "I say, do we want this sort of thing, or don't we?" The Superintendent said he thought that the man would probably go away of his own accord if he was left alone. So the eccentric held an audience in the House of Lords, the very considerable crowd that was coming in to take part in the debate on the American loan neatly dividing to avoid disturbing him and joining again, until the pressmen left him, having insufficiently appreciated the remarkable quality of his utterances. A young reporter asked him, "But don't you think it mattered that William Joyce betrayed his country?" and he answered in the accents of Sir Harry Lauder, "William Joyce didna betray his country. Ye canna say a man betrays his country when he goes abroad to better himself. Millions of people have done that and nobody's accused them of betraying their countries, and that's what William Joyce did. He had a fine position waiting for him in Germany, and he just took it." Surely this was a mind as fresh as Shaw's. His was a voice which was to be heard again, nearly twenty years later. Strangely enough, it was the only voice lifted on that occasion which was to be heard again, echoing through the decades.

Down in the street, Quentin Joyce and Angus MacNab and the Scottish Fascist were waiting, eager to speak to the press, eager to give praise to their martyr. That was why they had not looked so very greatly upset when the appeal was dismissed; they were like the people who, leaving a deathbed so painful to them that they could not have borne to contemplate it for another instant, find relief by flinging themselves into elaborate arrangements for the funeral. Angus MacNab, in his easy and gentlemanly but hollow and eccentric voice, was telling a reporter how calm William Joyce had been when he saw him in prison during the week-end. "He was in excellent spirits," he said, his eyes gleaming mystically behind his spectacles, "and he was discussing, quite objectively, and with all his old brilliance, the psychology of the four judges. He was wonderful. . . . But I must leave you now and go and tell my wife what has happened. My name? Angus MacNab, and please do not spell it M-c-N-a-b. The correct spelling is M-a-c-N-a-b." And Quentin Joyce was talking freely in his careful voice, which, without being mincing, was more gentlemanly and more English than any English gentleman's voice, because this ambitious and Anglophile family consciously ironed out the Irish brogue from their tongues. Some reporters were asking him to write an article or make some statement about his brother, which he was refusing to do, evidently out of loyalty to some code of family relationships. He seemed to be saying primly that it was for his sister-in-law to tell the story of Joyce when she was free, since a wife was nearer than a brother, and as such must have her rights. It was plain that he and all this group had felt themselves not less but more disciplined than the rest of the world, solid upholders of order. He went on to speak of some demonstration the Fascists would make against the sentence. "And believe me, there will be plenty of us," he kept on repeating, while the Scottish Fascist nodded. A year later, and for many years, this man was to insert in the *Daily Telegraph* an "In Memoriam" notice for William Joyce. But there were not plenty of them outside Wandsworth Prison on the morning of January 3, 1946, when William Joyce was hanged.

That prison lies in a shabby district in South London, so old-fashioned that it begins to look picturesque to our eyes. It is a mid-Victorian building with a façade of dark stone, inspired by a brooding and passionate misunderstanding of Florentine architecture, and it is divided from the highroad by a piece of ground not belonging to the prison, consisting of some cabbage patches and a dispirited nursery garden, planned whimsically, with thin streams trickling under toy bridges and meandering between the blackened stems of frosted chrysanthemums. The prison looks across the highroad to a monstrous building—built in the style of a Burgundian château and set in the midst of a bald and sooty park—an endowed school for the children of soldiers and sailors with the curious name of "The Royal Victoria Patriotic School." This title had become ironical during the war, for persons who escaped from the occupied countries were detained there often for dreary weeks, until they had satisfied the authorities that they had not been sent over by the Germans. An avenue runs between the cabbage patches and nursery gardens to the prison's great doorway, which is of green panelled wood with a heavy iron grille at the top, set in a coarse stone archway. A small notice board hangs on this door, and on it was pinned an announcement that the sentence of death passed on William Joyce was to be carried out that morning. On these occasions there is nothing whatsoever for a spectator to see except at one moment, when a warder comes out of a small door which is cut in the large one, takes down the notice board, and replaces it after two other notices have been added to the first: one, a sheriff's declaration that the prisoner has been hanged; the other, a surgeon's declaration that he has examined the prisoner's body and found him to be dead. But about three hundred people gathered to see that minute shred of ceremony.

They gathered while it was still dark and the windows of the cells were yellow in the squat utilitarian buildings which stretched away from the Italian façade, and waited through the dawn till full daylight, stoically bearing the disappointment that the hour of the hanging was at the last moment postponed from eight to nine. Some of those who waited were pressmen, lamenting that there was no story here; and there was just one yellow Movietone truck. Some people had brought their children, since the little dears, they said, had clamoured for the treat. Others were people drawn by personal resentment. An old man told me that he was there because he had turned on the wireless one night during the V-1 blitz when he came back from seeing his grandchildren's bodies in the mortuary and had heard Haw-Haw's voice. "There he was, mocking me," he said. There were many soldiers who had strolled out for a little after-breakfast diversion from a nearby demobilization centre. As time went on, all these people danced to keep their feet warm on the frozen earth.

There were some who did not dance. Most of these, however, were not particularly interested in William Joyce. They were opponents of capital punishment, who would have stood and looked disapproving outside any prison where anybody was being hanged. The most conspicuous of these were two tall and gaunt Scandinavian women dressed in black, who indulged in silent but truculent prayer. Quentin Joyce and his friends were not there; they were attending a Requiem Mass. During William Joyce's imprisonment he became reconciled to the faith in which he was born. But there must have been many Fascists who would not attend that service, either because they were not Christian or because they were not close enough to Joyce's family to hear of it. Of these a handful waited outside the prison, and of these only one grieved openly, standing bareheaded, with no effort to hide his tears at the moment of Joyce's hanging. Three others slipped through a gap in the trees of the avenue and stood in the nursery garden, where some rows of cabbage stalks veiled with frost flanked a rubble rockery, naked with winter, and at that moment they practised a highly tentative reverence. Their bodies betrayed that they had had no military training, and they wore the queer and showy sports clothes affected by Fascists, but they attempted the salute which looks plausible only when performed by soldiers in uniform. It was the poorest send-off for a little man who had always loved a good show and done his best to give one; who, so the prison gossip went, halted on his way to the scaffold, looked down on the violent trembling of his knees, and calmly and cynically smiled.

3

DURING the trials there had flowed into the mind of the community a conviction that Joyce had not been guilty of any offence against the law. This was in part due to the inadequate reports of the proceedings which were all that the press could find space to publish because it was starved of newsprint. The public read almost nothing about the Joyce trials which was not so brief and disjointed as to be unintelligible, and it came to a conclusion which was summed up in the pubs in some such terms as these: "Of course he can't be guilty of treason," was said in all the London pubs. "He's a dirty little

bastard, but we've no right to hang him, he's an American."
And so it went on. "A miscarriage of justice," said the clerk in a
government office, handing out a legal document concerning
Joyce to an inquirer some months later, "that's what the verdict
was. I hold no brief for the little man, though he was a wonderful speaker. I'm no Fascist, but I always used to listen to him
when he spoke up our way by the Great Northern Hospital; but
it stands to reason that giving an American a British passport
can't change him into an Englishman. A miscarriage of justice,
that's what that was."

But this was not a tenable point of view. It had no legal basis,
since Joyce had got himself out of the safety of American citizenship by obtaining an English passport. It had no basis in the
world of fact, which is sometimes, we must admit, divided from
the world of law. William Joyce was not an American in any real
sense; and indeed during the war the United States had passed
an Act concerning Naturalization confirming this view of the
reality of citizenship.

In 1940 the United States had declared that persons who
owed the sort of allegiance to another country which William
Joyce and his father had owed to Great Britain could not retain
their American nationality. At the time Joyce was tried it
appeared by an act afterwards declared unconstitutional that
Michael Joyce's American naturalization would have been nul-
lified because he had resided continuously for more than three
years in the territory of the foreign state of which he had been
a national before he was naturalized a citizen of the United
States. William Joyce would have lost his American nationality
under the same act, had it been passed earlier, because he had
served in a British military unit (after the age of eighteen) and
because he had participated in British elections. But there was
some merit behind the public's regret that Joyce had been
sentenced to death, ill-argued though it was. We were all afraid
lest the treatment of Joyce had been determined by our emotions
and not by our intellects; that we had been corrupted by our
Nazi enemies to the extent of calling vengeance by the name of
justice.

The legal profession also showed a discontent with the
verdict which was startling. For of the nine judges who had
considered the case, one at the Old Bailey, three at the Court of

Appeal, and four at the House of Lords, together with the Lord Chancellor, only one (a Lord of Appeal, Lord Porter) had dissented from the verdict of guilty, and he did not fundamentally disagree with his colleagues in their view of allegiance. His objection related to a passage in Mr. Justice Tucker's summing up at the Old Bailey, which he regarded as a misdirection of the jury on a minor technical point. But the lawyers were, like the public, misled by the inadequate press reports. One thinks of lawyers as having a collective consciousness and becoming aware of all legal proceedings as they happen, but that is childlike faith. "I'd thought," one said, "that Joyce's appeal in the House of Lords was going well for him." His reason for thinking thus was a remark addressed by the Lord Chancellor to Joyce's counsel: "Surely the proposition is elementary that allegiance was only due from an alien while he was in this country." Read out of its context, this sounded like an encouraging invitation to pass on after a point had been proved. Heard, the sentence conveyed with crystalline peevishness that the counsel was hammering home the obvious, and it was followed by the statement, "The question, surely, is whether there are any exceptions to this rule."

The lawyers, like the rest of us, had insufficient information, and they also were afraid lest the law had been tainted by revenge, and this they felt sharply and personally, since it was their mystery which was being profaned.

Such scruples were honourable, and it would be an unhealthy community which did not recognize them. But the situation was not simple. A number of people were saying, "William Joyce was a vile man but he should not have been hanged"—and smiled as they said it, claiming to speak in the name of mercy. But they were hypocrites. They were moved by hostility to the law, being destructive by nature.

Nowhere has the law been finally analysed and defined. To make laws is a human instinct which arises as soon as food and shelter have been ensured, among all peoples, everywhere. There have been yellow people who have flashed on horseback across continents, apparently too mobile to form customs, apparently preoccupied with slaughter and devastation. There have been black people who have squatted on their haunches through the centuries, their customs degenerating to superstition round them.

These have been thought by men of other kinds to be without law, but that was an error. Both kinds of society had reached a general agreement as to how to order their lives and ordained penalties against its violation. But neither they nor any other society could define exactly what they were doing when they were making that agreement and ordaining those penalties. Demosthenes said that every rule of law was a discovery and a gift from the gods, and he added that it was also an opinion held by sensible men. Nine hundred years later the great Justinian prefixed that same definition to his Digest of Laws, only changing "gods" to "God." Both seemed guilty of paradox, for assuredly men are not gods, and the last thing a god or God could fairly be compared with is a sensible man. Yet pagan and Christian alike realized that the law should be at once the recognition of an eternal truth and the solution by a community of one of its temporal problems; for both conceived that the divine will was mirrored in nature, which man could study by the use of his reason. This is the faith which has kept jurisprudence an honest and potent exercise through the ages, though the decline in religion has made it necessary to find other and secular names for its aims and technique.

A number of the British who thought that Joyce should have been acquitted had wholly lost this conception of the law. It seemed to them an interference with life, although life is what likes to make laws. They like to lay unfair stress on the inability of the courts to adapt themselves immediately to the age, which indeed is one of their characteristics. Politics and the law are always lagging behind the times, because the course taken by our existence is unpredictable, and it takes days and months and even years to present Parliament and the courts with knowledge of the eventualities they have to meet. Such people saw William Joyce as having smartly outmanœuvred the law and as deserving of safety in recompense for having worsted that decrepit enemy. They even enjoyed the technical nature of his defence, which linked onto the delight that is often felt in people who have found a way through the law in grosser exercises than treason. Many people at the turn of the century were ready to cheer the cold shark Horatio Bottomley, because he had exploited the unforeseen situation created by the existence of a class which had a certain amount of investable capital and was ready to invest it without taking advice from a banker and stockbroker. It touched them neither in their hearts nor in their sense of self-preservation that most of Bottomley's victims were people like themselves, whose savings were their only shield from actual want in old age. Simply they derived pleasure from thinking of him as drinking three bottles of champagne a day and keeping a racing stable on the proceeds of a form of financial crime which the law then had not learned to check. It opened to all of them the prospect that one day they might find some such opportunity of gain, easier than honesty, and unpunishable, and that life would be proved moral nonsense.

Half a century later the emphasis was not on wealth but on license of conduct. Those who hankered for a meaningless universe wanted Joyce to go free so that they could see a man whose crime they knew by the testimony of their own ears escape the law. Joyce himself would have had none of this. As might be expected, he was not with those who said that he was a vile man but should not have been hanged. What might not have been expected was that his attitude was the exact reverse. He maintained that he was not a vile man, but thought England was right in hanging him. He would have taken it as proof of our national decadence that since the year he died no spies have been sentenced to death.

4

THE life of William Joyce is worth while studying in detail because he represents a type of revolutionary who is for the moment obsolete, though it is possible, if the later models fail, that he may yet be found in currency again. He begins by being a touching figure. For there is no sight more touching than a boy who intends to conquer the world, though there is that within himself which means he is more likely to be its slave. Young William Joyce was such a boy and took the first step to conquest all right, for he was brave. Perhaps he really lay deep in the heather so that he might tell the Black and Tans whether

the three men they were looking for were still in the farmhouse
in the fold of the hills; perhaps he only pressed on the Black and
Tans information that was of no service to them. But he did go
through the forms of attachment to a dangerous cause because he
was ready to die if death was nobler than life. That he was
mistaken in his estimate of where nobility lay is not a great
count against him, since he was only fifteen. And behind his
political folly was a grain of wisdom. He liked the scarlet coats
of the English garrisons, but it was Mozart himself who asked in
a letter if there was anything in life finer than a good scarlet
coat, and all scarlet coats take up a common argument. They
dissent from the dark earth and the grey sky; they insist that the
bodies that wear them are upright; they are for discipline, either
of drill or of the minuet. It was not to be held against the boy
that he preferred the straight-backed aliens in scarlet coats to his
compatriots who slouched with hats crushed down on cowlicks
and collars turned up round unshaven jaws as they went about
their performance of menial toil or inglorious assassination. His
family—and he was loyal to his own blood—cultivated that
preference. That the smart soldiers created the slouching assas-
sins he could hardly have been expected to work out for himself
at that age.

He came to London before his family; and his destiny sent
him down to South London, and there was significance in that.
South London is not the London where England can be conquered. It is not London at all, even calling itself by a vague and
elided locution. "Where do you live?" "South the River." The
people on the other bank never speak of their landscape as
"North the River." They may go down East, or up West, but
they move within London, where the Houses of Parliament are,
and the Abbey, and Buckingham Palace, and Trafalgar Square,
and the Law Courts, and Saint Paul's and the Mansion House,
and the Bank and the Mint, and the Tower, and the Docks. The
house where William Joyce first took up his dwelling on the
other side of the Thames stood in one of those streets which
cover the hills round Clapham Junction like a shabby striped
grey counterpane. It was a tiny little house, and he was there
only as a lodger while he got the formalities arranged for his
studies at Battersea Polytechnic. It was from there that he sent in
the completed enrolment form to the University of London

Committee for Military Education, thus taking what he believed to be his first step toward the conquest of England. It was going to be of no consequence at all that he and his family had had to leave Ireland. He would conquer the larger island instead.

When his father came south in the following year, he became, with superb adaptability, a grocer; and he took the step, unlooked for in a dazed immigrant, of establishing his family in a house as delightfully situated as any in London. Allison Grove is a short road of small houses which has been hacked out from the corner of the gardens of a white Regency villa in the greenest part of Dulwich, a queer cheap insertion in a line of stately properties. It has its own great sycamore tree and many syringas, and the most agreeable surroundings. Not far off is Mill Pond, still a clear mirror of leaves and sky, and beyond it Dulwich College amidst its groves and playing-fields. To the south a golf course makes a wide circle of mock country, bound by suburbs rising on round hills. To the north, behind the line of mansions into which Allison Grove intrudes, lies the handsome Victorian formality of Dulwich Park, with its winding carriage drives and its large sheet of ornamental water. An Irish family that had to come to London could not have more cleverly found a part of London more spaciously and agreeably unlike itself, and the house was cleverly found too. One side of Allison Grove had been built in Victorian times; the harsh red brick had been piled up in shapes as graceless as outhouses and to heights obviously inconvenient for the housewife. But the houses were amply planned for their price; and one of them gave room enough for the Joyce parents and William and his two younger brothers and his little sister. The neighbours, who thought the Joyces outlandish but likeable, though curiously arrogant, all noted that William was the apple of the family's eye, and they could understand it, for the boy had an air of exceptional spirit and promise. But during the day at Battersea Polytechnic he must have suffered many defeats, being tiny, alien, and ineradicably odd. In 1923 he was to experience what was to his inordinate pride, the pride of a very small man, the crushing defeat of failure in two subjects in his Intermediate Science examination.

His reaction was characteristic. There was nothing disgraceful in his failure. He was only seventeen; his schooling had been much interrupted, first by his disposition to argue with his Jesuit teachers, since as the son of a Catholic father and a Protestant mother he never accepted Roman Catholicism easily. Later he was distracted from his books by civil war and change of country. He could have tried again. But on this failure he immediately abandoned his intention of becoming a Bachelor of Science and turned his back on Battersea Polytechnic. It is to be noted that more depended on his failure or success than he can have expected when he was a child. With exile his father, Michael Joyce, had entered on a declining scale of prosperity. He had come back from America thirteen years before with a substantial captial sum; he was to grow poorer and poorer, and when he died in 1941 left only £650. He himself attributed his impoverishment to the failure of the British government to compensate him adequately for the burning of his house and the destruction of other property of his at the hands of the Sinn Feiners. This complaint was, in the opinion of a detached observer with some knowledge of practical affairs, well founded. William Joyce must have felt he could not afford to waste time. It is interesting to speculate just what effect this step had on his destiny. His ambition was very strong, and it just might have happened that if he had become a Bachelor of Science he would have recognized the easy and brilliant future which this age offers to the Communist scientist.

As it was, he went to the Birkbeck College for Working Men, which is a part of the University of London, a physically sombre though intellectually vigorous institution, hidden in the dark streets between Holborn and the Law Courts; and there he studied the English language and literature and history. He made an excellent, though odd, student and passed with first-class honours, though for the first two years of his course he was subject to a new distracting influence. In 1923 he joined the British Fascists. This was an odd instance of his inability to get the hang of the world he meant to conquer. Mussolini had come to power in 1922, and warm admiration was felt for him by numerous persons of influence in England; and a young man might well have sincerely shared that mistaken admiration and at the same time have wished to use that admiration as a means of personal advancement. But joining the British Fascists was not the way to make that advance. This body was never numerous and had few links with the influential admirers of Mussolini, having been promoted by an elderly lady, member of a military family, who was overcome by panic when she read in the newspaper that the British Labour Party was sending a delegation to an international conference in Hamburg. Her creation was patronized by a certain number of retired Army men and a back-bench MP and an obscure peer or two; but the great world mocked at it, and it had as aim the organization of amateur resistance to any revolution that might arise; it was a charade representing the word "barricade."

If William Joyce wanted either to hold a commission in the Regular Army, or to teach, or to become a journalist, membership in this universally unfavoured movement was certain to be prejudicial to his hopes. It may be said that he was still young, but many a boy and girl of seventeen, determined to rise in the world, has cast a canny eye on such strategical pitfalls. He, however, had from first to last none of the adaptability normally given by ambition. But there were more positive factors than mere obtuseness at work here. The party, as well as holding meetings of its own, made a practice of interrupting and breaking up the Communist meetings which were being held in London, especially in the East End, often with the aim of explaining and defending Bolshevik Russia. Joyce, according to a tutor who coached him at this time, took these affrays with extreme seriousness. He spoke of the Communists with real horror—as, in fact, Orangemen would speak of Sinn Feiners. There was working in him a nostalgia for the Irish situation. Later, in the air raids, we were all to learn that danger is a better stimulant than champagne until the fatigue is too great. William Joyce had experienced that gaiety when he was too young to know real fatigue. Hence he enjoyed, with a constant driving esurience, street fighting.

No sport could be meaner. The thin boy wearing spectacles is cut off from his friends, he is hustled into an alley, his arms are twisted, his teeth are knocked in. But the sport was recommended to William Joyce by the memory of his courage in its springtime, and excessive deaths in Russia gave him his excuse. He was led into temptation.

In 1925 he left the British Fascists. This may have been because he became involved in certain internal dissensions which appeared, inevitably enough, in the movement; dog of a certain

sort is always eating dog. Or it may have been because he feared
to fail in his arts course as he had failed in his science course,
and sacrificed his hobbies. But before long he had another and
more urgent distraction.

A week after his twenty-first birthday, on April 30, 1927, he
married a girl of his own age, a chemist's assistant, the daughter
of a dentist, who was remarkable for her pleasant good looks.
Because she was a Protestant, he, the son of an Irish Roman
Catholic father, the pupil of the Jesuits, married her at the
Chelsea Register Office. He set up house in that district and
started on a phase of his life which gave him and his family a
great deal of satisfaction. After he had taken his degree, with
first-class honours, he continued in his studies in a postgraduate
course in philology and later began a course in psychology at
King's College. He had no difficulty in paying his way, for he
had already, as a student, joined the staff of a tutorial college
and was regarded as one of its best teachers. He had a real
passion for teaching. He had a trick, another teacher remembered, of getting command of the minds of pupils who could not
get going by teaching them chess.

It must be remarked that all these achievements brought
him not an inch nearer any position of real power. He could
never by any chance have been invited to join the staff of any
school or college of conventional type, because of the curious
atmosphere of illiteracy which hung about him. Only unedu-
cated people accepted easily that he was learned. Educated people were always astounded to hear that he had been at a university. Even his handwriting, which was spiky and uneasy, suggested that he rarely took up his pen. Though he then went to
work for the Conservative Party, not only speaking for it but
learning the technique of organization, and showing aptitude for
both activities, it got him nowhere. He was not acceptable, in a
deep sense. A police officer who had known William Joyce for
many years and had liked him said hesitantly, for he was speaking a few days before the execution, that sometimes Joyce had
reminded him, even in the days before the war, of a real
criminal, of the sort that make lags, convicts. It was not that he
had then committed any crime, but because he, like the lags,
"did not seem to fit in anywhere."

Between 1930 and 1933 his enthusiasm for the Conservative

Party flagged, and during this time he renewed his connections with British fascism, which had now much more to offer him and his special case. A number of obscure people in London were at that time conscious that a disaster was overhanging Europe. Those who foresee the future and recognize it as tragic are often seized by a madness which forces them to commit the very acts which make it certain that what they dread shall happen. So it was natural that some of these should join with the young men who were gratifying a taste for street fighting under the plea that they stood for order and fascism, while others joined with the young men who were gratifying a taste for street fighting under the plea that they stood for order and communism. Both were undermining the civilization which gave them power to pursue these curious pleasures. In this way the Fascists and Communists had destroyed order and enabled Mussolini to seize power, and the same process was then taking place in Germany.

In Great Britain a Fascist movement of some apparent substance had been formed by Sir Oswald Mosley, who was inspired by that impatience with evil which often produces evil. In 1931 he appeared at a by-election at Ashton-under-Lyne to support the candidature of a member of his new party, which was to be a socialist party more drastic and dashing than the Labour Party. His supporter was standing against a Conservative and an orthodox Labour candidate. When the results were announced at the town hall on election night he looked down at a sea of jeering faces who were exulting at this defeat for several reasons. Some were guffawing because a rich baronet should profess socialism and because a man who was brilliant and handsome had suffered disappointment and humiliation; others because such a man had split the orthodox Labour vote and let in the Conservative. So Mosley said to a friend, "These are the people who have got in the way of everybody who has tried to do anything since the last war." It was a sensible enough observation; but making it in his pride violated the just pride of others. He abandoned the attempt to wrestle with the vulgarity of the vulgar by argument and by example and decided to court them in their own fashion. Thereafter his agitation might have deceived the vulgar into crediting himself with a like vulgarity, and it looked as if he might seize power through their support.

Joyce was, therefore, valuable to Mosley for just those qualities which would have prevented him from becoming an Army officer or a don. So the Fascist movement was ready to give him a place in a hierarchy, with which there went acclamation, a certain amount of money, travel abroad, and company which was of a certain distinction. The movement was not in all respects as Joyce would have had it. Though it happened to be led by Sir Oswald Mosley, he was in fact its follower rather than its leader. It had sprung up because people who, living in an established order, had no terror of disorder had read too much in the newspapers about Mussolini and Hitler and thought it would be exciting to create disorder on the same lines. If it had not arisen spontaneously it would have been fomented by foreign agents. It was a dynamic movement with roots that went deep and wide, and it did not impinge at any point on the world inhabited by the existing executive class. With the people that controlled politics, or commerce, or the professions, it had nothing to do. It grew beside them, formidable in its desire to displace them from that control, but separated from all contact with them as if a vast plate-glass window were between them. To no movement could the isolated William Joyce more appropriately have belonged.

It was Sir Oswald Mosley's peculiar function to give false hope to the British Fascists, to seem to lead them out of limbo and introduce them into the magnetic field of national power. Ill-informed about all conspicuous persons, they did not know that he was an outsider; he also had been born outside and not inside his environment. He had been born into the old governing class of the Tory aristocracy but had brought his own plate-glass window into the world with him; and he had penetrated into the new governing class of the Labour Party to the extent of holding office in the first Labour government, but had formed no tie of liking or trust which would prevent it from preferring any other of its members to him. It is probable that William Joyce, with his incapacity for drawing any social inference whatsoever, was as blind as the rank and file to the qualities of failure inherent in Sir Oswald.

Within two years after Sir Oswald had founded the British Union of Fascists, William Joyce became his Director of Propaganda and deputy leader of his party. He lived then in a home which, though cheap and unfashionable, possessed its picturesque distinction. He was staying in a flat in a road clinging to the lip of an escarpment in the strangest spot in the strangeness of South London. It was far south of the river, where the tameness of town overspreads heights which, though insignificant in elevation, are wild in contour; and if it covers them with the tame shapes of houses it has to stack them in wild steepness. But above this suburban precipice the buildings themselves were wild with the wildness sometimes found in Victorian architecture. Outside the windows of his flat in Farquhar Road, two towers ran up into the sky, and between them the torso of the Crystal Palace was at one and the same time a greenhouse and a Broad Church cathedral. In summertime the night behind this didactic architectural fairy tale was often sprayed with the gold and silver jewels of Messrs. Brock's fireworks, while a murmur of ohs and ahs and cheers rose from the crowds that walked in the gardens among the cement prehistoric animals which had been placed there in the mid-nineteenth century as illustrations to some thesis regarding the inevitability of progress and the usefulness of knowledge. A little way up the road was the Crystal Palace railway station, the most fantastic in London, so allusive, particularly in its cast-iron ornamental work, to uplifting Victorian festivity that it would not be surprising to find its platforms thronged by a choir singing an oratorio by Parry or Stainer. The windows on the other side of the house where Joyce lived looked down on the whole of London, across the Thames, over the imperial city, up to the green hills of Hampstead and Highgate. Tufts of treetops and a lack of roofs told where there were public parks; Joyce would point them out and say he had spoken in all of them. At night the lights of London make a spectacular theatre, and it is said that keen eyes can distinguish the light which burns above Big Ben to show that the House has not yet risen. It was from this flat, on July 4, 1933, that William Joyce addressed the application for a passport which cost him his life. He desired it for the purpose of travelling to France and Germany.

It was a consciously illegal act, as he was not British. Or was it not quite that? The statement he made after his arrest makes it appear that he had never been sure about his nationality—which is to say, that he never made sure about it, that he never paid the visit to a solicitor which would have told him everything. He took a gamble on it. He took yet another gamble on standing for the two-seat constituency of Shoreditch as a Fascist candidate in the municipal elections of 1937. But success was far away; 2564 people voted for him and 2492 for another Fascist, out of a total poll of 34,128.

He took another gamble when he gave rein to his passion for street fighting in his new post and in cold deliberation and with burning appetite applied himself to the technical problems of creating disorders; for a conviction might mean deportation, if he were discovered. It was about this time that Michael Joyce, who had long been reconciled to his beloved firstborn, tore up his American passport and all documents relating to his American citizenship before the round astonished eyes of his son Quentin, muttering his secret and commanding that it should be kept a secret, clairvoyant in his perception of the existence of the awful danger threatening his blood, but wrong, as clairvoyance nearly always is, concerning its precise nature and the point in time and space where that danger waited. He thought it was to be a common exile of his family across the sea, and must have seen it near at hand about eighteen months after William Joyce took his first post with Mosley, when he and his chief, together with the Fascist officer for Sussex, Councillor Bentinck Budd, and a ranker named Mullan, appeared at Lewes Assizes on a charge of riotous assembly at Worthing. They were acquitted after a trial that lasted for two days.

The incident at Worthing had followed a rhythm by which the normal course of life in provincial towns of England, and even in London itself, had been disturbed again and again during the past few years. First the local Fascists would announce well in advance that Sir Oswald Mosley was coming to hold a meeting in the largest local hall. Truculent advertisements and parades would prevent the town from forgetting it. The idea of violence would suddenly be present in the town. The proper course for those who were anti-Fascist was to abstain from all action on the day of the meeting, to stay in their houses and ignore it; but the idea of violence would enter into them also, and they would feel under a compulsion to attend the meetings and interrupt and provoke the stewards to throw them out. Then relatives and friends would know what they were thinking, and grow tense with dread. On the day of the meeting Sir Oswald Mosley and his party would arrive in a town already in the grip of hysteria, and there would come with them sinister paraphernalia: a complete counterfeit of all necessary preparations for the battle which could be regarded as defensive. There were men in uniform carrying weapons, truncheons made of shot-loaded sections of hose-pipe sealed with lead, armoured cars; ambulances complete with doctors and nurses—making a picture that meant danger, that aroused fear, that provoked the aggression which is fear's defence. The anti-Fascists, who had at first expelled the idea of violence from their minds and then reluctantly readmitted it, gathered, unstrung by this abhorred mental guest, round the hall in which the Fascist intruders were holding their meeting, spinning out words to cover the emptiness of a programme that contained nothing but anti-Semitism and an intention to establish dictatorship against the general will. When the Fascists came out they paraded in front of the crowd, bearing themselves insolently, until they provoked hostile demonstrations. Having provoked these, they assaulted the demonstrators, who struck back. So the civil order which generation after generation of Englishmen had insisted on creating in despite of tyranny and the lawlessness of their own flesh, lay dead in the street.

At Lewes this foolish and horrible story was told once more. The meeting had been over at ten. A hostile but inactive crowd had been waiting outside the hall. Mosley's lieutenants came into the street, bearing themselves in the jackbooted way, with elbows bent and clenched fists swinging. They began to speak in offensive tones to the people standing by. One paused in front of a boy of seventeen, a post-office messenger, and said something to him. The boy did not answer, and the Fascist asked, "Don't you understand English?" The boy, looking at the Fascist's black shirt, said, "I don't understand Italian," and the Fascist hit him. At Lewes Assizes, Sir Patrick Hastings, while cross-examining this boy, asked him, "Can you think of anything more insulting than what you did say?" It is of course a barrister's duty to get his client out of the dock, and Sir Patrick was defending the four Fascists; and he had the right to ask any question he thought proper. But it is interesting to remember that Mosley had visited Fascist Rome not long before and had taken the salute with Mussolini at a review.

Sir Patrick was no doubt encouraged by the atmosphere of

the court. There were sound reasons why this should not be
wholly unfavourable to the defendants. It was obvious that the
Fascists could not be regarded as solely responsible for the riot.
That the anti-Fascists had sinned as well as being sinned against
was shown by the number of tomatoes they had thrown at
Mosley and his lieutenants; these could hardly have been found
lying about the street of Worthing at ten o'clock at night. And,
truth to tell, some of the anti-Mosley pamphlets sold in the
streets contained a great deal of nonsense. They implied that
Mosley had promised Malta to Mussolini and parts of the British
Empire to Hitler. And, as it would have been impossible for
either dictator to give Mosley effective help to seize power in
England, and as once he was the dictator of England he would
have been their superior in resources, it is hard to see why he
should have made any such commitment. It is possible that some
of the anti-Fascist organizations were providing an opposition
hardly less irresponsible and professional and dangerously itiner-
ant than the Fascists.

During the trial the judge made certain interventions. A
witness for the prosecution affirmed, when questioned about an
incident in a certain street, that "the whole affair seemed to be a
joke on the part of the crowd." This statement made Mr.
Justice Branson request, "Tell us one of the jokes. I am always
interested in good jokes." The witness replied, "They were
singing 'Mosley's got the wind up' and that sort of thing." Mr.
Justice Branson majestically inquired, "Do you call that a
joke?" He also had passages with the police witnesses. It appeared that a prominent Fascist member and his wife in Worthing had sent several passionately apprehensive telephone messages to the police station before and during the meeting. One
was sent from the hall where the meeting was being held. "Tell
Superintendant B——— to send some men down to restore order.
If it is not done I shall go out and take the law into my own
hands." The constable who received this message took no
action, because his superior officers were already on the spot
outside the meeting. Mr. Justice Branson commented severely on
his failure to act. Later a sergeant was examined who gave a
picture of the debauch of savagery with which the police force of
this seaside town had had to deal that night. In a typical passage
a witness described how he had seen Fascists rush to the door-

way of a chemist's shop, and followed them and when they had run away had found a person lying on the pavement unconscious, and then had turned round and seen another person, who was one of the witnesses in the trial, lying in the road, also unconscious. Mr. Justice Branson interrupted this witness to say, "I understood you to use the phrase, 'The crowd which first chased down South Street.' Was there a crowd which chased down South Street?" The sergeant answered, "There was a large number of people." Mr. Justice Branson asked, "Why do you change your language? One expects in these cases that police will give their evidence fairly and frankly. Just bear that in mind in answering the rest of the questions."

It was not surprising that William Joyce was acquitted at Lewes. There was no evidence to connect him with the riot that had taken place, and it was said by Sir Patrick Hastings that his name did not appear in any of the depositions. The other three defendants were also acquitted. At the close of the case for the prosecution the judge said he must take the responsibility of telling the jury that it should find a verdict of not guilty. As the jury expressed its full concurrence with its direction, and announced that it had been its intention to request that the evidence for the defence should not be heard, since the prosecution had failed to make out its case, and as the cases of assault which had been brought against some of the defendants in the local courts had been dismissed, the effect of the trial on William Joyce must have been intoxicating. Nevertheless, the Lewes trial may well have exercised a powerful influence on William Joyce's determination to travel the road that led to the gallows.

Indeed, the courts of law, civil as well as criminal, provided considerable encouragement for any ambitious Fascist at that time. But in the civil courts it was hardly the lawyers who could be held responsible. Virtue has its peculiar temptations, particularly when it is practised as a profession. The good are so well acquainted with the evil intentions of the wicked that they sometimes write as if the wicked candidly expressed their intentions instead of, as is customary, veiling them in hypocritical dissimulations. This has on many occasions led to the award of heavy damages against the good in cases brought under the laws of libel and slander by the wicked. The anti-Fascist press was not mindful enough of this danger when it dealt with Mosley, whom it considered to be wicked. In one libel action Sir Oswald Mosley won, and rightly won, a verdict entitling him to £5000 in damages, and his costs. It must have seemed to William Joyce that society had gone a long way towards certifying that fascism was not incompatible with its institutions, and it must have seemed to him that the opposition was unscrupulous and antisocial.

The daily routine of his work must have encouraged him in this delusion that he and his kind enjoyed the acquiescence, even the fondness, of society. It was unfortunate that the police liked him. They did not show him this favour because they shared his faith. It is a mistake to think that the police favoured the Fascists over the Communists—as they certainly did—on political grounds. There were, of course, policemen, as there were generals and admirals, who were deceived by the Fascists' use of the Union Jack and slogans about Britain into thinking them conservative patriots instead of international revolutionaries. There were others who regarded the Communists as bloodstained bolsheviks and admired the Fascists as their enemies. But there were many who thought, and both common sense and wisdom was with them, that if the Communists had ignored the Fascist meetings and refrained from interrupting them, the Fascists would have been checkmated, since they would not then have been able to exercise violence and plead that they were defending the right of free speech. They would then have had to attack Communist meetings or make unprovoked assaults on Jews in order to get their street fighting; and in that case policemen who arrested Fascists would have been able to get them convicted.

As it was, they were constantly forced by the Communists' actions into arresting Fascists who were discharged by magistrates because they pleaded that they acted under provocation; and there is nothing a policeman likes less than seeing the charge against a man he had arrested being dismissed. This is partly, though not entirely, a matter of pride. It also concerns his promotion. If there is any blame to be attached to the men involved in these proceedings, it should not fall on the police but on the magistrates, who were so very often satisfied that the Fascists had been provoked. But for magistrates and police alike, the situation was exasperating. If a man went to a meeting held by a party which advertised its loyalty to King and country through every material and spiritual loudspeaker, and which was notorious for its easy resort to violence, and he remained seated during the singing of the national anthem, police and magistrates alike felt a disinclination to concern themselves with what subsequently befell him. They were, of course, wrong. Their business was to suppress violence, however it had been provoked. But such citizens, and all those who played the Fascist game by accepting their challenge, were either irritating masochists or troublemakers obeying Communist instruction.

If the police liked Joyce it was because he persuaded them he was alleviating this ugly situation. He was a fine disciplinarian. His men were truly his. On them he now could play all the tricks of charm that take in young hero-worshippers: the recollections of a previous encounter, stated with a suggestion that an ineffaceable impression had been made, a permanent liking engendered; the sternness broken by a sudden smile. He had also learned the trick of turning his puniness into an asset of terror; a little man can be terrible when he outstares a taller and stronger subordinate who has been insolent to him, and coldly orders another subordinate, still taller and stronger, to inflict a brutal punishment on him. "Joyce really had his men under control," said a member of the police force, "and he was always fair to us. We could never come to an understanding with the Communists; if we saw the leaders it was hard to get on terms with them, and if we did persuade them to alter a plan they didn't seem able to make their men carry out the alteration. But if I went to Joyce and told him that his men were doing something that wasn't fair on the police, trying us too hard or interfering with our time off, he'd have his men right off that job in half an hour, and there'd be no grumbling. And he always kept his word, we found him very straight."

This officer—and he spoke for many of his colleagues—thought Joyce a far abler man than Mosley. It is possible that William Joyce was, at that time, a person of real and potent charm, offering the world what Blake said pleased it most, "the lineaments of gratified desire." He saw his path to greatness clear before him. He experienced the sharp joys of public speaking and street fighting nearly every night, and every month or so the more prolonged orgy of the great London or provincial meetings. Moreover, the routine of fascism freshened and liberated the child in its followers. Mosley had taken a black old building in King's Road, Chelsea, formerly a teachers' training college, where he housed his private army of the whole-time members of the British Union of Fascists, and there life was a boy's dream. Uniforms were worn that were not really uniforms, that at once claimed and flouted authority, as adolescence does; there was discipline, savage (and therefore sadistically sweet) while it lasted, but perfectly eluctable, not clamped down on a definite period of time by the King's Regulations; corridors were patrolled by sentries beetling their brows at nothing, executive officers sat at desks laden with papers alluding to mischief as yet too unimportant to justify authority in taking steps to check it; dead-end kids that could call what was dead alive and the end the beginning, innocently and villainously filled rubber truncheons with lead. There is nothing like infantilism for keeping the eyes bright and the skin smooth.

At this time, too, Joyce must have been intoxicated by new experiences of several kinds. His family now denies that he ever went to Germany before 1939. But others believed that he made the journey more than once and shared in the long, sterile orgasm of the Nuremberg Rally, held on the great barren place which once had been rich farmland, where crowds drunken with the great heat entered into union with a man who was pure nihilism, who offered militarism and defeat, regulation and anarchy, power and ruin, the cancellation of all. That was a deep pleasure, surrounded by shallower ones: the drives through the entrancing country, scored with the great works which German Joyces had ordained by a wave of the hand, the visits to the fine villas which German Joyces had made their own and stuffed with works of art, the eating and drinking from the Gothic and Renaissance tables of German Joyces, where the heavy goblets stood on Genoese velvet. In his own country he frequented the homes of the wealthy Mosleyite supporters, and there perhaps knew less than the absolute enjoyment Germany could have given or did give him.

Few of the upper-class supporters of Mosley were intellectually distinguished in any way that induced the relinquishment of social prejudice. Only an eccentric, equally distinguished as a physicist and a steeplechaser, and a peer whose enthusiasm for fascism was part of his passion for the grotesque and wholly

conditional upon its failure to realize its objects, come to mind
as probably unbiased by class feeling in their response to charm;
and of what they would have considered charm William Joyce
had none. Of course he had his wit; everybody who met him in
England or Germany agrees that he never talked for long without putting a twist on a sentence that surprised the hearer into
laughter. He had also the same pleasantness that was remarked
on so often by the officials who had charge of him during his last
days. But he was not, as they say, a gentleman. The other upper-
class supporters of Mosley were for the most part professional
soldiers and sailors, usually in their fifties; and of these some
asked William Joyce to their houses out of a sense that they
should recognize his services to the movement. He was to them,
nevertheless, like an officer risen from the ranks. Awkwardness
occurred. One week-end he was a guest at the country house of
an Army man who kept a large stable; and on Sunday morning
the host let his guests try some of his less valuable horses.
William Joyce, who had learned to ride as a boy in Mayo and
Galway, handled his horse so well that he was allowed to try
another one, a fine and difficult thoroughbred. The host's father,
an old gentleman so deaf that he could not tell whether he was
shouting or whispering, stood among the other guests and
watched. "How marvellously Mr. Joyce rides!" a lady bawled
into his ear. "Yes!" he bawled back, "but not like a
gentleman." Nobody was sure whether Mr. Joyce had heard.

When a man's social horizon widens, his sexual horizon
rarely stays where it was. There was a rackety recruit to fascism,
a wealthy young man who had suffered the initial handicap of
being expelled from an ancient school, not for any perversion
but for precocity induced by the enterprise of an American
actress who took a cottage near the school for the summer term.
He invited Joyce to a shooting-party, where he met the sister of
an Irish peer and was profoundly impressed by her. She felt no
corresponding emotion and probably never knew of his. It may
have been such disturbing encounters which first suggested to
William Joyce what might not have occurred to him if he had
stayed where he was born, that he need not always stay married
to the same woman. From the beginning, it is said, his life with
the girl he had married when they were both twenty-one had
been a cycle of romantic ecstasy and quarrels and impassioned

reconciliations; he would turn anything into a fight. He took it for granted, too, that he should spend an amount of time with men friends which must have made home life exiguous. During his time of service with Mosley his relations with his wife grew more and more purely quarrelsome, and in 1936, although they had by then two little daughters, this marriage was dissolved.

At a Fascist rally in Dumfries, William Joyce met the woman who was to be his second wife, a pretty and spirited girl. Like his mother from Lancashire, which had been his second home as a boy, Margaret White was the daughter of a textile warehouse manager and an enthusiastic member of the BUF. A devout Protestant, she was a secretary and a trained dancer, who often performed at cabaret shows given at festive gatherings of North Country Fascists. She was slender and graceful and took her art seriously, but she gladly threw away her ambitions to serve her husband and his ambitions. Though outsiders thought that Joyce's second marriage followed the same pattern of ecstasy and dissension and reconciliation as his first, there was apparently a deep and true love between him and his wife which was to endure to his death. There is indeed to be recognized in the conventional prettiness of her face a certain not conventional solemnity and submissiveness, as if she knew she should bow to a great force when it visited her; and it appears certain that she believed William Joyce to be that great force.

He left South London, which had been his home since he was a boy with the exception of a few brief periods; which was still the home of his father, Michael Joyce, and his mother, Queenie, and his brothers and sister; which was his appropriate home. Where the drab rows of little houses and the complacent villas shamed their builders by losing their drabness and their mediocrity because of the hills on which they were set, there he should have gone on living, this puny and undistinguished little man who was wild with a desire for glory. He moved to the north side of the river, but not to imperial London. When he married his second wife he was living in one of the dreariest spots in the dreariness east of Brompton Cemetery: a place where the cats limp and have mange, and the leaves bud brown in the spring. It was the first of his London homes which was characterless. He might have chosen it when he had ceased to care whether the routine of life was pleasant because he was so preoccupied with the crisis of the future.

5

SHORTLY after his marriage William Joyce began to contemplate deserting Mosley and becoming an agent of Nazi Germany. He did not get on well with his leader. It can be taken as certain that, if the police thought him more able than Mosley, he held the same opinion with some intensity. Moreover, it is impossible that Joyce was blind to the gulf that yawned between one part of the Fascist movement and another. The wife of one of the few Fascist leaders who were in the inner ring with Mosley was asked, "Did you and your husband ever ask Joyce to your house?" She answered in horror, "Oh, no, never. That was the great thing that worried us all, about what we were to do after Tom"—as Mosley was known to his familiars—"had become dictator. We didn't know how we were going to get rid of all those dreadful common people we had had to use to get power." It is unlikely that the sentiments behind the remarks would have remained hidden from the cold eyes of William Joyce, and that he would have missed the political implication behind them; and he may have asked himself just why Mosley had chosen him as deputy leader of the party. It would have seemed more natural that the position should be filled by one of the high-ranking Army or Navy officers who supported the move-ment, rather than by an insignificant little man with no social influence, for whom Mosley had no personal liking. William Joyce was tough enough to put the question in that form, and shrewd enough to answer it by admitting that his charm for Mosley was the obvious unlikelihood that he would set up as a rival for leadership of the movement.

There was also a difference between their outlook on policy, which became more marked as time went on, and in which the advantage lay with Joyce so far as simplicity was concerned. Mosley had started his movement before Hitler came to power;

Mussolini had been his inspiration. But very shortly after 1933 the emotional interest of the British Fascist movement shifted to Germany. This was in every sense natural, for what makes every Fascist and Communist movement go round is the pickings for the boys; and the boys in Italy had never had anything like the swollen and novel pickings that came to the boys in Germany. Mosley seems, like many people, to have believed that Hitler was a man of supreme ability, and perhaps felt some personal liking for him. That he married his second wife in Hitler's presence may have signified either real affection for Hitler or a desire to build up an alliance by intimacy. William Joyce on his side venerated Hitler as he had never been able to venerate Mosley. While William Joyce was cold but naïve, Mosley was hot-headed but sophisticated; he could argue with his own passions in defence, not of the truth, but of his own ends. Hence Mosley could bear to proclaim the Nazi doctrine of a totalitarian and anti-Semitic state without overt propaganda for Hitler. His line was to admit admiration for Hitler and Mussolini, but to deprecate any excessive interest in Continental affairs and profess belief in isolationism. "Mind Britain's Business" was his slogan; and he assured the public that if Hitler was given a free hand in Europe and was returned his mandated colonies, while we at home suppressed the Jews, the peace of the world would be guaranteed, and the British Empire would be immune from attack. But he was careful to say that if Hitler should ever attack the British Empire, its people would, of course, defend themselves, and would be victorious. William Joyce wanted to preach acclamation of Hitler as the saviour of the world on such unconditional terms that by implication it must be the duty of every good Briton to resist any British government which took up arms against him.

Both these policies would work out to the same result. If Great Britain had pursued an isolationist policy and let Hitler conquer Europe as Mosley wished, Hitler would have had no reason to refrain from crossing the Channel and setting up what government he pleased; and there the matter would have remained, for it would have been extremely difficult for America to come to the aid of an invaded Great Britain which had acquiesced in the invasion of all the rest of Europe. In these circumstances it would certainly have been the Fascists from whom Hitler would draw his quisling government. On the other hand, if the Fascists had devoted their energies in peacetime to the proclamation of the greatness of Hitler, as Joyce wished, and preached collaboration freely and frankly up to the declaration of the war (within the limits set down in the law of treason), then again it would seem the Fascists would furnish the quislings when they were needed. Of the two policies, Joyce's policy frankly admitted the international character of fascism, which makes a man ready to be a traitor to his country, his county, his town, his street, his family, himself, and loses its dynamic power if it does not act by and through this readiness for treachery. Moreover, it was designed on the plane of heroism, and for that reason, had England been defeated in 1940, might have been more corrupting, since a quisling has more power if he has shown himself a brave man. This was outside the framework of Mosleyism.

But policy was not the only subject of disagreement between Mosley and Joyce at this moment. Joyce was, for the first time in his life, troubled about money. He had been brought up in a household where there had always been enough to maintain the simple satisfaction of all needs. He had supported himself and his wife adequately on his earnings as a tutor, which he had been able to stretch by taking on extra classes. For his chief pleasures, which were public speaking and street fighting, he did not pay but was paid. In his lesser pleasures he could afford to pay. For example, he had a fine radiogramophone and a large library of records, chiefly operatic. Now, however, he had to make a home for himself and his second wife and support his first wife's children, and Mosley was paying him a small and inelastic salary. He needed an increase in pay just at the very time when Mosley was least likely to give it. Mosley must have been in genuine financial difficulties. It is said that he was spending nine-tenths of his income on the cause, but that went nowhere in maintaining a private army of anything from twelve hundred to two thousand, together with a great number of subsidized hangers-on. It is true that he was financed by some industrialists, and by some City firms, even including one or two who by reason of their origin should have been most careful not to compromise themselves in this direction. But these industrialists were not the great magnates who were persistently rumoured to be contributing to Mosley's funds; they were for the most part old gentlemen at the head of minor firms with only moderate means at their disposal. If ever the bigger City firms were more generous they were also more canny, and both alike were beginning to be less forthcoming. They had contributed because they had believed Mosley to be a stabilizing force in society. But do what he could, he could not prevent his movement from looking what it was, revolutionary. The increasing brutality of the brawls with Jews and Communists was betraying the nature of its inspiration.

Also, time was to reveal that the right sort of recruits were not coming in. It is true that the movement enlisted Sir Arnold Wilson, an extremely able colonial administrator. Another writer of some standing and much charm supported the party, but it was too generally recognized that he had not been sober for thirty years for his political opinions to carry much weight. There should have been some appeal to the Kipling tradition in Francis Yeats-Brown, a soldier and the author of a best-seller about Army life in the East, but he was handicapped by his devotion to Oriental mysticism in its quainter manifestations. About this time a Fascist leader was driving a banker whom he regarded as a possible convert back from a week-end which had seemed very profitably spent, when he realized that they were passing the home of this officer-author and suggested that they should stop and call on him. The banker was delighted. But the butler repelled them. The major was in, and the butler would take a message to him, but he could not possibly be seen. The Fascist persisted and finally the butler, who was a traditional butler, for this was a traditional home, broke down and said, "It's no use, this is the day he spends sitting on the roof with his Yogi having his perpetual enema."

British fascism did hardly better with its aristocratic supporters. One of these bore a title founded by a historic personage of the first order. If anybody alluded in his hearing to his great ancestor "the great Duke of———" his brows would contract and he would say huffily, "The first Duke of———." Later he was to give his life nobly in the war against fascism, and this anecdote relates to a superficial oddity and not to the sum of him. It is worth while recalling only to explain the difficulties that Mosley was having in creating an impression of normality.

Even with his numerous service members he had his difficulties. He had to handle these with care, lest possibly an officer of personal attractions and gifts for oratory and administration should dispute his leadership. But all the same, it was a pity that his most active service supporter should be stone-deaf, although it is true that deafness has more than once played a decisive part in our great island story; our pro-Bulgarian policy, which so disastrously endured for generations, was largely the work of a *Times* correspondent who travelled through the Balkans ceaselessly but without being able to hear a word that anyone said to him. Worst Mosleyite disappointment of all, however, was a wealthy and aristocratic young man, now dead, who created a most favourable impression at one of the Nuremberg rallies but was, like the friend named Guy Burgess who had accompanied him, a Communist deputed to infiltrate the Mosley movement.

Naturally enough the movement was short of subscriptions. Joyce was paid no advance on salary commensurate with his services to the movement and he was therefore left in a state of insecurity and with a feeling that Mosley had failed to fulfil the promise he had seemed to make to his obscure followers, the promise that those outside should find themselves at last inside, that the powerless should find themselves as equals among the powerful. Sometime in the beginning of 1937 a police officer who knew Joyce found himself alone with him in a compartment in a late train from the Midlands which had had a breakdown. For a time they talked of impersonal matters, then, as the delay lengthened, fell into silence, which the police officer suddenly found himself breaking with the question, "Joyce, what do you really think of Mosley?" He had no idea why he asked that question; he had heard nothing of any breach between the two. The little man, who had been huddled in fatigue, now fixed the police officer with eyes cold as ice. Joyce was famous among the British Fascists for his power to curse, and for the next ten minutes, quietly and steadily, he used it, then sank back into apparent slumber. The police officer paid him the classic compliment of saying that he never once repeated himself, and added that "there was nothing ordinary in it," and he summed up its content as an opinion that "Mosley was letting them down by doing his job so badly." A few weeks later it was announced that Mosley had dismissed Joyce from his post as the Director of

Propaganda and deputy leader of the Party, for the reason that he was under a necessity to cut down on his salaried staff.

Within three weeks of leaving the BUF, Joyce had founded his British National Socialist League; and very soon afterwards he had an office in London and an official organ, *The Helmsman*. This was quick work; it also cost money. It is true that it did not cost much money, but then Joyce had almost none. He had gone back to his work as a tutor and was doing well, but not so well that he could earn much more than would support himself and his wife and meet other obligations. The British National Socialist League could never boast a membership that was more than a fraction of the strength of the BUF, and never pretended to live on its subscriptions. The only subscriber to British National Socialist League funds who has been identified with any certainty was the old Scottish stockbroker whose sister was later to visit Joyce in prison, and he gave generously, but nothing that went into thousands. Joyce himself declared that he was financed by certain industrialists, but it seems most unlikely that any industrialist shrewd enough to have maintained his business would have thought it worth while to subsidize this lone little man who, however great his gift for organization, had now only a handful of followers to organize. There was, on the other hand, a great deal of German money lying about in England at that time, to be picked up by anybody who chose to take a certain amount of trouble.

How little that trouble needed to be, how that money could petition to be picked up, can be illustrated by the case of the two young women with strong right-wing views who thought it would be amusing to write and publish a newsletter. After a couple of numbers appeared they were approached by a man holding a teaching position in a certain university, who told them that he would finance their newsletter to the extent of two or three thousand pounds, provided only that they published a certain amount of approving references to Hitler. If William Joyce accepted money from such sources, he was breaking no law. In the United States it is a crime to take money from the representative of a foreign power without registering as a foreign agent, but in England such an act is lawful and it would be easy to name a number of English persons on the Right and the Left who have benefited by transactions with Continental governments anxious to have friends in England. The United States law is, however, rendered nugatory by the power of bribery to take forms other than cash payments. There, as in England, publishing houses specially founded for the purpose can commission propagandist works, and the managements of societies for friendship toward specific countries offer well-paid jobs, while alien governments can buy whole editions of books or subscribe for thousands of issues of a journal. It is not impossible that Joyce accepted money, directly or indirectly, from those with whom he conspired, but it is quite certain that he did not commit treason for the sake of gain.

Some time after Joyce had left the British Union of Fascists and set up his own movement, he and his wife had moved to a very pleasant home, the most expensive home he occupied in his whole life: the top flat of a doctor's house in a soberly agreeable square in South Kensington. It would never have been let to him had he presented himself as the prospective tenant. But it was taken by Angus MacNab, whose obvious good breeding and gentleness impressed the doctor and his wife very favourably. He explained to them that he was setting up in business as a coach in partnership with a friend named William Joyce, and at a second interview brought with him Mrs. Joyce, whom they thought not so well bred as he was, but pretty and agreeable. On these samples of the household they concluded the transaction, and were disconcerted when its third person arrived with the removal van, which contained a prodigious amount of books and some poor sticks of furniture, and proved to be a queer little Irish peasant who had gone to some pains to make the worst of himself. The wearing of uniforms by private persons was by then illegal; so he and MacNab always wore black sweaters of a shape calculated to recall the Fascist black shirt. He wore a suit and trenchcoat in imitation of Hitler's turn-out, and they were deliberately kept dirty and shabby; he cropped his hair in the Prussian style and never wore a hat; he always carried a very thick stick; and he bore himself with a deliberate aggressiveness. The doctor and his wife instantly took a dislike to him, which they were to find not unjustified when they saw more of the household. They liked his wife and thought he treated her tyrannously, overworking her and giving her no thanks, in the peasant way. He was tiresomely exigent about his meals; and not only had she to cook them, but she had to wash up afterwards and then run off to help at the league office in the daytime, and in the evenings at meetings. But the doctor and his wife had to admit that she adored him and that he evidently made her very happy.

They had other complaints against him. Their new tenants were indubitably noisy. Joyce had always loved noise. A young man who knew him during his first marriage tells how he learned chess from him in a tiny room just big enough to hold two chairs, a table, and a radiogramophone which blared continuously at full blast. It was torture for the pupil; Joyce took it as natural. Here the household banged doors and stamped about when they came in excited from their meetings, and sometimes gave rowdy parties. To one of them they invited the doctor's wife, who happened to be alone that evening. She was not reassured. Some of the guests were wild Irishmen—the same that attended his trial. These were for the most part from families with the same roots as the Joyces, who had been supporters of the British occupation of Ireland and who had had to leave the country for safety's sake when Home Rule was granted. One among these was the son of a man who had performed an act of charity towards a man dying of gunshot wounds beside the road without inquiring into his political affiliations, was consequently victimized by his neighbours till he was obliged to take refuge in England, and there died in poverty, leaving his family aggrieved because they had received no adequate compensation from the British government. The doctor's wife was unaware of the pathetic antecedents of these merrymakers, but she was disconcerted by the vehement quality of the merriment they made, and she came to her own conclusions about a gentleman with long hair who was wearing a scarlet cloak and a pectoral cross, and who introduced himself as the monarch of an Eastern European nation. It was not revealed to her that he had once been sentenced to a term of imprisonment for the publication of obscene poetry, but she felt there was something a little odd about him.

Nevertheless, the doctor and his wife did not attempt to terminate the lease. They were moved to this forbearance partly by their kindly feeling towards Mrs. Joyce, who, they foresaw, would suffer greatly in one way or another through her marriage. They also liked MacNab, who was amiable and fantastical. Once when Joyce had gone off with the key to the flat and a pipe had burst inside it, MacNab, explaining that he had been a leading member of the Oxford Alpine Club, swarmed up the back of the Kensington house, by pipes and window ledges and gutters, till he found a window open on the fifth story. But the doctor and his wife developed more serious reasons than these for tolerance. One of their sons was taken ill and had to miss a term or two at his boarding-school, and during this period MacNab and William Joyce coached him, one in Greek and mathematics, the other in Latin and French. The parents found the boy was getting better teaching than he had ever had in his life, as they discovered that these two strange men really cared for the things of the mind, really possessed unusual intellectual capacity. After that they sometimes asked their tenants down to their sherry parties; and they found to their surprise that though William Joyce was so obviously odious in so many ways, so vulgar, so pushing, so lacking in sweetness, many of their guests found his conversation interesting and amusing and even charming. They were baffled. They did not know what they wanted to do about their odd lodger, and the doing of it might not have been easy. The rent of the flat was paid with perfect regularity. It would have been difficult to break the lease except on very contestable grounds, and contest was certainly not out of Joyce's line.

So it seemed as if this exile was to lose his rootlessness in a place that asked roots to grow and promised the grown plant pleasantness. Joyce's flat looked down on a communal garden of the sort that makes South Kensington so pleasantly green; the houses which back on it have their dining rooms built out into this garden. In summertime the ladies of these houses often sat with their friends among tubs of flowers on the flat roofs of these dining rooms, taking tea and looking down on their well-schooled children, who played on the lawns below. In late summertime, in the year 1938, William Joyce sat in his pleasant home and applied for the renewal of his passport. It might be assumed that he had been sent for by someone who wished him to go abroad. It might also be assumed that he had not expected this summons, for he had let his passport expire without applying for its renewal. It had run out on July 6. This was September 24: five days before the Munich Agreement was signed. Nothing is gained by the postponement of an application for the renewal of a passport. At whatever date the application is made, it is renewed from the date of its expiry. It is possible that William Joyce felt no exultation at all while he was filling in his application form. He had faced danger as a boy, but that was nearly twenty years ago. Ever since then he had lived cradled in the safety of the civil order of England, which he and his Fascist friends and Communist enemies were vowed to destroy, and safety becomes a habit. He must have liked the green dignity of this garden part of Kensington; it was like the home of his boyhood, which was also in one of the green corners of London, down in Allison Grove. He must have liked the setting of his life, and also its core. He liked teaching and he had his meetings, and he was still deeply and romantically in love with his wife. If he had given an undertaking to leave that home when a certain voice called him, then he must daily have known a real distress.

That time Joyce was let off and the wind of danger blew and fell again; and immediately after Munich Joyce lost his most valuable colleague. Just about this time Joyce began to lose the friendship of his landlords; and the German radio sounded too loud through the house, the hiccupping piano achieved the Horst Wessel song too often. The breach widened when Hitler walked into Czechoslovakia; the doctor and his wife were standing in the hall, aghast at the news, when Joyce came in, and asked him, "Now what do you think of Hitler?" Joyce said, without a smile, "I think him a very fine fellow," and went on his way up to his flat. MacNab came in a little later. The doctor and his wife pressed him for his opinion, and he too approved. The curious friendship between the two households, so unequal in social background and in character, faded from that moment, though the doctor and his wife still showed kindliness to Mrs. Joyce. Joyce, working alone, worked frantically. He spoke to every society that would let him inside its doors, in the warmer weather he had an open-air meeting every day, and sometimes several in one day. It was as if he was trying to leave an impression on the public mind that could be counted upon to endure; and indeed he partially succeeded in this aim. An enormous number of people in the low-income groups heard him speak, some during the years when he was with Mosley, and even more during the period when he was his own master.

Many people in the higher-income groups had also their contact with Joyce, but they did not know it. Anybody who was advertised as a speaker at a meeting appealing for funds or humane treatment for refugees from Nazi persecution would receive by every post, for many days before the meeting, threatening messages, couched always in the same words, and those words always so vague that the writers of them could not have been touched by the law. They were apt to come by the last post, and the returning householder, switching on the light, would see them piled up on the hall table, splinters from a mass of stupidity that might not, after all, be finite and destructible, but infinite and conterminous with life. Their postmarks showed they came from Manchester, Bristol, Bournemouth, Bethnal Green, Glasgow, Colchester. All over the country there were those who wished that the stranger, being hungry, should not be fed; being naked, should not be clothed. Goats and monkeys, as Othello said, goats and monkeys; and the still house would seem like a frail and besieged fortress. This device was the invention of William Joyce. The people who heard him in the streets sometimes saw this alliance with crime displayed. A number of his meetings were provocative of the violence he loved; he was twice tried for assault at London police courts during the year preceding the outbreak of war, though each time the wind that sat in so favourable a quarter for Fascists blew him out with an acquittal. But at many others of his meetings he used all his powers: his harsh, sneering, cajoling, denatured, desperate voice; his quick and twisting humour; his ability to hammer a point home on a crowd's mind, to persuade the men and women he saw before him of the advantages of dictatorship, the dangers of Jewish competition and high finance, the inefficiency of democracy, the greatness and goodness of Hitler, and his own seriousness. His audiences were not much interested in his arguments and were shrewd enough in their judgment of him. Many remembered him seven years afterwards. Only a very few said, "I liked him." Most said, "He has the most peculiar views, but he really was an extraordinary chap," or some such words. "Extraordinary" was what they called him, nearly all of them. This impression might not have served Joyce so ill had the days brought forth what he expected. If the Germans had brought him with them when they invaded England and had made him their spokesman, many Londoners might have listened to him with some confidence because in a scene which conquest would have made terrifying in its unfamiliarity he was a familiar figure.

William Joyce seemed to hear a second summons from abroad eleven months after the first. During that time his circumstances changed. In July he had left his agreeable home in South Kensington, at his own instance. In June he had suddenly written to the doctor saying that, with much regret, he must confess himself unable to carry out his three years' lease, which had still another year to run; the number of his pupils had, he explained, suddenly showed a sharp decline. The doctor answered, possibly not without some feeling of relief, that Joyce was at full liberty to sublet the flat, and this Joyce undertook to do. One day, before the Joyces left, the doctor's wife met Mrs. Joyce on the stairs and, with the extreme sweetness and generosity this couple always showed their strange tenants, paused to tell her how sorry she was that their connections must end for so sad a reason. She said, "All our fortunes vary, you know. One goes up and one comes down and then one comes up again, so you mustn't worry if things are bad." To her astonishment Mrs. Joyce burst into tears, flung her arms round her neck, and sobbed out, "You do not know how bad they are, you have no idea how bad they are."

About this time Joyce was importuned by a strange visitor; a man who, like so many of the British National Socialist League, was Irish, rang the bell marked "Joyce" that was beside the doctor's bell at the front door. Joyce came down, opened the door, looked at the visitor, slammed it, and went upstairs again. The visitor went on ringing and began to pound on the knocker. MacNab came down, white-faced, and opened the door, parleyed with the visitor, but, like Joyce, retreated. Out on the porch the visitor rang the bell and hammered on the door and began to shout. The doctor's manservant went out and tried to send him away; he cried out that he must see William Joyce, no one else would do. The door was shut, he remained outside, crying out in accusation, in imploration, in panic, as one who knew a great shame was to be committed and could not stop it. The police would have been fetched, but at that moment the doctor arrived, a tall, authoritative man, and took him by the arm, and turned him round towards South Kensington Station, and told him to follow the road to it. He went off, mumbling about a catastrophe.

What is significant is that Joyce, for all his volubility, could not find an explanation for this incident.

Paying their rent up to the last minute, leaving no trades-men's bills unsettled, the Joyces moved to a lodging as poor as any he had known since he had left home as a boy. It was a basement flat in a short street of dreary and discoloured houses, mean in size, which lies on the Warwick Road side of Earl's Court Station. Over their roofs, making them more dwarfish, looms the stadium, in formless height, morbid with the sick pallor of concrete; and at the end of the street is the wall of Brompton Cemetery, pierced with openings covered by wire netting, which disclose the sparse tombs among the long grasses on the cemetery's edge, and the distant white crowd of stout Victorian dead round the central avenues. This was not only a melancholy home for Joyce; it was minute, no broader than a henhouse. It might have been chosen by a man who believed himself about to go on a long journey and to need no more than a place to keep his clothes and his baggage till the time came to pack the one inside the other.

William Joyce must have been sure, in the summer of 1939, that there was going to be war, for we were all sure of that. And with half of his mind he knew what part he was going to play in it; but with only half, for again he let his passport expire. He did not apply for its renewal until August 24; and that date destroys William Joyce's last claim on our sympathies. For it is one day after Hitler signed his pact with Stalin. Then this man who all his adult life had hated Communists must have known that his leader was an opportunist and not a prophet; that he himself was apostle of a policy and not a religion; that there was nothing in the cause to which he had devoted his life that was equal in worth to the ancient loyalties. Now he should have seen what was on the underside of the banners stamped on the over-side with the swastika that hung between the sky and the stadium at Nuremberg. Now he should have recognized that the words he had been saying since 1927 were "Evil, be thou my good." But he would not open his eyes or unstop his ears and he stood fast and chose damnation. It is here his happy marriage helped to contrive his doom. He had made his decision to go over to Germany with the knowledge of his wife. To have gone back on it would have been a confession that he had been unwise when he made it; and he may have feared that such a reversal might have looked like a failure in courage. There are risks the most loving will not take with the beloved.

It is said that William Joyce went to Germany on the eve of the war on an off chance and offered his services to a surprised propaganda machine. But that some people from England were anticipating his departure for Berlin, and tried to stop it, is proved by the recollection of one who, in September 1939, was still a schoolgirl. One summer evening she was walking in the Fulham Road with her uncle, a young man who was a member of the British National Socialist League, when they met William Joyce, who was well known to both of them. He seemed strangely excited, and he told them, laughing extravagantly, that when he had been driving his car on the previous day he had been pulled in by the police for a trifling breach of the traffic regulations. The schoolgirl and her uncle were puzzled by his emotion. The uncle said, "But this is nothing. All sorts of people get run in for motoring offences." Joyce answered, waving his hat and clapping it back on his head, "Do you call this a motoring offence? I would call it a holding offence!" and went on his way. A "holding offence" is a device often and properly used by the police. When the police suspect a man of a serious crime but cannot prove him guilty of it, they watch him to see if he commits some minor offence, such as a breach of the traffic regulations. If they are lucky and he acts according to their expectations, then they can serve him with a summons and until he has faced his trial can exercise a certain amount of control over him. During this time they can prevent him from leaving the country. Late in August 1939, in a street near Queen Anne's Gate, William Joyce met an acquaintance who had long ago been his neighbour in East Dulwich, and they halted and had a chat. When they parted Joyce's acquaintance noted that he turned into the building beside which they had halted, and realized that this was the Passport Office. Even before that the name of William Joyce must have been posted at every port; and as soon as he fetched and had in his possession a renewed passport the warning signal should have been repeated. But a few days afterwards the police were searching for him all over the country; the old lady in Sussex was questioned, and her house was watched. William Joyce left England by the ordinary Continental route from Victoria Station without hindrance. Here was either a breakdown of routine fantastically fortunate for him or another traitor, working with him on the same pattern of treachery.

6

IN Germany autumn is not as it is in England, a time of sleepy mellowness. The red and gold of the foliage is hard to the eye, the air is like iron; those who sail on the waterways which run all the way from the Wannsee to the Baltic find their lips seared, though they may not feel very cold, by the air which has come down from the Arctic. Into this season, in its fierce and icy brilliance, which is one of Germany's particular enchantments, William Joyce was brought by his treachery. One day his little feet twinkled up the area steps of his basement flat near Earl's Court. His eyes must have been dancing. No matter what his misgivings might have been, the risks of the adventure must have delighted him. It must, indeed, have been intoxicating for him to go through London, where he had never been of any importance, where he was at best a street-corner speaker better known than most, and know that, if he won his gamble, he would return to it as the right hand of its conquerors. There would be then no building he would not have the right to enter, bearing with him the power to abolish its existing function and substitute another. There would be no man or woman of power whom he would not see humiliated, even to the point of imprisonment and death. The first should be last, and the last should be first, and many would be called and few would be chosen, and he would be among those that were chosen. He left the damp and the fog which would soon close in on London, and the obscurity which had closed in on him ever since he was born, and he went out to the perfect autumn of Germany and the promise of power. Very soon he was established in a home in the Kastanien Allee—Chestnut Avenue—in that most delightful suburb of Berlin, Charlottenburg, where there are broad streets of wide windowed flats and little avenues of villas in flower gardens. On September 18, 1939, exactly fifteen days after the outbreak of war, he joined the German radio as an announcer of the news on the English service and had very soon become a reader of the news.

His voice was very soon recognized by the doctor and his wife in South Kensington, who had already begun to wonder about their former tenants. When an officer of the National Fire Service had come to examine their attics for combustibility they had found an inexplicable addition to their home. In a cistern loft, accessible only from the flat the Joyces had occupied, a bed had been put up and was there with its bedding. There was plenty of room to put up a bed in the ordinary rooms of the flat; the loft could be entered only by a very small trapdoor, and it must have been very difficult to get the bed up through it; there was almost no space to spare round the bed. It must have been put up there during William Joyce's tenancy, for somebody who had to be sheltered without the knowledge of the doctor and his wife. We shall never know who this was. Now William Joyce had lost a friendship which he had found it hard to win, and perhaps it occurred to him already in Germany that he might have made a bad bargain. He had not been given a warm welcome by his new friends the Nazis. They showed no consciousness of his experience as an agitator, and they underrated his remarkable powers as a broadcaster and gave him nothing to do but read news bulletins. But he was used to being thought little of by people when he first met them. That the news he was broadcasting was often fatuously untrue, and rendered all German propaganda suspect by its untruth, was probably unknown to him. When he told England that in September or October 1939—long before any bombs had fallen on the British mainland—Dover and Folkestone had been destroyed, he may well have believed it. It is worth while noting that this period of Joyce's service to the Nazis was given an interest in England which it lacked for him. The local details by which Joyce was supposed to show that he had a direct channel of communication with England, such as allusions to stopped town-hall clocks and road repairs, are not in fact found in the records of his broadcasts. They were invented as part of a whispering campaign designed to weaken public confidence, which was carried on by Fascists, some of whom, if not all, belonged to organizations other than

Joyce's British National Socialist League. Ignorant of the inaccuracy of his broadcasts, and the use that was being made of them, Joyce may have been bored with his work; but he cannot have felt such a passive emotion about the conditions in which he worked.

He must very soon have looked round the office of the English section of the Rundfunk in panic. It is said that the Duke of Wellington, on seeing some troops for the first time, exclaimed, "I don't know if these fellows frighten the enemy, but, by God, they frighten me!" So might William Joyce have exclaimed when he first saw the colleagues who had been artlessly assembled by Dr. Goebbels' propaganda machine. The most sympathetic was an elderly lady called Miss Margaret Frances Bothamley, who before the war had helped to found a body called the Imperial Fascist League and run it from her flat in the Cromwell Road. She was in a state of extreme confusion. She had brought with her to Germany photographs of the King and Queen and the Princesses, with which she ornamented her flat; and she believed that in her youth she had made a secret marriage with a German music-master named Adolf, whom she appeared to identify with Hitler. During the first months of the war Joyce was forced to recruit a member of Miss Bothamley's organization who had been spending the summer in Germany: a colonel's daughter who belonged to one of the most famous literary families in England on her father's side and was related to a most exalted peer on her mother's side, but who had, through a series of unhappy accidents, found herself in her late forties lost in less distinguished worlds. She began by being an enthusiastic pro-Nazi, but, being fundamentally not without honesty and decency, turned against the regime and annoyed Joyce by sitting about in the office and doing knitting with an air of silent criticism.

There was also Mr. Leonard Black, who must have been a disappointing colleague for William Joyce. He was under thirty, and he had a long history behind him of inextricably confused idealistic effort and paid political adventure. He had at one time been a member of the BUF, but had left it and had later been a paid organizer in the service of the Conservative Party, while at the same time—which was odd—carrying on pacifist agitation. Then he went abroad and taught English at various branches of the Berlitz School of Languages, and was so doing in September

1939. It was his story later that the day before war was declared he went down to the station and tried to buy a ticket to England and found they would not sell him one for German money, and, as he had no foreign currency, went home. Few of us do not know the mechanism employed. He had wanted to stay in Germany. He said, "I ought to go and see about that today. But tomorrow will do just as well. I have a lot to do now. I will go tomorrow." He did that until one day when somehow it became possible to put aside all engagements and take the necessary steps; and on that day it happened that those necessary steps could no longer be taken. Then he returned home, saying, "Well, I have done all I could. Nobody could have told that today it would be too late. It is not my fault." And at the back of his mind a voice must have said with cold cunning, "Yes, I will be able to tell them that, if things go wrong and I am called to account," while another voice said, "Look, you Nazis, I have stayed with you." Most of us—except the people who are in fact intolerable nuisances by reason of their incapacity for compromise—have at some time or other behaved according to this formula. William Joyce, having just abandoned this formula at the great crisis of his life, was unlikely to feel sympathy with Leonard Black or other recruits of his type.

He owed the presence of Black in his office to the activities of a certain Herr Albrecht, whose business it was to see what Englishmen stranded in Germany would do for their hosts. He sent for Mr. Black and a friend of his called Mr. Smith and questioned them as to their readiness for cooperation. Mr. Black went home and wrote Herr Albrecht a typically ambiguous letter. "Dear Herr Albrecht," he wrote, "I write to make it perfectly clear that I have not offered to work for the Gestapo. I would never think of doing that, and I absolutely refuse to sell my country. There is a certain price I will not pay. The most I would do is radio propaganda." And he ended with a postscript which bears a significance beyond his intention. "Mr. Smith," he wrote, "will not even do radio propaganda." Mr. Smith, using that term in its generic sense, did not even do radio propaganda. Only a small proportion of the civilian internees or prisoners of war lost their loyalty; and of those that did, many found themselves too noble to be the instruments of their own ignobility and went back to their camps, where some of them were punished till they died, and all suffered grave torment. They were not many, the men who could split their minds in two and pretend that while they were serving Germany they were making contact with anti-Nazi elements and sabotaging Nazi activity, which was the defence that nearly all of them kept at the back of their minds and produced at their trials. All such men hated William Joyce, who did not split his mind, who desired to make England Fascist and, to procure that end, was ready to help Germany to conquer England, and never denied that desire or that readiness, either during the war or after it.

He sat among the hatred of these poor silly creatures and knew a more humiliating hatred from some others who worked in his office. A certain number of Germans had been drafted into the office, men who had a special knowledge of the English language and English life. As such men had usually acquired their knowledge through having English relatives or having been educated in England, many were anti-Nazi. They despised Joyce as a traitor to his own country and an enemy to their own country, the true Germany; and they were gentlemen and cruelly knew he was not a gentleman. But there was another painful element in the office, which must have cut William Joyce far deeper. The Nazis were prone, in all sorts of circumstances, to make a peculiar error. When one of their enemies became their friend, they went on treating him as an enemy. However ready he might be to serve their interests, however much they might need his help, they continued to savage him. The great historic example of this curious trick is their treatment of the Russian soldiers and civilians who, by tens of thousands, gladly surrendered to them as they invaded Russian territory in 1941 and 1942. These people, who might have been their most valuable aids then and forever after, they packed into cattle trucks and sent off to camps where they were starved and tortured. Later they were fetched out and invited to fight alongside the Germans, but by that time their enthusiasm was not what it had been, and the treatment they received in training and at the front failed to revive it. The Germans acted on the same perverse principle towards the British broadcasters, who were all favourably disposed towards them to start with, and, having burned their boats, had every reason to remain firm in the faith. But at the head of the British section, which they had as if in mockery called the Concordia Bureau, they placed a certain official who was detested by his staff, English and German.

Two Germans were to tell a British court what this man had been, in evidence that was disinterested and, indeed, unaware of its own portent. When Mr. Black was tried at the Old Bailey early in 1946, the prosecution called as a witness one of the German technicians who had recorded his talks. He was an SS man, a lank and hollow-cheeked young man, who might have been carved in wood in the thirteenth century, and he spoke a peculiar wooden German which might come to be natural in a man who had been drilled all his youth in tyranny and then marched along a straight road for many years in the direction of defeat. He was called Krumpiegel; surely one might as well be called Rumpelstiltskin. As he gave evidence, there stood beside him the interpreter who was then one of the chief glories of the Old Bailey, that slender and distinguished old gentleman of Spanish Jewish descent, Mr. Salzedo. He was very courteous to the defeated barbarian but plainly savoured a certain satisfaction as, in his silvery voice, he translated the comic expressions used by barbarity. "Did Black look happy when he was at the Concordia Bureau?" asked the defending counsel. Mr. Salzedo translated: "He says that he does not consider happy (*glücklich*) an appropriate word to use in connection with Black's personality, but for the greater part of the war he could fairly be described as contented (*zufrieden*)." The defending counsel continued: "But did Black seem to be contented in his relations with the head of the bureau?" Krumpiegel looked more wooden than ever; he folded his arms behind him, said some words, and looked blank as an ill-treated child that has told the truth about its tormentors and does not believe that it will not be punished for it, whatever the grown-ups say. Mr. Salzedo translated: "He says the chief's relations with his employees were never a source of gratification." There came later to give evidence for Mr. Black one of the anti-Nazi Germans who had worked in the Concordia Bureau, a sad being wearing an air of desolation more usually presented by places than by persons, a human Golgotha. A question made allusion to this same chief. The anti-Nazi paused before answering. In accomplished, springless, exhausted, pedantic English, he said, "He was . . . the . . . prototype . . .

of the Nazis." The Concordia Bureau had been battered by huge irrational waves, tides obeying the moon of Hell. Joyce must have been devoured by rage to find himself subordinate. But there he had to sit, at this command, with his idiot compatriots around him. There was one last irony in his situation, of which, fortunately, he was unaware. Among the English who had come to Germany to broadcast for the Nazis, some were Communist agents. The party thought it wise to have eyes and ears here also. One of these at least denounced several of the genuine British Fascists to the German authorities as spies. But in the first years of the war, no doubt these poor wretches refused to worry about what were obviously only temporary conditions. When there were gathered in as Nazi harvest first Norway, then Denmark, then the Low Countries, then France, there was nothing on earth to prevent the fall of England; and all the poor misfits in the Concordia Bureau must have had their heads stuffed with infantilist dreams. In dreams a fast car, long as a bus, would be sent down to Dulwich to pick up the family and bring them to Joyce's office; which would have been in Buckingham Palace, or in the War Office, or Downing Street. . . .

It would, in fact, have been in none of these places. Inexorably the law that to him that hath it shall be given would have come into operation again; there would certainly have come forward as quislings after the first few days of the German occupation this popular historian and that expert in foreign affairs, this civil servant and that leading Communist, and these would have been given precedence over William Joyce, who would have found himself fulfilling just the same subordinate role in the new dispensation as in the old. But that he would not have suspected. He must have imagined himself saying to his father and mother, smiling, "Well, this is my room. Do you like it? And the next one is mine too, that's where my three secretaries work." He would have talked his young brothers and his sister into taking good jobs and would have found admiring Angus MacNab a post that would keep him close to him. In the evening his wife would have worn fine new dresses, like the wives of Göring and Goebbels, in a home he had no doubt long since chosen as he passed it in his little car, on the way back from a meeting. Joyce's unbeloved aide, Mr. Black, had friends at Brighton, and in his daydreams would have extended his protection to them, for he was generous. They were afterwards to put up bail for him at the London police court.

Miss Bothamley, no doubt, would have explained the beneficent intentions of the invaders to Queen Elizabeth and the Princesses; and the colonel's daughter, who was a kindly creature, would have looked after the interests of her former husbands. It must have been a sickening blow to the inhabitants of the Concordia Bureau when weeks and months passed, and the Nazis still did not invade Britain. Then came the air raids, and the apotheosis of William Joyce. He was a revolutionary, which is to say that he hated order and loved it. For the revolutionary wants to overthrow the order which exists because he believes that he can substitute for it another which might be superior. This may be an absence of order which, by a mystical logic, he has proved more orderly than the presence of order. Or it may be an order which, if he be the suicidal type, he subconsciously knows will be inefficient and will thus restore nothingness to a universe so obstinately created, so stuffed with things. But whatever the revolutionary dreams of in the sense of reconstruction, his will is directed towards the destruction of a system which cannot be destroyed. It has come into existence as a result of the interaction of innumerable forces, some invested in man, some diffused through earth and air and fire and water. Not in the short space of even the most massive revolution will the nature of man or of earth and air and fire and water be substantially modified. So when they set to work on a new system it is inevitably very like the old. In revolution there is first destruction of what has been created, followed by its re-creation, on less favourable terms, owing to shock and waste. The appetite for death that is in us all is immensely gratified, and that is all.

The French Revolution has given pleasure to all subsequent generations, because it was an outstanding event which afterwards proved never to have happened. A number of revolutionaries overturned the monarchy of France because of its tyranny and its financial and economic inefficiency, in order that they might substitute a republic which should give its people liberty, make them equal, and join them in fraternity. When the din settled, France was ruled by a self-crowned emperor who wielded power more absolute than any French king had ever been given by the priests who crowned him; and the society which reconstituted itself after his fall conferred on its people increases of liberty and equality and fraternity no greater than were won by other nations untouched by revolution. The Russian Revolution, which is plainly going to be a source of still greater satisfaction, achieved a more perfect balance; for, with an enormously greater expenditure of blood than France ever saw, it slowly reconstituted the Tsardom it destroyed, identical in spirit, allowing for the passage of time, and reinforced in matter. The scientific genius of Peter the Great even rises again from his tomb for the delectation of Sir Charles Snow. William Joyce was among those who set their hands to the Nazi Revolution, which with an infinitely greater expenditure of blood than either France or Russia had seen was to tear down Europe, which was then twopence coloured, in order that it should be built up again, penny plain.

Now that the RAF was let loose on Germany the Berlin night above Joyce's head was sprayed with such gold and silver and precious stones as he had seen when he stood with his young wife at the windows of his flat near the Crystal Palace, watching the firework displays. An American correspondent who broadcast from Berlin up to the time of Pearl Harbor has described how one night he could not leave the Rundfunk building because of the bombs, and took shelter in the cellar in the company of Joyce and his wife, and how Joyce snarled out in his queer voice a stream of amusing and inventive curses on the raiders. With gusto he sneered at the English over the radio, telling them how their planes were wasting their bombs on the sham cities, Doppelgänger Berlins and Hamburgs and Essens laid out on fields with lights, where mock fires were started to make believe they had hit their targets, and rolling on his tongue the "gross registered tons" of the English shipping which were being sunk by Nazi submarines.

Very early in this new air war a bomb fell on Michael Joyce's house in Allison Grove. Nothing remained of it except a hole in the ground beside the remains of a neighbour's basement. At the time of his son's trial long grasses, and lilacs and syringas grown wild-branched for lack of pruning, gave the place a certain elegiac beauty. The family lost all their possessions except a trunkful of old papers and a few pieces of furniture, and they went to live at a rest centre until they were found another house. To strangers they seemed arrogant and unmoved by the shame of being kin to Joyce, who by now had been identified by many people, particularly in this district, as the news reader on the German service known all over England as "Lord Haw-Haw." But when a worker in the centre came to Mr. and Mrs. Joyce and told them that she was a friend of the doctor and his wife who had been Joyce's landlords in South Kensington, and that she herself had met Joyce, the old man and his wife broke down. William had always been the difficult one of the family, they said, but they had never thought he would be led away into doing anything so terrible as this, for he had always been a good boy at heart. It was perhaps his trouble, they pleaded, that he was too brilliant. They were ultimately found a house, a characterless little modern villa in an uninteresting part of Dulwich, which must have been too small to hold a family of such numbers and such strong individualities. It is not easy to understand why Michael Francis Joyce, who was by then over seventy, and his wife, who was growing very frail, did not go to the country under the evacuation scheme. But there was no reason why Lear should have wandered on the stormy heath instead of taking shelter from the storm. Men sometimes feel that if a certain hammer falls it is their part to act as anvil. Michael Francis Joyce lived among the amazement of the news and the bombs until he died five months later, on February 19, 1941.

It is not known whether Joyce heard of the destruction of his family's home and the death of his father at the time of these events; but it is not impossible that he did, however loyally his relatives kept their obligation not to communicate with him, for the Joyces had connections and friends in both Eire and the United States. Certainly he showed signs of stress, notably in his relations with his wife. That he and his wife loved each other deeply cannot be doubted, but as the war went on his manner towards her became noticeably unkind, and their marriage seemed for a time to be at an end. His position in the Rundfunk would have been by itself enough to drive a man of his temperament to distraction. He was learning that traitors are in the same unhappy state as prostitutes: their paymasters think they have a right to employ them, but hate and despise them for being so employed. Moreover, his work itself was growing more degraded in kind. From the beginning he had been engaged in the unhandsome business of recruiting announcers and speakers in the camps of British civilian internees; but a gloss could be put on its unhandsomeness. Some of the internees were British only from a legal standpoint, such as the people who had been brought up in Germany since childhood or who were the children of mixed marriages; and of these a number were sincerely glad to have an opportunity to perform any service asked of them by what they considered as their fatherland. But as the war went on William Joyce was obliged to do more and more of his recruiting among prisoners of war, first drawn from the Mercantile Marine, then from the regular services, the Army, the Navy, and the Air Force. In only a very few cases could Joyce have the slightest reason to suppose that the men he was approaching would have any ideological bias towards fascism. What he was doing was to seek out men who as prisoners of war were undergoing an extreme physical and mental ordeal, and to bribe them by promises of freedom and food and drink and the society of women into sacrificing their honour—which was no empty phrase in this connection. When they went to the microphone with William Joyce, they broke their oath of allegiance to the head of their state and cut themselves off from their comrades for reasons that were apparent and contemptible, and they committed in little such an act of cruelty to their kin as Joyce had committed to his, on his own grand scale. They transferred their loyalty to the people who were dropping bombs on their parents and wives and children. It was an ugly business, and it grew uglier in the handling.

At first few prisoners yielded to temptation. The British authorities had foreseen the situation and had made provision for it. In theory, all soldiers, sailors, and airmen were warned before they left England that the Germans would ask them to broadcast, pointing out that they could thus reassure their families regarding their safety, and they were ordered to refuse in all circumstances. But even though this theory often broke down, the British officers who were in charge of prisoner-of-war camps under the German staff constantly warned all ranks of the attempts that would be made to seduce them, and kept an eye on those who seemed likely to succumb to seduction.

Moreover, certain men, mostly noncommissioned officers, were given training before they went abroad which prepared them for the ordeal of fooling the Germans and serving as British agents. Few of these Pimpernels came into action at once; so the Germans could count on getting only an odd prisoner or two who, dazed by shock or by natural imbecility, consented to be interviewed before the microphone regarding the circumstances of his capture. The Germans did not take serious steps to improve this position till 1942, and the big drive they made did not show its results until 1943 and 1944. There were never many traitors, but there were some, and this was inevitable, because the number of prisoners of war was so large that it was bound to include a few representatives of the Fascist minority in Great Britain, and rather more than a few rogues and madmen. Moreover, some sane men were losing their balance under the pressure of the conditions peculiar to the life of a prisoner of war, the worst of which is the uncertainty concerning the duration of his imprisonment.

The most interesting example of the sincere Fascist traitor was a pilot officer in the RAF, a man of forty who joined the SS and wrote broadcasting scripts for Joyce. He uttered a revealing remark when a court martial sentenced him to ten years' imprisonment for an extreme act of treason which might well have cost him his life. He said indignantly to his lawyer, "This just shows how rotten this democratic country is. The Germans would have had the honesty to shoot me." The Nazis made curiously little use of this honest and lettered fanatic or any of his kind. They seemed more at ease with the rogues and the madmen and the sane men off their balance, whom they took great trouble to procure. They established holiday camps, at which the conditions were comfortable and even, to the eyes of many privates and ratings, luxurious; and the German welfare officers in the ordinary prisoner-of-war camp approached men whom they had marked down as likely prospects and told them that, as they had of late been working especially hard or seemed to be in poor health, it had been decided they should go for a month to one of these special camps. It would very often be true that these men were overworked and ill, and therefore the invitation seemed to them a welcome sign of humanity in their captors, and when their own officers told them not to accept it, the advice seemed a sign of their inhumanity. Most of the men thus tempted kept their heads, but some did not. These were exposed during their sojourn in the holiday camp to gentle propaganda, and at the end of the month were returned to the normal discomfort of their original camp. After they had had a few days in which to brood on the change, Joyce or one of his agents paid them a visit and suggested that a permanent return to comfort might be arranged if only they would read some scripts before the microphone. It would be explained that these broadcasts would be extremely pro-British and would simply aim at the affirmation of German good will towards Great Britain, and this was often true, for this was the early radio policy of Dr. Goebbels.

All these proceedings were quite uneconomic. The money was laid out to little purpose, and there we have come on an early instalment in a serial story which has become progressively more dismal. Expenditure on weapons may at least bear indirect fruit in the form of advances in scientific knowledge, but every year more and more money is spent by the great powers in maintaining an army of traitors and spies, many of whom serve imperfectly the purpose for which they were hired and can make no contribution to any higher purpose. How this operated in the Second World War on the German side can be judged from the tale of Mr. Walter Putney, the son of a Barking widow, a junior engineer on HMS *Vandyke*, who was captured at Narvik. He was an eccentric creature with some real but superficial ability, but he cannot have done much for the Nazi cause. Putney consented to go to the famous British prison camp at Colditz to spy on the occupants, but there he broke down and gave way to a Dostoevskian weakness for confessional collapses and told all to a senior British officer. It was typical. Prison camps are not funny places, but poor Putney made them so. It is a complicated story, and how little use and how much bother he can have been to the Germans can be judged from what happened to him after the peace. There then began for him the nightmare that all the traitors knew at that time: they were treated like unloved children whose parents are doing a moonlight flitting, stuffed into a van and told to hold their noise or else. The SS sent him with a mixed bag of traitors down to Italy, and there they were moved about from town to town until he and a Dutch broadcaster stole a motorcycle and rode towards the German front lines, where they managed to be captured by Italian partisans, who, thinking they were ordinary prisoners of war, handed them over to the American Army. It repatriated Putney to London, where he gave an immensely long statement to Scotland Yard, which had had only incomplete reports on him and decided it could not be bothered about him, as it had so much more important business on its hands. His life and liberty were handed back to him on a platter.

He then proceeded to get himself, all over again, into terrible trouble. What happened illustrates a curious strain of silliness present in nearly all traitors. He fell in love with a young typist; and his emotion had the curious effect of making him write a complete account of what he had done in Germany. This was many thousands of words long and was almost the same, sentence by sentence, as the statement he had given to the police weeks before. He put this in an envelope and gave it to the typist, telling her she was to send this to a solicitor if he should be arrested, a possibility he had not been able to dismiss. He then had the extreme imprudence to fall out of love with her before recovering the envelope. She opened it and read its contents, which were a complete surprise to her. From motives not so much of greed as of anger, she told him she would take the letter to the police if he did not give her a sum of money far too large for him to raise. This threat need not have meant anything to Putney, as the document was a replica of the statement he had already made to the police. However, it inspired him to go to the nearest police station and, in a dramatic monologue delivered with great force and brilliance, appeal to the law to protect him against this attempt at blackmail.

The dazed constabulary appealed for guidance to Scotland Yard, which had, by an unhappy coincidence, just received much fuller reports of what Putney had been doing in Germany; and he was arrested and charged with high treason, because he was suspected of betrayal of the secrets of his fellow prisoners at Colditz, though on that charge he was acquitted. But on the other charges, which related to his broadcasting and the preparation of leaflets for the SS, he was found guilty and sentenced to death. He was returned to Wandsworth Jail, where William Joyce was awaiting execution, and was put in another condemned cell, but hardly noticed it, being rapt in a new interest.

The police like no crime less than blackmail, which is indeed an icy sin, far farther from love than murder. As soon as they had Putney's case well under way they prosecuted the typist for demanding money from him with threats, and immediately Putney became inflamed with a desire to give evidence in her favour. The girl, however, pleaded guilty and was bound over. It is probable that disappointment over this rejection clouded Putney's relief when, after his appeal had been rejected, he was reprieved.

It is to be noted, as characteristic of the problems of security and espionage and treachery, that this eccentric had occupied the time and energies of a large number of Germans. It had taken a welfare officer and an official called a Gruppenführer and William Joyce to recruit him. Once he was incorporated into a system he was dealt with by a small army of men who had university degrees or service rank—Dr. Springben, Dr. Kurt Eggers, Dr. Menzel, Dr. Ziegfeld, Dr. Adams, Dr. Hafferkorn, Dr. Wansche, Dr. Hempel. They lavished interviews and correspondence and telephone calls on him, and at least two SS agents (including one bearing the delightful name of Herr Wockenfuss—Mr. Distaff-foot) seem to have followed him about for long periods. It is hard to avoid suspecting that the organization of British treachery had become a racket, and that a number of Germans were exploiting it to find themselves easy and remunerative jobs at a safe distance from the front; and that their success was not paid for in efficiency. In spite of all this wealth of personnel, German security was not good. Labour in Berlin being short, four British prisoners of war were sent to do the cleaning in a villa used by the German Foreign Office; and all four spent some time sitting on the floor and reading the contents of the wastepaper baskets, being highly trained intelligence agents, who had, what was more, the means of communicating their discoveries direct to England.

All this must have disgusted William Joyce, with his pride in his own competence. It is possible that he may have been revolted morally. He does not seem to have been a sneak, and he cannot have liked a stratagem employed by the Germans to overcome the reluctance of prisoners to turn traitor, which is worth noting because, like the uneconomic nature of treachery from the employer's point of view, it has endured until the present day. There were British subjects who said that they might have considered broadcasting but were restrained by the fear of what would happen to them if the British won the war; and they were told that this was no real obstacle. "You can always say that you thought you would have a better chance to escape once you were out of the camp and that you meant to send messages home over the air in code, or put sugar into the petrol tanks of vehicles, and were in general carrying on a private war against the Nazis. Nobody will be able to say you did not."

The traitors accepted this idea, which is proof that excessive egotism is an ingredient in treachery. It never occurred to any of them that if this advice was proffered to him it would be proffered to a number of other people. Hence, at court martial after court martial, soldiers and airmen turned up with defences which were often word for word the same, a coincidence which could not but be remarked. This ingenuous practice has been carried on from the time when traitors were Nazi to the new age of the Communist traitor, and still persists. The Germans and the Russians who have briefed the traitors in their employment must have known that the prescription is unlikely to work, but they do not care. They did not care even then, when they overcame Mr. Putney's timidity by helping him to find an alibi in advance. He carried on a prolix and animated correspondence with his family in London, suggesting in veiled terms, by misspellings and snatches of verse, that he was incorporating in his broadcasts information to the Royal Air Force about the weather over Germany and the probability of German raids over England. If he ended with "Good night," there would be no raid, but if he said, "Good, good night," the German bombers would be over. His family, highly respectable and well-meaning people, gave them to a Red Cross official, who forwarded them to the proper quarters. Putney stuck to his story to the very end, and only when he was under cross-examination in the Old Bailey did he realize that the British authorities knew that his broadcasts were not live but recorded, and that the recordings were not always used the same day that they were made. In consequence his warnings must always have been valueless, and that he must have known; and the Germans must have known that the British authorities would know that Putney knew this. The lot of traitors is very hard indeed.

The Concordia Bureau was getting shabbier and shabbier; it was providing broadcasters for what was known as the New British Broadcasting Station, which pretended to its listeners that it was operating on British soil. One broadcaster, with a duplicity which would never have been suspected in one who privately was full of idealist pretensions, frequently tried to convince British listeners by assuming a Cockney accent and the sort of wheeze affected by impersonators of Dickens' characters in order to breathe: "You'll probably 'ear us tomorrer night at the same hour, but it's getting 'ard, the police are always on our 'eels nowadays." Another speaker called himself Father Donovan, but was obviously not a priest, since his chorus-boy falsetto would have led to his rejection by the broadest-minded seminary, and in fact he was a seaman in his late twenties. It is unfortunately not open to us British to laugh at this ridiculous enterprise, since the Allies engaged in similar follies. There was "clean" broadcasting, which told the truth, and "dirty" broadcasting, which took the proposition that the end justified the means and bolted with it. The bolting went so far that there were sent over the air in the Allies' name such nasty fantasies as broadcasts purporting to come from microphones secretly installed in the bedroom of an enemy leader who was raping a girl. These broadcasts are not only objectionable in principle, but also injurious to the morale of the people whose officials sent them out. Either the people detect the fraud and learn to distrust their own government, or they do not detect the fraud and come to believe such falsities as the existence of sympathetic and constructive resistance movements in the country they are fighting, when in fact these do not exist.

William Joyce was labouring under the strain of ugly imposture, and with idiot companionship. A fair sample was an eccentric and passionate Salvation Army officer who, knowing either less or more about Eva Braun than we do, believed that the personal purity of Hitler was about to redeem the sinful world. He also lost some of his better comrades. He had not liked the colonel's daughter on his staff. But after sitting about the Concordia Bureau for years knitting in a sullen manner, she made her departure in a way which must have compelled his respect. She gathered her tattered integrity about her, sold all she could lay her hands on to pay back to the Germans every mark they had ever paid her, and was swept off into a concentration camp, from which she was to emerge, at the end of the war, into twelve months of prison and such subsequent exclusion from the society of her kind, such bleakness and hopelessness, that one may count her as having paid her bill and more. She was the victim of denunciation by a fellow traitor. The organization was ravaged by contending forces.

The troubles of the Concordia Bureau were not merely internal. Though a small staff worked for the German Foreign Office, the Concordia Bureau was a part of Goebbels' Propaganda Office, which was the hated rival of the German Foreign Office. The primary cause of the rivalry between these ministries was the fact that the Propaganda Office was a Nazi creation and the German Foreign Office was full of Junker stuff whose roots had not been torn up during the Weimar Republic because they had been so deeply planted in the soil of Germany under the Hohenzollerns. The rivalry had deteriorated, as all else in German life, and had become something very like a struggle between two gangs to get the bigger share of loot in a "protected" area. Perhaps because of simple departmental jealousy, and perhaps because of the large number of jobs connected with the Concordia Bureau, the Foreign Office took more and more interest in the bureau as the war went on. The office must have looked like any manifestation of the civil service. Actually insane cantrips were taking place. The German official described as "the prototype of the Nazis," was now a prey to ungovernable rages and once had it in his mind to send the inoffensive Mr. Black to a concentration camp, for what reason no one could ever discover. The people who intervened and saved his life were members of the German Foreign Office staff belonging to the group concerned in the attempt on Hitler's life in 1944. They were apparently anxious to take control of the Concordia Bureau out of Goebbels' hands. There were political cross-currents here which resulted in the arrival of a visitor to Berlin whose presence must have seemed to William Joyce a gross personal slight.

7

JOHN AMERY, who at the time of his trial had lived thirty-three years and had been in trouble for most of them, was the son of a gifted Englishman who had rendered liberal service to his country, and his wife, who was loved by many for her kindness.

John Amery was not insane, he was not evil, but his character was like an automobile that will not hold the road. As a child, he would be taken by his parents to a hotel at some holiday resort, and would be discovered in a corner of the gardens or in the lounge, after dinner, amusing the guests with some mimicry or musical fooling. But the entertaining monologue would become a dribble of nonsense, the dance would go on too long, and there would break in a hint of frenzy. The child would turn from a pet to a pest, and sooner or later there would be trouble of an odd, unpredictable kind, arising out of behaviour which was not cruel or cowardly but slapped the normal process in the face. What is one to do with a boy of fifteen who from school issues prospectuses for a film-producing company and collects money from investors, not with the intention of embezzling it, but inevitably with that effect? What is one to do with him when he is so pitifully delicate that it is not possible to subject him to the discipline of work? One can but say hopefully that he will not always be fifteen. This is, however, not necessarily true. There are some who are always fifteen. When he came to Berlin he was, as the years went, about thirty. He had been convicted seventy-four times for automobile offences, which included some quite unforeseen embroideries on the commonplace process of travelling from one point to another with the aid of an internal combustion engine. Marriage he had complicated as effectively as transport; credit to him was what orchestral tone is to a conductor, and his business enterprises were unimaginable. He once stranded an entire motion-picture outfit in Africa in circumstances which struck even the motion-picture industry as extraordinary. When he was twenty-four his loyal but exhausted family let him become bankrupt. He failed for £5,000, and his assets were nil. He went abroad on a generous allowance, so generous that it meant some sacrifice for his parents.

This was in 1936, when the Spanish Civil War offered a theatre for both left-wing and right-wing gallants. John Amery was a not unsuccessful volunteer on Franco's side. He had a fairly continuous career serving as a gun-runner and as liaison officer with the French Cagoulards. When the war broke out he remained on the Continent, still travelling between Paris and Madrid, and it is believed that the traffic which he carried on then took a reverse direction, and that his Cagoulard friends now received alms and money from certain Spanish elements to aid them in their opposition to the war against Hitler. It is useless to conceive of Amery as either a mercenary trafficker or a dogmatic Fascist. He was in France when it fell and fled to the south; but the Vichy government treated him as an unwelcome guest. It was trying to preserve its credit with the French people by dissociating itself from the frankly pro-German Cagoulards, and, being irritated on its prudish side by his revelry, treated him as an unwelcome guest. Its distaste for him increased, and at the end of 1941 it put him in prison for eighteen days and released him on condition he live in the mountainous district round Grenoble. He was at the time, so those that saw him say, very addled, very bored with the provincial life to which he was thus restricted, and in need of money. It is not surprising, therefore, that he offered his services to the Italians, who never answered his letter, and then to the Finns—then engaged in their anti-Soviet war—who declined them.

But the local German armistice chief, Graf Ceschi, took him under his protection. Amery said that this association was not of his seeking, that the overtures came from the Graf, and in view of what happened this is not incredible. In the autumn of 1942 a German officer took him and a French woman who was perhaps his wife to Berlin. There they were received by a Dr. Hesse, who belonged neither to the German Foreign Office nor to the Propaganda Office but to Hitler's personal staff. Thereafter, for a period of several months, John Amery was the most petted and best advertised English propagandist that had ever been put on the German radio. Immense trouble was taken to draw the world's attention to his broadcasts, which were repeated several times in an evening on one particular night in the week. He was given luxurious hotel accommodation, with a heavy expense account. He was sent all over Europe to address internment camps and give interviews to the local press, and he was photographed and filmed as if he were a Hollywood star.

In many ways Amery must have got Joyce on the raw. Amery was an Englishman, and the conflict between England and Ireland had never quite resolved itself in Joyce's mind. He adored the English, he had fought for them as a boy, or had at least performed some services which he thought of as fighting for them, and he genuinely believed that as a Fascist he was labouring to confer benefits on England. All the same, it was to England that he had come as a boy and had been sniggered at as a queer little bog-trotter with a brogue. It was England which had been ungrateful to his father and refused to compensate him for the loss of his property in Ireland. It was in England that he had been denied the power and position which he felt to be his right by virtue of his intellect. Ancient hatreds, however much they may be adulterated, often revert under stress to their first purity. When William Joyce cursed the raiders who were bombing Berlin, he cursed them as an Irishman cursing the English. Now here an Englishman had come, late in the day, and was put ahead of those who had been drudging in exile for years.

Moreover, Amery was a gentleman. He had been born on the imperial side of the River Thames, heir to every advantage which William Joyce had craved, and he had thrown all of them away. Joyce had a right to despise Amery morally; for though he liked a glass of whisky as much as the next man, he kept himself hard as nails for his work, and paid his debts. As for his intellectual superiority to Amery, that must have stung him. He had a limited but avid mind and he had tried to put some thought into his broadcasts whenever the Germans gave him the chance. Words flowed from Amery's mouth in the conventional groupings of English culture, but he had no intelligence, only a vacancy round which there rolled a snowball of Fascist chatter picked up from Doriot and Déat. Yet here he was installed in a suite at the Kaiserhof, while Joyce had only a flat in the suburbs, with an unlimited expense account which meant opulence compared to Joyce's unimpressive salary; and here was the German radio cupping its hands round its mouth and shouting to the whole world that it must listen to Amery's broadcasts, though they could have no propaganda value whatsoever.

That Amery was an excellent broadcaster, that the radio, which is one of the greatest liars in the world, transformed him into a pure and eager boy, burning with sincere indignation at the moral evils of bolshevism, was beside the point. He was known to every newspaper reader in England as the problem child of distinguished parents, who had made countless appearances in the police courts, and the sole result of putting him on the air would be to make English listeners feel sympathy with his family and a reiterated conviction that the Germans were terrible cads.

Worse still as propaganda was Amery's project, known at first as the Legion of Saint George. This was a body to be drawn from British prisoners of war who were to fight alongside the Germans against the Russians to save Europe from bolshevism, and the idea of it made the former director of Mosley's propaganda squirm in his seat. None knew better than he did what chance there was of raising such a legion. He knew that only a sprinkling would join and that these would be mad or bad. He knew also that a recruiting campaign whose appearance would be interpreted by the ordinary soldier as a call to the joys of peace rather than to the tasks of war would make English treachery a laughingstock; and traitors have their pride, like other people. He must have perceived that the Germans were in some ways very stupid, and perhaps he doubted whether they were going to gain the victory which was necessary if he was ever to realize his ambitions or even save his life.

Yet German propaganda was perhaps never less stupid than in the exploitation of John Amery. For propaganda has many uses beyond persuasion. What it sometimes aimed at in this case can be deduced from the character of Amery's gospel, considered in conjunction with the date. Though Amery's speeches held a few drops of anti-Semitic poison, his real preoccupation was hatred of Russia and communism. He made it a condition that the Legion of Saint George should be regarded as an exclusively anti-bolshevist force and should be used only on the Russian front. His conception of the war was as a struggle between holy nazism and corrupt communism, contrived by the Jews, and he wanted not peace but another war in which the West should sink its differences in order to attack the Soviet Union.

Now in the autumn of 1942 the Germans were beginning to feel nervous. It had appeared from the end of August that the situation in North Africa might not end as they wished, for Rommel's great offensive had been halted, and that because of a lack of aircraft. The Allies' air attacks on Germany were becoming more and more formidable. The Japanese were not doing so well as had been hoped. A group of Germans in and around the Foreign Office were not certain that Germany was beaten, but then again they were not certain that it was going to win. So they formed the idea that it had better sacrifice some of its ambitions and get rid of some of its liabilities. If they could stop war with Russia, so rashly initiated in 1941, Germany would have its energies free to fight Great Britain and the United States. But if it was to start peace negotiations with Russia, these must be kept secret, for two reasons. One was that if Great Britain and the United States heard of them they might use argument and force to dissuade their ally from the proposed desertion; and the other that, even if they failed, they would surely cut off the stream of supplies which they were sending out to the Soviet Union. But these shipments would go on to the last moment and would be shared with Germany when it again joined forces with Russia. It might throw dust in the eyes of Great Britain and the United States if, just at the time when these secret negotiations were opened, the Germans started a new anti-bolshevik campaign. They made their first overtures to Moscow, and John Amery was fetched out of his retreat in Savoy in October 1942 and broadcast during the first part of 1943 and began his recruiting tour of the camps. Nobody else could have drawn such widespread attention to an anti-bolshevik campaign. If William Joyce had made these broadcasts and gone on that recruiting tour, not a soul would have taken the slightest notice. It was the unique and fatal distinction of John Amery to be the one person out of the earth's population who could serve the German purpose; and the Nazis did not mind looking fools so long as they could create the impression that they were still actively anti-bolshevik.

It is to be remarked that from the middle of 1943 the fortunes of John Amery suffered a marked decline. The negotiations between Germany and Russia had broken down. Only a small group had ever participated in them. He was no longer welcome in Berlin; and when he lost most of his personal belongings in one of the famous raids which, on every night between November 22 and 26, 1943, assailed Berlin, he was awarded a decoration for exceptional bravery and packed off to Paris. From there he was sometimes sent to the occupied countries, such as Norway, Belgium, Czechoslovakia, and Yugoslavia, out of sheer nastiness; to prove that the British were degenerate, that a leading British statesman could have a son who betrayed his country and hiccupped as he did it. Soon they stopped letting him do even that, and in September 1944, with savage and indecent irony, they sent him down next to act as confidant to Mussolini, now at liberty and a poor figure of fun after his undignified rescue from Allied hands. "Enter Tilburina, stark mad in white satin, and her confidant, stark mad in white linen." What is the sin against the Holy Ghost? It is perhaps to deal with people as if they were things: to pick them up and set them down, without respect for their uniqueness, for their own wills.

In Germany, William Joyce sat and waited for the end. He moved about; most often he was in Berlin, but sometimes he was in Eupen and at Luxembourg, at the end he was in Hamburg; but always there was over him the same sky, the sky which is clearer than the English sky and is not loaded with dreary fogs, but has its own nocuments, which are madness and defeat. He was involved for the last year or so with Amery's creation, the Legion of Saint George, now known as the British Free Corps. After Amery had been ejected from Berlin, having served the Nazi purpose, the legion had been handed over to the SS and its name had been changed; and thereafter its recruits either were drawn from Joyce's broadcasters or broadcast for him afterwards. This must have been sheer torture to him. Some of them were pathetic. One, Kenneth Edward, had been taken by the Germans off a torpedoed ship when he was fourteen and kept in a prison camp for two and a half years, had been recruited by John Amery, whom he believed to be Foreign Minister of Great Britain who had somehow been ejected from his country and was being kindly assisted by the Germans to regain his rights. Another had given a false age when he volunteered for the British Army in 1941 and was just seventeen when he was captured in Italy, and he believed that the British Free Corps was six divisions strong. Some had another significance, such as Herbert George.

He had not the excuse of youth as these two had; but on the other hand it could be said that he had been in such trouble all his life that he had had no time to grow up. He was of medium height, but had the look of a Disney dwarf, but not a happy one, for too often the Thames-side police courts had claimed him. Once a chicken had been stolen; then a gas-meter slot had been opened and emptied; once someone had missed a shirt and a scarf. It was too much. He had attempted to commit suicide, and when he had served the mild punishment inflicted on him for that offence he enlisted in the Army, but they would not have him, he was discharged as daft. This was, however, only the beginning of a military career which was to be unique. He had always been interested in politics, and when the Spanish Civil War broke out he volunteered to serve in the International Brigade and actually fought in Spain. He soon deserted, and the incident was purged of the sordid by the candour with which, having crossed the Pyrenees and reached the Channel on foot, he sought the London offices of the International Brigade and re-ported as a deserter. Hurt at his reception, he went to sea and continued as a sailor after the war broke out. In 1940 he was taken off an oiler torpedoed in Norwegian waters, and was in one prison camp and another until 1944, when he received a letter from his mother telling him that his wife had had a baby. After thinking this over for some time he decided that it could not be his baby and was deeply distressed, and when two mer-chant seamen came to enrol recruits for the British Free Corps, he enlisted, just as a sad little dog, finding himself far from home in streets where they throw things, with rain falling and the dusk thickening, will follow any passer-by. Herbert George is not a negligible figure. There are so many of him.

Some of the British Free Corps had a great deal more excuse than the poor little man. Six of them, known as the Big Six, had natural endowment and education enough to realize what they were doing. One, the son of a Lithuanian merchant settled in England, had been at an English public school. It was surprising that he should have been in the British Free Corps, for he was a Jew on his father's side. He may not have known this, for he had been brought up out of contact with his father's family, though the Germans must have known it, if any intelligent officer examined his papers. He joined because he wanted to find himself a niche in the international society which he thought would be erected after the inevitable defeat of the Allies. Another of the Big Six, Francis McLardy, a qualified pharmacist, had been a member of the British Union of Fascists from 1934 to 1938, but this need not have been a determining factor which made him a traitor. He had been a sergeant in the RAMC and, having been captured at Dunkirk, was sent to work in a prison-of-war hospital in Poland.

There he was caught breaking a rule and was told that he was to be sent to the worst camp in Poland, which was famous for its abominations. Rumour had it that there the starved prisoners fell on the bodies of their comrades that dropped dead and tore out their livers, their kidneys, and the soft part of the thighs, and ate them. An American prisoner who was found in the camp when it was liberated has testified that this happened, though not many people could bring themselves to do it because the bodies were so lousy. To avoid being sent to this camp, McLardy wrote to the authorities and expressed that he wanted to join the Waffen SS and fight the Russians. That he was moved by the desire to save himself from this hell cannot be regarded as an absolute excuse, for thousands of men, finding themselves in the same position, chose to suffer the pains of hell rather than serve the men who made them. But few of us would care to judge him. It is to be noted that McLardy was perhaps the nearest to a Mosleyite traitor that the Second World War provided. The other adherents of the BUF who appeared among the traitors had lapsed from membership some time before the outbreak of war, and their cases prove nothing except that silly young men were apt to join the BUF in some circumstances and in others were apt to become traitors. Neither here nor in any other theatre of war was there proof that the BUF had issued instructions to any member of the armed forces.

The most obvious trace of ideological action in the camp was furnished by two priggish little negativists named Denis John and Eric Reginald. Denis John was the son of a stoutish middle-aged man, with watchet-blue eyes and a quiet way with him, who owned two baker's shops in North London, notably bright and clean for the grey streets of those parts—a German, the son of a German immigrant, who had had the sorrow of feeling it his duty to fight the Germans in the First World War. His son could not feel it his duty to fight them in the Second World War, for his parents' marriage had broken up when he was seven years old, and he had been brought up by a German grandmother and had been at school in Germany, and there had been a lot of trouble. He did not want to be a baker, for one thing; and he was a Lohengrin or Siegfried, with clear-cut features and waves of blond hair like golden wire, and he drew to himself the attentions of some young people with more money than he had, who, according to his family's friends, did him no good. When the time drew near when he should register for military service, he felt a natural reluctance to fight against Germany, which, strangely enough, he, a German's grandson, knew and loved better than his father, who was a German's son. If he had gone to the proper authorities they would have explained to him the means by which people in his position could appeal for exemption from military service as conscientious objectors.

But one of his new friends persuaded him to go to the offices of a pacifist organization and ask for assistance in evading military service, and it was arranged that he should take advantage of a scheme which exported registered conscientious objectors to do farm work in various districts, including the Channel Islands. It is not clear how Denis John was brought under this scheme; he never claimed to have become a conscientious objector, and cannot have been registered as one, for he had never even been called up. He was under age. But Denis John was sent off on a travel warrant issued by the Ministry of Labour to Jersey, which in neither this war nor the previous war would ever have seemed the safest of refuges, but was particularly unsafe on the day of his departure, which was May 17, 1940, seven days after the Germans had invaded the Low Countries. It is not at all surprising that by August Denis John was working for the Todt organization, the Nazi sappers; and the pacifist organization must have been unusually silly if it felt any astonishment, though it showed no guile in planning these events. There was not even the sense of a treasonable agreement behind these imbecile proceedings. The Germans were not prepared to accept these unhappy children, and Denis John and a number of others were dragged about Europe, from camp to camp, for five years, exposed to every sort of degrading influence, till he and Eric Reginald landed in the British Free Corps.

They joined it apparently only because the recruiting leaflets had caused an uproar in the English prisoner-of-war camp where they happened to be, and they wished to show how superior they were to the common herd. They were the best of a shameful crew. Most of the legion had left their original camps after being warned by their senior officers that they were taking a step which would cut them off from the society of their own kind, and passed into a state of degradation which made it inevitable that society would carry out its threat, not from nursed intention but as a result of the natural recoil from something that stinks. The Germans had, of course, far too much sense to keep on with the legion because they thought they could raise enough men to form a fighting unit for use on the Russian front or anywhere else. They wanted them for quite another purpose.

They put these men in villas in various pleasant parts of Germany, and dressed them in German uniforms with badges bearing the letters BFC and the Union Jack to show that the wearers were British soldiers, and let them go rotten with idleness and indiscipline and debauchery. They did a little drill and learned German and, as one of them said, "otherwise did nothing except lay around, and go into the town, where we drank and associated with women." There were never many of them. It appears that of the hundreds of thousands of prisoners of war in Germany only thirty-odd volunteered for the corps. But even so small a number, split into groups and sent into the German towns, drunken and with prostitutes on their arms, did something to raise national morale in 1944 and 1945 and persuade the Germans that it was all true, what they had been told, and that they could not possibly be conquered by those degenerate people the British. It is worth while looking at these drab and debauched people because this type of traitor was not to pass away but was to reappear on the other side of the world in another phase of time.

With what horrified embarrassment this crowd of scalawags was regarded by William Joyce, who had been so proud of his association with the Worcestershire regiment, who carried himself like a midget sergeant-major, can be judged from the effect they had on a young man called Thomas Haller Cooper, who was very different from William Joyce except in his detestation of what comes "all along o' dirtiness, all along o' mess, all along o' doing things rather more or less." Cooper's father, a photographer in southwestern London, had been a soldier in the army of occupation after the 1914–1918 war and had brought home a German bride. When he was nineteen his mother took him back to Germany, as a woman taking her child to present him at the temple, herself returning to London. The year was 1939. A short time before war broke out he joined the Adolf Hitler Division of the Waffen SS and served in Poland, and then in Russia, where he was wounded. When he was convalescent he was recalled to do traitor's work, visiting the English prisoner-of-war camps and talking with the prisoners and giving them corrupting literature, and finally was made an NCO in charge of the British Free Corps and practically became camp commandant. At first he enjoyed the work, and many of the members of the British Free Corps liked him. There was probably a real geniality, an honest tenderness, between them. Cooper had come from the Eastern Front, the others had come from years of hunger and confinement; they found themselves clean and well fed and could exchange tales of woe in what was their native language and his father's tongue, in a good villa that was more than comfortable, that was cosy, among the woods, the sweet aromatic German woods. He was a good-looking young man, tall and slender and dark, with that neatness which amounts to a form of piety, a cry to Heaven for approval. He had the look of the more thoughtful of many young Germans who became Nazis: the look of the white-collar man who cannot climb up because he has no special talent to make his own ladder and society will not let him use its existing ladders, which are reserved for other people.

Spiessbürger is the German word for it. He was loaded with frustrated ambition. He had been a clerk in London and had tried hard to get out of the groove. He had a great love of the East and, though he had not a very good record at school, had worked hard at learning Japanese and Chinese, and as he reached his later teens had tried to find employment in branches of the government service which might take him to the Far East, but was rejected because his mother was a German. For the same reason he had been rejected as a candidate for the English and colonial police force. The conflict in the boy's mind regarding the nationalities of his parents must have been painful, the more so because his mother was a woman of distinctive character. Her home was distinguished from all other dingy houses in the road by the wealth of flowering bulbs, jonquil and narcissus, crocus and grape hyacinth, which crammed the bow windows. This interesting parentage was, however, denied him by the Germans. He was presented to the British Free Corps as the son of Mr. Duff and Lady Diana Cooper, a remarkable fatuity, since the sophisticated members must have realized that the only child of the most publicized character of our time was not yet of military age.

Cooper travelled all over Germany with his charges. (It is one of the curious features of the Nazi regime that it made the German passion for travelling into a guiding principle of its administration. Prisoners of war, whether loyal or traitors, were moved round and round and round the country long before the time when they had to be hustled out of the way of invading Allies. It was as if in England we had moved the prisoners we held in the Isle of Man to the West Highlands, to Wales, to the Isle of Wight, and so on.) Always the billets were good, comfortable villas with gardens, set among the woods and heaths. The custody of these louts was not the enterprise Thomas Haller Cooper had foreseen when he was detailed to it, and he found he could keep himself sane by withdrawing into his favourite and unusual studies. In his room, instead of the usual portrait of Adolf Hitler, there hung a fine Japanese print. He had a solemn and sentimental love affair with a respectable young girl called Gisela, to whom he expounded Oriental philosophy in immensely long letters. He was really only a boy. In company he would murmur, as if in absence of mind, such phrases as *Om mani padme hum*; being overheard and questioned as to what they meant, he would start, give a translation, and explain that such phrases were always running through his mind, since he was, as a matter of fact, a Buddhist. At the same time he showed himself to be a Western-reading schoolboy under the skin by boasting quite untruthfully that he had had to come to Germany be-

cause in an East End street fight he had killed a Jew. Unfortunately his confidant was a British agent.

But no amount of sitting about in the sun among the pines
and mooning over Oriental grammar and writing to Gisela could
reconcile him to the degradation of his charges. He tried to
apply a mild form of SS discipline to them, and they mocked at
him and staged a mutiny. He behaved with courage. But when
D-day came and went, and the gales blew and did not blow away
the Allies, and the Atlantic Wall was as if it had never been,
then he was frightened. He said, "I have been a bloody fool,"
and announced his intention of working thereafter "for the
other side." But again it was to a British agent that he said
those words. Thereafter this strong and proud young man had to
cringe and smirk and flatter in the hope of survival. He was
obliged by orders of his superiors to visit prisoners of war and
thrust kindnesses on the prisoners under the sceptical eyes of
noncommissioned officers, terrible beings, worst when they were
little creatures burned up by Indian suns till there was left in
them not a scrap of blandness. These looked straight at him and
without speaking said things about rats leaving sinking ships.
But these missions were easier than his duties at base with the
British Free Corps, who daily grew more drunken, more desperate, more maudlin in the arms of their whores. Often they
openly cursed him and disobeyed his orders, and sometimes he
let it pass, because he did not dare to do anything else, but at
the same time he was prodded in the back by his superiors, who
did not know yet whether they were beaten. If they were beaten,
they meant to pull off their jackboots and run; but it was hard to
find this out for certain, and in any case they had obeyed orders
for so long that they had forgotten how to take the initiative.
Everybody's brain was boiling.

Sometimes authority thought that, yes, it would pull off its
jackboots, and left Cooper to do what he would with the British
Free Corps. Then he and his louts sat in a kind of vacuum.
Then authority would change its mind and would buzz about
Cooper's ears again and ask what he was thinking of to let
discipline run down, and he would disentangle the louts from
their weeping whores and insist they do a little drill. On the
night of February 13, 1945, authority finally lost its head. The

British bombed Dresden, as a result of an order which has since been studied exhaustively but which remains mysterious; and they slaughtered thousands of refugees and turned to rubble one of the fairest cities bequeathed to our time by people possessed by virtues which we lack. Authority then announced to the unit that it was to be sent to Russia. At this news the British Free Corps took to its bed as one man. Authority then turned on it and alleged that in some way the corps was responsible for the bombardment and clapped them all in prison. Some of them had been there already. The baker's son, Denis John, and his companion, Eric Reginald, had joined the British Free Corps only to flout the prejudices of their fellow prisoners of war, and, once they were in the corps, organized a revolt against the confirmed rebels, such as the poor little Herbert George, he who had always been in trouble, chickens, the gas-meter, the International Brigade. For that they were sent to a *Straflager*, a punishment camp, and learned what it could be like to be entirely protected, either by the police or by the recognized authorities of a prisoner-of-war camp. After seven weeks they had petitioned the German authorities to let them go back to the British Free Corps on any terms and were allowed to do so. The corps, on hearing it was faced as a whole with a *Straflager,* revolted. Authority was overcome by panic, pretended to take seriously the complaints against Cooper. He walked off with a straight back, on his way, and he must have known it, to the Old Bailey.

William Joyce now sat in his office, conducting his business with a quiet sacramental order. He had become wholly reconciled to his wife. D-day had been a crushing blow to him. All through his life he had been anxious, with the special anxiety of a very small man, not to make a fool of himself, and the first consequence of such wariness is to dread making prophecies that prove untrue. In his broadcasts he had mocked again and again at the idea of an Allied invasion of the Continent; and they had often been followed by songs, abominable and amusing lyrics coldly and lightly sung, which jeered at the Englishmen who were to attempt invasion and would lie dead under the Atlantic Wall. But now the Atlantic Wall had been broken. He had made a fool of himself.

Also he realized that, if the Atlantic Wall was broken, it did not matter how much effort it had taken to break it; henceforth it was insubstantial as a dream. Henceforth it was not to be Germans who were to kill Englishmen. There were perhaps to be more Germans killed by Englishmen than Englishmen killed by Germans, perhaps Germany itself was to be killed, perhaps William Joyce himself was to be killed, certainly William Joyce was to be killed. That possibility had always been clear in his mind. In his preface to his book, *Twilight over England,* published in Holland in 1942, he had written: "When, however, the writer is a daily perpetrator of High Treason, his introductory remarks may command from the English public that kind of awful veneration with which £5,000 confessions are perused in the Sunday papers, quite frequently after the narrator has taken his last leap in the dark." He must also have been conscious of what had happened to him. He had proved that there are no half-measures in treachery. If a man does not love his country enough to concede its right to self-government, he will end by not loving it at all, by hating it. Again and again Joyce had spoken with icy approval of the murder wrought by Germans on his fellow countrymen. He had not felt this unnatural emotion was important, for it was temporary, he would go back to England as a bearer of benefits and would be reconciled to his own people. But now he had to wonder whether they would forgive him; not forgo punishment, that he knew could not be, but forgive him.

As a revolutionary he must have known a sort of peace as catastrophe flowed towards him from the east and the west during the first months of 1945. There had been much doing, and the fruit of it was to be nothingness; there had been a fullness of life, there was to be an emptiness of death. To this end he had worked since youth, and he would have been disappointed by victory. But that he himself should die must have brought him the torment that the prospect of death brings to us all. That is the weakness of the revolutionary idea; human beings only want to play with the idea of death. They do not want to die.

Waiting for the end, William Joyce sat in his office and distracted himself by doing his work extremely well. His last broadcasts were, in form, ably and carefully written political essays, much superior to anything he had put over the air up to that time. In substance they were self-exculpatory. They

warned England that she was being ruined by her participation in the war and, destitute, would have to face a new
and insatiable imperialist Russia; and rebuked her for having fought Germany instead of aiding her to fight against the
bolshevization of the world. This was nonsense. The week before
Germany had brought England into the field against her by
invading Poland she had signed a pact with Russia, and she
remained in close friendship with her for the best part of two
years; and no intelligent Englishman had wanted his country to
go to war with Germany, because none was unaware that, if the
price of defeat would be the reign of the Gestapo in England,
the price of victory would be the disruption of Europe, the
destruction of its political and economic and intellectual harmony, which is the highest level man has yet attained. It was the
horrible and unique achievement of Hitler to force the West to
fight the most terrible of wars without the sustenance of faith in
victory. So the tired man, night after night, stood in the
Hamburg studio of the Rundfunk and warned his fellow countrymen of a danger which they had always anticipated and which
now no longer could be avoided. There came a night when he
spoke as if he were either very tired, or drunk, or perhaps both.
On April 30, 1945, he made a broadcast in which, speaking
slowly and with dignity and obstinacy, he admitted defeat. It
ended with the sentences: "Britain's victories are barren; they
leave her poor, and they leave her people hungry; they leave her
bereft of the markets and the wealth that she possessed six years
ago. But, above all, they leave her with an immensely greater
problem than she had then. We are nearing the end of one phase
in Europe's history, but the next will be no happier. It will be
grimmer, harder, and perhaps bloodier. And now I ask you
earnestly, can Britain survive? I am profoundly convinced that
without German help she cannot." Saying these words, he
plainly thought himself a statesman, but he had said nothing
that could not be answered with a phrase from an old comedy,
"Tu l'as voulu, George Dandin!" This was the last time that
the insatiable hunger of his voice was to travel over the air.
English soldiers came into his office a day later and found it not
disordered but empty.

8

EACH traitor took a different path to the end. Some hid themselves and were never found, and one of these was of some importance. But most of them found their way to the court martial or the Old Bailey, and there revealed more of themselves than might have been expected. For most of them were destitute, and had to take advantage of the Poor Prisoners' Defence Act, and a lawyer chosen under this act has not the usual amount of control over his client. He cannot tell him to go to the devil and find another lawyer, should he disregard advice; hence many traitors made the mistake of giving evidence on their own behalf and gave away much that might otherwise have been concealed.

Most of them walked to the Allied lines and presented themselves as escaped prisoners of war. The men who followed this course enjoyed a false sense of security which lasted for some time. Their stories were naturally accepted, and those of them who had acquired a good working knowledge of the German language during their captivity were useful as interpreters to the advancing British and American troops. Such men continued in this magical state of immunity for a matter of weeks or months. Till VE-day, and for a long time after, the Army had many other things to do than to chase unimportant traitors; and during this period of disorganization the men were sheltered by the rule of the British Free Corps and the British section of the Rundfunk that all traitors except the most important should work under assumed names. This did no more, and the Germans must have known it would do no more, than give them a short respite before arrest.

Little Mr. Black smugly reported at the British Embassy in Brussels, making no secret of having worked at the Concordia Bureau but claiming that he had merely sought cover for doing kindnesses to victims of Nazi persecution. One of the more hopeless members of the British Free Corps carried on him to the end the photographs of thirteen German prostitutes, as well as mementos of a steadier attachment. John Amery was captured by the partisans in Italy; and when he was questioned by a British Military Intelligence officer he asked for a typewriter and proceeded to type a statement some thousands of words long, which was brilliantly composed, put the noose around his neck, and gave the history of two different people. One of these was a wise young man of lofty principles who sought to reconcile England and Germany in order that together they might fight the rising tide of communism, and to that end travelled about Europe, a weary Titan urging common sense on statesmen who for some reason would not heed the voice of sanity; the other was a crazy Harlequin enmeshed in unfortunate adventure. "After a few days in Paris and travelling under the names of Mr. and Mrs. Browne, I arrived in Berlin early in October 1942," he wrote. For a time this inveterately companionate "I," who was always travelling under the names of Mr. and Mrs. Somebody, was to be alone. "On April 7–8," he wrote, "my beloved friend and political revolutionary, Jeannine Barde, died." The poor creature's death was said not to be natural. By some accounts she killed herself, life being rendered unendurable by the sour flavour of treachery, the air raids, the humiliations of dependence on the openly contemptuous Nazis, who knew that these two had no alternative employers. By other accounts she died because of a blow received at a wild party. The Germans' feeling for etiquette was outraged by Amery's failure to attend her funeral, though as like as not it was through unbridled grief that he absented himself. But to the wandering wit sorrow is no prison. "In the end of September," he wrote, "I returned to Paris. Once more much political talk, and on October 4 I remarried at the German Consulate. Politically, the situation remained almost unchanged." And at the end of the statement comes Harlequin's supreme antic. This man awaiting a capital charge writes: "Moreover, the colonel commanding the Piazza di Milano, who brought me from Saronno to Milan, undertook at the time to have returned my property that was seized by the partisans when they arrested me. Of this nothing has so far been seen. It consists of one suitcase (important documents and personal effects), one overcoat, one fur coat, and two silver foxes, a 20-litre petrol tin, full, one Lancia Aprilia motor car No. 78410 MICDI."

A statement well worth reading was contributed by Herbert George, the Disney dwarf. He described how he met a German girl called Hilda Henschel, and after speaking to her "found she was pro-English. I told her I wanted to escape, and she said she would help me. I told her I had studied the theory of piloting a plane and eventually she told me she could find out where I could get hold of a plane, which she did. The plane was in an aerodrome about thirty kilometres away from Hildesheim. On the night we had a nasty raid and the airfield was damaged so I could not carry out my plans." He returned to England, and at his Thames-side home rejoined his wife in perfect domestic bliss, although he had taken steps to divorce her when he was in the prisoner-of-war camp; and, determined to pick up all the threads, he became the life and soul of the local Communist Party. The poor little man had to leave this happy and busy life for two years' hard labour.

It would have seemed a pity to bother about this odd little soul, but such segregation was in his own interests. It was certainly a great relief to the licensed trade of his Thames-side town. On Saturday nights Herbert George would come into a bar and, after a drink or two, would be filled with a desire to entertain the company and would therefore relate his adventures, first in the International Brigade and then in the British Free Corps. This never worked out well. His imprisonment must also have been a relief to the officers of the local Communist Party, who were doubtless serious-minded men. This odd creature, and all the other odd creatures, then went into a world abhorrent to contemplate: a world of cold cells, of dirt, of mind-slaying monotony. Not that it would have mattered so much to this most resilient of prisoners.

William Joyce left his Hamburg office and went out, in the company of his wife, to seek a safety which, by then, he knew could not be found. First he slipped into his pocket a passport made out in the false name of Wilhelm Hansen. It is significant that the imaginary Hansen was described as a teacher. Joyce liked teaching; he was proud of his gifts as a teacher. It was dated November 3, 1944, but the date may have been as false as the name. It is unlikely he would have given in and taken this precaution till the last possible moment. Then it would be easy, for all over Germany people were sitting in government offices forging papers to deny their curious Christs at the third cock-crow. Joyce's wife had a separate passport. It had occurred to them that anything might happen: the worst might happen; they might have to part. So they started on their journey, and, like all the traitors who then closed the door behind them on the misery and futility which had grown thicker and thicker round them for the previous five years, they stepped out into the spring. But for the Joyces there was not any season of respite, for they could not, like their underlings, go into the British or American lines and tell a lying story and be given work, and be at ease for a little and hope for the best. Joyce, who at that time had only a vague suspicion that there was any doubt about his British nationality, knew that there was no hope for him at all if he fell into Allied hands; he had issued too definite a challenge.

So the Joyces went out into the forest, the beautiful German forest toward the Danish frontier. It is said that they spent a night in a town or village; and sometimes they found a bed in a barn or outhouse on the wood's edge, and by day they sat on the soft pine needles. They were now united in their earlier love. But their joy in each other must have been transfused. Each must have said, "No, it was not your fault we came from England, it was mine." At all times they were horribly uncomfortable. The Allied troops were everywhere, and they were under a real necessity to hide. They fed at irregular intervals on what they could get, and William Joyce had always been exacting, in his sergeant-major way, about his food. They both grew very thin and could not keep themselves clean or neat. Joyce developed a skin disease affecting the scalp.

On May 28, 1945, they had been on the run for some weeks. That evening he was walking among the trees near Flensburg when he came on two English officers, Captain Lickorish and Lieutenant Perry. Had he gone on his way they might not have noticed him, for he was by then a miserable figure, and they were busy searching for kindling wood. But he halted and watched them, and in the end he had to speak to them. He had been reared by his father to regard the British Army as a symbol of the power and glory of earth; he had hoped to be a British officer himself; he had boasted as a boy that he had served under the orders of British officers. Also they were men of his own people, from whom he had been exiled for five years and more. He called to them in French, "Here are a few more pieces." Nothing was more certain to catch their attention. They stared at this strange little figure who was talking French to them in the depth of the German forest. He said in English, "There are a few more pieces here." He was lost. At once his voice betrayed him.

The two officers conferred together, and Lieutenant Perry said, "You wouldn't happen to be William Joyce, would you?" Joyce put his hand in his pocket, meaning to draw out his forged passport, and the lieutenant, nervous as every member of an invading force must be, thought that he was feeling for a revolver and drew his own and shot him in the leg. Joyce fell to the ground, groaning, "My name is Fritz Hansen." But so little store had he set on his sole means left him for escaping detection that he had not troubled to memorize his own false name. His passport was made out to Wilhelm, not Friedrich, Hansen; and he was still carrying his real military passport, made out in the name of William Joyce.

One of the officers went away and made contact with authority, and eventually Joyce was taken to the military hospital at Lüneburg. Mrs. Joyce had been arrested and taken to a prison camp, spent and dishevelled, saying in her habitual manner, which was jaunty and mechanically cynical, that she and her husband had expected this for a long time and that there was no use making a fuss about it. They were not to see each other again until after he had been sentenced to death. The news that Joyce was coming to the hospital arrived before him, and his stretcher was carried from the ambulance through a crowd of soldiers who were chiyiking and crying out, "This is Jairmany calling." This must have been the first intimation to him that he was considered by the British public as a comic character, and there could be no more perplexing anticlimax. On May 31 an Intelligence officer came and sat by his bed and interrogated him. To that officer he dictated this statement:

I take this opportunity of making a preliminary statement concerning the motives which led me to come to Germany and to broadcast to Britain over the German radio service. I was actuated not by the desire for personal gain, material or otherwise, but solely by political conviction. I was brought up as an extreme Conservative with strong Imperialistic ideas, but very early in my career, namely, in 1923, became attracted to Fascism and subsequently to National Socialism. Between the years of 1923 and 1939 I pursued vigorous political activities in England, at times as a Conservative but mainly as a Fascist or National Socialist. In the period immediately before this war began I was profoundly discontented with the policies pursued by British Governments, first, because I felt they would lead to the eventual disruption of the British Empire, and because I thought the existing economic system entirely inadequate to the needs of the times. I was very greatly impressed by constructive work which Hitler had done for Germany and was of the opinion that throughout Europe as also in Britain there must come a reform on the lines of National Socialist doctrine, although I did not suppose that every aspect of National Socialism as advocated in Germany would be accepted by the British people.

One of my dominant beliefs was that a war between Britain and Germany would be a tragedy, the effects of which Britain and the British Empire would not survive, and I considered that a grossly disproportionate influence was exerted on British policy by the Jews, who had their reasons for hating National Socialist Germany. When, in August 1939, the final crisis emerged I felt that the question of Danzig offered no just cause for a world war. As by reason of my opinions I was not conscientiously disposed to fight for Britain against Germany, I decided to leave the country since I did not wish to play the part of a conscientious objector, and since I supposed that in Germany I should have the opportunity to express and propagate views the expression of which would be forbidden in Britain during time of war. Realizing, however, that at this critical juncture I had declined to serve Britain, I drew the logical conclusion that I should have no moral right to return to that country of my own free will and that it would be best to apply for German citizenship and make my permanent home in Germany. Nevertheless, it remained my undeviating purpose to attempt as best I could to bring about a reconciliation or at least an understanding between the two countries. After Russia and the United States had entered the war such an agreement appeared to me no less desirable than before for, although it seemed probable that with these powerful allies Britain would succeed in defeating Germany, I considered that the price which would ultimately have to be paid for this help would be far higher than the price involved in a settlement with Germany.

This belief was strengthened from month to month as the

power of Russia grew, and during the later stages of the war I became certain that Britain, even though capable of gaining a military triumph over the Germans, would in that event be confronted with a situation far more dangerous and complicated than that which existed in August 1939; and thus until the very last moment I clung to my hope of an Anglo-German understanding, although I could see that the prospects thereof were small. I know that I have been denounced as a traitor and I resent the accusation as I conceive myself to have been guilty of no underhand or deceitful act against Britain, although I am also able to understand the resentment that my broadcasts have in many quarters aroused. Whatever opinion may be formed at the present time with regard to my conduct, I submit that the final judgment cannot be properly passed until it is seen whether Britain can win the peace. Finally, I should like to stress the fact that in coming to Germany and in working for the German radio system my wife was powerfully influenced by me. She protests to the contrary, but I am sure that, if I had not taken this step, she would not have taken it either. This statement has been read over to me and it is true.

(*Signed*) William Joyce

This was a remarkable statement to be dictated by a man who had been brought into hospital three days before, not only wounded but suffering from malnutrition and exposure. Of course it was nonsense. It would certainly have been in Great Britain's interest to form an alliance with a strong and sane Germany, in order that the political and economic balance of Europe should be maintained. But it was to nobody's interest to be yoked with Hitler, who was for internal and external unrest. Had Great Britain submitted to Nazi Germany, few characteristically British people would have survived to have the benefit of Nazi leaders in a war against the Soviet Union. They would have died in British versions of Buchenwald and Belsen. That was why, whether Britain could win the peace or not, she had to fight the Second World War. Nevertheless the statement was remarkable as the effort of a beaten and exhausted man.

Sixteen days later Joyce was flown to England. One of the soldiers in the plane asked him for his autograph as they were crossing the Channel and he wrote him a scrawl—"This is the most historic moment in my life, God bless dear old England" —which reeked of that illiterate quality never dispelled by his

university education. He was taken to Brixton Prison and there
he did well. He had, after all, escaped from the alien forest, he was
no longer forced to take part in an alien tragedy out of which he
might well have contracted. He had food to eat, a roof over his
head, and the English about him, the unexcitable, matter-of-fact,
controlled English whom he admired. There were no Nazi officials
here and no concentration camp. He had always liked the police
and got on well with them, and his passion for discipline was so
great that he may have found a sort of pleasure in conforming to
prison routine. Into this cold grey snugness came his family,
most often his beloved and loving young brother Quentin. From
them, it is true, he must have learned that though his parents
had not actually been killed by the forces whose cause he had
espoused, they had been tormented by them in their last hours.
Though he may have heard of his father's death not long after
it happened, it must have been now that he heard for the first
time of the death of his mother. That tiny and spirited being
had been persuaded to go into the country after her widowhood,
but had returned to London to be with her sons and daughter,
and when she was stricken with a painful disease she was taken
to Saint Mary's Hospital, Paddington, where she lay dying during the summer of 1944, while the V-1s broke over the town.

But to distract Joyce he now was faced with an intellectual
exercise more complex and more unusual than any he had engaged
in when he was free to study as he liked. When he had entered
prison he believed he had no defence to the charge of high
treason which had been brought against him. But his solicitors
drew his attention to the passage in his statement in which he
had alluded to his belief that his father had been a naturalized
American citizen and had forfeited his naturalization by failing
"to re-register." If his father had been a naturalized American
citizen when he was born, they told him, then he himself was an
American citizen by birth, and nothing which had happened
afterwards could affect that. Did he ever believe that safety lay in
that resolution of his doubts regarding his status? It may be so.
But it is said that, in conversation with a prison official, he
described the defence which was to be put up for him and
added, with a faint smile, "It will be amusing to see if they get
away with it."

Perhaps the gentle cynicism was honest enough. He had lived by his ambition. That part of his ambition which lived on his lips and in the forefront of his mind, had been utterly frustrated. He was not going to be king. In all the world there was not one man, not the most pitiful blind beggar nor the most eroded leper, of whom it could be more certainly said that he would never, till the end of time, exercise the smallest grain of power. The other ambition, which lived in his heart and in the secret governing chamber of his mind, was as utterly fulfilled. The revolution had succeeded. He had seen Hamburg and knew that more than a city had been destroyed; he had a nice historic sense and perhaps he recognized that a civilization had been murdered. Into his cell, each morning, came something like the white light which comes at dawn into a house where a corpse lies awaiting burial. If the dead was loved, then those who wake and see such light feel grief; if he was hated, his enemies wake to emptiness and bereavement, because the hunt is over. If the corpse was both loved and hated, then those that still live feel aching conflict; and if the corpse did not die a natural death but has been helped on its way, then their own consciences tell them that they should pay for their guilt with their lives. The successful revolutionary feels all these things about life, which he has killed in part. Hence his own death is truly a release from pain, and Joyce went serenely to his trial, which was the pattern of such trials as must happen in the hereafter. For we shall be judged at the end unjustly, according to the relation of our activities to a context of which, being human and confined to a small part of time and space, we know almost nothing. It is said that in few murder cases has it been wise for the accused person to give evidence on his own behalf. But here was a trial where a person under a capital charge could not conceivably give any evidence bearing on his guilt or innocence. He might, indeed, have embarrassed the prosecution to the point of impotence if he had given false evidence that he had not used his passport for the purpose of leaving England for Germany; and he must surely have known enough of the means employed for getting German spies in and out of England to have been able to spin a plausible tale. But he was not a perjurer. He had chosen to play out his drama in the real world. If sentence was to be passed on him, let it be based on the truth. But that condition was all he could contribute to his own trial. He could not speak of his own knowledge concerning his father's naturalization, or his status at birth, or the kind of allegiance he owed to the Crown, or the consequences flowing from possession of a passport. He might have been the poor soul in a theologian's dream, waiting to hear if the divine caprice poured wine of grace into his cup and made it saved and unbreakable, or left it empty and damned.

He was found guilty and he was taken to Wormwood Scrubs, a prison standing on the western edge of London next to a school and a hospital on flat and greasy fields where the seagulls gather. It has a peculiar character, for it was built about seventy years ago in the full flush of the late Victorian enthusiasm for social reform, with the intention of reclaiming prisoners serving their first sentence by providing them with beautiful surroundings. It is a work of great vigour, which recalls at one and the same time Ravenna and Pisa and a giant model of a lodging-house cruet, and it has the merit of presenting extraordinary shapes which the inmates may well find appropriate to their own extraordinary destinies. A prison built as simply as the ordinary hospital or school might well seem heartless to convicts who know that they have lost their liberty by no event as natural as falling sick or growing up, and the oddity of the Scrubs is like a recognition by authority that their life became quite strange and different from other people's when a demon entered into them and they said "Yes" when they should have said "No." It was there Joyce waited for the hearing of his appeals, in which he did not believe, and changed to the man we saw at his later trials, who no longer troubled himself about his demon's unfortunate reply but pondered on an answer he must make to another question.

As it happened, the prison was seized by a spasm of madness and ejected him. The news that Joyce was within its walls spread amongst the other prisoners, and they raged against his presence. Perhaps they were trying to upset the social verdict of worthlessness passed on them at the same time as their legal conviction; perhaps they were idiotically responding to the call of tradition, for throughout history treason has always been the crime most abhorred by the English, as parricide has been the crime most abhorred by the French. Perhaps it was true of the criminal population, as it was of the rest of us at the end of the war, that the sanest were a little mad and the half-mad quite demented. Whatever their reasons, they howled against him with the simplicity of wolves. In his cell he heard the riot, lifted his eyes from the book he was reading, and forced them back again, but finally laid the book aside and said hesitantly to the prison official who was sitting with him, "Those people are not calling out against me, are they?" He received an evasive answer, but was later to learn the truth, for one day as he was taking exercise some prisoners in cells overlooking the yard realized his identity and, though they knew they would be punished for it, shouted curses at him and threw down on him what missiles they could find through the windows. It is said that some of the craziest convicts formed a plan to make a dash past the warders at a favourable moment, to seize William Joyce and to murder him.

There was little reason for fearing that this plan could have been carried out, but this was not the atmosphere in which a man under sentence of death could be left to await the hearing of his appeal. So Joyce was taken away from Wormwood Scrubs and sent to Wandsworth Jail, a shabby old prison, black as a coal-tip, set among the trodden commons and the discoloured villas, the railway viaducts and the long streets of little houses, which lie "south the river." The last days of his life in London were to be spent only a mile or two from the house in Longbeach Road where it had begun. Now his second wife, with whom he had lived only in his aspirant exile north of the Thames, was received into the district which was his real home.

A man condemned to death has the right to see whom he chooses, and the authorities brought his wife over from Germany and lodged her in Holloway Prison, sending her over the river to visit him almost every day. They took great delight in each other's company, and on the morning of his hanging she retreated into a frenzy of grief which for long did not abate. It was necessary afterwards to send her back to Germany, for she had automatically become a German subject when her husband became a naturalized German. There it was necessary to put her in a camp from which she was not released for two years, for she was passionately pro-Nazi and could no more be let loose than any other Nazi propagandist; and, indeed, had she been allowed to return to England and her own family, she could not have been left at liberty, for her own sake. These two people had contrived their own ruin with a finality that not their worst enemy could have achieved by unremitting malice. Iago was a gentle child compared to their suicidal selves.

9

BUT there remains a mystery about William Joyce and all his kind of Fascist leader. Why is it so important to them that they should stand on the political platform, hold office, give commands with their own voices, and be personally feared? A man who is not acceptable as a national leader is given by our system the opportunity to exercise as much political power as is necessary for his self-respect and the protection of his right. He can vote in Parliamentary and local elections; and he can serve his country as a private Member of Parliament or as a member of a local authority or as a member of a special committee. Why should William Joyce and his kind howl after impossible eminence when in the common run they had no occasion for humiliation? There are other means of establishing exceptional value. If Joyce was not loved by the mass he was loved well by some near to him, and to some was a good lover; to his brother Quentin and to his second wife he was light and warmth. He was also a very good teacher. Happily he transmitted knowledge, and was happy to see it happily received. That surely should have been enough for him: to be a good brother, to be a good husband, to be a good teacher. Many are given less. Yet he hungered for the mere audience, for the wordless cheering, the executive power which, if it be not refined to nothing by restraint, is less than nothing.

Perhaps right was on his side. Perhaps it is not enough to be a good brother, or to be a good husband, or to be a good teacher. For human relationships are always qualified by questioning. A brother, and a wife, and pupils have their own selves to maintain, so they must sometimes defend themselves and keep back their secrets. They will sometimes pass over to the attack and seek out the secrets of the brother, the husband, and the teacher, and often time changes them so that there is no acceptance, only this questioning. It would be better for a man to have a relationship with a person who knew all about him and therefore had no need to question him, who recognized that he was unique and precious and therefore withheld no confidence from him, who could not be changed by time, though by his steadfastness he might change time and make it kind and stable. Those who believe in God enjoy such a relationship. It would be impertinent to speculate about Joyce's relationship with God, about which we know nothing relevant save that he left the Church in which he was born, returned to it before his death, and in the meantime had inscribed himself on the Nazi records as a "believer." But it can be taken that his mind had been trained over the trellis erected round him by society, and that that trellis was cut in a non-Christian or even anti-Christian pattern. Whether he enjoyed his relationship with God or not, he must often have believed that it did not exist.

Those who have discarded the idea of a super-personal God and still desire an enduring friendship must look for it in those fields of life farthest removed from ordinary personal relationship, because human personality lacks endurance in any form of love. The most obvious of these is politics. There a leader can excite love in followers who know nothing of him save his public appearances. That love is unqualified; for no party can cause its enemies to rejoice by admitting that its leader has any faults, and what parties profess they soon sincerely feel, especially in crowded halls. That love swears itself undying, too; for no party can afford to let itself be overheard contemplating the exchange of its leader for another.

Therefore many men who would have been happy in the practice of religion during the ages of faith have in these modern times a need for participation in politics which is strong as the need for food, for shelter, for sex. Such persons never speak of the real motives which impel them to their pursuit of politics, but continually refer, in accents of assumed passion, to motives which do indeed preoccupy some politicians, but not them. The chief of these is the desire to end poverty. But William Joyce had never in his life known what it was to be hungry or cold or workless, and he did not belong to the altruistic type which torments itself over the plight of others; and indeed there was probably no callousness in this, for surely if he himself had been destitute he would have been too completely absorbed in his rages and his books to notice it. His was another hunger, another chill, another kind of unemployment. But the only people in the generation before him who attacked the governing class had been poor or altruist, and since their attack had been successful their vocabulary held a tang of victory, and William Joyce and his kind borrowed it.

Therefore they spoke of economics when they were thinking of religion; and thus they became the third wing of a certain triptych. In the third and fourth centuries of this era Europe and North Africa and Nearer Asia were racked by economic problems caused by the impending dissolution of the Western Roman Empire. The study of economics was then barely begun; there was as yet no language in which the people could analyse their insecurity and design their security. But several men of genius and many of talent had been excited by the personality of Christ and excited by the bearings of his gospel on the discoveries made by the ancient philosophers. Hence the science of theology was developed to a stage where intelligent people could grasp the outlines with which it delineated universal experiences and applied its phraseology to their particular experiences. Therefore those suffering economic distress complained of it in theological terms. They cried out to society that its structure was wrong, in terms which, taken literally, meant that the orthodox Christian faith was mistaken; they rushed from the derelict estates where they starved as peons and sought the desert, where they could eat better on brigandage, and said that they did this because they had had a peculiar revelation concerning the Trinity. The hungry disguised themselves as heretics. Now, in our day, those suffering from religious distress reverse the process and complain of it in economic terms. Those who desire salvation pretend that they are seeking a plan to feed the hungry. Between the two wings of the triptych shone the rich panel of European civilization, created during a happy interim when, for various reasons, man found it easy to say what he meant.

It is undignified for any human being to be the victim of a historical predicament. It is a confession that one has been worsted, not by a conspiracy of enemies, nor by the hostility of nature, but by one's environment, by the medium in which one's genius, had one possessed such a thing, should have expressed itself; as harsh as it is for an actor to admit that he cannot speak on a stage, for an artist to admit that he cannot put paint on canvas. So the victims of historical predicaments are tempted to pretend that they sacrificed themselves for an eternal principle which their contemporaries had forgotten, instead of owning that one of time's gables was in the way of their window and barred their view of eternity. But William Joyce pretended nothing at his trials. His faint smile said simply, "I am what I am." He did not defend the faith which he had held, for he had doubted it; he did not attack it, for he had believed in it. It is possible that in these last days fascism had passed out of the field of his close attention, that what absorbed him was the satisfaction which he felt at being, for the first time in his life, taken seriously. It had at last been conceded that what he was and what he did were matters of supreme importance. It was recognized that he had been involved by his birth in a war between the forces in the community which desired to live and those which desired to die, a war between the forces in himself which desired to live and those which desired to die. It was an end to mediocrity.

He said that he had had a fair trial; but he had had two trials. On the floor of the courts where he was put in the dock there was tested an issue of how far the letter is divorced from the spirit, an issue which must have come up again and again since the birth of law. Centuries ago, or in the part of the world least visited by civilization, it might be debated whether a man can live all his life among a tribe and eat its salt and in the hour of its danger sharpen the spears that its enemies intend for their attack on it, and go free because he has not undergone the right ceremonies which would have made him a member of that tribe. But in the upper air above the courts it was argued whether the God with whom man can have a perfect relationship is the dream of disappointed sons imagining a perfect Father who shall be better than all fathers, or is more real than reality. This other trial was not concluded, for it began with some remote birth and will not now end till the last death. It is this uncertainty which gives life its sickening and exquisite tension, and under that tension the fragility of William Joyce was as impressive as his strength. He sat in the dock, quietly wondering at time as it streamed away from him; and his silence had the petitioning quality we had heard in his voice over the air during the war. He had his satisfactions. He had wanted glory, and his trial gave him the chance to wrestle with reality, to argue with the universe, to defend the revelations which he believed had been made to him; and that is about as much glory as comes to any man. But treason took to itself others not so fortunate.

⇛ I I ⇚

The New Phase

1

It TOOK SOME TIME for the law to digest the Fascist traitors. John Amery was brought to trial at the Old Bailey on a charge of high treason; but it was at first not thought that he was going to suffer the same fate as William Joyce. His case was postponed several times in order that evidence might be collected for his defence, which rested on a claim that he had become a naturalized Spanish citizen, and it was known that a relative had gone to Spain to collect proof of that claim. His mother applied for a seat in court, and, while the officials felt some sympathetic apprehension in granting the application, they supposed her to have reason to know that she would joyfully witness her son's acquittal. But she did not appear, and the trial, which was one of the most dramatic the Central Criminal Court has ever seen, ended in an enigmatic tragedy.

The court was crowded, and the atmosphere was hopeful, for nearly a whole side of one of the three tables in front of the bench was taken up by a number of trim and florid young men who were said to be Spanish lawyers who had, presumably, brought proof that John Amery could not have committed treason against England because he was not a British but a Spanish subject. But at eleven o'clock, half an hour after the trial should have started, there was no judge on the bench, no jury in the box, no prisoner in the dock. Then Amery's counsel, Mr. Gerald Slade K.C., later Mr. Justice Slade, who had been William Joyce's counsel, and now dead, and Mr. John Foster, now Sir John Foster and a Q.C., left their seats and went through a door in the glass walls of the empty dock and, stooping to gather up their black gowns, down the stairway into the cells. After half an hour there was a flurry of messengers and the trial began. The judge entered in shrivelled and eccentric majesty: Mr. Justice Humphreys, small in the depths of his red and purple robes, a very old man, with wit on his tongue and a fiercer wit on his face, where there was often written what he would not let himself say in case institutions he respected fell.

In the dock, John Amery looked like a sick little monkey and was yellow with fear, but behaved well. The indictments against him were read out. He was charged with having made treasonable broadcasts and speeches and having attempted to seduce British subjects from their allegiance, and was asked whether he pleaded guilty or not guilty. It had been supposed that he would answer "Not guilty." Then the jurors would have been called in and sworn, and counsel would have addressed the court, and the routine would have rolled on for perhaps as long as four days. But when the question was put to him he answered, "I plead guilty to all counts," and the trial lasted eight minutes.

A murmur ran through the court which was horrified, which was expostulatory, which was tinged with self-pity, for this was suicide. If he pleaded guilty he must be sentenced to death, for there is no alternative sentence for treason, and it is not in the power of any judge to substitute a term of imprisonment. There is only the possibility that the Home Secretary may advise the Crown to reprieve the condemned man; and this happens only in certain circumstances, not to be found by any eye in the case of John Amery. In effect, the young man was saying, "I insist on being hanged by the neck in three weeks' time." Very strangely, what he did felt like an act of cruelty to the whole court. That was why it felt self-pity. It rejected the life that was in all of us. Now it could be perceived that the legal tradition whereby a man under a capital charge must be urged by every possible means to plead not guilty is no meddling excess of humanitarianism, but is an expression of the fundamental belief of living things in life. It recalled that saying of Charles Dickens which so profoundly impressed Tolstoi, that whatever power gave us life, and for whatever purpose, he was sure it was given to us on the understanding that we defend it to the last breath. It is true, of course, that there are conditions in which a man can die without betraying his life, because his death will give it the spiritual value without which it is worthless, but these conditions were not to be found in the case of poor young Amery.

The old judge leaned forward and said to the clerk of the court, "Before that is recorded—" and broke off. Then he said to Mr. Slade, "I never accept a plea of guilty on a capital charge with-

out assuring myself that the accused thoroughly understands
what he is doing and what the immediate result must be, and
that he is in accord with his legal advisers in the course he has
taken." Mr. Slade answered, speaking with obvious fidelity to a
prepared statement, "I can assure you of that, my lord. I have
explained the position to my client and I am satisfied that he
understands it." This passage had the quietness of the worst sort
of nightmare. It was as if he had said, "Yes, this man chooses to
be walled up, and all proper arrangements have been made to
get suitable bricks." The old judge's eyebrows and the corners
of his mouth made a queer pattern. Yes, life has to be defended
to the last ditch, but what a damned thing it is! He said, "Right.
Let it be recorded." Then the clerk of the court asked John
Amery if he had anything to say. The young man answered,
weakly and politely, "No, thank you." The attendant placed
the square black cloth on the judge's head, but the judge did
not deliver the death sentence. Instead he leaned forward and
asked, "You do not want to say anything?" Still in the same
well-bred and dying voice, the young man said, "No, thank you,
sir." It was quite clear that he was morally satisfied and that he
was congratulating himself on having at last, at the end of his
muddled and frustrated existence, achieved an act crystalline in
its clarity, an act which fulfilled the conditions in which a man
can choose to die without betraying life. Yet none of the
hundreds of people who were watching him with the intensest
interest had the faintest idea what that act was, with perhaps the
exception of the lawyers, who were bound by professional etiquette to keep silent.

It was immediately spread about that John Amery had suddenly insisted on pleading guilty for the sake of his family, to
spare them the prolonged anguish of his trial. But this could
hardly be the whole explanation. For if the Spanish lawyers were
there, they must have attended to give testimony in support of
his story that he had been naturalized as a Spanish citizen, and
he had simply to stand by while the case moved towards his
acquittal, which would have been the best way of sparing his
family's feelings. There was, in fact, another complication,
which could be guessed from the curious circumstance that the
Spanish lawyers did not all belong to one party. Anyone who
watched them during the period of waiting before the trial be-

gan could see that they were split into two groups. So, it turned out, they were. One group had come to give evidence in support of John Amery's claim to be a naturalized Spaniard, and the other to controvert that evidence.

How that situation arose was indicated some months later to a traveller in Spain who found himself at a dinner party with a member of the Franco government. This traveller remembered that a relative of John Amery had gone out to Spain with letters from the British authorities asking the Spanish government to give all facilities for searching the records for proof of this claim to naturalization, and that shortly afterwards a law officer, bearing credentials from the same fount of authority as Amery's relative, had also gone out to Spain, apparently on some errand of investigation, though it was not known what that might be. It occurred to the traveller that perhaps the Spanish politician might have known one or both of these visitors, and he mentioned their names. "Now tell me," asked the Spaniard, "just what happened in that case. What made the British government change their minds about John Amery?" "Change their minds?" echoed the traveller. "Yes," said the Spaniard petulantly. "First they wanted not to hang him, and then the next thing we knew they wanted to hang him." There had been a Spanish misunderstanding of British processes.

It must be remembered that John Amery probably believed himself to be a Spanish subject. It was certainly true that when he was gun-running for Franco he had received a *laissez-passer* for Spanish territory which, once he had heard of the defence raised by William Joyce, would very easily have been transformed by his feather wits into a formal certificate of naturalization. He assured his lawyers that he was indeed a Spanish citizen, and his relative went to Spain to look for the relevant documentation in the belief that it existed, and quite unprepared for any unusual act of complaisance on the part of any Spanish official. It would not have crossed his mind that it was necessary, and when he was given the required certificate he took it back to England in all good faith. But shortly before the trial the private papers which Amery had left behind him on the Continent had fallen into the hands of British Intelligence officers. They found that the date on the Spanish certificate of naturalization put Amery in Spain on a date when, his passport showed, he had been in another country. Hence a British official also made a journey to Spain.

The judge spoke some words to Amery before passing sentence, expressing hatred of his crime. Many people thought the judge heartless, forgetting that a very old man might well feel himself on an equality with a prisoner under sentence of death, and might even think that the prisoner would find a precise evaluation of his position, given by one so likely to understand it, more interesting than tenderness from a stranger with whom he had less in common. True, there was a certain ineptness in his enlargement on a passage in the depositions which described how Amery had visited the camp at Saint Denis to enlist internees for his renegade British Free Corps and had been warned by some of the men that he was committing high treason but had taken no notice. This is not a point worth making, for by that time Amery had been sealed in his magic circle, and he must have believed that he was giving the internees an opportunity to join the winning side. Yet, if what the judge said had little application to Amery, he seemed to say it because his mind had been shocked into flight to some place near the source of our general destiny. He said slowly and querulously, "They called you traitor, and you heard them." It was as if he spoke for all men, marvelling at our knowledge of good and evil and our preference for evil. That was a timeless moment; but the case had its aspects which showed the power of time. It seemed extraordinary that Amery had been allowed to plead guilty. That he had wished to do so was not a satisfactory explanation, for he was too volatile to have resisted whole-hearted pressure, had it been applied. It was widely said that his counsel, Mr. Slade, had concurred with his client's wish because he thought that should Amery plead not guilty the jury would be prejudiced against him if he did not go into the box to give evidence on his behalf, and would be still more prejudiced if he went into the witness box and babbled in his customary fashion; and Mr. Slade hoped that Amery would afterwards be reprieved because he was the son of a loved and valued public servant. The prosecuting counsel, Sir Hartley Shawcross, did all he could to dissuade Mr. Slade, pointing out that the social climate would never permit such a concession to one of the governing classes, and of course he was right. Mr. Slade was in the wrong century.

As the historical plays of Shakespeare indicate, it has never been the custom in this land to exempt the great or their kin from the gallows, and the specific privileges granted to nobles in this connection are trial by their peers and a silken rope. In the eighteenth century the kind of mercy for which Mr. Slade hoped was sometimes practised, but throughout the nineteenth century the tide flowed in a contrary direction; and by the time the First World War was over few people in any class would have considered it proper that a great man should be rewarded for his greatness by exemption of his son from the penalty which would certainly have been inflicted on the son of a poor man.

This dangerous lapse into archaicism was due to deep-seated peculiarities in Mr. Slade's character. In court he was the coolest and most resourceful of craftsmen, and he was a notably successful chairman of the Bar Council; but he was not the orthodox barrister he appeared. For one thing, he always believed his clients to be innocent, not in the highly technical sense with which lawyers must hold that belief, but with the Wordsworthian simplicity which is the privilege of the layman; and in general matters he was apt to turn his face against the judgments of his fellow men even when these seemed well calculated to serve our common convenience. It distressed him that the civilized world had agreed mealtimes, since a man should eat only when he is hungry, and different men, and indeed the same man on different days, might be supposed to feel hunger at different hours, according to the energy they had expended. Such a man might easily fail to grasp public opinion on a matter such as the favouring of a convicted person because of his birth, rarely discussed because no longer considered arguable. The error probably cost Amery his life. For had he pleaded not guilty and gone into the witness box, his demeanour would probably have made it possible to reprieve him on the ground of insanity.

At that trial time could be seen moving at quick-march pace; at other trials it seemed to be standing still. There were two which took place in the world of Kipling, of "If" and "Recessional." The first concerned a Kenneth Edward, who at the beginning of the war had been a charming and moderately naughty boy of thirteen in a Cornish town, the son of a policeman employed in a naval dockyard. In 1940 he went to sea as a deckboy on an ammunition ship, and within the year was on a

steamer which was sunk by a German raider. For six weeks he
was a prisoner on the raider, and then he was landed in France
and passed through a succession of internment camps. In one of
them there was an elderly Englishwoman who was released and
persuaded the camp authorities to let her take the boy home
with her. As he grew nearer military age the Germans took him
back again into custody. He described what happened then in
these words:

> Then I was sent to a camp near Drancy near Paris, in which
> I found myself alone with a lot of Jews. I stayed in this camp
> with them for three months and then I was transferred to St.
> Denis with all the Jews on August 29th, 1942. On June 9th I
> escaped from St. Denis and I could not get away from Paris so
> I gave myself up on the 10th of July 1943. When I returned to
> camp I had a dog's life from the Jews because they believed I
> gave one of their number away seeing he had escaped and was
> hiding unbeknown to myself quite near to where I was and he
> was caught three days after: I stayed in camp then in a hut to
> myself because even my best friend would not speak to me
> until it was found out that I never gave him away. Soon after a
> man came to our Camp and he called himself John Amery. He
> called some men to a hut in the Camp and spoke to them about
> a Legion of St. George that had been formed in Germany. Then
> he put some big Posters in the Camp, which said that a said
> Legion had been formed and the strength of this Legion was a
> little 1800 men POW and those RAF planes that had come
> from England to fight Bolshevics which I can truly say I did
> not understand what it meant until a few months ago, he said
> it was our duty to come and fight for England and Europe. So
> I spoke to the Camp Captain Gillis a German who said it was
> good and that most of my friends had vol. but he could not
> tell me their names, so I thought if he said it was good it must
> be so. I told him I would join too.

A fortnight afterwards he was taken to a private house in Paris
where he was introduced to a German named Plack, of the
Foreign Office, and John Amery, who was introduced to him as
the Foreign Secretary of England. They took a great deal of
trouble to persuade this illiterate child with no military training
to enlist in the legion, and this was not folly. A gay and good-
looking boy, in high spirits because he had regained his liberty,
and bubbling over with talk of the fine time the Germans were

giving him, might have been a very successful recruiting agent in British prisoner-of-war camps.

About three weeks later Kenneth Edward succumbed, and the camp authorities handed him over to an English member of the legion named Tunmer, who took him to Paris. There they lived in a house managed by French collaborationists in the bleak surrealist district on the outer edge of Auteuil, where gaunt buildings tower over the fortifications, not far from the fantastic viaduct of the Pont-du-Jour. Tunmer took him round the sights of Paris and gave him some money to spend on amusements and promised him as nice a time in Berlin. There was doubtless a real tenderness and pity in the older man's dealings with the boy, for after eight days of this holiday two men in civilian clothes came to the house and took Tunmer away. He was a British agent. Later that same day John Amery paid Kenneth Edward a visit to see how he was getting on. When the bewildered boy told him what had happened he showed signs of surprise, and, on the plea that it did not seem safe to stay in the house when such things were going on, he rang up the Gestapo.

The immediate consequences were alarming. Kenneth Edward was questioned about Tunmer and thrown into prison for a week. Then he was taken to Berlin under guard, where he was met at the station by Amery, his Cagoulard wife who had succeeded Jeannine Barde, and Herr Plack. They greeted him affectionately and took him back to Amery's rooms, a suite in the Kaiserhof, a luxurious hotel looking out on a great square. Kenneth Edward was dazzled by all this splendour and was greatly impressed by John Amery's good looks; and he had a good time playing with Amery's dog. Amery gave him three hundred marks and was with him for some hours, telling him lying stories about the growing strength of the legion and preaching a crusade against bolshevism. Finally he took him over to the Foreign Office, which was not far away, where a Dr. Hesse inquired of him with what must have been inhuman irony as to his readiness to fight the Russians; and afterwards Plack took him to a boarding-house.

But he did not see Amery for a month. Plack kept him supplied with money and cigarettes, and he drifted about Berlin with nothing to do. Then Amery summoned him to the suite at the Kaiserhof and introduced him to Thomas Haller Cooper and a group of German officers who had been engaged for some time past in spotting likely traitors in the prison camps. "Drinks," Kenneth Edward reported in one of his statements, "were supplied by Amery." The British Free Corps was launched onto the sea of alcohol on which it was to sail until its shipwreck. At the end of the evening Amery said to the boy, "You will soon be with your unit now, and will start training with the Corporal." But no call came for him, and it was the last time he was ever to see him. For the next three months Kenneth Edward was to live in a peculiar limbo. Berlin was constantly raided by the RAF. Plack ceased to take any interest in him, and he was so poorly fed that he missed the Red Cross parcels he had had in camp. He was unable to write to his family or receive letters from them. As he spoke very little German he was repeatedly put under arrest; he thought it happened on as many as twenty-three occasions. Again and again he wrote to Amery, asking him what he was to do, but received no answer. The last time he was arrested his captors put him in a cell and beat him with a blackjack in revenge for the damage the RAF was doing. In desperation he went to the Foreign Office and reminded the authorities of the interview he had had when he first came to Berlin; and on January 1, 1944, he was sent to a house on the outskirts of Berlin where there was a handful of men who had volunteered to join the British Free Corps and were now under the command of Thomas Haller Cooper.

Kenneth Edward was not very kindly received. As he put it, "I wasn't very trusted and had been brought in by Amery." That there was some feeling against him was indicated by his position as the one and only private in the British Free Corps. All other volunteers, without a single exception, were made officers. The explanation he gave was probably correct. The Germans had by this time found that John Amery was more than they could stomach. Nevertheless, they used Kenneth Edward by sending him on recruiting tours through the camps. But they had fallen into the pit which is dug for all corrupters of youth. Despoiled innocence loses its innocent charm. The happy and pretty boy they had enlisted to speak fair things to melancholy prisoners was no longer happy or pretty, and his words had little power to lift the heart.

He made no recruits; and, on finding himself, in the month of

May 1944, in the course of a tour, at the merchant seamen's camp
near Bremen, he heard something of the security officer who was
in charge, Captain Notman. This man was what the mass of men
since Homer have wished to be: comely, strong, courageous,
trusted and trustworthy, not without guile, and much loved.
Learning his repute, Kenneth Edward wrote him a letter in which
he threw himself on his mercy:

> But it's not been for the last month that I have realized I am
> a traitor to England and by what I am doing I am causing my
> Mother the greatest agony she has ever felt so I implore you not
> for my sake but for my Parents' sake to help me get out of the
> mess I am in. I'll face anything if I can get out, but if it is
> possible to see Brigadier-Major Interne I think he will see that
> I don't get down the mines Because I am scared for my health
> and I would (I have realized) like to come to Milag with Real
> Englishmen, I thank you Sir.

When Captain Notman got this letter he came out of his office
and talked to the boy, whose presence in his camp on these tours
he had till then ignored. But he could do little for him. He
advised him to stay in the legion, which was probably the best
advice the boy could have been given at this juncture, when the
Germans had begun to savage the traitors; and he told him that
as Switzerland was the neutral power charged with the responsibility of protecting the interests of British prisoners of war, he
might as well go to the Swiss embassy in Berlin and put his case
before the officials there.

This Kenneth Edward did, but nothing came of it. Prisoners
of war who lose their status by treachery are not a class which
can be protected by international action, since it is impossible to
make the threat of reprisals against a similar group within the
frontiers of the aggrieved state, which is the only weapon guaranteeing the protection of prisoners of war. Kenneth Edward had
to resign himself to the squalid lotus-eating of the legion. A
leading English traitor gave him his patronage, but this cannot
have been much help, for the man was of unamiable character.
In his loneliness the boy made another attempt to get in touch
with Amery and the Placks:

Dresden, 4.11.44

Dear Sir,
   I write you a few lines and hope that you may receive them.
Well Mr. Amery it is a long time since I saw or heard from you

last and I sometimes wonder how you are getting on. I hope you are in good health the same as this leaves me. I saw in the French papers that you were wounded on your way to Lyons, but I am glad to know that you have recovered. I am still in the British Free Corps we expect to go to the front in two weeks's time, but I don't think there is anything in it. We are doing Pioneer Training for the past six weeks and I like it very much. I speak a great lot of German so I can tell a few where to get off. How is your wife and dog? I hope they are still in good health. Have you heard from Mr. and Mrs. Plack. How are they? Would you tell them I should like to be remembered to them and I would like to have a line from them some time, I cannot write to them because I have not there present address, also would you be so kind as to give Mr. Adami my best regards. I must close now because it is time for me to go on Garde duty. All the Boys sends there Best Regards so goodbye for the time.

Yours truly,
(Signed) Kenneth Edward

The forced cheerfulness of this letter contrasts with the misery of the letter he had written six months before to Captain Notman, which can be assumed to be honest, since it was an attempt to get behind prison bars, where a hard fate might befall him if the British were defeated. But there was no answer. Inevitably he was one of the unhappy residue of the corps dragged to the Russian front by Thomas Haller Cooper, who, just released from uncomfortable custody by the Germans, nevertheless went forward in Wagnerian ecstasy to die for Germany and actually got himself and his reluctant charges into a battle near Schöneberg. There Kenneth Edward, not a Wagnerian type, surrendered to the Russians. Intelligence officers came on his traces when they were trying to find the leading British traitor who had taken the boy under his wing, but he had vanished into thin air and had never been seen since; he was perhaps one of those traitors who were Soviet agents working in disguise. Amery's papers were examined and the security officers of the camps reported on the legion's recruiting campaigns. So it happened that, in the following February, Kenneth Edward was tried at the Old Bailey with three other merchant seamen, one of them the eccentric Herbert George.

It was an unimportant case, like a number of others brought

in order to assert the sacredness of prisoners of war and protect them from molestation in future wars. If it be objected that he was young, it should be remembered that many boys no older had shown themselves sturdier of soul. He was given nine months' imprisonment, the lightest sentence passed on any traitor, and his robust health and resilient character took him through it. But his trial lingers in the memory of those who saw it because of his reaction to the sight of Captain Notman in the witness box. For a minute it could be seen that he would forget the terror and the loneliness and the beatings and the bullying, but not the injury which had been inflicted on a deeper part. Captain Notman was the kind of person he respected, brave, honourable, upright; and poor Kenneth Edward had appeared before Captain Notman in the past and was appearing before him again, as committed to a way of living which the captain held in contempt. If by some odd chance somebody in court had quoted:

> If you can keep your head when all about you
>   Are losing theirs and blaming it on you,
> If you can trust yourself when all men doubt you,
>   But make allowance for their doubting too;
> If you can wait and not be tired by waiting,
>   Or being lied about, don't deal in lies,
> Or being hated, don't give way to hating,
>   And yet don't look too good, nor talk too wise:

there might have been tears shed in the dock, unnoticed by Captain Notman, who would have been listening appreciatively to the verse.

In the Kipling world too was the trial of the only traitor that gave the Royal Navy reason to hang its head. He was a young stoker of faint personality and incurious mind, and the chief charge against him was the betrayal to the Germans of information about radar equipment in the type of motor torpedo boat in which he served, and about the naval and harbour facilities of Portsmouth, neither of which subjects could he have had at his fingertips. But he was up to his neck in dubious goings-on. A slender boy, not unlike the Duke of Windsor, with a long neck, hair pale gold in the light and mousy in the shadow, and pouches under his blue eyes, he made a poor show in the dock, sagging like a plant in need of staking. When he was cross-examined he was pitifully unresentful of injustice and misunderstanding, and borne down by noise.

But he was true to an exalted resolution. He had been a coward in Germany, and he knew what cowardice was. That he knew because other people were brave. He had a comrade who was very brave: a dark boy with bright brown eyes who threw back his head and laughed when he was asked if the Germans in the camp had beaten him for covering up a friend's escape. That *had* been a pasting. So Stoker Rose was determined not to be a coward in England. He was not going to lie to save his skin; and in excess of abnegation he bent his neck beneath the yoke laid on it by his cross-examiner. At last, when he had covered himself with a web of admissions, the investigating officer said to him, "I suggest to you that right from the start you knew that what you were doing was wrong. Is that not so?" The boy did not answer for a long time. His face became greenish-white; then the discolouration cleared and left it steadfast, though still languid. "Yes, sir," he said. It was the truth, and he told it when he was being cross-examined on a capital charge.

The moment was, from his point of view, satisfactory. He had always known that he should have resisted the Germans to the point of death, and he felt cleansed by his confession of long-standing cowardice, which was of the sort more usually made to a priest or to a parent than to a lawyer in court. Plainly he felt about this investigating officer as young Kenneth Edward had felt about Captain Notman. He was saying, "I am inferior to this man who is questioning me, because I did not uphold the values that he has always upheld." A minute later his own counsel asked him, "Did you do what you did with the purpose of betraying your country?" He answered with a new strength, "Absolutely no, sir." "Why did you do it?" asked his counsel. He answered, "I had no alternative," and added with a laugh, "I was frightened to death." "You mean," said the counsel with a smile, "you were frightened of your life." The exact truth eased them both.

This was an attempt to keep the natural man in check, fully justified by the presence of the natural man at his worst in the witness box. The legal departments of the armed forces have a horrid weakness for tainted evidence. John Gordon, an Irish-Canadian, was serving a sentence of twenty-five years' imprisonment for treachery; he had taken a day off to take a hand in condemning to prison or to death a young man with whom he had lived in companionship for two years. Because prison was a horror to his goatish disposition and he had been there for six months, he stood like a dead man not so efficiently raised as Lazarus. When he was asked a question his mouth worked under the stubble of his moustache and hung open; his hands were usually clasped behind him, sometimes he brought them forward and rubbed them together. They were marked as if by untidy stigmata. Staring upwards at nothing, he repeated names of men with whom he had lived for years as if they were words in an unknown language.

But the next day he was well enough. He saw the court as comprised of persons who, like all persons gathered together in public, purported to believe in virtue. Or did they really believe in virtue? Perhaps so. He could believe in virtue too if he forced himself. Then let them all be virtuous together. At his own court martial he had been described as "the ears and the eyes of the Germans" and had been the informer to end all informers, and now he unctuously set about persuading the court that his collusion with the Germans had been all for the sake of his comrades. "There were a hundred and one little things we could do for the prisoners," he declared priggishly. But in this orgy of self-justification he spared time to say a good word for the lily-like stoker. He described how the boy had gone more than once to see certain German officers and begged to be released from his post as "trusty" and allowed to resume his status as an ordinary prisoner of war, and had wept when he was refused. This creature was indeed half a child himself. "What did you do with your time?" he was asked. He answered, "We played cards. We read books. We went walks in the woods. And sometimes," he said with sudden gusto, "we went swimmin'." One saw his hairy and sweating body raising a diamond spray of water in the sunlight; one heard the harsh and meaningless cries with which he would have banished tranquillity in order to proclaim his pleasure.

This depraved child, companion to Caliban, had brought suffering on himself even before he was sentenced to this long term of imprisonment. The wounds on his hands were due to a beating with barbed wire he had been given by a working party of prisoners of war who had discovered that he was an informer. They had also left his face a bleeding jelly and broken several of his ribs. They counted this as an eye for an eye and a tooth for a tooth. He had brought as bad and worse on their comrades. When all is said and done, Caliban is dangerous.

One day the court rose early and the spectators went out into the Portsmouth Naval Barracks at a time when the men were in their quarters; man's fear of Caliban was made visible. At every window in the huge towering blocks there was a row of intent and unsmiling faces, crowded together at the side which gave the best view of the courtroom door far below, like beads pushed along the wire of an abacus. They were watching to see the stoker led out. There were thousands of them, and they had paid generously for his defence. But none was speaking. The silence was absolute. A giant body was apprehensive lest it had lost its virtue, which it required as much as its strength if it were to be strong. This was the spirit of the "Recessional":

> Lord God of Hosts, be with us yet,
> Lest we forget—lest we forget!

and it was presently to vanish from all treason trials.

The prosecutions of British persons charged with treacherous relations with the enemy during the Second World War under the Emergency Powers (Defence) Act, 1939, ended with a nonpareil, a case quite unlike any that had come before or were to come afterwards. One of the most famous litigants of the last half-century was tried and convicted for broadcasting for the Germans in occupied Paris: a man of exceptional gifts, who had been brilliantly successful in business, had offered up his life in martyrdom to an idea connected with insurance finance. Roughly speaking, he thought it wrong of insurance companies to invest in commodities, and he crusaded against the practice with a fervour which would have been excessive had it been the prime cause of cancer, and which brought ruin on himself and his family. He had been attracted to Germany because he believed that the Nazi government was sound on this issue—and he was hardly conscious of any other—and on the outbreak of war he and his family were caught there and were engulfed in a series of horrible misfortunes, which finally swept them into occupied France. There he took service with the Germans from sheer need; and after the war the British authorities might have overlooked his offences, had not he been betrayed into provocative actions by his indignant feeling that too much importance was being ascribed to matters which, in his mind, were only marginal to the great problem of insurance finance. It is to be hoped that in the hereafter a world will be constructed for him where the Pearl and the Prudential, the Scottish Widows and the Eagle, all alike toe a celestial line and invest their surplus as he thinks decent.

Then an ideological hush fell on the Old Bailey. But not for long. Treachery is not a peculiar product of the war between Great Britain and Germany. It is a business which has been carried on since the beginning of history. Faint cries from the past tell us how the Illyrians were ashamed when those of their blood without pride worked for Rome, and how Central Europe blushed over the renegades who joined the yellow barbarian hordes; and the Republic of Venice entered on its books the figures of its competition in the traitor market on the Mediterranean coasts with the great corrupter, Islam, who for centuries made aliens like William Joyce beys and pashas and tutors to the children of its great, and picked the Christian Free Corps from the galley-slaves. The traitors who stood in the dock in the Old Bailey were enduring their two-hundredth incarnation or so, allowing three generations to a century and putting the first complicated civilization in the fourth millennium before Christ. There is always loyalty, for men love life and cling together under the threats of the uncaring universe. So there is always treachery, since there is the instinct to die as well as the instinct to live; and as loyalty changes to meet the changing threats of the environment, so treachery changes also.

Six months after the hanging of William Joyce, the most remarkable representative of the phase of disloyalty which ended with the defeat of Germany, there followed him into the dock at the Old Bailey Dr. Alan Nunn May, Lecturer on Physics in the University of London, who represented the new phase of disloyalty. The community condemned in the person of William Joyce the extrovert who sought to find in politics what in other ages he would have found in religion and made his search on the field of fascism, with its marches, its bands, its shouting, its bright colours, its blows, its violence. Dr. Alan Nunn May was the personification of the introvert who makes the same transference but is better pleased by the secrecy and drabness of communism, which is fascism with a glandular and geographical difference. He was a scientist, and in that was as representative of his breed of fascism as Joyce had been of his. For the new Fascists, who stepped forward after the war to carry on the old business of disloyalty under a different label, were, in England, under scientific domination. It had been the claim of the violent men who formed the Nazi-Fascist movement that they should be entrusted with power because they were endowed with a greater amount of physical strength and vitality than the mass of the population, an amount which would enable them to seize power if it was denied them. It was now the claim of the scientists who formed so influential a part of the Communist-Fascist movement that they were endowed with a greater amount of special technical knowledge than the mass of the population, an amount which would enable them to seize that power if it were denied them. There is a similarity between the claims of the Nazi-Fascists and the Communist-Fascists, and no less similarity between the methods of putting them forward. The claims depend on an unsound assumption that the man who possesses a special gift will possess also a universal wisdom which will enable him to impose an order on the state superior to that contrived by the consultative system known as democracy; which will enable him, in fact, to know other people's business better than they do themselves.

If this assumption seems less patently absurd when it is applied to a scientist than to a pianist or a painter, the reason is simply the dizzy novelty of science. The study of physics or chemistry is no more likely than the study of harmony and counterpoint to develop social omniscience in the student; nor have these or any other branches of science made any contributions to the technique of government which would give their students any right to intervene as experts. It frequently happened then that the BBC asked certain Communist scientists to speak about the age we live in, and they were all remarkable for the vanity with which they claimed that the advance of science has at last made it possible for man to contemplate a planned and abundant economy for the world. But modern science had and has done almost nothing to give man the precog-

nizance necessary for planning and still less to guarantee any
kind of useful abundance. It cannot foretell or control the
foundation of all economy, which is weather. It has not yet
found a way of providing cheap houses, or a cheap and convenient source of light and heat and energy, or a cheap and reliable
food supply. The groundless boasts were, like the equally groundless boasts of the Nazi-Fascists, covers for a threat. Mussolini and
Hitler, when they said that they and their followers could govern
because of their physical strength and ruthlessness, meant that
they and their followers had enough physical strength and ruthlessness to beat and shoot anyone who refused to be governed by
them.

The Communist scientists, who said that they and their associates could govern because of their technical knowledge, meant
that they and their associates played a sufficient part in the
development of processes used in modern war and industry to be
able to blackmail society if it would not accept their dictation.
One demand was as absurd as the other. Obviously any fragile
doctor or research worker has as much right as any brawny
Fascist to have his say in the conduct of the community; and
obviously any teacher or any factory hand or any housewife is as
necessary to the state as a scientist and has as much right to self-
government. If it be asked why some scientists, who of necessity
must have a certain amount of intelligence, should be Communist-Fascists, it can be answered that the British and American
scientists came from a group which had been deprived of its
defences against absurdity, and especially against totalitarian
absurdity, by its social origins.

British and American scientists are drawn from the intellectuals of their two countries: that is, from a section of the English
middle classes, or from American groups profoundly influenced
by the culture of that section. Intellectuals may be defined as
persons whose natural endowments and education give them the
power to acquire experience of a rich and varied order, usually
linked in some degree or other with learning and the arts, and,
furthermore, to analyse their experiences and to base generalizations on the results of the analyses conducted by them and their
fellows. They are essentially gregarious. They pool their experiences, they conform in their conclusions. Nobody can be an
intellectual all by himself. That is why William Joyce, though

he had an intellect capable of passing exacting academic tests, could never be called an intellectual. His Anglo-Irish loyalist tradition and his early Irish background made it impossible for him to fit into the conventional groove. Intellectuals are thrown up for the most part by the middle classes. This was not so in earlier times, in Tudor or Caroline or Georgian days, but it has been the case in the last hundred years. Though there have been notable exceptions, such as Bertrand Russell, the old landowning class bound its young too closely to the services and to politics and to estate management to give them much time for the life of debate; and the industrialists have always been too busy. Intellectuals thrown up from the lower classes immediately pass, in this country, into the middle classes.

It is the function of intellectuals to enable society to adapt itself to changing conditions—which is, indeed, to attack the essential problem of politics. But while there are few functions so important, there are few so constantly subject to degeneration. A lazy intellectual, or an intellectual who has adopted the vocation with insufficient equipment, can pretend that he is discharging that function simply by attacking the status quo, without giving any indication of what he proposes to substitute for it. This actually gives him an advantage over the constructive intellectual, for in destruction wit and irony can more easily come into play. He will often have dynamic force behind his wit, because the intellectual who had not a religious sense of the duty of selflessness burned till recently with the grievance that unless he was a man of fortune he could not gain a position of power. He felt this more and more as the nineteenth century went on, for the industrial revolution had created a new field of power other than that which had been cultivated by the landed aristocracy.

There is an ominous significance in Matthew Arnold's rage against the philistinism of the manufacturing classes, which was defiling the English mind as the smoke from their factories' chimneys was defiling the English sky, and his anguished, nostalgic love of the traditional English culture based on classical studies and therefore dependent on the existence of a leisured class under no compulsion to follow utilitarian studies. Arnold rightly supposed that there were far more aristocrats than manufacturers who could understand and value him. It was most sinister, though it then seemed most innocent, that in his distress he looked for comfort to a country other than his own: to Germany, which in that age was the country from which there had come the Prince Consort, Christmas trees, the music of Mendelssohn.

Every decade of the nineteenth century was to produce more and more Matthew Arnolds, who were to feel furiously that by all traditional standards they formed the superior class of the community, the sages and the prophets, and that they were wholly disregarded by a rising class of industrial tyrants. They dealt with their fury in two ways. Either they clung to the old landowning aristocracy, with something often difficult to distinguish from snobbery but actually concerned with deeper matters. For an example of that form of adaptation we can turn to an alien who, when his discontent took the usual form of looking to another country for salvation, looked to ours. The English landowning aristocracy, transplanted to America, had found it physically impossible to cover the vast and ever-expanding terrain and was a weakly growth except in certain localities; whereas the industrial revolution had been, as gardeners say, a good grower, and its flowers of philistinism were lush. Henry James simply turned his back on the distressing scene and went to England and basked in the sunshine which still, though with diminishing strength, warmed the terraces of the great houses. His correspondence illustrates the curious historical fact that the nineteenth century, which knew few material vestiges of the system of patronage, can show many more respectful letters from intellectuals to aristocrats than can the eighteenth century, when peers were real patrons and paid cash.

But if the intellectual chanced to be neither a rich American, nor a writer successful enough to be lionized, nor a scholar holding authority in a public school or university, he could not range himself with the landed aristocracy, because he would be too obscure to attract its attention. Friendless, he would rage alike against the old class which had held power and the new class which was taking it from them; and he would find relief in attacking the capitalist system which maintained them both. In this enterprise he found certain important allies. Chief among them were the humanitarian members of all classes, who were becoming revolted by the cruelties inflicted by capitalism on those who were unable, for one reason or another, to share in the benefits it was conferring on the country as a whole; and the industrial workers, who were gathering together to demand a larger share of the profits which industry was creating. This meant that the intellectuals joined the procession which was formed by a union between the humanitarian section of the Liberal Party and the idealistic but legitimately acquisitive Labour Party. They were, however, not entirely contented. The Liberal Party consisted largely of Whig aristocrats and philistine industrialists, who carried more weight than the humanitarians and took no notice of their intellectual friends; and the Labour Party was dominated by industrial workers who had a deep distrust of intellectuals and thought them just another type of toff. English intellectuals might have become as purely academic and politically ineffective as their French colleagues at this period, had they not found exceptional leaders in Sidney and Beatrice Webb.

Both these gifted people were animated by a special discontent. Sidney Webb had a deep understanding of the administrative problems of the modern state; and it was most unlikely that he would ever be in a position where he could communicate this understanding to society, because he belonged to the lower middle class, and, though he had many endearing qualities, lacked the social charms which opened the doors of great houses. Beatrice Webb had talents of the same sort to an unusual degree, and they burned with a fiery brilliance because they had been set alight by a fierce resentment. Her diaries frankly confess what she was: a member of the wealthy industrialist class, bitterly jealous of the landowning aristocracy which had a longer title to power and often failed to conceal that they looked on her class as intruders. She despised the proletariat, and few people have written of the rank-and-file socialist more savagely than she did. But even more did she dislike people who lived in houses with useless parks round them, people who gave their little boys ponies, people who had their own private libraries and picture galleries. Now she and her husband recognized that the modern state was becoming so complicated that it would have to be governed by a bureaucracy of experts, and they embarked on a long campaign to form the young intellectuals of their day into an army of experts which should be the cadre of this

bureaucracy, while at the same time they influenced the policy of
the Labour Party so that it would call this army into action as
soon as possible. They were, in fact, planning to pick up power
when it fell from the hands of the industrialists as it had fallen
from the hands of the landowners.

They were aided by the support of the two most interesting
young writers of their time, H. G. Wells and Bernard Shaw, who
also were animated by discontent. Wells was full of justified
proletarian resentments. His mother was the housekeeper in a
great house, and he knew the agreeable life from which those
without property were excluded. He had been phthisical in his
youth and had suffered a grave internal injury when playing
football, and had felt the panic realization of insecurity which
was then the lot of the sick poor. Worst of all, he had an exceptional intelligence and had to fight to get it trained. He was also
to know the intellectual's sense of impotence in the form most
relevant to the special case of the Communist-scientist. By a
miracle of courage and persistence he wrested from society a
degree in science, and with his quick, glancing mind grasped
sooner than most of his colleagues what innumerable windows,
looking on what fantastic views, were going to be opened by
modern scientific discovery.

He was therefore repelled by the lack of imagination shown
by the nonscientific minds of the age, who were, indeed, quite
strangely blind to both the threats and the promises which were
being held out to society by science, even when they might themselves have derived profit and security from examining them. It
is staggering to realize for how long British industry grudged
spending money on research, and how, though the need for
mechanization of our armed forces was worked out on paper not
many years after the South African war, professional soldiers
were still resisting it till quite a late date after (not before) the
First World War. Wells had, therefore, a number of legitimate
grievances against society, and so had Shaw, though his were
fewer, less searing, and more dryly historical. He was the son of a
poor gentleman, and was in his youth so literally penniless that
he often lacked clothes fit to be worn in the street; he was also
Anglo-Irish, member of one of the ascendancy families whose
ascendant days were numbered. He was white-hot, and Wells was
red-hot, and they were as good as a combined fireworks-and-

bonfire show for drawing sightseers, who, as they gaped at the astonishing brightness, necessarily drew into their lungs much of the political atmosphere of the group.

The Webbs were not successful in some of their dearest enterprises. Their army of experts was apparently not trained on quite the right lines and furnished few of the contemporary leaders of the Labour Party. But the Webbs did much positive work. Till they set up in business, the English local government system was an uncharted jungle, and they took it over as if they were a highly efficient Woods and Forests Department. Their views on our penal system were also far in advance of their time and were both sensible and humanitarian. It would be incautious to ascribe to the influence of the Webbs any great part in the making of the Beveridge Report, on which our present welfare state is founded, but it must be remembered that Lord Beveridge was for many years Director of the London School of Economics, which the Webbs brought into being, and no one could direct that mighty engine of research without being in some degree also directed by it. The Webbs also urged their followers to whip up their energies and follow all sorts of political activities, including standing for local government offices, and for that reason the English left wing has been preserved from the lack of practical experience which makes the northern liberalism of the United States so sterile. They were positive indeed, and so, following different paths, were their literary supports. Wells revolted against them, partly because he found any form of cooperation impossible, partly because he was by temperament and conviction a democrat and he saw that the logical consequence of their bureaucratic theories was dictatorship. Giddy with excitement over life, he went his own way, alone in his time dreaming dreams of the future which matched its strangeness when it came, bringing to life characters rich as life itself makes them, spilling over into history and theology and by the use of the technique of free thinking coming to an oddly Christian conclusion: that there is a glory, and that man by himself cannot lay hold on it.

Shaw, just as excited, but pale, went on with his lifework of injecting the tired English prose of the late nineteenth century with the genius of the eighteenth-century prose, which had been laid up, not in lavender but in some more pungent herb, over in

Ireland. He refused to follow the fashion set by the Victorian and Edwardian playwrights and look at man through the wrong end of the opera glasses; his plays showed characters not merely as involved in social and sexual imbroglios but as making a choice between salvation and damnation. Many of the rank and file of the Webbs' followers were positive in their own lesser ways, as civil servants, teachers, doctors, lawyers, bringing a certain new initiative and conscientiousness to their work. The women among them were moved to much usefulness; many of the voluntary institutions for the care of mothers and children which were taken over by the National Health Service were founded and carried on by such women. But positive as both the leaders and followers were, they lived in an atmosphere of negativism. The foundation of their creed was the assumption that there was nothing in the existing structure of society which did not deserve to be razed to the ground, and that all would be well if it were replaced by something as different as possible. They were to do it quietly, of course; but the replacement was to be absolute. To them the past was of value only in so far as it gave indications of how to annul the present and create a future which had no relation to it.

The condition of these people's children was paradoxical. They were brought up in a state of complete immunity from any form of physical want. Not only did they never suffer from hunger or cold or lack of clothing, they lived in a society from which such deprivations were being eliminated more quickly and more thoroughly than ever before. They were surrounded from birth by the affection and extremely conscientious care of their mothers and fathers, who took parenthood very seriously indeed. They were exempt from fear of war as we now know it, for the airplane was still a toy, the British Navy was the supreme munition of the world, and it was an article of faith in this group that all foreigners (except, for some reason, the French) were pacifists. These children were, in fact, more fortunate than any groups which had ever existed previously, save certain scattered patricians during periods when the wind blew war away from their cities and trade was good; and even over them these English children had a huge advantage so far as freedom from violence and disease is concerned. Yet they were taught and believed that they were living in the worst of all possible worlds but that they need not despair, as it would be the easiest thing they and their parents ever did to tear it down and make a better one.

The homes where these children were reared were cheerful; Victorian frowstiness had been turned out of doors. The walls were distempered in light colours, the furniture was made of unstained wood which could be scrubbed, the curtains were of bright washable materials. Behind this simplicity there was an ideological complexity. The furnishing annulled the eighteenth and nineteenth centuries; it cancelled the immediate past which had produced the people who were using it. It had gone back to peasant art, because it was held that all that was true and beautiful lay so near the surface that primitive peoples had possessed it completely and it was only our wicked recent civilization which had perversely lost it. Clothes were peasanty too, rough tweeds for the men, hand-embroidered smocks for the women, and never orthodox evening dress; and the abundant, carefully prepared, simple, and often vegetarian food was served on peasant pottery.

The ideological complex came out into the open in the books lying about in their homes, of which the most treasured were the green volumes, tooled with gold lettering, which contained the plays of George Bernard Shaw. The prefaces of these were prized more highly than the plays, for they were battlefields where the values of our traditional culture made their last stand and bled and died, all except altruism and truthfulness and austerity, of which he and they thought well and claimed the monopoly, believing that they, and they alone, were the saviours of society. Of the other virtues, patriotism, it is to be remarked, was the first to get its dismissal. It was naïve for a man to feel any conviction that his own country was the best, or even as good as any other country; just as it was naïve to believe that the soldier of any foreign army committed atrocities or to doubt that any English soldier or sailor or colonial administrator failed to do so. The difference between the Webb-minded group and William Joyce can be judged from the letter he wrote to the University of London Committee for Military Education when he was a lad and was seeking admission to the Officers' Training Corps. No boy or girl in that group could possibly have written with a straight face of loyalty to the Crown or professed a desire to draw the sword for beloved England. Many were to learn better, and prove it with their lives, in 1914 and 1939; but earlier their attitude was anti-patriotic. Here the whole group, adult and juvenile, was agreed; but there was one point on which the rank and file went farther than their leaders. Both Shaw and Wells wrote books on religion which showed that they were neither atheists nor even agnostics but heretics. Most of these households, however, had adopted materialism, but not at all tragically, like the mid-nineteenth-century sceptics whom Mrs. Humphrey Ward describes in *Robert Elsmere*. On the contrary, it braced them like a cold bath.

This society had its own brightness and charm and virtue. But the position of its children was very difficult indeed. Not only were they taught to think of themselves as living in a miserable capitalist world when in actual fact they and most of their neighbours were not miserable at all; they were also taught to think of their parents and themselves as a courageous minority who were attacking the impregnable fortress of capitalism against fearful odds, and this also was not true. The capitalist system as these people knew it was about to collapse, not in consequence of their attack, but because it could not operate confidently (and confidence was necessary to its efficiency) except on an expanding market, and the rising ability of the Americans and the East to satisfy their own needs was contracting the market at the very same time that the system was having to meet the cost of the social services and of the rearmament made necessary by the threat of emergent Germany. England would have had to socialize itself during the last half-century even if there had not been a single socialist alive; and though it would have discovered socialism for itself, it welcomed every socialist who would save it that trouble. It therefore happened that few, if any, socialist intellectuals ever suffered a pennyworth of inconvenience owing to their faith, and that, indeed, an ambitious young man or young woman might find it a considerable material advantage to hold that faith.

Thus the children of this group were doubly sealed in fantasy and were bound to be discomfited by the passage of time. There is nothing spiritually easier than being in opposition, and those suddenly translated from that ease to the ordeal of responsibility must feel like oysters suddenly prised from their shells. That was the condition of these children when they became adult and found a socialized state forming itself round them. They no

longer could feel brave in demanding that coal should be nation-
alized, for all-party action had granted that long ago; now they
had to go on the Coal Board and face opponents who were in the
favourable position of being in opposition to state power. Many
of these children were strong enough to find no difficulty in facing
this reality in their adult years, but some were not and sought to
go on playing the rebellious part for which their parents had cast
them, even when the times were not safe for play-acting. Some of
these were lucky and were able to continue the pretence that they
were rebels by ascribing a rebellious quality to actions which were,
in fact, the pink of conformity. Such people feel that they habitually show courage in reading a left-wing weekly, even when there
is a left-wing government and there cannot be imagined any safer
occupation on this globe than reading or writing this publication.
But other people cannot buy their fantasy so cheaply. They are
conscientious and feel that, if they were taught to be rebels, then
they must go on being truly and effectively rebels. The faith that
inspired their fathers and mothers to rebellion was socialism, and
since that is now the established practice of their land they must
find another dissident faith.

It is obvious that such minds, at once fantasy-bound and lit-
eral, will turn happily to communism. It is on the left, where
they learned in their infancy salvation lay. It has a materialistic
basis, and one of its first claims is that it transcends the claims of
patriotism, which, if one has been brought up to believe that
patriotism existed only to have its claim transcended, gives it the
authority of a fulfilment of the prophets. Thus communism can,
alone of the parties, truly gratify nostalgia. The Conservatives
cannot re-create the great days of colonial expansion. The Liberals cannot re-create the smoky but glowing dawn when manufacturers and factory hands alike knew that the expansion of
industry gave power into their hands. The Labour Party cannot
put itself back into the glorious drunkenness of permanent opposition, but the Communist Party can still do that. It can put
people farther left than anyone else, and it can relieve its supporters from any nasty fear that a general election may impose
on them responsibility for government. That is to say, it can
carry its converts back to the golden days when the flowering
almonds along the avenues of the Hampstead Garden Suburb
were saplings, and revolutionary activities could be carried on

serenely in the lee of an unthreatened British Navy. This is especially magical for those who were not born until those almond trees were tall and sturdy, and have only their elders' reminiscences to tell them how delightful it was to follow a gallant liberal line in the midst of a stable conservative community. Communism offers a haven to the infantilist; and since it is perfectly possible for a highly gifted intellectual to be an infantilist, it appeared not surprising that a prominent English scientist should be a Communist and therefore, since every Communist is bound to regard disloyalty to his country as one of his party duties, disloyal.

2

IN many ways the trials of William Joyce and Dr. Alan Nunn May were as different as black and white. Both prisoners were poorly built; but Joyce had made himself a little knuckleduster of a man by hard exercise, whereas Dr. Nunn May had plainly never noticed that he had muscles. When Joyce was in the dock the court was full of his simple and forthright and ungifted followers, open in their grief. When Dr. Nunn May stood in the same dock his complicated and secretive and able associates were discreetly absent, because only the party was of importance. It had been the singularity of Joyce's case that it depended entirely on evidence regarding matters of fact and law, which he could have neither confirmed nor disproved, since he was unaware of them until the time of his trial. His destiny had depended on outward events. But there was no evidence at all against Dr. Alan Nunn May, except his own statement, which set down facts convicting him of guilt which were known only to himself. This was in harmony with Soviet policy as it was at that time.

In 1948, in a Philadelphia bar during the Progressive Party convention which adopted Henry Wallace as a presidential candidate, a Russian forgot and talked. He said: "In England, now that the war is over and espionage trials take place in open court, persons detected in espionage on behalf of the Soviet Union are instructed by whichever of our organizations it is which has been using them, to plead guilty and to admit to the police their participation in the particular crime of which they are accused, and nothing more. In the United States such persons are at present instructed to proceed in precisely the opposite way and to deny everything. This is a compliment to England. It is felt that British procedure is so efficient that if a false plea of not guilty is entered, it will be detected by the lawyers, the judge, the jury, and the press, and other matters may be stirred up which will extend the scope of the inquiry into the doings of the Communists. It is probable too that the case will be settled so quickly and will take such a clear form that the public will see what is going on, and it is therefore best to limit the matters disclosed. In the United States, where legal proceedings are likely to be prolonged and confused, and all sorts of considerations may prevent the truth from appearing, it is worth while putting up a plea of not guilty, no matter how absurd this may be in view of the real facts. This policy would, however, be altered and would fall into line with the policy advised for English suspects if courts in the United States became more vigilant, as altered circumstances may make them at any time."

It is true that both Alan Nunn May and the Soviet spy who was next to be tried did indeed plead guilty, and that in all such cases tried in America the accused persons have denied their guilt often on such a wholesale scale that they have got themselves into unnecessary trouble by denying minor points which the prosecution was able to establish with ease, thus throwing doubt on their credibility. But there is nothing to suggest that Dr. Alan Nunn May had received such instructions, when he told the story of his misdoings, which were indeed deplorable on his own showing. He had voluntarily entered the service of the British government during the war, as the senior member of the nuclear-physics division in the unit devoted to research on the atomic bomb, and had gone to Canada to work under Sir John Cockcroft in the atomic-energy project, as a group leader in the Montreal laboratory of the National Research Council. During the course of these proceedings he signed a statement acknowledging his liabilities under the Official Secrets Act. He then used his position to collect information and hand it over to a Russian agent who forwarded it to Moscow. Later he and his friends claimed that he took this step because he had come to the conclusion that his researches were contributing to create a situation dangerous to mankind unless steps were taken to ensure that the development of atomic energy was not confined to America.

This is the line his defenders have followed, but it is not an honest account of the situation, for it is marked by an important omission. It omits the important factor that other members of the Communist Party had long recognized him as one of themselves, working underground. During the war the English Communist Party carried on a singularly disingenuous campaign for deep bomb-proof shelters, which contributed no single valid idea to the sum of our knowledge of defence, and neither achieved nor proposed any untried method which if it had been adopted would have saved a single life, but which fulfilled its real intention of spreading distrust of the shelters provided by the authorities and suggesting that the Communists alone were taking thought for the safety of the public. Douglas Hyde, who was then news editor of the *Daily Worker,* describes this campaign as "led by our scientist-members, among whom was Dr. Nunn May." It must be remembered that a member of the Communist Party is obliged to act on all instructions originating from the authority in charge of the section to which he belongs and would have had to hand over to any person named in those instructions any material directed, no matter what relevance his action had to the dissemination of scientific knowledge.

Dr. Nunn May was therefore, though not guilty of treason, in other ways on exactly the same legal and moral footing as William Joyce or any of the British traitors who had been inspired by adherence to the Nazi creed. Nor would his convictions regarding atomic energy explain why, as he himself confessed, he gave information about quite other matters. As well as handing over notes regarding atomic energy, of what scope and nature is unknown, and two samples of uranium, he also gave information regarding electronic shells, and these were not the innocuous electronic shells known to physicists, but armaments. This last information was conveyed to Moscow in a telegram from Colonel Zabotin, the military attaché in Ottawa, which read thus:

On our task Alek [the code name for Dr. Alan Nunn May] has reported brief data concerning electronic shells. In particular these are being used by the American Navy against Japanese suicide-fliers. There is in the shell a small radio-transmitter with one electronic tube, and it is fed by dry batteries. The body of the shell is the antenna. The bomb explodes in the proximity of an aeroplane, from the action of the reflected waves from the aeroplane on the transmitter. The basic difficulties were the preparation of a tube and batteries which could withstand the discharge of the shell and the determination of a rotation speed of the shell which would not require special adaptation in the preparation of the shell. The Americans have achieved this result, but apparently have not handed this over to the English. The Americans have used a plastic covering for the battery which withstands the force of pressure during the motion of the shell.

It would be interesting to know if Dr. Alan Nunn May's passion for the universal dissemination of scientific knowledge led him to take steps to break down the barrier which he described as existing between the Americans and the English in this matter.

Furthermore, Dr. Alan Nunn May rendered the Soviet authorities yet another service which is extremely difficult to interpret as springing from a desire for the dissemination of scientific knowledge. There came to Canada in 1945 an Englishman in his middle twenties, one Norman Veal, a flower nurtured in the parterre of the Hendon branch of the Young Communists' League. He had worked in the meteorological service of the Air Ministry in England from 1939 till the end of 1941, when he was transferred to the atomic-energy project in England; he worked there until January 1943, when he was sent to the atomic-energy project in Canada as an instrument-designer. After two years he approached the Soviet authorities, anxious to help. Interviewed later by the Canadian Royal Commission, he explained that his political views changed from day to day, but if he had met a Russian agent, and the agent had asked him to turn over to him information which he (Mr. Veal) had gained while working in the National Research Council and which was secret—well, it would naturally depend on the circumstances and the situation at the time, and he would certainly not have done it in the last year or so, because he thought he could put an end to secrecy in scientific work by supporting the United Nations and its work for international scientific cooperation, but yes, "prior to that period," if he had felt anything he could do would help to shorten the war, he might possibly have done it, and in spite of signing the declaration regarding the Official Secrets Act, "I think I can honestly say I might have given information, assuming that I had any information that was worth having." What is terrifying about this testimony is that there is no indication that young Mr. Veal could have told the difference between a Soviet agent and a Nazi agent. A child could have played with him.

The canny Russians were not blind to his artlessness. They consulted Dr. Alan Nunn May, who gave them what information he had about him, stating that "Veal occupies a fairly low position and knows very little," and pronouncing him "inclined to be careless," as he had begun a conversation with Dr. Nunn May on conspiratorial matters in the presence of a third person. This really cannot be disguised as activity designed to enfranchise science from lowly bonds.

In any case it is difficult to understand why these scruples about illegitimacy of engaging in researches which were not to be published did not occur to Dr. Nunn May when the post was first offered to him, as he was then made fully aware of the nature and conditions of the work he was to do; nor why, when these scruples did arise in his mind, he did not take the obvious step of resigning from his post, which would have caused serious inconvenience to the authorities, and explaining his reason to his fellow scientists and to the general public. The one thing he could not do from any point of view was what he did: to disclose the result of his researches in spite of the understanding between him and the government that he was to be bound by the requirements of the Official Secrets Act. No society, whether capitalist, socialist, or communist, can survive for ten minutes if it abandons the principle that a contract is sacred.

It has subsequently been pretended that Dr. Alan Nunn May forgot this elementary social principle in his desire to give help to the USSR so that it might the better defend itself against Germany and Japan. But he made no such claim in his own statement, though such a claim was made to defend him on his release from prison; and indeed it is patently absurd. He handed over the samples of uranium and his information about the theory of atomic energy in the early days of August 1945, three months after VE-day, and some days after the atomic bomb had been used at Hiroshima, when the defeat of Japan was quite certain. The telegram sent by Colonel Zabotin to Moscow regarding the information received from Dr. Nunn May later fell into Canadian hands. It contains a specific reference to the Hiroshima explosion. Dr. Nunn May cannot have thought the USSR would use the information he had given it except against the United States and Great Britain.

To the very end, to the moment when the sentences were delivered, the contrast between the two trials was maintained in its acuteness. The guilt of William Joyce was over and done with; the guilt of Dr. Nunn May was a continuing force. By the time Joyce came to trial it was impossible that what he had done could harm anyone. He had tried to do evil and had failed. But the samples of uranium and the notes Dr. Nunn May gave the Russian agent threw such light on the research into atomic energy that they were immediately flown to Russia on a flight undertaken solely for the purpose; and if ever Russia drops an atom bomb on Great Britain or America, the blame for the death and blindness and the sores it scatters must surely rest in part on this gifted and frivolous man. But whereas nobody in court at Joyce's trial, except his kin and friends, was greatly moved when the sentence of death was passed on him, the spectators were plainly appalled when the judge passed sentence of ten years' imprisonment on Dr. Nunn May, though none of them was his follower. The Attorney-General, Sir Hartley Shawcross, showed that he was heavy-hearted under the necessity of making the prosecuting speech, and he waited for the sentence with an apprehension rarely shown even by a defending counsel.

It was the light about Dr. Nunn May's head which made the thought of his imprisonment intolerable; the sense of a network of perceptions and associations and interpretations which made the Nazi-Fascists seem like hogs rooting among the simple unimproved beechmast of the world. William Joyce had great courage; but though it is a terrible thing not to have courage, to be courageous carries a man out of that terror but not a step farther, unless he has other qualities to transport him. Millions of men have been brave, but have been nothing more, and the brute creation also is brave. Dr. Alan Nunn May was precious to us as Joyce was not, because he was something which man must be and is not yet, save here and there, and with great difficulty.

They were actually on a perfect parity in the dock. They had even been on the same side in 1939 and 1940 when the Stalin-Hitler pact was signed and put an end to the pretence that there is any real difference between fascism and communism. But the kind of mind possessed by Dr. Nunn May had seemed to hold out a promise which, it could now be seen, was not to be fulfilled.

3

THE conviction of Dr. Alan Nunn May was followed by an active campaign for the remission of his sentence. In so far as this was conducted by those bound to him by ties of blood and friendship it was, of course, above criticism. But other and less commendable elements were involved in it. A number of scientists gave their support to the demand for his release on the ground that his offence was negligible. Of these scientists, some would hardly have cared to argue the case. It would be very natural for a man to feel great horror at the thought that a gifted comrade, with whom he had probably had pleasant social relations, was being sent to prison for ten years. It would also be unpleasant for a scientist not to join in such a demand in a laboratory where the feeling was running strongly in favour of Dr. Nunn May, and abstinence would be taken as a sign of inhumanity or reactionary views. Moreover, some scientists were so genuinely distressed by the imposition of secrecy on scientific workers by the government, which had been weighing on them more and more heavily since the beginning of the war, that they envisaged Dr. Nunn May's treachery simply as a protest against that secrecy.

There is much to be said for the principle here involved. It is ridiculous to think of small groups of persons with rare gifts working on related facts of high importance to our species, at points dotted over the globe, and failing to pool their discoveries. But the universe is constantly forcing us to do ridiculous things for the sake of our survival. It is ridiculous for a man to crawl along the ground on his stomach when he has two legs and can walk, but if an enemy is looking for him he will be very foolish if he does not. It is very hard, however, to believe that these scientists held the principle that research must never be secret to be absolute, as they pretended. They did not demand that the scientists of England, including the German Jewish refugees, should smuggle the results of their labours over to Nazi scientists during the war. Nor have they burst into cheers on any of the later occasions when it became quite certain that the Nazi scientists who had escaped from Germany at the end of the war had imparted many of their secrets, particularly regarding the construction of jet planes, to the Perón government of Argentina, though that broke down one national barrier at least, which is no more than Dr. Nunn May could have claimed to do. There was something genuine in this scientific attitude, but a great ideal more that is humbug.

The irrationality of this campaign has since been proved at very great expense indeed. Although the scientists involved asserted that Dr. Nunn May had been right in giving away the secrets of atomic energy to the Soviet Union on the ground that all scientific discoveries should be shared, at the same time they asserted that the surrender of these secrets was of no consequence, since science was universal, and therefore the Soviet scientists were bound to discover all that we knew about atomic energy through their own researches, and the only thing to be said against Dr. Nunn May was that he had taken unnecessary trouble. Again, there is something in this claim, but much more humbug. Obviously, since the subject matter of science is the human environment, it often happens that a number of scientists are attracted by the same problems and arrive at the same conclusions. But not always at the same time. Darwin and Wallace made neck-and-neck recognition of the pattern of evolution, but often there is a time-lag. The genetic discoveries of the Austrian monk Mendel were confirmed by the researches of three men who knew nothing of one another or of him: De Vries, Correns, and Tschermak. But he wrote his great paper in 1865; they provided their triple confirmation in 1900. It would be unlikely that a time-lag would be so great today; but it could be great enough to inconvenience a competing power, as we have learned since with blushes. The Soviet Union was able to send up its first disconcerting *sputnik* and all its dazzling successors, never losing its cutting edge of priority, because work had been done on fuels in its laboratories which had no parallel in ours. It is quite possible that, had Dr. Nunn May and his allies not been disloyal, the West might have enjoyed an effective monopoly of atomic weapons which would have given the world a far longer breathing-space than it was able to enjoy.

The real motivation of this campaign was twofold. A large number of those who took part in it were animated by a feeling for which psychiatrists have a name, that they formed an elect class which should be allowed to do as it liked. Their real argument for the release of Dr. Nunn May was quite simply that he was a scientist, and that therefore it was ridiculous to consider that he should have been bound by the undertaking he had signed regarding the Official Secrets Act, and that if he thought it right to give away the result of his researches to a foreign power it was disgraceful that a society which consisted in the main of nonscientific inferiors should call him to account.

This is an attitude which had already been detectable in various writings by scientists on the subject of atom-bomb policy, in which it is assumed that this should be left entirely in scientific hands. The claim that because scientists had invented the atomic bomb they should be given the right to decide what should be done with it, and the claim that because Dr. Nunn May was a scientist he should be allowed to break the law without paying the penalty, rest on the assumption already discussed that because a man has scientific gifts he is likely to be superior to his fellows in all intellectual respects, including that kind of general farseeing ability, tender towards the future of the individual and the race, which we call wisdom. This assumption is based on no evidence whatsoever. All our experience suggests that, though special gifts rarely appear in individuals below a certain level of general ability, that level is not very high, and gifted individuals may appear anywhere in the scale above it; and quite obviously the possession of special gifts, such as scientific or musical aptitude, which demand technical training beginning at an early age and a long and exhausting working day, will prevent the possessor from developing his general ability. The very fact that a man took a leading part in perfecting the atom bomb might unfit him for forming an opinion as to what should be done with it; and

Dr. Nunn May must surely have been too busy in his laboratory to have worked out a social cement which could replace the idea of contract.

The second strand in this campaign was, of course, Communist. Few of the scientists concerned with it in its more dignified manifestations were Communists, and few of the well-known Communist scientists took a prominent part in organizing it in any way that would take the eye. But there was often a sense of Communist influence guiding a hand which without doubt thought itself writing of its own and innocent free will. An appeal to the Home Secretary urging him to reduce the sentence passed on Dr. Nunn May may seem strange at first reading, as it contains statements about the convicted man's offences which could not possibly soften the Home Secretary's heart, as the files showed him that these statements were wholly untrue. But it becomes an intelligible document if, and only if, it be recognized that the person who wrote this appeal had been naïve enough to accept direct or indirect suggestions from some other persons who did not care a button about Dr. Nunn May but who were extremely anxious to whitewash a criminal known to the public as Communist, and thus deceive it regarding the essential nature of the Communist Party. The same spectacle of enthusiasm for a friend and for science exploited as political propaganda was manifest in the demand of various branches of a certain association that Dr. Nunn May should be released on grounds as wide of the mark as the claim that "the information divulged was of a purely scientific character, unconnected with the manufacture of the atom bomb, or other form of weapon."

Communism made its contribution to this movement. There was also a certain amount of open and undiluted Communist propaganda which maintained quite starkly that Dr. Nunn May should be regarded as innocent because his treachery had benefited the USSR, which, as one propagandist stated, "had torn out the guts of the German Army practically singlehanded." Such persons could not envisage the act of handing over to Russia a defence secret possessed by Great Britain as a crime at all, because Great Britain had no right to defend itself against Russia. Among this sort of fanatic the idea that Dr. Nunn May had handed over the information about the atom bomb before and not after the defeat of the Nazis was widespread; and it is not possible that all those who spread it so widely could have been ignorant that this was a lie. But what was interesting about all grades of these campaigners was their ingenuous readiness to show that, if they were for the dissemination of truth in science, they were all against it in the press. Fierce efforts were made to prevent the publication of the true facts of the Nunn May case, whether in a newspaper or in a book.

The public, indeed, had the greatest difficulty in learning those facts; and it was as effectively prevented from learning some other facts which made the case much more disturbing by showing that Dr. Nunn May was not an individual working in isolation but a cog in a complicated machine. For in 1946 the world was still in a state of disorder, travel was impossible except for those who pleaded a special mission, and the transmission of news was almost as gravely impeded by lack of newsprint, the eating up of space by items dealing with the peace, and the concentration of correspondents in the devastated Continental areas. Hence it happened that for a long time there did not reach British newspapers any easily assimilable reports concerning the Canadian spy ring of which Dr. Nunn May was a member. One night in September 1945 a Russian cipher clerk named Igor Gouzenko, employed in the Soviet embassy at Ottawa, on the staff of the military attaché, snatched an armful of documents from his files which would bear witness to the existence in Canada of a treasonable conspiracy organized from the Soviet embassy and working through a group of Canadian and British citizens, and went out into the city with the intention of handing over these documents to some responsible person connected with the Canadian government and of seeking asylum for himself and his wife and his child. By this action he put himself into the position of the German refugees who aided the Allies against the Axis, and laid himself open to the charge of treachery. He had the same answer to that charge as they had. Allegiance is given only in exchange for protection, and he felt that Stalin gave his people as little protection as the German refugees felt that Hitler gave his. It is true that British and American Communists would claim that their governments also did not give their peoples protection. That is, indeed, the essence of the contention between the Communist Party and the states of the world.

It might well have happened that Mr. Gouzenko's actions had

no consequence, except for him and his wife and child. For although he spent part of that night and the whole of the next day visiting newspaper offices and ministries and police stations, he found nobody who appeared to take the slightest interest in him or his documents. Actually the police were sufficiently interested in his story to shadow him, but not as closely as he could have wished. In the evening he returned home to his flat entirely discouraged and in great fear; and he approached his neighbours and asked them to take charge of his child in case he and his wife were murdered. The neighbours responded sensibly and kindly and took in the whole family, but might have thought him a lunatic or a liar, had not the Russians, with that peculiar gift for blundering which is a far greater protection for the West than any Western merit of character or intelligence, sent along the second secretary of the USSR embassy, a member of the staff of the military attaché, the military attaché of the Russian Air Force, and a cipher clerk. These four gentleman proceeded to enter the Gouzenkos' flat by breaking in the front door, and when the police were called in to stop this crass burglary and asked the burglars to produce their identification cards, they produced their own quite genuine ones. No more convincing proof of Mr. Gouzenko's story could have been provided; and indeed it is hard to imagine what other proof could have been provided.

The material filched from the Soviet embassy by Mr. Gouzenko was finally investigated by a royal commission appointed for that purpose by the Canadian government; and its report is the most complete picture of Communist treachery that we possess. It is hardly necessary to say that it cast no discredit on the Soviet Union whatsoever. Not till the Earthly Paradise is established and man regains his innocence can a power which has ever been at war be blamed if it accepts information regarding the military strength of another power, however this may be obtained; and of course it can be blamed least of all if the information comes to it from traitors, for then it is likely to touch on the truly secret. There is no need to blame any but the Britons and Canadians who formed this spy ring, but they must be blamed, for they felt no qualms whatsoever, but great pride and pleasure, in handing over to the representatives of the Soviet Union any information it required of them, no matter how brutally this treachery might conflict with their duty to their employers, public or private, nor what dangers it might bring down on their fellow countrymen.

This group cannot have been actuated by the desire to enfranchise science, for it included others than scientists and dealt with matters which could not possibly be regarded as scientific. Nor can it have been inspired by hatred of fascism, for the nucleus of the group was in being before the war, and during the Stalin-Hitler pact the Canadian Communist Party showed peculiar gusto in cooperating with the Russians. Miss Kathleen Mary Willsher, for example, was a graduate of the London School of Economics who was the trusted assistant registrar in the Ottawa office of the High Commissioner for the United Kingdom. From 1935, with no discernible breach on account of the Hitler-Stalin pact, she handed over to a Communist agent information which she obtained during the course of her day's work in the High Commissioner's office, such as a complete account of the size and functions and organization of his staff, and a report of Lord Keynes's confidential conversations in Ottawa in 1944 on the subject of postwar credits. It can hardly be maintained that information on either of these subjects can have helped the Soviet Union to fight Hitler.

But it is true that the bulk of the members of the group, so far as the Gouzenko papers enable us to identify them, were scientists and that their proceedings were alarming. Prominent among them was Dr. Nunn May; and nobody who has read the Canadian commission's report can visualize him as an individual engaged in a solitary battle with his conscience over the question of secrecy in science, so plainly do the extracts from Gouzenko's files and their confirmation in his own statement show him as a Communist snugly working among his Communist fellows under party discipline. But even more conspicuous and alarming was Dr. Raymond Boyer, a French-Canadian of forty, a handsome, popular, spoiled, sulky millionaire, the foremost chemist in Canada, one of the foremost chemists in the world. He had for some time been a subscriber to the funds of the Communist Party, and he gave before the Royal Commission just the type of evidence which the Russian at Philadelphia indicated that Communist headquarters advise persons to give who are standing trial for Communist activities before a vigilant and competently conducted tribunal. It appeared in the files brought in by Gouzenko that he had given the Soviet agents the formula of a new method of producing an explosive known as RDX. He made a full confession of just that: of how he had handed over to a Soviet agent the formula of a new method of producing an explosive known as RDX. Alike in his laboratory and as a witness he showed exceptional ability. He told nearly nothing.

This restraint was in marked contrast with the loquacity which had evidently characterized Dr. Boyer and his friends at all other times. These scientists talked and talked and talked. Dr. Boyer had talked about RDX. Dr. Nunn May had talked about his own work on atomic energy and about the great experimental plant at Chalk River, Ontario. Their friends talked about radar; they talked about the anti-submarine device known as Asdic; they talked about all the explosive propellants that were being developed and improved; they talked about the VT fuse, which knocked the Japanese Air Force out of the air; they talked about the locations of research stations and production plants; they talked about everything they knew, with a freedom which amounted to what psychologists name "total recall." It might even be termed gabbiness. Now this strange disease did not affect all scientists working in Canada. The afflicted group formed only a small proportion of the whole. But it was large enough to have a great quantity of valuable information to give away, and though the mass of its members and supporters were drawn mainly from the lower grade of scientific workers, it contained some men of outstanding ability, even allowing for the extent to which Communists in every walk of life, and particularly in science, deliberately inflate the reputations of their fellow members. But what was really remarkable was that this epidemic of gabbiness was spreading amongst scientists all over the world.

It is perhaps not fair to call it an epidemic. The mass of scientists proved immune to the germ. They adhered to the normal pattern of behaviour and, in some cases at the bidding of their consciences and in others from fear of the police, did not consider themselves free to communicate to a foreign power, or to a political party which was an agent of a foreign power, information acquired in the course of their employment and which they had undertaken not to divulge. But it is equally true that all over the globe there sprang up these groups of scientists which, in the middle of the war, claimed the right to publish as they thought fit all information arising out of their labours, without either consulting their own governments or informing them afterwards. In Great Britain this group had little opportunity to manifest itself during the war, but it was organized to become richly vocal as soon as peace was achieved. In America it was peculiarly happy and carefree. During the war Communist influences romped round the wartime atomic project at the radiation laboratory of the University of California at Berkeley, and a group of young scientists kindly and innocently formed what was practically a dining club to offer hospitality to Soviet agents. Never before has treachery been so sunny and lighthearted, presenting itself not as Judas, conscious of the last suspension from the elder tree, but as some innocent little figure in straw hat and sailor suit.

Typical of this new dispensation is a figure who was cleared of guilt, a Californian scientist who dined at a restaurant in San Francisco with a Russian official on the eve of his departure for home, and talked so loudly about his work that he was clearly overheard by two officers of the Federal Bureau of Investigation who were dining at an adjacent table; and who, when he had to appear before the Committee on Un-American Activities some years later to explain this incident, made little jokes about his violin-playing. His conversation was not deemed criminal; but the gaiety with which he faced suspicion of treachery gives some indication of the curious mental climate in which he and his associates had their being, a climate most dangerous to the general weather of the world. The consideration which chilled us when we contemplated Mr. Norman Veal chills us again. Few of these people were experienced in the ways of the world, and a number revealed themselves in evidence as even simple-minded when they left their own field. Those among them who were really Communists would, of course, have gladly handed over their country's secrets to the Nazis during the Stalin-Hitler pact. But both they and the fellow travellers would have chattered away to anybody who told them he was a Soviet agent; not one of these chatterers could have told Hans from Ivan. Indeed, it is to be wondered why this garrulity was not exploited by acquisitive persons whose only ideology was self-help; for some of the information handed over by the Canadian spy ring could have inspired them to successful financial speculation. Indeed, we cannot be quite sure that this did not happen.

It is one of the oddest manifestations of our governmental failure to cope with the giant inconvenience of communism that, for a full year after the publication of the Canadian Blue Book on the spy ring, it was impossible to obtain it in England. It should have been reissued by our Stationery Office, and government spokesmen should have directed public attention towards it, for it made it quite apparent that we had to deal with a closed corporation of the most inconvenient kind any community had ever had to fear. At a time when munitions had become more deadly than ever before, the designers of the deadliest among these were peculiarly subject to emotional disturbance which would lead them to handing over their designs to our only potential enemy, Communist Russia. The situation had arisen because they were members of a negativist generation in England, finding a new and picturesque way of falling out with their neighbours; but there was another and a special cause due to their occupation. They were not mere dilettanti of revolution, who made trouble on the scientific field if they happened to be scientists. They were making this extreme form of trouble because they were scientists.

The reasons apart from social background which make this class of intellectual find a special attraction in communism must be conceded to be strong. There would seem to be an obvious cause in the underpayment of those scientists, not employed in well-endowed universities or by prosperous industrial corporations, who are sometimes paid below their deserts. In England it is possible for a first-class scientist who has slipped into an unpopular and industrially unserviceable branch of science to find himself earning a salary of £2000 or £1500 a year. A number of men with gifts above the average may earn, not merely at the beginning of their working lives, but in their middle and closing years, salaries ranging between £1000 and £2000 a year. In America the popular imagination conceives of the scientist as sure of remuneration enabling him to maintain a high standard of comfort. But this is not an invariable rule, and even though the American scientist probably has ideal conditions for his work he may have a justified financial grievance. The situation is more embittering because learning is in some American communities denied the prestige still accorded it in England. There is much room for discontent here. One of the less fortunate American scientists, working in a university in an industrial town, will not be able to afford to buy a new car, though an old car is the recognized symbol of outer and inner failure; his wife will not be able to hire domestic help or a baby-sitter because she will be outbid by the wives of the executives and operatives in the neighbouring factories; he will be conscious that he has not much command of respect in a society whose reverence goes to Ford and Kaiser. It would be strange if these circumstances did not stimulate a certain hunger for political power.

There must be here necessarily a sense that the existing political institutions are not working well. For the economic lot of scientists would be satisfactory if industry paid them a high wage, which the university and the government had to take as the norm; and the scientist believes that industry is in such need of his service that its reluctance to pay him high wages is proof of its own inefficiency, and of the general wastefulness of the capitalist system. But in fact the situation precludes any simple arrangement by which scientists can be drafted from their universities to fruitful employment in industry. There are all sorts of unexpected and unexplained features in technological development which make such planning difficult. Some prosperous industries need to be maintained by continuous research, but others have the slenderest need for it; for example, zip fasteners are manufactured in vast quantities and are essential to the production of women's cheap ready-made dresses, and are the result of a few patents taken out by only two inventors. Some large corporations have found their handsome and costly laboratories attracted and stimulated research workers to give them just what they wanted, but others again have found their research investments a dead loss and have been more fortunate in developing inventions made within much smaller organizations, where the research workers, until the kill was made, were not very highly remunerated; or even by single and independent research workers. Other industries have found that their most useful material has been derived from work done in academic institutions with no cooperative needs in mind. The economic landscape abounds in such irregular contours, and there is no level site on which there could be speedily run up an organization by which scientists could supply industry's need for scientific help as the Ministry of Health and the Board of Trade perform their functions, with the same guarantee of security for the functionaries. But the legend is strong that it is only the ineptitude of our present system which prevents such an organization from being built.

This is the more unfortunate because there is already a strong reason predisposing scientists to think that they could be better moulders of the state than professional politicians. A scientist knows that he can understand a great many things which are mysterious to the nonscientific man. A great scientist knows that he can understand a great many things which are mysterious to lesser scientists. He would have to possess the gift of humility in very full measure, were it not to occur to him that maybe he could solve quite easily the economic and social problems which have so long perplexed nonscientific men. He is the more prone to form this opinion because the long years of his training and the long hours of his working day restrict the scope of his experience, and prevent him from realizing the disorderly quality of economic and social problems. He is apt, too, to live in the company of his fellow scientists, without meeting men of affairs and thus learning appreciation of their special talents and virtues. It must be very tempting for any scientist to think that he can solve any major political conundrum, say the housing problem, by applying to it the same methods he uses in his laboratory: by assembling the necessary apparatus, handling his material with dexterous and economical movements, observing accurately all the changes set up in that material, and subjecting his observations to a process of logical analysis.

But, in fact, houses come into being on quite another plane of creation. Any house not built by a tyrant with unlimited power to draw at will on materials and slave labour must represent a struggle between conflicting interests, only to be resolved by frequent compromises of a sort never called for in the course of a scientific experiment. There is an initial conflict between the person who is going to live in the house and the person who is going to pay for it, which exists even though these are the same person, sometimes to the extent of making it impossible for him to live in it when it is finished, because he has spent so much on it that he has nothing left for upkeep. This conflict becomes more bitter in the hard times when housing becomes a major political problem (which are the only times when scientists would wish to emerge from their laboratories and solve it), because the landlord, who is often a hybrid composed of the state and a local government body, is therefore at war with himself as well as with his tenant, who also often is at war with himself, because he is also a hybrid composed of a subsidized pet who is paying less than the economic rent of his house, and a taxpayer and ratepayer who is paying the subsidy and keeping himself as a pet.

Moreover, as building is rationalized and more and more of the component parts of every house are made by specialist firms, and more and more people than the actual labourers who work on the site are involved in its construction, each of them acts as a brake on its rise from the sod. For though these people's demand for higher profits and wages may be controlled, their not less natural demand for more leisure and less tension cannot be so controlled, and their refusal to work long hours or overstrain themselves slows down the speed of building and adds to its cost by amounts which may not be less than those involved by a spectacular rise in wages and interest, and must always be less convenient for actuarial handling, since they are indirect and highly variable and often unpredictable. The authorities who are building the house must attempt to counter this tendency by encouraging the firms least affected by it, but without forgetting their concern with efficiency or the accepted principles of industrial welfare. Bricks and mortar cannot meet and marry until there have been countless wrangles of this complicated sort; and it may well happen that an administrator responsible for a housing project may be uttering a worthy *apologia pro vita sua* when he says to himself, "Well, I am building these houses very badly indeed. If you judge them with the conception of a house as 'a machine to live in' at the back of your mind, they are all wrong from the foundations to the chimney cowls. But I am building them, they are going up, soon people will be able to shelter in them, and thank God for that." This is not a justification permitted to either the artist or the scientist, who must build his work of art or his research right from start to finish, and let the

people seek their shelter where they can find it. The martyrdom
of the man of action is that he must take pride in botched work;
the martyrdom of the man of science and the artist is that they
must never take pride in their work at all, since, being the work
of human beings, it is imperfect.

This does not show the scientist at a disadvantage. The man
of action is his peer when it comes to making mistakes.
C. F. Kettering, renowned for his part in developing the operational efficiency of the automobile by his contributions to the
discovery of ethylized fluids, tells the story of the great industrialist who inquired from his director of research how long a certain
piece of research would take to complete. When the director told
him that it would take his team of six men two years to get it
done, the industrialist bade him take on six more men and finish
the job in a year. Every variety of human being, as well as every
individual, has its peculiar faults; it is unfortunate that the
Russians know about the faults of the scientist well. It happens
that throughout the nineteenth century and the early years of
the twentieth century the Russian mind was strongly attracted to
science. This was due in part to the experimental nature of the
Slav; it is significant that the practice of artificial insemination
was invented by the illiterate horsemen on the steppes and was
developed to a very high pitch of efficiency by the not too literate masters of the stables of the Tsars and their employers. It is
also significant that Peter the Great believed in nothing but
what the Americans call "know-how," that Catherine the Great
was injected by the French philosophers with faith in all kinds
of learning, including the physical sciences, and during the nineteenth century the German people, having begun to manifest
their terrible genius for producing a vast excess of the very best
specimens of the white-collar class, exported a number of them,
including many scientists, to Russia.

Consequently an understanding of the scientific character is
one of the Russian traits which were profound enough to survive
the Revolution and pass unaltered into the USSR. Hence the
bolsheviks have steadily pursued a policy based on their aware-
ness of the occupational risk to which the scientist is subject: this
temptation to believe that he is called to wear a double crown
and surpass Caesar as well as Archimedes. The USSR has therefore posed to the scientists of the world as the one country which

gives their tribe real power. In point of fact, as Nazi Germany showed, a totalitarian state must keep art and science in strict subjection, since it claims that its creed represents the finality of wisdom, and it cannot permit artists and scientists to set forth on researches from which they may bring back disconcerting revelations of reality quite inconsistent with that creed. It is significant that the word "objectivity," which to all free artists and scientists means a necessary precondition of their work, meant in Nazi Germany and means in the Soviet Union a vice implying disloyalty to the state. But foreign scientists are invited on flattering and delightful visits to the state which give them experience bound to be uniquely intoxicating.

When a certain prominent English scientist visited Moscow during Stalin's lifetime, the great man always received him. It is impossible to imagine his being granted a similar favour by the King of England or by the President of the United States or France, or that they, geared to their administrative duties as they are, would have anything interesting to say to him, geared as he is to his highly specialized scientific duties. It is even more unlikely that Stalin, geared to a highly specialized type of administrative duty and wholly alien from the West, should have found any basis for an intellectually profitable exchange. But though the adult self of the scientist would learn nothing from the interview, his childish self, which wishes to live more than his life, would rejoice at being raised by a ruler to be his companion.

At home too there is the same elevation into another sphere, the same promise that ordinary human limitations are to be transcended and the Communist scientist shall discharge two functions and live two lives. During the past quarter of a century, both in England and in France, there have been conspicuous examples of Communist scientists who, though far from brilliant or even sensible outside their own fields, have been carefully built up into popular political oracles. It is hard to think of any agency which would so transform the destinies of their non-Communist colleagues. It cannot be charged too heavily against the scientists that they are self-seeking in accepting these benefits from Russian sources or that they show themselves blind to the suffering of the millions who are incompetently governed by the bolsheviks. For it must be remembered that they believe that political problems should be solved by the same methods as scientific problems, and that if it is impossible to build a new house without a struggle between conflicting interests unless the builder is a tyrant with unlimited power to draw at will on material and slave labour, they will consider the Soviet Union sensible in becoming such a tyrant and will feel there is no degradation in receiving presents at its hands.

It has to be remembered that at this time history has done a great deal to inflate the scientist's suspicion that not merely does he know other things than are known to the nonscientist; his knowledge is greater and more valuable. Fundamentally it was courage which had won the war, but only because it had had science for its servant, and that servant had in the end realized its own private dream by achieving atomic energy. Men were becoming like gods, and some more like gods than others. Thus it happened that shortly after Hiroshima a scientist, not a Communist but very much of the Webb-determined world, was talking with horror of the efforts that the soldiers of America and Britain were making to get the control of atomic energy into their hands. It should, he maintained, be left with the scientists, to whom the world owed the knowledge of atomic energy. One of his hearers (thinking, as it happened, of an American scientist who was not Communist but Fascist in his sympathies) asked what guarantee there was that, if scientists controlled atomic energy, extremists among them might not hand over their secrets to the most aggressive of soldiers. He, the least arrogant of men, replied by a simple claim that he and all his kind were born without sin. "How can you suppose that any scientist would do such a thing?" he asked, his spectacles shining with anger. "Science is reason. Why should people who live by reason suddenly become its enemy?" He put into words an implication which often can be recognized when Communist scientists write on other than technical matters. The comradeship of scientists with the Soviet Union, even if it amounts to a transference of national loyalty, cannot be wrong and cannot lead to any harm, because scientists cannot be wrong and cannot do harm, because they are scientists, and science is right.

We are re-entering by a new door into the old world of fanaticism. The Webb-minded world which had produced this generation was predominantly materialist, but no persons and no people can get rid of religion by becoming atheist. The troubling ideas in the depth of man's mind, which religions try to formulate and clarify, do not cease to trouble when these attempts are abandoned. All that happens is that men continue to debate these ideas in terms borrowed from the dominant art or science of their time, and swear that it is of this art or science that they speak. Today politics and economics preoccupy us, and we carry on that discussion in political and economic terms. Joyce and his type of Fascist conducted their part of it in vague and general terms, seeking to find in political activity the kind of recognition of their individualities which in any other age would have led them to an altar. But among the intellectuals, who find verbal formulas irresistible, not only the problems set by the pious persist; the solutions they found, the texts which came to their lips, are with them still, changed but recognizable.

Not one stone may be left upon another. . . . What was that nonsense about? What we are so sensibly saying now is that the capitalist system is evil and must be destroyed. The Day of Judgment approaches when it shall be declared who are the sheep and who are the goats, and we shall be raised to sit on His right hand. . . . What moonshine! Let us turn to sense and proclaim that there shall be a revolution and then the state will be governed by us. What the faithful must believe has been decided at the councils of the Church. Really superstition is a terrible thing. We ask our enlightened selves only what it was that Lenin said. If any man preach any other gospel unto you than that ye have received, let him be accursed. Bigotry is a vice, but do not take that leaflet! The woman who is giving it away is a Trotskyite.

Mysteriously, such sectarianism acts as fuel to the soul. Four years after the trial of Dr. Nunn May, in the beginning of 1950, there followed him into the dock a Communist scientist traitor beside whom he was a timid amateur. He had all the arrogance of the scientists, or rather of the scientists at that date; they were not so arrogant before and they are not so arrogant today, but then a Spanish hidalgo would have seemed modest beside them. He also derived a particular fervour and sense of divine mission from a transplanted heresy. The sternest orthodoxy would allow Quakerism its special grace and it is a shame that any shadow should fall on it. But it is only the truth that Dr. Klaus Emil Fuchs was born in a Quaker home, and that, materialist though he was, he was inspired to his breach of faith with England, which had sheltered him as a refugee, by his memory of the doctrine of the Inner Light.

4

IN 1874, in the little industrial town of Beerfelden in the Odenwald, that district of wooded hills which lies between Darmstadt and Heidelberg, there was born a child named Emil Fuchs. He grew into a man who exerted a great effect on his fellow men. Though short and full-faced, he had great physical charm, he could speak in private and in public with burning intensity, he was inflexible in his courage and singlemindedness, he never ceased to seek the truth, and in the opinion of some of the people who liked him best he was not very intelligent. He became a Lutheran pastor and held ministries in various places until 1918, when he settled down in the industrial centre of Eisenach. His functions must have altered, for he joined the Society of Friends in 1925, but he remained in Eisenach until 1931, when he became professor of religious science at an academy for the training of teachers in Kiel. He was politically very active and was the first pastor to join the Social Democratic Party. After 1921 he became very well known throughout Germany as a speaker for a group known as the Religious Socialists. He married young and had several sons and daughters, and there were few homes in which parents and children seemed to live on a smoother plane of happy equality.

As the Nazi threat grew stronger in the late twenties and the early thirties Dr. Fuchs considered what he should do and decided that it was his duty as a Christian to oppose Hitler. Throughout the whole of the Nazi regime, in peace and in war, he stood by this decision without making the smallest compromise, though he was cruelly persecuted. Meanwhile his youngest son, Klaus Emil Fuchs, who had been born in 1911, was helping to create the situation for which his father was preparing himself by prayer. He was a university student, first at Leipzig and then at Kiel, and at both places he was involved in the useless and silly and violent political activities by which German undergraduates did so much to destroy the civil order and social coherence of their country and bring down the Weimar Republic. At Heidelberg he joined the students' group of the Social Democratic Party, but quarrelled with them because they supported a policy of naval rearmament, and he had been brought up to be a pacifist. But shortly afterwards he quarrelled with his father's pacifism and joined the Reichsbanner, a semi-military organization composed of young members of the Social Democratic and the Democratic Parties (as it might be in England, the Labour and the Liberal Parties).

This was a union of parties which should have been effective as a bulwark against the Nazis, had not so many Germans behaved as young Klaus Fuchs was going to behave when he moved to Kiel.

There he transferred to the university branch of the Social Democratic Party, but quarrelled with the party when it decided to support old General Hindenburg as *Reichspräsident,* for fear that if it ran its own candidate this would split the anti-Nazi vote and Hitler would be elected. Fuchs then offered himself as a speaker to the Communist Party, and at the same time joined an organization, frowned upon by the Social Democratic Party, in which members of the Social Democratic and the Communist Party attempted to convert those members of the Nazi Party whom they believed to be sincere and open to appeals to their better feelings. Then, when Hindenburg was elected, Papen, who was a soft man ready to succumb to the Nazis, was made *Reichskanzler* and he dismissed the elected Prussian government and put in the *Reichsstatthalter* as a kept government. Klaus Fuchs's reaction to this news was to run along to the Communist Party headquarters and enrol as a member because the Social Democratic Party was doing nothing effective.

In fact, what had happened was that the Communists had been attacking the Social Democratic Party instead of the Nazis, telling all the young idiots like Klaus Fuchs that it was Codlin who was their friend and not Short; and there were so many of these idiots that the Social Democratic Party was too weak in prestige to do anything at all. This had been the intention of the Communists, who desired Hitler to come to power because they believed that he would soon fall and they would then come to power. Hence the doom of Germany, and all of us.

Klaus Fuchs then became busy and happy, in the suicidal way of Germans, in carrying on a silly and mischief-making campaign regarding the internal affairs of Kiel University. The Nazi students had started an agitation protesting against the high fees; and the organization composed of Social Democrats and Communists, of which Klaus Fuchs had now become chairman, decided to call their bluff and started negotiations with the Nazi students, proposing that they should form an alliance to carry on a campaign for lower fees and should organize a strike of the students. The Nazi students hedged, and after a few weeks Klaus Emil Fuchs issued a leaflet describing the negotiations and pointing out how little the Nazis had been in earnest. Then the Nazis, to get back their prestige, used some dispute between the faculty and the students as an excuse to call a strike against the rector of the university.

By this time Hitler had been made *Reichskanzler* and the Nazi students were able to enlist the support of the SA, who demonstrated in front of the university. Klaus Emil Fuchs was physically weedy, with a large head and a narrow, rickety body, but he had inherited his father's courage, and every day he walked up and down in front of the SA to challenge his Nazi fellow students to do their worst. On one occasion they threatened him with violence, but he escaped. Then, on his way to an illegal conference of anti-Nazi students held in Berlin, he read of the burning of the Reichstag in the newspaper and realized that the Communist Party would have to go underground, and he took the badge of the hammer and sickle from his coat lapel and prepared to work in secret.

For some time he hid. Then the Communist Party arranged for him to go abroad, as a refugee, telling him that he must continue his studies, because there would come a time, after there had been a revolution in Germany, when people with technical knowledge would be required to build up the new Communist Germany. The Communist Party had a finger in every pie during that period. It engaged in street fights with the Nazis. But that was for show. Its policy had not been to fight. It was not fighting Hitler, it was fighting the Social Democratic Party. But it gained a large measure of control over the organizations distributing the offerings of goodwill which were made by the liberals of the world to the victims of the Nazis. Klaus Emil Fuchs was first sent to France and then to England, where he was befriended by the Society for the Protection of Science and Learning, and sent to Bristol University, to get his doctorate of philosophy in mathematics and physics.

Afterwards he got a scholarship at Edinburgh University and there took his doctorate of science, and was given a Carnegie Research Fellowship. He carried on the work it enabled him to do after the war broke out, for he went before an Aliens Tribunal and pointed to his membership in the Communist Party as proof that he was anti-Nazi. It is not possible to know in what terms his statement was made, for by an administrative act of incredible folly all or most records of the proceedings before the Aliens Tribunal were destroyed after the war. Quite apart from their bearings on espionage, these records would have been of priceless value to the historian. But in May 1940 the Nazis invaded the Low Countries and France, and it became necessary for the British to intern all aliens, for the safety of all parties. He was one of a group of alien scientists who were taken to Canada and placed in a camp on the Heights of Abraham outside Quebec. There was a strong and open Communist section in this camp, led by Hans Kahle, a veteran of the Spanish Civil War, who is described in Douglas Hyde's *I Believed* and in Mrs. Haldane's *Truth Will Out*. He later became police chief in Mecklenburg in the Eastern Zone of Germany. Fuchs was his recognized second in command.

In 1942 Fuchs was allowed to return to Great Britain, and he went to Glasgow University to continue his researches. Very soon Professor Rudolf Peierls, a young and very eminent German-born psysicist, working at Birmingham University on atomic research for the British government, asked for his assistance. So Fuchs went to Birmingham and in June signed the usual security undertaking and a month later applied for naturalization as a British subject, in due course taking the oath of allegiance to his Majesty the King. The names of his sponsors have not been disclosed; it is the custom to regard such persons as acting confidentially. It was, however, strange that later these particular sponsors did not feel under an obligation to reveal themselves, considering who they were. At about the same time he decided to inform the Soviet Union about the work he was doing, and he established contact with another member of the Communist Party. For the following eight years he maintained continuous contact with persons personally unknown to him whom he knew to be charged with the duty of transmitting to Russia all the information he gave them; and he told them all he could about his work, without hesitation. For some months he worked happily with Professor Peierls, making his home with him and his family in Edgbaston. In 1943 Professor Peierls went to America and worked on the American atomic project for three years, and so did Klaus Emil, the British government guaranteeing his loyalty. When they returned Klaus Emil was made head of the theoretical physics division of the atomic-energy establishment at Harwell, and he held this post, regularly communicating to Soviet agents information regarding the researches carried on in the establishment, until he was arrested in February 1950.

Meanwhile his father was treading a stony path with great courage and endurance. When Hitler came to power Dr. Fuchs was deprived of his professorship at Kiel and later was imprisoned in a concentration camp for nine months. He was not singled out for punishment owing to any act of his own; he was taken in a blanket catch of dissenting ministers. But he did nothing to ward off his fate, though he was invited by the Ministry of Education to come into the Nazi Party on easy terms, and as soon as he was released, though he was under surveillance by the Gestapo, he and two of his sons started a car-hire service which was a cover for an escape route for refugees. After three years the cars were confiscated. At various times his sons fled the country, and a daughter of his, who was a painter, became subject to recurrent attacks of mania after she had helped her young husband to escape, and finally threw herself off a moving train and was killed. In complete loneliness, except for his motherless grandson of four, Dr. Fuchs lived through the war years, maintaining his opposition to the regime, and performing such courageous acts as addressing disaffected Nazis gathered together in private houses.

When the war came to an end his life brightened. He was reunited with his scattered children, and though he was now over seventy he embarked on an active life as a Quaker preacher and teacher, travelling all over Germany to find and reassemble the remnants of the Society of Friends and to welcome those who wished to join it. In 1948 he went for a year to lecture at the American Quaker Centre, Pendle Hill, and then returned to Germany to take up his work again, which was lying more and more among the members of the German branch of the body known as the Fellowship of Reconciliation. All these associations are above suspicion. The Quaker movement has been subjected to many attempts at Communist infiltration, but these have been checked by wise and hardheaded leadership. It is possible that the professed Quaker who makes propaganda aimed at weakening the defences of Great Britain or America is a disguised Communist, but it would be unlikely that a Communist would be able to carry on any agitation useful to his cause inside the Quaker organization. Some of the members of the Fellowship of Reconciliation had dubious political antecedents, but investigation shows that most of these were due to family connections which it would have been hard to waive. But it so happened that from 1947 Dr. Fuchs and his followers had had one overmastering desire, and this certainly looked suspicious when the activities of Klaus Emil were exposed; for what they wished was that Dr. Fuchs should go and live and work in the Eastern Zone of Germany. This was, however, not because he and his followers liked the Russians, but because they did not. They saw Soviet rule as an extreme example of sinful man's tendency to bring suffering into the world by violating what is holy; and it was Dr. Fuchs's intention to save oppressed and oppressors alike by meeting the Russians with love and recalling them to peaceful ways by reminding them of Christ. When Dr. Fuchs became professor of ethics and religion in the University of Leipzig, his followers did not conceive this as a release into Utopia, but as a descent into Hell.

There could hardly be a more striking example of the difficulty of applying security tests to people above a certain level of mental complexity. On the face of it Dr. Fuchs's desire to go into the Eastern Zone, and the readiness of the Soviet authorities to give him a professorship, looked as if the old gentleman must be a full member of the Communist Party. But investigation was bound to show that he regarded himself as Daniel about to enter the lions' den, and that the Soviet authorities were employing him as they will employ anyone of good repute who is willing to associate with them. When that conclusion was reached, it would inevitably happen not only that no black mark was inscribed against the head of the theoretical physics division at Harwell, but that it was less likely that a black mark would be inscribed against him afterwards. If somebody had conceived a suspicion that Klaus Emil might be a Communist, it would be examined with the reflection that, after all, there would probably be nothing in it, since he came from a quietist family which extended its tolerance to Communists not because they were Communists but because they were human. It would obviously not be within the scope of a security officer to conduct his investigations on a plane likely to reveal that in the quietism of the father there was a strain which might, to his amazement and distress, emerge in the son as Communist treachery, though it was logical enough. A glimpse into Dr. Fuchs's mind is given by a remarkable pamphlet he wrote, called *Christ in Catastrophe,* which has been widely distributed by the Quakers in America and England.

It is an eloquent pamphlet, beautiful in its description of the joy felt by the mystic when he is aware of the presence of God. But it is also egotistical and smug and curiously unsympathetic towards the sorrows and achievements of others. It lays stress on the divine favours that were showered on Dr. Fuchs, and the mission which Christ gave him to carry on in stricken Germany. "Was it imagination that enabled people like me to know, from the beginning of all propaganda, that the spirit of Hitler was not God?" he asks. "Why did so many, very clever and orthodox theological thinkers, scholars, pastors, and leaders of churches not recognize evil?" He goes on to taunt those who "had Christianity as doctrine, very elaborate, very refined, very traditional," but "had not that experience in which the living Christ, the risen Lord, gives his call and task for this day and this time." There is not one word of praise to be spared for, say, the German Catholics, though the heroism of many of them was exemplary. There is also an unengaging passage in which he describes how, when he came back to Germany from a six weeks' visit to his son in Switzerland in 1947, he saw the faces of the people in the street with a new sharpness, and he describes them with singular lack of pity. He admits that "sometimes" he sees a face "in which it is written that this man, this woman, overcame suffering and despair, that behind the face is serenity, a conscience at rest and yet awake to love, truth, helpfulness," but concerning the rest he permits himself to make assumptions which, considering the time and the place, seem remarkably disagreeable. It also seems a pity, when describing the reactions of American newspaper-readers to "the lynching of a Negro in an unknown township in the South," to say, "they read, shudder a little and forget." A number of Americans, when they read of a lynching, shudder but do not forget; and engage in activities of a most purposeful kind to prevent another one from happening.

There is also a curious lack of shrewdness in the pamphlet. At one point Dr. Fuchs recounts how, after he had given a talk in a German town, a man of about fifty had come to him and told him, with tears in his eyes, that he longed to go to church and acknowledge God, but he could not because every time he came near the church he saw standing by the door the field chaplain attached to his regiment in the First World War, and heard him saying, as he said then, "Shoot them, beat them, kill them, win the attack!"—and was therefore prevented from entering the church. On inquiry, Dr. Fuchs found that the man was chairman of the Communist Party of that district. He regrets that the man had rejected Christianity and attributes his rejection to the fault of the chaplain in not understanding that a Christian must be a pacifist. But he does not remind the man that it is inconsistent for one who leaves the Church because it is not pacifist to go over to the Communists, who rejoice in the exploits of the Red Army. Indeed, he seems himself to forget the existence of the Red Army, for he talks of the Communist Party as promising a "world of justice, peace, and love." But at the same time he deplores that this man should have been so disillusioned by hearing the warlike utterances by the chaplain that he accepted it as proven that man will always fight, and therefore all of us have not only the right but the duty to fight in the same way for our ideals. But one cannot help feeling that if that were the man's own conclusion, it was illogical of him, and uncharitable to feel such bitterness against the chaplain because he had come to the same conclusion. The emotional force behind this passage, its incoherence, and its air of confidential moral authority, make a painful impression.

It was information received from America which led the British security organization to turn its attention to Klaus Emil Fuchs in 1950. It was strange that it had not been actively interested in him long ago. He had made no secret of his Communist sympathies when he came before the Aliens Tribunal which granted him temporary exemption from internment at the beginning of the war, and his fellow internees have never doubted that he was an active Party member, but though the Americans actually gave the information which touched off the fuse, their record was not more creditable than the British. The existence of a courier system transmitting information to Soviet headquarters in the United States had been reported to the Federal Bureau of Investigation by an ex-Communist spy named Elizabeth Bentley, who had repented and made a voluntary confession of all her activities in the autumn of 1945. Had her evidence been followed up it would have led to Fuchs. No fewer than three of the couriers appeared in 1947 before a federal grand jury summoned to investigate espionage, and cleared themselves by what now seem oddly unconvincing stories. In May 1949 Elizabeth Bentley again disclosed particulars of the courier system before a committee on immigration and naturalization which is a subcommittee of the Senate Judiciary Committee. In the United States, as in Great Britain, the weakness of security is not that it does not collect information but that the information it collects is not used. It is interesting to note that Alger Hiss was first accused of espionage in 1939, and that no effort was made to conduct an official investigation into the charges until 1948. This was equally unfortunate whether he was innocent or guilty.

The arrest of Klaus Emil Fuchs on February 2, 1950, and his appearance at Bow Street on February 10 and at the Old Bailey on March 1 told the world that a new page had been turned in the book of history. On that page were written two facts. First, Great Britain and America had lost most of the protection they thought they enjoyed against their only potential enemy, the Soviet Union, in their monopoly of knowledge concerning the atomic bomb. Thanks to Klaus Emil Fuchs and Alan Nunn May, its basic elements were now known to the Russians. We had still an advantage arising out of our knowledge of the practical problems concerning the manufacture of atomic bombs, and our superior industrial equipment; but even so we enjoyed no protection which the Russians might not destroy by further spying of a sort

which they evidently found easy to organize and that on a scale
which a totalitarian state finds far easier than a democracy; and
the blame lay on these Communist scientists. And the second fact
written on this page of history was the complete unmanageabil-
ity of the Communist scientist, who was an even stranger animal
than we had imagined.

When Klaus Emil Fuchs was approached by the security
officers, he began to talk in a manner which cannot exactly be
called light-minded, for indeed one might as well call *The Sorrows of Werther* light-minded, but which was not what would
have been expected from a man charged with this particular
offence. It has to be conceded that he had been found out and
that he must have been extremely disconcerted. It also has to be
conceded that his statement was typically German in the way
that English people find most difficult to understand. He spoke
with the subjectivity bequeathed to the German people as a
legacy from their romantic movement, which makes them pass
round their emotions as if they were nosegays exhaling perfume;
and he showed that obsessive interest in political activities of the
more violent sort, combined with a complete lack of political
sense, which has too often brought Germany to the brink of the
abyss and sometimes over it. If this be remembered, it seems less
strange that Klaus Fuchs should have begun by assuring the
security officers that he had a very happy childhood, a matter
concerning which they cannot have expressed any anxiety. They
were members of the regular police force, who rarely care about
such things. In the same vein, he recalled that when all his
schoolfellows wore imperial badges on the anniversary of the
founding of the Weimar Republic, he alone put on a republican
badge, and had it torn off. In minute detail he recited all the
political fatuities of himself, his friends, and his enemies, committed at Leipzig and Kiel Universities, with a respectfulness
that no Englishman of thirty-eight would extend to his own
doings at the age of twenty. We must indeed make allowances
for his plight and for very considerable differences in national
characteristics. But all the same his statement is odd and displeas-
ing.

It is terrifying, the apology of a man who took on himself the
responsibility of giving away our defence secrets to another
power. It betrays Fuchs as a man who had never emerged from

adolescence and who, on matters outside his special province, could not rank as an intelligent adolescent. It has an egomaniac quality. He was addressing the representatives of the state, whose business it is to consider the interests of all, but he importuned them with particulars of his internal condition to which nobody could give attention unless he was representative of a God with infinite time and love to bestow on each individual. It also appears that he believed he could solve any problem; it was as if he imagined himself to be Sophia, heavenly wisdom. An occasional consciousness of sin did not affect his self-confidence, and he makes it plain that he regarded it as his part to forgive, not to seek forgiveness. He also shows extreme inhumanity.

His great decision of treachery was made in the political sphere; yet his statement shows unusual political ignorance. He could not understand events even when he had been up to his neck in them. It is well known that in the early thirties, when the German Communists accused the Social Democrats of not opposing Hitler, they were hoping thereby to draw anti-Nazi enthusiasts away from the Social Democratic Party, and thus to split the Popular Front, so that Hitler had to come to power. Their Intelligence service and their judgment were alike so weak that they believed that Hitler's regime would be short-lived and expected to use its ruins as the foundation of a Communist Germany. All sorts of witnesses have testified to this effect, and it would be virtually impossible for a non-Communist to write of these years without alluding to this party policy, or for a Communist to write of them without defending it or denying that it existed. But plainly Fuchs was so little in touch with political discussion that this interpretation of what had happened round him had never reached him. He writes of these events as they had seemed to him when he was a naïve twenty.

He draws an alarming picture of this political naïveté working in with the only one of his own characteristics which seemed to him doubtful: his readiness for deceit. At Kiel University the left-wing organization he had led had started an agitation against the high fees; and in this it pretended to cooperate with the Nazi students, to whom it had presently proposed that they should jointly declare a strike of students, well knowing that the Nazis would turn tail when it came to the point. After the negotiations had gone on for some time, Fuchs suddenly issued a leaflet disclosing the nature of the negotiations and pointing out that the Nazis had shown they were in earnest. He had been highly praised for taking this step at the Communist conference he attended in Berlin just after the burning of the Reichstag, but it had been an unfair thing to do. He should first have warned the Nazis that he would issue such a leaflet if they failed to take action by such and such a date. "I omitted," he said, "to resolve in my mind" this point; and perhaps, he thought, it was then that he had begun to accept the Communist view that scruples "of this kind are prejudices which are weaknesses and which you must fight against." Even those of us least inclined to sympathy with communism must feel it unfair to saddle the party with the responsibility of discovering that a politician may often find a lie a most useful help in time of trouble.

He goes on to describe how when he first went to England he tried to make a serious study of the basic Marxist philosophy.

> The idea which gripped me most was the belief that in the past man has been unable to understand his own history and the forces which lead to the further development of human society; that now for the first time man understands the forces of history and he is able to control them and that therefore for the first time he will be really free. I carried this idea over to the personal sphere and believed that I could understand myself and that I could make myself into what I believed I should be.

Presenting a report on progress to perfection, he goes on to relate respectfully the ill-informed and elementary opinions he had held concerning foreign affairs up till the time he was interned, and then suggests that it was a pity that the internees were for a long time not allowed any newspapers. It does not occur to him that, if newspaper reading had been encouraged and the war had gone against us for any length of time, it might have been difficult for the guards to keep discipline and even to protect the non-Nazi internees against the Nazi internees. "I felt no bitterness at the internment because I could understand that it was necessary and at that time England could not spare good people to look after the internees, but it did deprive me of the chance of learning more about the real character of the British people." It is implied that he might have spared them if he had known more about them. It never crosses his mind that it was not for him to spite them or spare them, or that at any time it might be right for him to submit to lawful authority and not to transcend it. What has happened here is that the Lutheran right to private judgment has moved over into the secular field. Fuchs is claiming the right of private judgment to supersede public judgment altogether. Sometimes a man must say to society, "I think that what you are doing is wrong, and I intend to make you stop and do what is right." This is one of the chief instruments by which society moves towards civilization. But private judgment cannot supersede public judgment every time, which is what Fuchs was prepared for his own to do, with a confidence equalled till now only in those devotees who believe divinity to be within them.

It is the heavy task of the heretic who rejects the authority of the Church to make a whole new spiritual cosmos by his own unaided efforts. He cannot sit back and face a metaphysical vacuum; if that had been possible for him, he would not have been a heretic. Fuchs began work at Harwell, handing over the results achieved by himself and his colleagues to the Soviet authorities, and built up a system which justified him:

> In the course of this work I began naturally to form bonds of personal friendship and I had to conceal from them my inner thoughts. I used my Marxist philosophy to establish in my mind two separate compartments. One compartment in which I allowed myself to make friendships, to have personal relations, to help people and to be in all personal ways the kind of man I wanted to be and the kind of man which, in a personal way, I had been before with my friends in or near the Communist Party. I could be free and easy and happy with other people without fear of disclosing myself because I knew that the other compartment would step in if I approached the danger point. I could forget the other compartment and still rely on it. It appeared to me at the time that I had become a "free man" because I had succeeded in the other compartment to establish myself completely independent of the surrounding forces of society. Looking back at it now the best way of expressing it seems to be to call it a controlled schizophrenia.

In fact, he had rediscovered the fact that it often serves a man's immediate ends to lie and cheat: nothing more than that. Further on in his statement, in an equally muddled passage, he tells us that later he rediscovered that to lie and cheat and deceive is wrong, destructive to oneself and to one's environment. Many quite stupid little children would have told him as much, and although they had learned it by rote, it would still have been worth his while to listen to them. But his vanity was too great for him to entertain the idea of ever listening. It was for him to be listened to. Perhaps the most terrifying sentences in his statement were these:

> In the post-war period I began again to have my doubts about Russian policy. It is impossible to give definite incidents because now the control mechanism acted against me also in keeping away from me facts which I could not look in the face, but they did penetrate and eventually I came to a point where I knew that I disapproved of many actions of the Russian Government and of the Communist Party, but I still believed that they would build a new world and that one day I would take part in it and that on that day I would also have to stand up and say to them that there are things which they are doing wrongly.

He had decided that the Western World was unfit to survive and betrayed it to the Soviet government; but the Soviet government also was not worthy, he would have to correct it in its turn. Here we are back in the religious zone again. George Fox believed that he was filled with the Inner Light and that he then "knew nothing but pureness, innocency and righteousness." He was followed by James Nayler, whose followers called him Jesus and "the dear and precious Son of Zion, whose mother is a virgin and whose birth is immortal." The materialist in Klaus Emil rejected omniscience as impossible; yet it firmly claimed omniscience, and it was willing to manifest omnipotence as the occasion arose. It happened to be the atom bomb of which he had disposal; but if it had been some weapon approaching still nearer to the absolute of destructive power he would have disposed of it as blithely. He was unrestrained by any tenderness. He makes no mention of the sufferings of his family under the Nazi regime; he expresses no concern about the horrors of atomic warfare which, owing to his action, henceforward threatened Great Britain and Western Europe. Though he says that what he has done may "endanger" his friends, he apparently means only that he might endanger their prospects of continued employment at Harwell. Though he admits that he recognizes his deceitfulness as wrong, he is unabashed, as Madame Guyon was when she had to sign what amounted to a retraction of her quietist doctrines. She had previously explained that it never seemed necessary for her to find a defence for her conduct "for I no longer have a conduct, and yet I act infallibly."

The trial of Klaus Emil Fuchs took place before the Lord Chief Justice, Lord Goddard, at the Old Bailey on March 1, 1950, and it had the reticent quality which appertained to trials of Russian agents in England at that time. The authorities preferred that the public should see as little as possible. They wanted to lift the cloth hanging over the cage just long enough to see the kind of bird inside and sentence it accordingly, and then they popped back the cloth. It was all over in ninety minutes. Klaus Emil came into the dock, a pale, neat young man, like innumerable middle-class Germans, with a bulging forehead and glasses, not much of a chin, and a weakly body. He was charged under the Official Secrets Act on an indictment comprising four counts: that on a day in 1943 in the city of Birmingham for a purpose prejudicial to the safety or interests of the state he communicated to a person unknown information relating to atomic research which was calculated to be, or might have been or was intended to be, directly or indirectly useful to an enemy; and that he had committed similar offences on a day unknown between December 31, 1943 and August 1, 1944, in the city of New York, and on a day unknown in February 1945 at Boston, Massachusetts, and on a day unknown in 1947 in Berkshire. His plea of guilty was entered. The Attorney-General opened for the prosecution and read passages from Klaus Emil's statement. A security officer gave evidence that he had taken down the statement, and an atomic scientist of high standing and unquestioned loyalty, who had been used by the security officers to examine Fuchs, told how Fuchs had admitted passing on information, and that in his opinion it was of a kind valuable to a potential enemy.

Fuchs's counsel made the debatable point that as the first three offences were committed during the time that Russia was fighting as an ally of Britain, it would be difficult to see how giving information to Russian agents could be interpreted as prejudicial to the safety or interests of the state; and he pointed out, too justly, that the authorities had bought this betrayal with their eyes wide open, for Klaus Emil had not concealed his Communist convictions when he appeared before the Aliens Tribunal. Then the Lord Chief Justice asked Klaus Emil if he had anything to say before sentence was passed on him, and he answered by a last flare-up of his celestial impudence. Complacently he complimented the court on having given him a fair trial. When the thin pipe of his voice was no longer heard, the Lord Chief Justice went on to deliver judgment. He enumerated the four main consequences of Klaus Emil's crime. He had imperilled the right of asylum which had extended to political refugees; he had not only betrayed the work he himself had done, which was the property of his employers, he had handed over the work of other scientists, who might therefore have fallen under unjust suspicion; he had imperilled the good relations between Great Britain and the United States by betraying work done in an American project; and he may have brought the irreparable ruin of atomic warfare on Great Britain and the United States. He then sentenced Klaus Emil to fourteen years' imprisonment, not for the sake of punishment, but to safeguard the country. "How can I be sure that a man of your mentality, as shown in that statement you have made," he asked, "may not at any minute allow some curious working in your mind to lead you further to betray secrets of the greatest possible value and importance to this land?" It was the maximum sentence that could be given under the Official Secrets Act.

Little can be said in defence of this policy of trying the criminal in a manner which concealed the nature of the crime from the public which had suffered from it. It helped the Communists, enabling them to present the scientist Communist spies as starry-eyed altruists who imparted secrets to other powers just because they were scientists and wanted their fellow scientists to have the benefit of their own discoveries, and were so unworldly that they did not know that they were doing any harm, and hardly knew what ideologies were about. This was the picture of Fuchs that was spread about the world after his conviction, and it was as untrue of him as it was of Nunn May. Fuchs had been deep in the Communist movement long before he came to England. We know this from the testimony of Harry Gold, a courier who handled Fuchs's material in the United States. Gold reported that at the same time that Fuchs was giving him material he had derived when present at the first atomic explosion at Alamogordo, Fuchs said that he was greatly worried because the British had got to Kiel ahead of the Russians, and he was frightened lest British Intelligence officers find the very full dossier collected by the Nazis concerning his Communist background and ties, which Fuchs himself described as "very strong." He was not a doctrinaire Communist, not a passive intellectual; he was a good party underground worker who knew all the tricks. He knew all the rules and sternly rebuked Gold on one occasion for breaking one of them by arranging a meeting in a public place. The material he transmitted to the Soviet Union always astonished Harry Gold, who was a qualified scientist himself, by its quantity and its quality. Of one consignment he says that "there were fifty, sixty, a hundred pages of very close writing on yellow pads, sometimes white. And he had a very small crabbed hand—it not only contained a tremendous amount of theoretical mathematics, it contained the practical set-up."

Fuchs had indeed much material to transmit, for he knew much concerning the gaseous-diffusion process, which was an important method for producing bomb material. To obtain a satisfactory chain reaction it was necessary to separate the easily fissionable uranium-235 from the more abundant uranium-238, which constitutes 99.3 per cent of pure uranium. There are several techniques for doing this, such as the electromagnetic, centrifuge, and liquid-diffusion processes, but none eventually proved to be as practical as the gaseous-diffusion process. This had been developed in England largely at Birmingham University by the team of which Fuchs was a part, while the Americans worked on it in a complex of laboratories and plants grouped under the name of K-25. There, on their own, for the British built no plant of this kind, they worked out an entirely novel process.

It was based on the theory that if a gaseous uranium compound was pumped against a porous barrier, then the lighter molecules of the gas, which would contain U-235, would pass through more quickly than the heavier molecules containing U-238. The problem was to make porous metal membranes, with sub-microscopic holes punched in them, some millions to the square inch, which functioned within an airtight vessel called the diffuser. As the gas was pumped through a long series, or

"cascade," of these tubes, it tended to separate, the lighter parti-
cles going ahead and the heavier falling back. There is so little
difference in mass between the gaseous suspension of these two
kinds of uranium that it is impossible to sort the two out except
by using several thousand successive stages.

Fuchs was in possession of these facts through his own team's
work on the subject when he was in Birmingham, and through
the information placed at his disposal by the Americans. But at
the end of 1943 he went to America and saw the plant in action
and was given much detailed information. It is obvious that such
a process raised many engineering problems; for example, the
effects of gas corrosion on the hundreds of miles of pipes had to
be minimized, the flow of gas through the pipes had to be regulated, air had to be excluded from them, particularly at the
welds. Fuchs was informed of all the solutions that had been
found, and of the multifold mechanical equipment, the pumps,
seals, valves, and coolers, which had been conjured up to meet
these unique requirements. To create the scientific and technological treasure house revealed to Fuchs, the United States had
mobilized its academic and industrial and financial resources
with an unsparing hand. The Soviet Union was not in a position
to duplicate this effort from scratch. It had remarkable academic
resources, but its industrial and financial resources were not
comparable to those of the United States, and it could not have
created K-25, even if it had been a neutral and had not been
impoverished by war. Fuchs enabled it to make the A-bomb
without going through this expensive experimental phase, and
thus brought down on the unhappy world, years before it need
have happened, the dreariness of the cold war.

There were other aspects of Fuchs's treachery. The Americans
learned of it with resentment. He would not have been allowed
to visit the K-25 project, and receive information from it and
various scientific agencies who had received him as a trusted
colleague, had his antecedents been known. His German birth
would have been reckoned as valid an impediment as his communism, until he had been screened. General Groves, then in charge
of the atomic-bomb project in the United States, has recorded
acidly that he received an assurance that each of the British
scientists sent over to work in his project had been investigated
as thoroughly as he himself saw that all his own employees were

investigated. But in view of Fuchs's record he was of the opinion that at that time the British had made no investigations at all.

There was also some bitterness over a difference between American and English policy regarding compartmentalization. The Americans isolated their scientific workers in the individual projects (plutonium project, gaseous-diffusion project, and so on) and had not allowed them information on regarding one another's work. This was obviously contrary to the best interests of scientific research, which requires a wide scope for the imaginative mind, and it gave the affected scientists a lamentable feeling of frustration. The American authorities freely admitted the case against it, but said that it was a temporary evil made necessary by wartime perils. The English gave way to the protests of their scientists and never imposed the system. Now the Americans thought grimly that Fuchs's all-round knowledge had enabled him to get an over-all picture of the American atomic programme such as was allowed to only a few of the top members of their projects. This was the catastrophe which the Americans had tried to avert by compartmentalization, and the Englishmen had flouted them with just those catastrophic results which the Americans had foreseen.

There was further food for bitterness in memories of a not too fortunate episode in Anglo-American relations. At the end of 1943 the British government had sent over to America the scientists and engineers who had been working under Peierls and other scientific leaders, to study the developments of the gaseous-diffusion process and give what help they could. They spent four months on the task, and their American colleagues were surprised by what seemed to them their visitors' lack of enthusiasm and their unhelpful suggestions. They criticized various features in the process and proposed alternatives, all of which seemed to their hosts complicated and unpractical. Not one of these was adopted, then or subsequently, and this zero seemed odd enough in view of the undeniable ability of the members of the mission. No doubt the situation was largely the result of war nerves and overwork on both sides. But it would be natural enough if afterwards it was wondered whether this had not been an attempt at sabotage, and whether, if it was Fuchs who planned it, those who fell in with his plans were not silly and careless. A wedge had been driven between the two countries, and this, as they were inevitably to be allied for the foreseeable future, was more than a mere inconvenience.

This was the first manifestation of a change in the grand tactics of treason, which resulted from the transformation of the international situation by the Second World War. Espionage had hitherto borne a relationship to counterespionage as simple as that which keeps the burglar on evasive terms with the police. In the old multinational world a country instructed an agent to steal the military or naval secrets of another country, which would endeavour to defend itself against such thefts by the use of various types of security organizations; and the value of this agent to the country employing him would be measured by the usefulness of the secrets he stole and the success with which he hoodwinked the security organizations. But now, in a world where the Soviet Union faced the Western bloc, another system of scoring suggested itself. Anything which detached the United States from its allies weakened the Western bloc and strengthened the Soviet Union. Obviously the United States would not want to share its defence secrets or to engage in any expensive form of cooperation with an ally whose security organizations were proved to be inefficient or infiltrated by Communists. It followed that now the Soviet Union might get the best value out of an agent by using him to collect enough information in Western countries to establish him as a spy and then allowing him to be identified as an agent in circumstances which discredited the security organizations of the country where he had been working. This might break down the morale of that country and arouse distrust in the United States. We were in a new era, and the proof is before us if we look back to William Joyce, who had no such second string to his bow. His was not a two-power world, and if he (or another spy) had thrown his weight into one or other of the two scales the balance would not have even trembled. It might be thought the new dispensation was better than the old, because the new spy was a man of intelligence and even of great talent.

But this illusion cannot survive a reading of Fuchs's statement. We can never be sure that there will not arise some other gifted scientist, just a little sillier, just a little crazier, who would decide to set fire to the world in order to please the dematerialist Red Indian who was his spiritualist aunt's control, or the holy men in Mars whom he knew to be waiting for the signal of the flame that they might come down and bring us salvation. This is unlikely to happen, but it is within the realm of possibility. Even far short of this, very disagreeable things might happen. Behind the scenes scientists, the most eminent, were putting up the most bizarre efforts to exempt Fuchs from punishment because he was one of their company. An honoured public figure wanted Fuchs to be allowed to go scot-free and take a professorship at a university. Many, hardly less distinguished, whom one had thought of as harbingers of the future, suddenly appeared as ghosts from the past: identifiable ghosts. In their demands that the case should be hushed up, they revealed them-selves as reincarnations of the French officers who would not permit the exposure of the forgers and perjurers who had con-spired against Dreyfus, because nothing must tarnish the honour of the French Army. Nothing must tarnish the honour of scien-tists. This phase passed. Few of these men, except those who were crypto-Communists, would not now regret that they made this curious plea for privilege. Yet that phase might conceivably be repeated. If history took a turn which again placed our mili-tary destiny at the mercy of a sudden spurt of inventiveness by our scientists, they might make anew this excessive claim for power.

The Fuchs trial did nothing to acquaint the public with the true nature of his offence. Indeed, it did something to disguise it. A security officer gave evidence that he had taken down Fuchs's statement, and he made the same assertion that was made con-cerning Alan Nunn May at his trial, that before he took down the prisoner's statement there was no evidence on which he could have been prosecuted. Now, this must be technically true. But all the same there were substantial reasons why the idea of making a statement to security officers had seemed good to these two persons, and it was a pity to create an impression that here were two honest souls who confessed when they had no need.

The trial was not followed by any organization of petitions for the remission of Fuchs's sentence such as had been carried on five years before for the benefit of Alan Nunn May. Obviously it was better to let sleeping dogs lie. As always after an event which draws attention to the criminal side of the Communist Party's activities, in Britain and the United States a number of prominent Communists expressed disapproval of the party policy and disassociated themselves from it. This creates an illusion that the Communist Party is weakening and that these particular people have become innocuous. But some resentment was expressed by those dissidents who, though not themselves Communists, have been persuaded that it is reactionary to punish a Communist for even the most unlawful act. An American radio commentator, assuming that Abraham Lincoln look of country shrewdness, said: "I always heard that your British justice was the fairest in the world, but anybody could see that your Lord Chief Justice came into court with his mind made up about the case. Why, the minute Fuchs had stopped speaking he started right off with his judgment." It was explained to him that the Lord Chief Justice would have read Klaus Emil's statement beforehand, as it had been admitted without challenge before the examining magistrate, and would have been told that a plea of guilty was to be entered. But it was no use: the American came from a generation conditioned to grumble at authority, and it was no more use arguing with him than it would have been trying to staunch by logic the flow of saliva dribbling from the jaws of Pavlov's dogs when they heard the dinner bell.

Others likened Klaus Emil's statement to the confessions so monotonously proffered by persons tried in Soviet courts for offences against the state. They were moved by a desire to prove that the confessions in the Soviet courts were as freely given as it was known that Klaus Emil's statement had been. But the analogy does not hold good. The confessions in the Soviet courts are cut in the same pattern and astonish by their incompatibility with all that has been previously known about the persons who make them. But Klaus Emil's speech could not have been made by anybody who had not been a student in a German university in the early thirties, who had not read English left-wing weeklies and newspapers in the late thirties, who had not a quietist background. Only once is there adherence to a pattern, and that is one imposed by the Communist Party.

He remarked that when he accepted the position offered him in the atomic project "at first I thought that all I would do would be to inform the Russian authorities that work upon the atomic bomb was going on." It is a curious coincidence that in the propaganda distributed for the purpose of getting people to petition for the immediate release of Dr. Alan Nunn May, it was stated that "the real significance of his action was to inform Russia of the *existence* of the vast atomic energy programme." It is a strange echo. But for the most part the statement is highly individual and bears no trace of being a response to force or persuasion.

In prison he was interviewed by English and American security officers, who liked him and believed in his candour. But towards the end of May there was announced the arrest in Philadelphia of an American citizen named Harry Gold, a biochemist engaged in research concerned with a certain cardiac condition in Philadelphia General Hospital, on a charge of espionage, based on allegations that he had acted as a courier for Dr. Fuchs, receiving from him written and oral information about the work in the Los Alamos atomic project and handing it over to a Soviet official. It was believed in London that Gold's arrest was due to information given by Klaus Emil, but this was not so. He talked, and talked with great profit to the authorities, but not until after Gold had been arrested. It is a curious coincidence that Fuchs, who had expressed willingness to aid the authorities in the detection of his American courier, at last identified Gold from a film shown him in person by the FBI on the same day that Gold was arrested. He had previously seen photographs of Gold but had failed to recognize him.

This was the first of a series of arrests made in connection with this particular American spy service. Within six months they numbered eight. Most of them illustrated a tropism which few historians would have predicted. The parents of those arrested had left Russia to avoid persecution and had been received handsomely in the United States. They themselves had been nourished by the swelling abundance of the last half-century as America had known it; none was poor by European standards. They all had had good educations, most had graduated from universities, all had gone out to steady employment on a high level. At the first opportunity they set to working, year in, year out, with great pains and at great risk, in order to betray the United States to Russia. It is not easy to find out what moved them, for most of them refused to testify on their own behalf. The party direction had changed now that the eyes of the world were on such cases, and there were no longer the protestations of innocence, the attacks on the probity of the courts, the barracking of spectators, and all the elaborate procedure which had been part of the standard American Communist drill till then. Now the direction to American Communists was, as it long had been to English Communists, to get these trials over as quickly and quietly as possible.

But there were two among the accused who broke away from the party while they were under arrest, and talked. One was a young soldier, David Greenglass, who in 1945 had come back to his post in New Mexico from leave in New York with a bit of cardboard in his pocket, half the side panel of a box of gelatin, cut across in zigzags. Later Harry Gold had come down to New Mexico with the other half of that panel, and the soldier had matched his with it and had known that this was the man to whom he was to hand certain information he had learned in the course of his work on the atom-bomb project. After arrest this young man soon threw in his hand and testified against his sister and her husband, Ethel and Julius Rosenberg, who had got him into this trouble. The other accused person who became a government witness was Harry Gold.

He carried the apotheosis of the new traitor a stage farther. He was a little dark man, so swollen with good living that he lost fifty pounds during the first six months of his detention. He was born in Switzerland in 1910, of Russian parents named Golodnitsky, who brought him to America three years later. Through his adolescence he worked in a laboratory by day and at night studied at the University of Pennsylvania and New York University. Finally he took his Baccalaureate of Science, *summa cum laude,* at Xavier University, a small but old and renowned Jesuit College in Ohio. From then on he held well-paid and interesting research posts. But from 1935 to 1946, which included his undergraduate years at Xavier University, he was a Communist agent, stealing industrial secrets from his employers for the benefit of the Soviet Union, and undertaking courier work. It might have been expected that, when he came to tell of this work, the most interesting part of his story must deal with his relationship to Klaus Emil Fuchs. But his account of this told us few new facts, other than that there had been two meetings between them at Santa Fe, the second of which took place on September 19, 1945, the very same day that the less fortunate

William Joyce was sentenced to death for treason at the Old Bailey. These meetings are not among those mentioned in the indictment brought foward at Fuchs's trial, and presumably he had concealed them from the authorities.

It was at Santa Fe that Fuchs had expressed anxiety to Gold because the British and not the Russians had taken Kiel, explaining that the Kiel Gestapo had a very complete dossier on him and that he was afraid lest British Intelligence would find it and "become aware of his very strong Communist background and ties." It was interesting to hear this from Harry Gold's lips in March 1951, since in March 1950 Mr. Attlee had told the House of Commons that he objected to "loose talk in the press suggesting inefficiency on the part of security services. I entirely deny that. Not long after this man [Fuchs] came into this country— that was in 1933—it was said that he was a Communist. The source of that information was the Gestapo. At that time the Gestapo accused everybody of being a Communist. When the matter was looked into there was no support for it whatever."

That was a strange remark and typical of the defensive statements made by governments when spies have been detected in their countries. Not one single sentence had any relation to reality. Nothing could be more absurd than the idea that in the thirties the British government was in the habit of discussing the eligibility of German refugees with the Gestapo, or any other agency of the Nazi government, and we knew well that no refugee was ever kept out or regarded with disfavour because of Communist sympathies. On the contrary, those who dealt with refugees in those days remember that the authorities beamed on Communists as certain to be anti-Nazi. So little were the Home Office and security organizations interested in communism that it was not until 1939, when the British Communists opposed the war effort, that it was even sought to draw up a list of party members. But as for the statement, "when the matter was looked into there was no support whatever," Mr. Attlee must only a short time before have read Klaus Fuchs's own statement, with its abundant particulars of his Communist youth, and he must also have learned recently that Fuchs had never concealed his Communist activities, speaking of them freely before the Aliens Tribunal.

But Mr. Attlee went on to paint the lily by saying that "from that time onwards there was no support for it whatever," which was strange indeed, in view of Klaus Fuchs's close association with the well-known Communist Hans Kahle in the internment camp on the Heights of Abraham, under the nose of a notably capable security officer. It is unfortunate that espionage was then treated as a partisan matter. It meant that a Labour government had to defend itself from Tory attacks when it had to report a failure of security during its tenure of office, and a Tory government had to submit to similar attacks in a like situation. The time was ripe for both parties to admit that in modern conditions security organizations have so difficult a task that a certain amount of stark, final failure is inevitable, and that no matter what party is in power at the time both parties should join together in work for the future rather than engage in a dogfight over pretence that the Cabinet, and not the stupidity of a Western security agent or the brilliance of a Soviet agent, can be blamed for a breach in our safety. The defensive statements put up under the system were always foolish and have put many misstatements into currency.

As relevant to the main line followed by modern espionage was Gold's account of his life as an industrial spy. For eleven years he served the Soviet Union in this capacity with great diligence and audacity, on a curious psychological basis. He never joined the Communist Party and despised most of the Communists he met as "wacked-up Bohemians," except one, who fascinated him because he relieved the conventionality of life in Jersey City by wearing a neat black snake as a cravat. Reluctantly he associated with them, simply because he had to have somebody to conspire with against the United States, not that he hated his adopted country, but he had to have something to conspire against. Gifted with an unusual power of self-knowledge, which makes his long statement one of the best confessional set-pieces of modern times, he quite saw that his state of mind was odd, but he could do nothing about it, and he abandoned himself to his mask-and-domino passion.

For some time he worked at a Philadelphia sugar factory, where the research director was notably kind to him and helped him to rise from lab boy to qualified chemist, and presently, with the aid of false keys and frequent volunteering for night duty, he acquired many of the firm's secret processes regarding paints and lacquers and industrial solvents. Later he was withdrawn by the Soviet Union and sent, at its expense, to Xavier University. On his return to industry he did much courier work with other industrial spies. One of them was Alfred Dean Slack, a research chemist for Eastman Kodak, who handed over to him Kodak's information on colour films: a huge complex of technical information which had taken many men years to develop. Another of them, according to Gold, worked in a steel corporation and handed on to Gold over a period of five years countless blueprints and drawings of various industrial processes relating to high-octane gasoline, turbine airplanes, chemical production, and synthetic rubber, which were handed over to Amtorg, the Soviet trading agency, which rapidly photographed them and gave them back to Gold, so that they got back to the steel corporation premises after a few hours. This particular spy was being paid a generous salary by his employers. He would of course have defended his breach of trust by professing sympathy with the ideals of the Soviet Union; but idealism seemed hardly a relevant consideration, since the Soviet Union could perfectly well have acquired all these industrial processes by simply buying the patents.

Usually Gold's courier work was carried on among these industrial spies, with the single exception of Fuchs. But in June 1945 he was told to make a double event of a trip to New Mexico, by following up a visit to Fuchs at Santa Fe by a trip to Albuquerque to meet a low-grade technician who was employed on the construction of the atom bomb at Los Alamos, a young soldier, twenty-three years old, named David Greenglass. This was a more important assignment than Greenglass's quality suggested, for what he was supplying was a description and sketches of various patterns of "flat-type lens moulds." The lens involved was nothing like the lens as it is known to laymen, being a combination of high explosives which focused detonation waves as a glass lens focuses light waves, and so touched off the atom bomb. The design of this contrivance had presented new problems, and again the Soviet Union was receiving material from the traitors which would enable it to skip a lengthy and expensive experimental stage in the manufacture of the bomb.

When Gold arrived at Greenglass's house in Albuquerque, and presented half the side of a Jello package, and Greenglass took the matching half out of his wife's handbag, Gold greeted him with the words, "I come from Julius." This was the recognition line which he had been instructed to give by his Russian contact, Yakovlev, a clerk in the Soviet consulate. What is surprising is that it related to a person who really was named Julius: Julius Rosenberg, the husband of Greenglass's sister Ethel. Though Gold did not know Rosenberg, he too was an active figure in the Communist world. The son of a well-to-do working tailor, he had taken a degree in electrical engineering at the College of the City of New York when he was twenty-one and had thereafter had a pleasant enough existence. He went into the civil service and worked for five years in various Army Signal Corps plants, at reasonable salaries, while Mrs. Rosenberg earned money as a stenographer and a singer. He was also steadily engaged on odd jobs for the Communist Party, of which both he and his wife had been open members ever since their adolescence. The couple occupied a flat in an agreeable housing development in New York at a low subsidized rent.

Sometime during the war the Rosenbergs passed from the open party to the underground section and collected information from various spies working for the Soviet Union. They had always wanted to get into espionage. When Ethel's brother David was drafted into the workshops at Los Alamos, she and her husband sent David's young wife, Ruth Greenglass, down to New Mexico to tell him that he must give them all the information he could for Soviet use. Ethel was then twenty-eight and her husband twenty-six, and they were both competent and masterful characters; David was much less intelligent and was devoted to both of them, particularly Julius, and his wife was just twenty. The younger couple demurred, but eventually Julius and Ethel talked them out of their timidity and David made his small but important contribution to Soviet knowledge.

As soon as Harry Gold told his story it was inevitable that both the Rosenbergs and David Greenglass would find themselves in the dock. David saved his life and exempted his wife from prosecution by testifying against his sister and her husband, and they were sentenced to death on April 5, 1951. This is an ugly phase of history, but few modern events have been as ugly as this involvement of brother and sister in an unnatural relationship which is the hostile twin of incest. But the story appears even more pitiful if one inquires into the years between Green-glass's treachery and discovery.

In September, Gouzenko handed over to the Canadian govern-ment the papers he had filched through the Soviet embassy concerning the atom-bomb spy ring. The Soviet authorities then ordered all agents involved in this ring to disperse, sending the Russians back to Russia and telling the non-Russians to change occupations and get into nonsensitive fields. Rosenberg was in double trouble, for he had been removed from the government service in 1945 because security officers discovered that he was a Communist. At first he seemed in luck, for he had been working as a civil servant in a private firm which had let itself out to the government, and after the civil service had dismissed him this firm continued to employ him at a higher salary. But soon the firm ran into difficulties and closed down.

The Rosenbergs then went too impetuously into business. The Pitt Machine Products Corporation was the American equivalent of a small factory in Hornsey or Wandsworth, with six or seven thousand pounds behind it. Half this capital was supplied by a silent partner found by Julius Rosenberg. The other half was supplied by older relatives. It was arranged that David and an-other brother, Bernard, who were both skilled machinists, should work the machine shop and manage it, while Julius was the sales manager. All three were to draw equal pay. The business was a failure, as such factories in Hornsey and Wandsworth often have been. There was bickering. Rosenberg ascribed the failure to his brothers-in-law's slipshod management; they blamed his inexpe-rience as a salesman. By 1949 the till was empty. Bernard and David had to seek employment elsewhere, having lost their sav-ings and being burdened with the obligation to repay the loans made by the Greenglass relatives. This was felt as a special hard-ship by David, for the loan had been negotiated while he was still in the Army, without his consent. He had also felt forced to fall in with the plan, as Rosenberg was pressing him as an alternative to take a civilian job at Los Alamos and continue in his espionage.

He was also distressed by the condition of his wife. She had read of the trial of Nunn May and was terrified of the punish-ment that might be inflicted on her husband and herself. She had had a miscarriage which had injured her general health, and though she had a child of two she now had to go out to work but could not earn enough to pay a proper child's nurse. She then became pregnant again, and during her pregnancy sustained in an accident some severe burns which had not healed when she gave birth to her second child. She had just returned from hospital when Julius Rosenberg visited her. He had already arranged for the escape of other Communist agents, notably of Morris Cohen, a teacher of Russian origin, a man of great charm, and his wife, a handsome and gifted woman of Polish origin. Rosenberg showed Ruth Greenglass a copy of the *New York Herald Tribune* reporting the arrest of Harry Gold. He explained that this was the agent who had visited them at Albuquerque, and told her that she and her husband must flee the country.

Ruth said, "We can't go anywhere. We have a ten-day-old infant." Rosenberg replied, "Your babies won't die. Babies are born on the ocean and in trains every day. My doctor says that if you take enough canned milk and boil the water the baby will be all right." He then gave them $1000 and directed them to go with their children to Mexico City, where if they performed some conspiratorial mumbo-jumbo in front of the statue of Columbus in the big square there, a stranger would send them on to Sweden, where if they performed some more conspiratorial mumbo-jumbo in front of the statue of the great botanist Linnaeus there, another stranger would send them to Czechoslovakia. The Greenglasses gave in to the extent of having their passport photographs taken. Then they decided they could not go on. They used the dollars in paying off their debts. Ruth was now ill again, for her burns had become septic.

Presently Rosenberg brought them a further sum of $4000 and repeated his instructions for their journey. The Greenglasses simply gave the money to a relative to keep in a safe place, and when Rosenberg came back in a few days they found the strength to resist the man who had been the architect of their ruin during the last five years, and told him that they were going to stay where they were and face the inevitable judgment. Eleven days later the FBI arrested David Greenglass, and though what he had to do must appear forever horrible, it must be remembered that he had to choose between his sister and his wife, and he chose his wife, in circumstances when he must have felt a special tenderness for her. His suffering must have been increased by the protracted sufferings of Julius and Ethel Rosenberg, which disturbed the whole world. The death sentence was passed on them in 1951, but they were not sent to the electric chair till 1953. Even though this delay was caused by exercise of rights to appeal, it added to the ordeal of capital punishment, an act as discreditable to our civilization as the crime it punished. In the eyes of many, they met death as heroes.

5

F U C H S had reported to Gold at Sante Fe in 1945 that though British and American scientists had been as brothers in the early war years, there were by that time frequent signs of coldness. Not long after that there was a further fall of temperature when Alan Nunn May was brought to trial, and when Fuchs himself was detected five years later the air became icy. The United States forgot its own failures over Harry Gold and the Greenglasses and the Rosenbergs; and it preferred to remember that it had given Alan Nunn May and Fuchs very handsome access to American laboratories and classified material, because the British authorities had given them clearance which should have been withheld. Such sour feeling between the Western Allies was something the Soviet Union rejoiced to see; and it was still more pleased when, five months after Fuchs had been convicted at the Old Bailey, a physicist named Bruno Pontecorvo, Italian by birth but, like Fuchs, a naturalized British subject, left the British atomic-energy project at Harwell in suspicious circumstances. When his disappearance became known, it was learned that he was a Communist of many years' standing and the strongest ties.

Now, this did not raise much panic on the score of what he might have told the Russians. Pontecorvo's communism probably did not mean much to him, and it seems unlikely that he would ever have risked more in its service than he needed. He was attractive and exuberant, thirty-seven years of age and his great gifts did nothing to sober him and take away his delight in cocktail parties and mild flirtations, in his happy family life with his Swedish wife and three little sons, in tennis-playing and swimming, and in the pursuit of professorships at the instigation of a cheerful and unjaundiced ambition. It is probable that he joined the Communist Party for the same reasons as many another middle-class Italian of his day, because it professed to be the farthest extreme from fascism and because it looked after its own kind as tenderly as the Mafia or Tammany Hall and could be of great assistance to a young man in his professional life. In 1936, when Pontecorvo was twenty-three, he left Italy for France, where he worked till the Germans came in 1940, for the most part in the laboratory of the Communist scientist Professor Frédéric Joliot-Curie. There he must certainly have derived considerable advantage from his party connections, for in Joliot-Curie's orbit communism meant jobs for the boys, but the later years which he spent in the United States, Canada, and England could have been filled full by his brilliant talent and his gusto, without any political aid. If the party made demands on Pontecorvo, presumably he satisfied them. The chances are that he gave no overweight.

What shocked the British and American public when Pontecorvo went at that moment was not the thought of what he might have given away in secrets even had he been a fanatic. This was not an urgent consideration. The war was over, and what Fuchs and Alan Nunn May had not given the Soviet Union would by now have been independently deduced by Russian scientists. Nor was it the thought that the Soviet Union would thereafter be able to use his fine mind; he was getting to the age when many physicists lose their power of original thought, and in any case there are so many gifted scientists in the Soviet Union that one more makes no matter. What was distressing was the light the case threw on British security work.

Pontecorvo had left France in 1940 to go to the United States, where he worked for a private company on problems connected with the location of oil deposits by radiographic means; and then in 1943 he was invited by the British government to work on its atomic-energy project, at first in New York and then in Canada, at the heavy-water pile at Chalk River, at the same time as Alan Nunn May. In 1946 he took a position with the British Ministry of Supply atomic-energy organization, but it kept him in Canada until 1949. In 1948 he applied for British nationality and was granted it. In January 1949 he moved to Harwell as a senior principal scientific officer. This means that Pontecorvo was five times screened by British security organizations: three times after the Gouzenko revelations, twice after the conviction of Alan Nunn May. Yet apparently it was news to the chief security officer at Harwell when Pontecorvo went to him in February 1950, when the Fuchs trial was pending and told him he had a brother in Italy who was a Communist. This was indeed an extraordinary state of affairs. Pontecorvo was speaking of his brother Gilberto, who had been a Communist by 1939 and had played a conspicuous part as a politician and journalist in the party's service ever since. Moreover, that was not the only member of the family who was Communist. There were two other connections who were far more important. His older sister, Signora Giuliana Tabet, who was herself not a Communist, was a key worker in the party of that left-wing politician of indeterminate position, Signor Nenni; she was, to use the word applied to those British Members of Parliament who in the spring of 1948 consorted with this borderland figure, a Nenni-goat. But her husband, Signor Duccio Tabet, was an open Communist, an agricultural scientist who worked on the party staff. And Pontecorvo's cousin, Emilio Sereni, was one of the best-known Communists in Italy. He was a member of the Central Committee of the Italian party and from 1948 had been one of the 131 Communist deputies in the Italian Chamber of Deputies.

It does not need to be argued that this is far from being the ideal background for a senior principal scientific officer at Harwell, and the only point at issue is whether the British security organizations should have known of that background. The answer is that they should certainly have known of it. An apologist writing under instructions from the Atomic Energy Division of the Ministry of Supply naïvely stated that, "not having possession of a private army of investigators, British security was in no position to send men running all over Europe to check up on the family histories of every scientist employed by the government." But British security has a public army of investigators, and to check up on the family history of Pontecorvo they would not have had too run all over Europe but to spend a morning and a few shillings on taxi fares. Bruno Pontecorvo was born in Pisa.

British security had only to find somebody who knew Pisa to learn all about the political connections of the Pontecorvos. Pisa is a town about the size of Dover, and Pontecorvo's father was a prosperous textile manufacturer, and everybody took a friendly interest in the family's affairs. Once his connection with Gilberto Pontecorvo and Emilio Sereni was established, the problem could not have been simpler. There were many newspaper correspondents, students of foreign politics such as can be found at the Royal Institute of International Affairs, and government researchers who knew all about these people. At times when Pontecorvo was screened for naturalization and for Harwell, Emilio Sereni had occupied the not inconspicuous posts of Minister of Postwar Assistance and Minister of Public Works. It is hard to avoid the suspicion that someone in security knew the truth, and the whole truth, about Pontecorvo, and decided to ignore it.

If this should sound like a lament over an unachieved persecution, let it be remembered that had Pontecorvo been rejected by our security organizations he would have suffered no hardship whatsoever. If he had not been given British nationality, he would have remained an Italian citizen, which was no hardship after the war; and had he been excluded from government service in Great Britain or America, he would not have begged his bread from door to door. On the contrary, he probably would have secured a better-paid and more congenial position in a university or industrial organization. He had, indeed, accepted a professorship at Liverpool University when he disappeared. It must also be remembered that when a security officer rejects a Communist for government service in a sensitive area the most relieved person must be the Communist, unless he is an insane fanatic. He may even have been forced to present himself for this employment against his own natural inclinations; and it seems most improbable that the natural inclination of the gay and sociable Pontecorvo led him along any road which seemed likely to end at the Old Bailey.

It is even probable that he had no desire to take the other road which he was forced to follow at the beginning of September 1950. He and his wife and their three little children left Harwell on July 25 in their car for a camping holiday. He was due to return some time before the opening of a conference at

Harwell on September 7; he was not to take up his professorship at Liverpool until the new year. The Pontecorvos finally settled down on the coast between the Lido di Roma and Naples and appear to have seen something of their Communist relatives. On August 27 they turned back to Rome, which was natural enough. The children were aged twelve, six, and five and presumably could not travel too far in a day; and this left little enough spare time if Pontecorvo was to be at work before the opening of the conference. But they stayed on in Rome for five nights, though, it is said, they had to stay with relatives in conditions of considerable discomfort; and on the second day they went to the booking office of the Scandinavian Airways system and booked tickets for the whole family to fly to Copenhagen by an early-morning plane on September 1 and go on to Stockholm by the night train. The fare was $620, that is, £220. The Pontecorvos were at the end of their holiday, and the holiday allowance they could have exported at that date amounted to £205 in all. At Stockholm Mrs. Pontecorvo did not try to see her parents, though they lived in the neighbourhood of the airline ticket office where they took tickets for Helsinki in Finland. At Helsinki airport the Pontecorvos disappeared. They got into a private car and were seen no more, though in March 1955 it was definitely ascertained that Pontecorvo was in the Soviet Union. *Pravda* announced that he was a Soviet citizen and had been secretly awarded a Stalin Prize the year before; and he made a personal appearance with his passport at a press conference.

There is only one fact that can be deduced from this story. It is impossible to gather whether Pontecorvo had in fact acted as a spy and had at any time handed over to the Soviet Union any secrets he had learned in the United States or in Canada or in Great Britain, or whether he had known when he left England that he was not going to return. But it is quite evident that his flight was planned to attract as much attention as possible. Had he been either a law-abiding citizen or a Soviet agent, there was a simple way by which he could have left England and gone to the Soviet Union without getting a line in the newspapers or even causing gossip among his colleagues. He had only to go to Liverpool University at the new year, teach for a term, complain during that term that he or his wife or children were suffering from ill health, send in his resignation to the university authori-

ties, return to Italy, refrain from taking another academic position, and after a suitable period of quiescence take a plane to
Berlin or Vienna and slip behind the Iron Curtain. Nobody
could have stopped him from leaving the country, and the departure of a scientist who had been working, not at Harwell, but at
Liverpool University, would not have pricked the curiosity of
the newspapers. Even if there had eventually been gossip among
his colleagues, it would have been an extremely difficult task for
the most enterprising newspaper to trace a man of Italian birth
who had returned to Italy and was living as a private individual
and might have moved to any other country in the world, considering that there would be nothing against him definite
enough to justify the raising of a hue and cry. It is true, of
course, that this way of getting out of England without scandal
would have taken some time; Pontecorvo could not have hoped
to arrive in Russia before Easter 1951. But if the Soviet Union
was in a hurry for his services he could at least have written to
the authorities at Harwell, sending them his resignation and
announcing his intention to go to the Soviet Union. This letter
would have been sent to the head of the Atomic Energy Division
of the Ministry of Supply, who would have forwarded it to the
Minister of Supply, who was then Mr. Duncan Sandys. It would
then have had to be decided whether the contents of the letter
should be made public or not. The chances were, for reasons
well known to the Soviet Union, that the letter would not have
been published.

But instead of sending any such letter to the authorities at
Harwell, Pontecorvo wrote a postcard to a colleague there, informing him that he had been delayed by an accident to his car
and that he would not return till the actual first day of the
conference. This was written on August 31, when Pontecorvo
had made all plans to start on his journey to Russia on the
following morning, but it was couched in very convincing terms.
That postcard made it quite certain that Pontecorvo's failure to
appear at the conference would cause gossip at Harwell; and as
the weeks went by and nothing was seen of him, a sense of
mystery grew. It was by now exactly six months since Fuchs had
been convicted. Security must have had some idea of what had
happened, but that idea could not be clear-cut. That postcard
must have weighed with the security officers as well as Ponte-

corvo's colleagues, for reasons which are quite respectable. They had some cause to suspect that Pontecorvo might be detained in Italy against his will. It seemed probable that he had really wanted to take up the professorship at Liverpool, and he knew that security would leave him alone if he behaved himself. There was a good reason why he should want to stay in England, and still better reason why he should want to stay outside the Soviet Union. In 1935 there had appeared in the *Proceedings of the Royal Society of London* an article which was at once to become famous, entitled "Artificial Radioactivity Produced by Neutron Bombardment," and it was signed by six Italian physicists, Amaldi, D'Agostino, Fermi, Raetti, Segré, and Pontecorvo. In 1940 these scientists were awarded a patent relating to the results of their work which bears the title, "Process for the Production of Radioactive Substances." After the war the six holders of this patent laid claim against the United States government for ten million dollars' compensation for use of this process during and after the war. The case was still undecided when Pontecorvo left England. The hopes of the scientists were inflated but not in vain; the case was in fact decided in 1953 and the scientists were awarded the sum of $60,000 apiece. Pontecorvo was a happy spendthrift, and it seems unlikely that he would have chosen to go to the Soviet Union just when such a glorious opportunity for enjoying the luxuries of the Western world was gilding his future.

The security authorities may therefore have had some doubts as to the likelihood of Pontecorvo's defection, and certainly no English newspaper would have cared to commit itself. But on October 20, 1950, every newspaper in Rome, excepting only the Communist organs, carried huge headlines telling of the disappearance of Bruno Pontecorvo and the efforts which the British government was making to find him. Either the British government had asked the Italian police to find out what it could about Pontecorvo, and the Italian police had talked to the press; or else the Soviet Union, tired of waiting for the fuss to start in Great Britain, had itself tipped off the non-Communist press, while holding back any confirmation in its own press out of a shrewd suspicion that if the mystery was left unresolved the hubbub would continue all the longer. The English public found it hard to digest the news that Pontecorvo had been at

Chalk River with Nunn May and at Harwell with Fuchs; and the government spokesman who answered questions in the Houses of Parliament on several occasions had nothing to say which could disguise the huge and ridiculous proportions of the failure in security which had permitted Pontecorvo's employment or naturalization.

In the United States comment was unfavourable and prolix. It was also sometimes unfair. Four days after the Italian newspapers had revealed the disappearance of Pontecorvo, Mr. Gordon Dean, then Chairman of the United States Atomic Energy Commission, held a press conference at which he said that he believed "the record will show that he came over here with a British team during the war" and that "the process then was for the British to certify that he was a reliable man, or words to that effect, and could be used in the program." Mr. Gordon Dean had been misled. Pontecorvo's only tie with England when he went to the United States was that he had spent a week's holiday there five years before. He went to the United States under his own steam in 1940 and filed first papers for United States naturalization in 1941, two years before he was invited to become a member of the joint Anglo-Canadian research team, and the British extended this invitation to various scientists working in the United States atomic-energy project who were then or afterwards American citizens. It is to be remarked that the process of his United States naturalization, which is supposed to be subject to drastic inquiries into character and affiliations, went forward without a hitch, and the only reason that it was never completed was the failure of Pontecorvo to take the final steps. The British might well have taken this as a guarantee that Pontecorvo was a blameless character. No marks can be given Mr. Dean. All faces should have been red.

The British people looked at their government and their security organizations with distrust. The American people looked at the British people and their government and their security organizations with distrust. The Canadian security organizations looked at both the American and the British security organizations with distrust, which was embittered by certain past experiences. Alan Nunn May and several members of the atom spy ring revealed by Gouzenko had reached Canada only through British clearance; and when a branch of British security had visited Canada during the war to recruit Yugoslav Communists to drop in Yugoslavia as supporters of Tito, the Canadian authorities, knowing these men to be profoundly anti-British and anti-American and having had to restrain their pro-Nazi activities during the time of the Stalin-Hitler pact, rightly regarded these proceedings as idiotic. It was also unfortunately true that when Canadian Communists got into trouble with the authorities they were apt to slip over the border into the United States and get lost—as Sam Carr, the Communist leader involved in the atom spy ring, did for nearly four years—and that the American security organizations suspected of Soviet associations a distinguished Canadian civil servant and even more distinguished Canadian politician, whom the Canadian security officers thought to be innocent. In such matters as this a government must to some considerable degree depend on reports from its security organizations.

Consider the Prime Minister of Great Britain, the President of the United States, the Premier of Canada, all scanning reports sent in by security organizations which were on the defensive and had long been exasperated by their counterparts in other countries. Consider also that the Prime Minister of Great Britain, Mr. Attlee, had the most urgent reason for wishing atomic-energy security to be watertight, since he was producing the atom bomb while allowing his supporters to attack Winston Churchill as a monster because he had helped produce the atom bomb in wartime. Consider also that in the United States the Democratic Party, with Truman halfway through his last term as President, would wonder very much if it was safe to continue the firm alliance with Britain as part of his programme, particularly as it could not tell how many more Soviet agents might detach themselves from British laboratories; and consider also that Canada might wonder what had come over the mother country, and that some doubt might cause even greater discomfort in Australia, which had let itself in for a close cooperation with Great Britain on experiments with nuclear weapons, and which was from year to year more fiercely threatened by the Communist transformation of Asia.

It is doubtful whether Pontecorvo could have transmitted a scientific secret which would have enabled the Soviet Union to do the damage to its enemies which, without danger to itself and

at a trifling expense, it inflicted by making him take that spectacular flight from Rome to Russia.

6

THE flight of Bruno Pontecorvo was a perfectly
planned and perfectly executed manœuvre designed to destroy
American confidence in British security organizations so far as
their power to protect their atomic projects was concerned. Now
there was to be an attack on American confidence in British
security organizations so far as their power to protect their diplomacy was concerned.

Pontecorvo left Rome on September 1, 1950, and the news of
his departure was published on October 20. On May 25, 1951,
Donald Maclean, a counsellor in the senior branch of the Foreign Service and head of the American Department in the Foreign Office, and Guy Burgess, a second secretary in the junior
branch of the Foreign Service, left the United Kingdom from
Southampton on the boat for Saint Malo. They fled because
Maclean, who had been a Soviet agent for a very long time,
probably ever since he entered the Foreign Service in 1935, had
just been informed, probably by several persons, including another person in the employment of the Foreign Office named
Philby, that he had been detected and was under surveillance by
security; and Burgess, who also was a Soviet agent of long standing, though it is not established that his activities were ever
illegal, though they were certainly repulsive, had thought it
prudent to accompany him, for reasons not yet quite clear.

They left at very short notice indeed. Burgess had been appointed second secretary at the British embassy at Washington in
August 1950 and after a series of disasters had been sent back to
Europe and had arrived at Southampton on board the *Queen
Mary* on May 7, 1951. On board he met a young American
student named Miller and arranged to go with him for a holiday
in France, starting on May 25 and leaving by the cross-Channel
steamer *Falaise*, which sails from Southampton for Saint-Malo at

midnight. When that day arrived, he spent some of the morning with Miller and in the early afternoon hired an Austin car from a motor firm in Crawford Street, Marylebone, and drove it away, undertaking to return it on June 4. Afterwards he did some shopping and bought a suitcase and a mackintosh, and then saw Miller again and left him with the promise that he would call for him at half past seven. Then he went to the Reform Club, where he asked, oddly enough, for a road map for the North of England. Later he drove down to Tatsfield, a village in Surrey, near the Kent border, not far from Westerham, and he went to the house were Donald Maclean was living with his wife, an American, who was expecting a child in three weeks, and their two little boys.

Maclean had spent a day which was not less clear of any indication of the unusual. It was his birthday, and he had lunched with two old friends, a husband and wife, and had arranged to stay with them while his wife had her baby. He then went to the Traveller's Club and cashed a cheque for five pounds, returned to his desk at the Foreign Office, and in the early evening travelled down to his home at Tatsfield by train. It was Mrs. Maclean's story that she did not know Burgess and that her husband introduced him as an office colleague named Roger Stiles, and according to Mrs. Maclean her husband and Burgess left the house at nine o'clock and drove off in the hired Austin to Southampton. They arrived there just in time to get on the *Falaise* three minutes before it sailed, leaving the car on the quayside, which attracted some attention. It was the impression of one passenger that they were greeted by a man on board in the morning, and that the same man accompanied them ashore when, in a drenching downpour, they went down the gangway and got into a taxi. It apparently escaped the notice of all three that Burgess had left his luggage behind him on the ship. Then Burgess and Maclean, now without a companion, hailed a taxi in Saint-Malo and directed the driver to get them to Rennes in time to catch the 1:18 train to Paris. This cost them five pounds, although there were two trains from Saint-Malo which would have taken them to Paris by way of Rennes for the sum of thirty-six shillings. At one o'clock they got out of the taxi outside the Hôtel du Guesclin at Rennes. This hotel is situated close to the station, and not in the centre of the town, but nobody saw them taking a train. From that moment they vanished. It is now known that they then made their way to the Soviet Union by Switzerland and Czechoslavakia. But then and for four years afterwards the Foreign Office said it had no idea where they had gone, and it disclaimed any knowledge that they had been Soviet agents.

Now, this can hardly be described as a flight. It was more like a paperchase, the same sort of paperchase indulged in by Pontecorvo. However hurried Burgess might have been, he could have sent a message to Miller to say that he could not travel with him that night. But Miller was left in a state of bewilderment, to talk and spread the news of a mystery, to answer the questions of the police with the candour of distress. Burgess had a car of his own, and he could easily have got a friend or hired a chauffeur to drive him and Maclean down to Southampton and take it back to the garage. But he hired a car and abandoned it on the quayside, where it was bound to be traced back to the firm from which he had hired it in his own name. He must have arrived at the Maclean household between half past six and seven o'clock. We are told, though there is only Mrs. Maclean's word for it, that her husband and Burgess did not leave the house until nine o'clock. Why did the two men, who were under such a supremely urgent necessity to catch the boat, leave only three hours to cover the hundred miles that lie between Tatsfield and Southampton? If they had wanted to go quietly on board with the other passengers, they would have started earlier. One must suspect that probably they did start earlier and drive round until they could make a last-minute arrival which was bound to leave a lasting impression on the onlookers. When Burgess left his luggage on the *Falaise* he left irrefutable evidence that not only was it he who had hired the car that was to be found on the dockside, it was he who had abandoned it, and it was he who had gone to France. His new suitcase could be identified by the police far more easily than an old suitcase. To travel by taxi to Rennes rather than by rail was to give one last glaring clue to their pursuers.

It must also be realized that there was no reason why these two men should have left Great Britain at all. There was no evidence whatever that Burgess had committed any acts which brought him within the scope of the law in so far as it relates to loyalty. Mac-

lean had been under suspicion for about six weeks prior to his
disappearance, since mid-April. It was stated four years later,
when the government at last adopted a more or less candid attitude to the affair, that in 1949 British security had learned that
certain information had been transmitted to the Soviet Union,
and that at first there were six thousand persons who lay under
suspicion of guilt. This was an odd statement, because it is difficult to understand how the duties of six thousand persons could so
overlap that they were all in possession of information of such a
special nature that it was a matter of grave concern when it was
handed on to the Soviet Union. Even if there were six separate
pieces of information, this works out at a thousand civil servants
per secret, which seems a large allowance. However, the statement was made in good faith, and no doubt there is some meaning to it. As the result of two years' steady investigation, it was
concluded that Maclean was probably the principal agent of a
group of two or three. (This implies that the security organization must have cleared people at a steady rate of fifty-eight a
week, which surely means that the case against most of them
must have been so easily refuted that they could hardly rank as
suspects at all.)

But no evidence was discovered which would have justified his
prosecution under the Official Secrets Act. The security officers in
charge of his case had therefore resolved to question him
directly. Mr. Herbert Morrison, then the Foreign Secretary, sanc-
tioned this proceeding on May 25, the same day on which Burgess and Maclean left the United Kingdom. This has caused
some people to form a picture of Maclean and Burgess as having
learned of Mr. Morrison's action and making a precipitate decision to take flight. It must be realized that the security officers
would have debated whether to ask Mr. Morrison for this permission for some days before they interviewed him, and that a
refusal by Mr. Morrison would be most unlikely. Anybody who
was in a position to warn Maclean of Mr. Morrison's action
would almost certainly be in a position to warn him of the
debates which led up to that action. It is to be noted that Burgess booked the two-berth cabin on the *Falaise* on May 23, and it
would be a simple soul who thought that he had ever designed
to share it with poor Mr. Miller.

When Maclean received whatever warning he was given, he

had (like Pontecorvo) only to take one simple step, if he and the Soviet Union wished the matter to pass off quietly. He could have resigned his post in the Foreign Office and he could have refused to make a statement to the police or to anybody else. He must have known that the desire of the security officers to question him meant either that they had not sufficient evidence to prosecute or that they wanted to stave off a prosecution. For the rest of his life he would have been subject to a gentle though unrelenting form of surveillance, and that would have been all. His friends need have suspected nothing, for there were, as was to be made abundantly clear, good reasons, quite unconnected with the ideologies, why there would have been nothing surprising in a divorce between him and the Foreign Office.

If Maclean had small need to leave the country, Guy Burgess had none at all. The Foreign Office was most anxious that he should resign, and even considered ways and means of forcing his resignation if he should be difficult, but this was not because of any suspicion that he was a Soviet agent. It was on account of personal misbehaviour in the United States. The Virginia police had arrested him three times in one day for motoring offences of a dangerous nature. On the third occasion his car had been involved in an accident, and the police had found that he had surrendered the wheel to a man whom he had picked up by the roadside, who had no driving licence and was a homosexual with a police record. There was no reason why Burgess should not have settled down happily in his flat in New Bond Street.

But let us suppose that they both found themselves unequal to the strain of carrying on the perpetual exercise of great and small deceptions which make up the life of a foreign agent. They still could have managed their flight so discreetly that there need have been no scandal. Even though the first stage of their journey had been indiscreetly patent, they still could have killed comment if they had paused in their flight and posted in France letters giving the Foreign Office their resignations and announcing to their families that they proposed to spend a long holiday together on the Continent. Had they written such letters, not one line suggesting that they were Soviet agents could have been printed in any newspaper. In the unlikely event that any rumour of the two men's Communist activities had reached a newspaper office, press investigation would have led straight to the well-established facts that both had been in trouble at the Foreign Office for drunkenness, and that they had homosexual habits which would make it quite comprehensible that they should decide to spend a holiday on the Continent together or seek refuge there from Scotland Yard.

There was no need to account for their flight by communism, and any newspaper would find it advisable not to mention that as a probable cause, for it would be very irritating if a couple of homosexuals, bronzed and fit after a Continental holiday, were able to win enormous damages because an ideological motive had been wrongly ascribed to their expedition. Had Burgess and Maclean written those letters, had newspaper curiosity been diverted and allayed, the two might have quietly passed into oblivion. Others have faded away, nobody now can remember quite how or when. But Burgess and Maclean did not take time off to write those letters; they left a mystery behind them which became a stinking fog. The Foreign Office did not announce the departure of the two men, and this might have been a wise policy if it had stuck to it quite inflexibly; considering that the exit had been planned to get the missing men on the front page, it would have been a wise step to keep them off it by pretending that both men had resigned and that their departure might be a matter of moment to their families but left Whitehall cold. But unfortunately the Foreign Office did not remain inactive. It took an astonishing step. It asked the French police to find Burgess and Maclean for it.

This was in itself an idiotic request, for the Foreign Office knew that Maclean was a Soviet agent who had fled because he was threatened with detection and was therefore either safe behind the Iron Curtain or enjoying almost as comfortable invulnerability in France, since he had committed no extraditable offence. But it was idiotic for another reason. A secret that really is a secret may be safe at Scotland Yard or in the hands of the FBI. But there are European police forces which see no reason why they should seal their lips regarding matters of no importance to the governments of their own countries, and so, if news comes their way which relates to another country, transmit them to any foreign journalists who seem interested. At the beginning of June, Mr. Larry Solon, the chief Paris correspondent of the *Daily Express*, discovered that the French police had been asked by the British police to look for two members of the British Foreign Office who had disappeared in France. It is odd that this request of the Foreign Office seems to have reached the French police a week after the departure of the two men, by which time they would be bound either to have left France or to have taken effective means to conceal themselves.

On June 6 Mr. Solon had identified the two men who were missing and confirmed the story, and he telephoned the news to the London office of the *Daily Express* that night. It was published the next morning. Late that night Maclean's wife and his mother, Lady Maclean, received telegrams from him which had been handed in at a Paris post office. They were certainly from him: the one addressed to his mother was signed by a nickname. But they had certainly not been written by him: the word "leave" was misspelled, Mrs. Maclean was addressed as Mrs. Maclean Melinda, the number seven had a stroke through it in the Continental fashion. They were quite uninformative and added to the mystery rather than explained it. So too did a telegram handed in at Rome, which was signed by Burgess and addressed to his mother, and announced that he was "embarking on long Mediterranean holiday." These telegrams performed the same confusing and stimulating function as the postcard Pontecorvo sent to Harwell from Rome the night before he started on his journey to the Soviet Union.

Meanwhile the press was working on the story, and month by month facts were established which gave a highly disagreeable picture. It seemed that the system of selecting personnel for the Foreign Office had fallen into a state of chaos, and that our principal security organizations had been operating with an inefficiency which it had to be hoped was only that. It hardly mattered why Maclean and Burgess had suddenly fled from the Foreign Office, it was so grave a scandal that they should ever have been there at all. At last what had long been known in certain circles in London and Washington and New York was learned by the whole world.

Maclean should have left the Foreign Service long before. By 1940, when he was twenty-seven, he was known as an intermittent alcoholic. He was sent to Washington in 1944 and stayed there four years, and during that period he was considered, even by American standards, a heavy drinker. He was appointed counsellor to the British Embassy in Cairo in November 1948, and there his misbehaviour became more and more shocking. One evening in March 1950 he and his wife organized a felucca party on the Nile, during which he became dangerously drunk, seized his wife by her throat and tried to strangle her, had a wrestling match with an armed night-watchman and took his loaded rifle from him, and then fought an English diplomat who tried to get the weapon from him and broke the poor man's leg. Two months later he and a friend went on a stupid drunken prowl round Cairo, which lasted twenty-four hours. At one point they went in search of drink to the flat of a girl who worked as a librarian in the American embassy, and, finding that she was out, broke into the flat, took what drink they could find, smashed the girl's bath by throwing a radiator slab on it, broke some furniture, and dropped some of her clothes into the toilet bowl. Not unnaturally the news of this exploit enraged the American ambassador, who cannot have been pleased on hearing six months later that Maclean, who had passed the intervening period on sick leave in the care of a psychiatrist, had been appointed head of the American Department.

It is very difficult for an English person to believe that the official who made this appointment was not deliberately seeking to alienate the American State Department; and it is too much to expect an American to put any agreeable interpretation on it whatsoever. But there was an argument for keeping Maclean in the Foreign Office. His nature would not have been guessed by those who met him casually, for though he was charming he did not invite confidence. He seemed a perpetual adolescent. He was lanky like a lad who has outgrown his strength, and he had the brilliance of skin and eye which usually passes with youth and seems inappropriate in an adult. His gaiety had the feverish quality of overexcited eighteen, and at any moment it might have run up the scale to hysteria. He was a delightful person to sit next at dinner; he was intelligent, his manners were not only good but goodhearted, he was witty, his mind was cultivated. But afterwards doubts would cross his companion's mind. Could he really be the age that he was said to be, or responsible enough for the post he occupied? The answer was that he was a superb administrator.

He was born to be a civil servant; he had the watchmaker's

mind which understands the workings of a complicated machine and is not repelled by complication and feels pride as the shining cogs and wheels perform the process that runs parallel with time. One who should know has said that in all the history of the British embassy at Washington it was probably never so exquisitely efficient, so impeccably organized, as when Maclean was its First Secretary. He belonged to that rare and strange type of alcoholic in whom, when everything else is poisoned, the capacity to work keeps its virgin integrity. He could go out on a debauch which he himself would liken to an alley cat's prowl round the garbage pails, sleep, and then arise and address himself to some problem set his ambassador by Whitehall and collect the relevant information with an inspired competence not to be surpassed by any of his colleagues.

Of course this was not enough. If a man possessed the finest mind ever recognized in diplomacy, it would still be wrong to send him abroad as a representative of the United Kingdom if from time to time he brawled in the streets; and it would still be wrong to employ him at home or abroad if from time to time he became so demented by drunkenness that discretion could not be expected of him. It was also true that when he was drunk he engaged in homosexual coquetry and was therefore vulnerable to blackmail.

Certainly Maclean's brilliance afforded some reason why the authorities should have wanted to retain him at the Foreign Office; then they should have reckoned that it was insufficient in view of his other qualities. But there was no reason why Guy Burgess should ever have been employed by the Foreign Office. He too had a good mind, but the counterbalancing disadvantages were so manifest that that should never have weighed for a moment with the authorities. He had, of course, a certain charm, but this was of a special kind. He was thirty-nine when he disappeared, but he still recalled one of the schoolboys in André Gide's *Les Faux Monnayeurs*. He was at once obviously well bred and obviously squalid. He was short and stocky, always grubby, and often drunk. It could be seen that he belonged to the world of the favoured, who have wealth and respect by right of birth; but it was certain that in his time he had wakened up in some very queer rooms. He had many friends. These included some of the most unpleasant English men and women now living, but some were decent people, and some of these tried to justify their liking for him by saying that he was very kind, and no doubt he was. But his charm was of a more troubling sort than can be accounted for by good nature.

Sometimes, in a home for children unhappily not like other children, there is a small boy who always catches the visitor's eye. The brooding darkness of the child's face lights up with such an enchanting smile, his response to strangers is so quick and gay, he has such a quaint turn of phrase. Surely, the visitor says, there cannot be anything very much wrong with this delightful little boy. Well, yes, there is. It unfortunately happens that wherever he goes, fire breaks out. By constant watching it has been established that the only toy he cares for is a box of matches, and up the houses and barns and hayricks go, in crackling flames. That was Burgess's distinguishing mark: the flashing smile of the fire-raiser, full of secret pleasure in mischief and destruction. Even his most loyal friends had no illusion about his favourite toys. Some were affectionate and benevolent people who wanted to help and protect him against this innate viciousness; and some were people who were mischievous and destructive but would not risk their own safety and found a vicarious gratification in his recklessness.

It is the most sinister feature of the Burgess–Maclean episode that Guy Burgess never lacked employment. He came down from Cambridge, where he took a First in History, and did two years of postgraduate research. In 1936 he went to the BBC, where he remained until 1939; he handled a feature called *This Week in Westminster*. After this he moved to the *Times* but stayed there only a month and acquired a curious job which he retained for many years, as financial adviser to Lord Rothschild's Hungarian mother, who met him at a week-end party, was deeply impressed by him, and paid him £1200 a year to scrutinize her investment list. He was then given a position in MI6, one of the three principal security organizations in the United Kingdom, which is controlled by the Foreign Office. By this time Burgess was well known as a drunkard and a homosexual, and also as a Communist, though here the issue was slightly confused. He had been up at Cambridge at the same time as Maclean, and they had both belonged to the same study circle, and when Burgess came to London he had made no secret of his Communist faith. But in

1934 he went to Moscow in the company of a well-known Oxford member of the Communist Party and student of Marxism,
Derek Blaikie, who was afterwards to die in the war. He returned professing deep disappointment and pretended to have
left the party. For a period during the late thirties he professed
to be a member of some British Fascist organization and to have
taken part in a Nuremberg rally. Actually he had been instructed by the Communist Party to infiltrate the British Fascist
movement, in company with a wealthy young man mentioned
earlier in this book. But at the time he professed sincere conversion to the Fascist faith.

The security officer who screened him for MI6 presumably
found out that he was not a Fascist; for we were fighting the
Nazis, and here was a young man who, on his own telling, had
only recently been hobnobbing with Hitler. But if the security
officers found out that he was not a Fascist, presumably they
found out that he was a Communist; and this was a time when
the Stalin-Hitler pact was still in force and the British Communist Party was doing everything it could to aid the Germans and
defeat its own country. But either the security officers ignored his
communism, or their reports were ignored on a higher level.
Burgess was accepted, and he was given a post in an offshoot
called the Special Operations Executive. This was a cloak-and-
dagger body which dealt with sabotage in invaded territories and
the dropping of agents by parachute. It dealt with secrets which
had to be kept if the lives of our own men and our allies were
not to be thrown away.

In 1940 Burgess was charged at Marlborough Street with being
under the influence of drink while driving a War Office car. His
solicitor pleaded that he had just been in an air raid and had
been working fourteen hours a day "at rather confidential
work" which necessitated travelling to a station thirty miles out
of London. The magistrate dismissed the case on payment of
costs, and MI6 continued to employ him. Ostensibly he had left
it in 1941 to take up a position in the European propaganda
department, but he was still involved with cloak-and-dagger organizations. He was at one time entrusted with the business of
removing anti-Russian bias from Poles whom the British were
training for sabotage. It is not easy to exaggerate the blackness of

the mark that this appointment leaves against the security officers who passed him for this work.

Let us consider the situation: a large number of Polish patriots risked their lives to get out of Poland and make their way to Great Britain, in order to be instructed in the art of guerrilla warfare and then return to their own country and fight the Germans. Many of our airmen risked their lives to transport these men. These patriots were for the most part pious Roman Catholics, and they hated Russia because the Tsarist Russians had stolen their country and oppressed them in the past, and they suspected, with what turned out to be good sense, that the bolshevik Russians wanted to do the same thing in the future; and they brought to heterosexuality an enthusiasm which was sometimes excessive. Once in Great Britain, they submitted to military instruction with fervour and industry; but they were also considered as subjects for political instruction, which meant that they were handed over to Mr. Burgess, who was obviously not a soldier, obviously a Communist, and obviously homosexual. The situation was not tolerable. Let us imagine that Germany had invaded Great Britain in the Second World War, and a number of Englishmen of a conventional type escaped to the United States in order to be trained and brought back as guerrilla fighters, and they were told by the Americans that they must submit to political instruction involving reconstruction of their fundamental beliefs, and they were handed over for that purpose to an eccentric American, obviously not a soldier, obviously a Communist, and obviously a homosexual. The vast majority would have objected. But there was another objectionable feature of Burgess's employment in this field. Already it was becoming plain that the Communists among the exiles were compiling dossiers of their anti-Communist compatriots, and no intelligent onlooker could think that their intention was to make life easier for these anti-Communists. To put a known English Communist in a position where he would inevitably provoke anti-Communist exiles to express their opinions was to take a murderous risk.

In 1944 the Foreign Office put Burgess into its news department. This was at the period of the Greek struggle against communism, when there was such an evident attempt to distort the

news that every effort should have been made to preserve its
purity at one of the most important sources. In 1946 Burgess was
made assistant private secretary to the parliamentary under-secretary to the Foreign Secretary in the Labour government, Mr.
Hector McNeil, who formed a strong personal affection for him.
There was nothing sinister in this. Hector McNeil was a simple-
minded man who had been raised to high office with a speed
bewildering to himself and even more bewildering to others,
owing to the war. In 1941 he was thirty-four, a Glasgow journalist obscure even in his own town, when he was elected to Parliament and was made secretary to Mr. Noel-Baker, who was then
Minister of War Transport; and he was passed through the mill
so quickly that in five years' time he was second in command at
the Foreign Office. It was presumably not Burgess's communism
which recommended him to McNeil, who was vociferously anti-
Communist and orthodox Labour; and there were many reasons
for the friendship. He was intelligent enough to appreciate that
Burgess was an agreeable rattle, framed to lighten the hours of
overwork and relieve the loneliness of the outsider who was a
stranger in London and had had no time to make friends. It is
really hardly bearable to think of their relationship. It was as if
one had discovered a new novel by André Gide and read of a
horrible little Parisian schoolboy advancing on some earnest
provincial as the poor greenhorn carries his suitcase out of the
Gare de Lyon. Hector McNeil should have been protected by the
permanent officials of the Foreign Office.

But when he was made Minister of State in 1946 he was allowed to retain Burgess as his assistant private secretary for two
years. Meanwhile Burgess, who had throughout the years been a
temporary employee in the Foreign Service, appeared before a
Civil Service Commission board and was accepted as a permanent member of the establishment. This was a special concession,
for he was over the prescribed age. In 1948 he was transferred to
the Far Eastern Department, which was then a peculiarly sensitive area because of the differences which were developing between Great Britain and the United States regarding the rise of
Mao Tse-Tung and the fall of Chiang Kai-shek, and the emer-
gence of the Korean War. In 1949 his labours were temporarily
interrupted because, at one of the disorderly parties which he
was in the habit of giving at his flat, he was thrown downstairs

by a guest and had to be removed by an ambulance, suffering from a fractured skull, a broken jaw, and arm injuries.

After that he went for a holiday in Ireland and appeared in the Dublin District Court, charged with driving a car while drunk, but the magistrate, Mr. O'Flynn, was a man of sympathetic character, such as we would all hope to meet in time of trouble, and he described Burgess as "a man of brilliance who appeared to be overwrought" and dismissed the case. Later in the year Burgess went on another holiday and got into another sort of trouble. He went to North Africa and on his own initiative called on any local representatives of security organizations and expressed disapprobation of British policy in general and of the inefficiency of these officials and the bodies to which they belonged. Early in 1950 the security authorities gave the Foreign Office particulars of this jaunt and he was severely reprimanded. But there was such wildness in the offence that, even had it been his first, it would have merited dismissal.

On the contrary, in August of that year he was appointed second secretary at the British embassy at Washington. Maclean's last frenetic years at that establishment had been under the ægis of Lord Inverchapel, one of the most bizarre human beings ever to rise to the rank of ambassador, which is saying a very great deal indeed. But he had gone, not, it is sad to say, owing to punitive official action but because he had reached the retiring age. He had been replaced by Sir Oliver Franks, now Lord Franks of Headington, who had won distinction first in the academic world and then for war service in the Ministry of Supply, and who was a thoroughly civilized person. It is unlikely that Lord Franks would have enjoyed having Burgess as a member of his staff, even had the new arrival not been preceded by a report from a section of Intelligence warning the staff to watch the official who was being sent out to it by the personnel officer of the Foreign Office.

The security staff of the embassy soon realized on which side of this curious conflict in Whitehall opinion the right lay. Burgess was reported for drunkenness, driving offences, brawling argumentativeness at official parties, advertisement of very sordid homosexual adventures, and (twice) for negligence in the custody of confidential papers. It was now twelve years since he was first admitted to the Foreign Service and had started running up this record. At some point towards the end of seven months an incident occurred which is not in itself perhaps very important, if it be coldly scrutinized, but caused some curious results. It is said that he received a startling communication from another member of the staff, Mr. Harold Philby, a temporary first secretary who had been sent to Washington some months before Burgess; they were old friends and Burgess had lived in his home from August 1950 till April 1951. Philby is said to have received from London the secret report of the MI5 inquiry into the leakage of Foreign Office information revealed in 1949, which named Maclean as the principal suspect. He is supposed to have told Burgess of the danger overhanging their friend, and Burgess is supposed to have been the first to break the news to Maclean on his return to England. For that reason Philby has been named the "Third Man" of the Burgess–Maclean affair.

This is one of the most firmly established legends in the arcana of modern espionage, but it is an imprecise version of what must have happened. Mr. Philby was a dyed-in-the-wool Communist and had been so since his Cambridge days. As a young newspaper correspondent he covered the Spanish Civil War (and was decorated by Franco) but took an active part in organizing the Loyalists, and while many of these were not Communists his particular friends were among those who were. Throughout the Second World War he had worked with MI6. At Washington it was one of his tasks to act as liaison officer between British and American Intelligence. A Soviet agent with this experience of undercover work, gained one way and another, would have seen the importance of alerting Maclean at once; and as he must constantly have been reporting on his work in the Washington embassy to Soviet contacts in America, all he had to do was to inform them. They had only to get in touch with the Soviet contacts in England who received the material constantly turned in by Maclean. It is certain that Philby treacherously divulged to Burgess the contents of the report. But it is, on the other hand, probable that he told Burgess that Maclean was on the brink of being discovered and knew it, that he was about to make an escape to the Soviet Union, and that Burgess must accompany him.

Philby, for a mysterious reason, was exonerated by the British authorities; but the sweat poured down their foreheads as they did it. The scandal the Soviet Union had planned was therefore not as vast as they had hoped. But it was spectacular enough. The curiously public disappearance of Pontecorvo had thrown a searchlight on a long-continued failure of the atomic-energy security organization. The curiously public disappearance of Burgess and Maclean appeared to throw a searchlight on two even more disgraceful failures of three other security organizations. On both occasions the United States, forgetting its own failures in this field, visibly experienced doubts as to the wisdom of regarding Great Britain as a reliable ally with a right to share information. Delighted, the Soviet Union kept the pot on the fire to bubble and boil for years afterwards.

A fortnight after the diplomats' departure there had been the equivalent of the Pontecorvo postcard—a Paris telegram from Maclean, a Rome telegram from Burgess. The Maclean one had been handed in, it was related with a splendid melodramatic touch, by a woman "who was heavily made-up." These were followed by other mystifying communications. There is no reason why anybody in the Soviet Union should not send a bank draft to a resident in England, provided the Soviet government gives its consent. Maclean acquired two one-thousand-pound bank drafts by the circuitous method of getting someone to go to Saint Gallen in Switzerland and purchase them under a false name (a transaction about which the Soviet government must have been informed, too) and then had them sent not to his wife but to his mother-in-law, who was living with his wife. Though Swiss banks practise the extreme of secretiveness, news of this transaction leaked to the press. Lord Beaverbrook unearthed and published this information and deserves commendation on this score, for there was no reason why the public should not know this fact and there were many reasons why it should. It was also learned that there is nothing to prevent people in the Soviet Union who wish to write to people in Great Britain from stamping their letters and posting them and chancing their luck with the censorship—which Burgess and Maclean could have done with some confidence. But the two diplomats kept on sending their families letters posted in such places as Reigate and Herne Hill and Poplar.

Mrs. Maclean, who gave birth to a daughter three weeks after her husband's disappearance, continued to live at Tatsfield. She insisted against the will of the Foreign Office on taking her family for a holiday in the South of France that August, but otherwise obeyed the authorities' request that she should remain in England in order that she might help them in their inquiries. This was a strange request, as she had claimed to know nothing about her husband's disappearance except that he had brought Burgess to dinner and then gone off in his company. If the story was true she could not help the Foreign Office; and if it was untrue she did not want to help the Foreign Office; and the latter alternative seemed the more probable, as it would be natural for a Communist's wife to be herself a Communist. She made it no secret that she would have preferred to leave the country, as she was incessantly watched by reporters.

This was indeed the case, though her complaints were exaggerated. She alleged that her children were waylaid and photographed on their way to school, though the photographers could never be identified; and indeed there is a strict rule, agreed on by all the newspaper proprietors, against the molestation of children, which reporters and photographers dare not disregard. But there was certainly an unwinking eye kept on the Tatsfield home and it would have been a matter for regret if it had not been so. The press believed that the Foreign Office was lying when it said that it did not know where the missing diplomats had gone, because by that time a cloud of witnesses had arisen to give testimony that both had been Communists; and the press also believed that Mrs. Maclean was lying when she said that she knew no more than the Foreign Office. In both these beliefs it was right.

On July 15, 1952, Mrs. Maclean announced that she was going to leave England and live in France or Switzerland. Her last act on this soil was to cause a newspaper controversy by denying the authenticity of an interview with a reporter. The balance of evidence suggests that it was genuine, but in any case it was so trivial and so neutral that it was not clear why she considered the matter of importance. Perhaps the important factor was that, thanks to her well-meaning but foolish friends, the newspaper controversy lasted for weeks and was later revived for further use. She eventually settled down in Geneva with her children and her mother, and there she gave it to be understood that she was going to divorce Maclean on the grounds of desertion.

Among her friends were two people who are reputed to be conducting a movement for bringing ex-Communists back into the fold by enlisting them in a bogus Communist Party which claims to be free from Soviet control. She performed various mysterious actions which both the newspapers and the security organizations ignored.

On September 11, 1953, Mrs. Maclean and her three children vanished. There was no reason why she should not have gone to her husband quite openly. If she had driven her family down to the railway station, taken tickets to Vienna, and there passed behind the Iron Curtain, nobody in the world could have stopped her, or, indeed, would have wanted to do so. Instead the Pontecorvo pattern was repeated once more. She told nobody that she was going, not even her mother. She accepted an invitation to a cocktail party which she must have known that she could not attend, and she told her mother that she had met an old friend from Cairo, who in fact did not exist, and had arranged to take the children to spend the week-end with him and his wife at Territet, near Montreux. She knew that she was leaving for good, for she took all her clothes except a mink coat and an evening dress, but she told the mechanic at the garage where she left the car that she was coming back for it in a week's time. Six days later there came the equivalent of the Pontecorvo postcard, the Paris telegram from Maclean, the Rome telegram from Burgess. A woman, not Mrs. Maclean, went to the post office at Territet and handed in a telegram, using the baby's pet name, Pink Rose, as a sign it came from Mrs. Maclean, and a spelling mistake to show it was not Mrs. Maclean who had written it out, and containing a false promise that the boys would be back at school in a week's time.

The required uproar broke out. America was nudged in the ribs and asked if it had forgotten Burgess and Maclean and British inefficiency, at the exact moment when a discussion between America and Great Britain on the sharing of atomic secrets was taking a critical turn. Nor had interest an opportunity to subside. Mrs. Maclean communicated with her mother, Mrs. Dunbar, in a letter which had been posted, whimsically enough, in Cairo; Burgess communicated with his mother in a letter posted, with equal whimsy, in Borough High Street. Later there was published a book about the Macleans, written by a close friend of Mrs. Maclean, with the assistance of her mother, which contained some of the most intimate material ever published about living persons. It was not clear why Mrs. Maclean, who had been represented as a reserved character, had chosen to leave her husband's letters to her and her letters to him behind her in Switzerland along with the mink coat and the evening dress, nor why her mother had chosen to bring them into the light of day, though the effect was sordid.

7

THE press and the public wearied at length of the names of Maclean and Burgess, and the case would have fallen to the back of our minds had it not been for a curious turn and twist in Commonwealth relations. Throughout the years the British government had denied all knowledge that these two men had been Soviet agents. The government was not the same, for in 1951 Labour went out and the Tories came in, but the denials never altered. It is still hard to guess why our ministers persisted in this profitless deception. They cannot have continued to nourish the hope (if, indeed, they ever nourished it) that they could persuade the Russians that they had planted Burgess and Maclean on them as British agents disguised as Communists, for they had made attempts to purge the Foreign Service and security agents of Communist elements such as would hardly follow the planting of two bogus agents on the Soviet Union. Had these attempts been made in order to deceive the Soviet Union, they would have been made to appear vigorous, but that they did not; they were lackadaisical. As it was, the Communists who were thus ejected would certainly report the manner of their ejection to their chiefs. The government cannot have been actuated by a desire to avoid giving the full story with its disquieting conclusion that either our security organizations were corrupt and inefficient or their corrupt and inefficient superiors had ignored their reports, because it did not have to give the full story. A simple statement that the men had been Soviet agents and were behind the Iron Curtain would have involved it in no necessity to make further disclosures. Nevertheless, the government continued to suppress the truth, answering questions in the House with an air which suggested that the questioners were the sort of people who would call napkins serviettes; who were, though Miss Nancy Mitford had not yet popularized the term, non-U. The Tory government had not abandoned this practice in 1954, when an event which it could not have foreseen gave these denials a most inconvenient significance.

In April 1954 Vladimir Petrov, the third secretary at the Soviet embassy at Canberra, who was also head of the Australian branch of the MVD, sought political asylum with the Australian government and was presently joined by his wife Eudocia, who was also an MVD official. This was certainly a genuine defection, but it was almost as catastrophic for their hosts as if it had been a ruse of the Soviet Union. The Liberal Party was in power, and Petrov brought with him papers and information which cast reflections on certain members of the Labour Party, including some persons closely associated with its leader, Dr. Evatt. There followed a political battle of a fury not previously known in that country, nor ever known in ours. Dr. Evatt and his followers alleged that the Petrov papers were forged and Mr. Petrov had been procured to give false evidence in order to discredit the Labour Party at the general election of 1955. During the sittings of the royal commission which investigated the affair Dr. Evatt himself cross-examined witnesses with such heat that his permission to appear was withdrawn from him. The flames spread from the political to the religious field, for the Roman Catholic Church became involved through a strongly Catholic branch of the Labour Party, which now ranged itself against Dr. Evatt. It became necessary for the Liberal government to insist for its own sake on the authenticity of the Petrovs' evidence. It happened that Petrov had stated that he had been told by Kislytsin, the second secretary at the Soviet embassy at Canberra, an MVD man who had previously worked at the Soviet embassy in London, that he had handled many documents supplied by Burgess and knew that those documents had been photographed for transmission to Moscow and then returned to him; and that he had himself handled many documents supplied by Maclean when he worked in Moscow. But if what the British government was saying about Burgess and Maclean was true, then the Petrovs were lying.

There was some interchange between the Australian and the British governments which was apparently based on the assumption that what the British government had been saying was perhaps not true. By now Sir Anthony Eden was Prime Minister, and Mr. Harold Macmillan was Foreign Minister. On September 18, 1955, an article on Burgess and Maclean by Petrov which had been published in the Australian press was published in the English Sunday newspaper *The People*. A newspaperman, ringing up the Foreign Office to ask for comment on its contents, in full expectation that he would get the usual denials, was startled to be told that, yes, Maclean and Burgess had been long-term Soviet agents, and they were being investigated by security services when they fled from Great Britain, and they had left because they knew they were being investigated. It could not be said that now the truth was out, for the press, notably the *Daily Express*, had seen to that a very long time ago. Rather should it be said that the lying was over.

Public excitement and anger rose to a storm. It was perhaps one of their consequences that Hector McNeil, the able and hopeful provincial who had shown such promise, died of a cerebral haemmorhage. It might be argued that perhaps it was a pity that the truth was told, that it would have been better if complete silence had been preserved and the Soviet Union had been disappointed in its ambition to use the scandal as a wedge to drive between the United States and Great Britain. But there were three important reasons why the press should have told the story and forced the government to confirm it. There was first of all the immediate necessity to tell the world what sort of men Burgess and Maclean were: long-standing members of the Communist party, who were also disorderly and drunken neurotics. It was necessary to establish that they were old party members, to prevent the Russians from following their usual routine and presenting these men as selfless idealists who, in the course of their work at the Foreign Office, had become sickened by the warmongering policies of Britain and her allies and had therefore fled to the peace-loving Soviet Union. The importance of preventing this can be realized by remembering again the Communist press campaign regarding the atomic espionage. Actually no scientist ever handed over an atomic secret to the Russians who was not an old party member and an agent under instruction. But year in, year out the British public was falsely told that the atomic spies were scientists who had nothing to do with the Communist Party and had handed over the atomic secrets to the Soviet Union simply because they thought that scientific knowledge should be held by all countries in common. That deception must never be forgotten.

It was also important to give an honest picture of the two men's characters because it is a common belief, held by people not otherwise sympathetic with Communists, that Communists are idealists. In fact, the nature of communism is such that it must of necessity recruit far fewer idealists than any other party. Only an idealist too stupid to notice what is going on round him could feel happy in an organization which has no other aim than to seize political power against the will of the majority through the use of fraud. Karl Marx himself gave us the measure of the idealism we need attribute to Burgess and Maclean when he foretold that if a revolution was made in the name of the proletariat it would be joined by many members of the middle classes who doubted their power to maintain themselves in a world thus disorganized. It is to be remembered that when Donald Maclean joined the Communist Party at Cambridge he had good reason to feel anxiety about the future.

During his childhood he had known the sense of security which comes from an influential father, for Sir Donald Maclean was then Chairman of the Liberal Party, which had next to no votes but immense prestige, and he later acted as President of the Board of Education in the Ramsay MacDonald government and was therefore held in high honour by the Labour Party, whom he was helping to relieve from the embarrassing shortage of qualified ministers. But Donald Maclean's father was not a member of a rich or influential family, nor had he made a fortune for himself. He was a Cardiff solicitor who had waited till middle age to go into politics and to marry, and in 1932, when Donald had just gone up to Cambridge, he died at the age of sixty-eight, leaving a widow and five children, all still to be educated, and an estate of less than £25,000. This is indeed more than a mass of Britons are able to bequeath to their families, and many a young man in Donald Maclean's position has been unperturbed, but that is not the point. In the Victorian age a political leader would have hardly been able to reach such eminence unless he had sufficient means to leave his family an estate three or four times as large, and thus enable it to continue its life in an atmosphere of ease and respect. A creature so often the prey of despair as Donald Maclean might feel the old world had failed him and listen to a voice which pretended to speak for a new world which would not disappoint; and it might also hold the ear of Burgess and his friends, who knew themselves so gifted that such opportunities as were still offered by the old world should have been theirs, had they not been debarred by their strangeness. It cannot be said that that voice did not keep many of its promises. It gave them, indeed, a sort of fame.

There we touch the second reason why the press performed a public service by telling the true story. Plainly the system of selecting and controlling personnel in Whitehall had broken down, and Great Britain was in a fair way to lose what had always been reckoned by other nations as one of its greatest assets: an efficient and honest civil service, untainted by corruption. Apart from the national interest, this involved a grave injustice to many individuals. There were a great many men of the same age as Burgess and Maclean who could have performed the duties that they had performed in their various posts and who would have remained sober and refrained from breaking up American librarians' baths. Such men had some grounds for feeling aggrieved when they realized that they had failed to satisfy the authorities in some way not mentioned in the statutes of the Civil Service Commission; and it really hardly mattered whether these crypto-requirements related to homosexuality or communism.

The third reason for telling the story was perhaps the strongest. Everybody knew that there were Communists, but very few people really believed it. They knew with their minds, because they had gathered the information from books and newspapers, that the Communist Party is an association which requires of its members that they abandon their loyalty to their own country and obey all instructions issued by the Soviet Union, even when these instructions tell them to put the Soviet Union's interest first. They knew that there were a number of Communists in Great Britain, and some may have vaguely remembered the days of the Stalin-Hitler pact, when British Communists did everything they could to secure Britain's defeat by the Nazis. But this knowledge seemed to them outside reality, like a dream, the recollection of a film seen long ago, a detective story read in childhood. This was perhaps because, though there were cases of Communist espionage before the war, they seemed almost amusing, so unlikely was it that the Soviet Union should ever become a great aggressive power; and although there were more alarming cases of espionage in the war, those were tried in camera. The first case of Communist espionage which took an alarming form was the trial of Alan Nunn May, which took place in 1946, just five years before the disappearance of Burgess and Maclean.

It also, very unfortunately, happens that the Communist conspiracy repeats a pattern which was exploited by writers at a time when the corresponding reality was only faintly discerned by observers of society with specialist interests. Fiction ran away with the idea and seemed to take it for its own, simply because a secret society which is real has to be kept, so far as possible, secret. There are myriads of secret societies which stemmed from splinter forms of Freemasonry and from the Illuminati and multiplied before and after 1848; but they seemed tentative and unimpressive compared with the majestic machines which, omnipotent and omnipresent and unnamed, controlled the nations in the works of Eugène Sue; and he had imitators in every language when the disciples of the political philosophies of Blanqui and Nechaev still numbered only a few thousand. The huge international conspiracy was part of the bag of tricks used by most writers of the nineteenth-century invention, the detective story. Thus it happened that international conspiracy was established in the common mind as a feature of a vulgar district in the world of fancy, and it seemed quite ridiculous to think of it as a real threat. At least the day-to-day reporting of the Burgess and Maclean story by journalists, who on other occasions reported railway accidents and jewel robberies, and the controversies concerning Burgess and Maclean which raged between known public characters, made the newspaper reader realize that the Communist conspiracy was as much a fact as railway accidents and jewel robberies or the atom bomb, and that there were English people capable of becoming conspirators.

When the Petrov disclosures forced the British government's

hand a White Paper was issued, which was bound to be inept, but was so to an unnecessary degree. It suggested that Maclean's house at Tatsfield could not be watched by the police because it was in an isolated situation in the country. This is a remark which could never be worth making, except by a house-agent attempting to sell a castle in the Yorkshire moors to an exceptionally trusting foreign criminal. It also alleged that there was no legal way of preventing the two men from leaving the country. But it is certain that a bank clerk who was suspected of embezzlement as strongly as Maclean was suspected of treachery would not have been permitted to board the *Falaise*. A witness in an embezzlement case could not, without the jiggery-pokery of a "holding offence," have been prevented from going; but a suspected person could have been taken from the dock to a police station "to help the police in their inquiries." It also contained the naïve sentence: "No trace can be found in Burgess's subsequent career"—after he left Trinity College—"of direct participation in the activities of left-wing organizations; indeed, he was known after leaving Cambridge to have had some contact with organizations such as the Anglo-German Club." As Burgess was attached to the Foreign Office during a war with Germany, it was precisely those pro-German associations which should have been investigated so thoroughly that his communism was discovered.

There was a debate in the House of Commons, which was also bound to be inept, but, so far as the government spokesmen were concerned, was less so than might have been expected. Mr. Harold Macmillan and Sir Anthony Eden made handsome admissions of past governmental error. But the House was given serious news when it was announced that the security system of checking officials had been tightened since the disappearance, and that out of nine hundred officials who had been examined four had been asked to leave the service and six others were moved to work of less importance or asked to resign. If these men had committed offences which made them liable to prosecution and they had not been prosecuted, then there had been a "cover-up" which amounted to an assault on law by the bureaucracy; if they had been so guilty that it was impossible to continue their employment and also impossible to prosecute them, then an open society had not been able to defend itself against a secret society.

This conspiratorial situation was novel, and our Western world was unprepared to meet it. But both Mr. Macmillan and Sir Anthony Eden gave muddled counsel when they declared that Burgess and Maclean could not have been restrained by justice unless the law was altered and the citizen was deprived of his civil rights. Mr. Macmillan said, "It would be a tragedy if we destroyed freedom in the effort to preserve it." Sir Anthony Eden said:

> Would the House like the law altered? Would it agree that the law should allow any British subject to be detained on suspicion? Well, you have to face these questions when there is no evidence on which the man could be judged. Would you be willing that people should be held indefinitely by the police while evidence is collected against them? Of course not. But in this case detention would have been justified. British justice over the centuries has been based on the principle that a man is to be presumed innocent until he can be proved guilty. Have we to abandon that principle? Worst of all, are we to make an exception for political offences? The last thing I would wish to see in this country is the Security Service having the power to do some of the things which some of our friends in the press do not seem to realize would flow from such a policy. If we had that power under the law Burgess and Maclean would not be where they are today. What would have been the consequence to British freedom and to those rights which this House has always defended? I would never be willing to be Prime Minister of a government who asked these powers of this House.

This homily was irrelevant. Its irrelevance is worth noting, for this is the standard excuse put up by the security organizations when a Soviet spy is discovered. They have much better excuses, but they perversely insist on using this one. Yes, they say, this spy could have been caught, but only at the price of adopting McCarthyite methods. This is complete nonsense. It suggests that we must choose between Communist conspiracy and sacrificing our liberties. But there is no need to make such choice, indeed it cannot be made, at least not in the case of Communist espionage. There is no instance of Communist espionage which could have been more readily detected than it was had the police been free to disregard the acknowledged rights of the accused person. It has often not been possible to bring a charge against a suspect though the police and members of the public knew that he was guilty, but the required evidence could not have been produced even if the powers of the police had been extended in every conceivable direction.

Our civil rights are the result of a harmony. The individual knows that he does not want to be manhandled by the community, that he does not want to have his house searched by the police unless they can satisfy a magistrate that they have reason to believe it contains evidence of guilt, that he does not want to give the police statements except by his own free will, that he wants to be treated as innocent till he is proved guilty. But the community has long ago learned that if people are liable to have their houses searched by the police at will, the guilty will destroy evidence with a thoroughness that they would otherwise not apply, that forced statements are apt to be false, and that to treat innocent men as guilty does nothing to produce social order, since it engenders contempt for the law, and anyway lets the guilty go free to go on plundering the community. Conspiracy is the last offence which would tempt the community to disregard its age-old experience and throw away the civil rights which it has found so useful. It can only be traced by the observation of meetings, by the tracing of actual documents or their copies, or by unforced confession. None of this evidence could be more readily obtained by any tampering with freedom.

But all these considerations did not apply to Burgess and Maclean. The questions about the two men which the Foreign Secretary had to answer were quite simple. Why had Maclean been suffered to remain in the Foreign Office so long when he was a known alcoholic with Communist associations, and why was he appointed head of the American Department after having committed offensive action against an American's property during a drunken brawl in Cairo, which had led to protests from the American ambassador? Why was Burgess allowed to remain in the Foreign Office so long when he was a known alcoholic with Communist associations, and why was he appointed second secretary at the British embassy at Washington, when he had already been censured for disclosure of official secrets, and why was he kept there for seven months in spite of repeated acts of miscon-

duct and his superiors' protests? The state, like any other employer, has a right, frequently exercised, of employing or reject-
ing those who apply to it for employment and dismissing those
who serve it badly. It did not, in fact, require any further powers
to deal with Burgess or Maclean. It already possessed ample
powers which could have been turned to this purpose, and had
not used them.

The fault seemed to lie with the security organizations. These
number nine, and four of them were concerned with Burgess and
Maclean: the Special Branch, at Scotland Yard, which is responsible to the Home Secretary; MI5, the fifth division of Military
Intelligence, the counterespionage body which operates in strict
isolation from the rest of the War Office, but is responsible to
the Secretary for War; Q, which is an internal organization
within the Foreign Office, looking after its own; and, more re-
motely, MI6, the espionage body, which is a department run by
the Foreign Office under a civilian head and is responsible to the
Foreign Secretary. The question of responsibility is complicated.
Once a security organization reports to its minister, which it does
usually in the latter stages of an operation, the report is immediately referred to the Prime Minister, who is under no obligation
to inform his cabinet then or at any time, and can deal with the
matter entirely according to his discretion. In one postwar government it was not the habit of the Prime Minister to inform the
Secretary of War regarding atomic espionage. The ultimate
responsibility for all security matters used to rest with the Prime
Minister, but was transferred to the Home Secretary by a directive of Lord Kilmuir when he was Lord Chancellor. Unfortunately this directive was not brought to the attention of the
public, or even the Houses of Parliament. Few secrets in this
field have been kept so well.

It appeared that the security organizations had dealt
inefficiently with Burgess and Maclean. But it might also be true
that the security organizations had given the authorities sound
advice which they had disregarded. This has often happened.
Long before the war it was a matter of common knowledge that
the Special Branch reports regarding the desirability of aliens
applying for British citizenship were often thrown into the
waste-paper basket. But in the House of Commons ministers gave
such strange answers to questions that it became obvious that

this was not the explanation of this crisis. The security organizations had themselves been behaving very strangely.

When the diplomats disappeared Mr. Morrison stated that the first time he was informed that the head of the American Department had been suspected of being a Soviet agent was on May 25, the day he consented to the questioning of Maclean, and the day that the two men left England. But the suspicion had become a matter for administrative action at a lower level five weeks before this. This seems an excessive delay. There were signs of inaccurate briefing in these Parliamentary statements, too. Lord Reading, Minister of State in the Foreign Office, declared that "a very experienced under-secretary who supervised the department was watching Mr. Maclean with special closeness towards the end of the time before his disappearance just to see whether there was anything which indicated that Mr. Maclean was not performing his duties satisfactorily at that moment, and he came to the conclusion that there was nothing to which exception should be taken." This under-secretary was later identified by the Foreign Office as Sir Roger Makins, by then the British ambassador at Washington. This made him look uncommonly silly. But Mr. Macmillan, then Foreign Secretary, was afterwards to contradict this assertion. Sir Roger Makins had, it seemed, conducted no sort of inquiry into Maclean's behaviour at all and was completely blameless in this matter.

Mr. Philby had, as we have seen, informed Burgess when he was a guest in his house that Maclean was under suspicion. On October 25, 1955, Mr. Marcus Lipton, a Labour M.P. representing Brixton, asked in the Commons whether Sir Anthony Eden, then Prime Minister, had "made up his mind to cover up at all costs the dubious third-man activities of Mr. Harold Philby, who was first secretary at the Washington Embassy a little while ago." Sir Anthony denied this and suggested that Mr. Lipton had better raise the matter in the course of the debate consecrated to this subject, which took place on November 7 of that year. Mr. Macmillan then referred to the possibility that Maclean might have been tipped off by a friend, and explained:

In this connection the name of one man has been mentioned in the House of Commons. He is Mr. H. A. R. Philby, who was a temporary first secretary at the British Embassy in Washington from October 1949 to June 1951, and had been privy to much of the investigation into the leakage.

Mr. Philby had been a friend of Burgess from the time when they were fellow undergraduates at Trinity College, Cambridge. Burgess had been accommodated with Philby and his family at the latter's home in Washington from August 1950 to April 1951, and of course it will be realized that at no time before he fled was Burgess under suspicion.

It is now known that Mr. Philby had Communist associates during and after his university days. In view of the circumstances he was asked, in July 1951, to resign from the Foreign Service.

Since that day his case has been the subject of close investigation. No evidence has been found to show that he was responsible for warning Burgess or Maclean. While in government service he carried out his duties ably and conscientiously.

I have no reason to conclude that Mr. Philby has at any time betrayed the interests of this country or to identify him with the so-called "third man," if, indeed, there was one.

On November 10 Mr. Lipton, who after the debate had been instructed on the matter at an informal meeting of Q and MI5 men, made a personal statement in the House. He said that he regarded it as his "duty to withdraw unreservedly the charge" implied in his question and during his speech in the debate, and express deep regret that he had made this charge. There were many who were bewildered by these interchanges. A prominent figure at Scotland Yard had informed a journalist in the presence of two witnesses that Mr. Philby had indeed informed Burgess of the suspicion that lay on Maclean.

So from mystery to mystery the story went on. It was rumoured that the two men were in Prague, in Moscow, in Warsaw, or home again in London, in some prison behind the Iron Curtain, or dead. Then in February 1956 a celebrated correspondent, Mr. Richard Hughes, found himself in Moscow just at the time when Mr. Khrushchev and Mr. Bulganin were about to start for their famous visit to England. They were known to be anxious about the impression they would make, and it occurred to the resourceful Mr. Hughes that he might cash in on this anxiety by asserting through the proper channels that British public opinion would be much more likely to accept them as sincerely trying to improve Anglo-Soviet relations if, at last, the Soviet came clean about the missing diplomats. So, on February 11, in room 101 of Moscow's National Hotel, Burgess and Maclean were exhibited to Mr. Hughes and representatives of Reuter's agency, the Tass agency, and *Pravda*. It was not quite the end of the story. There was still a little juice to be squeezed out of the lemon, though only a very little.

8

HOW much harm did Burgess and Maclean do to their country? This can never be known. Every secret they learned during their official lives was certainly transmitted to the Soviet Union. Burgess must have learned much that was useful to his masters when he was running about London in the company of the odd-come-shorts who, like himself, mixed with unsuspecting heroes to form the army which was dropped on Europe to help the resistance forces. It is painful to think how much more he must have learned when he was personal assistant to Hector McNeil. The Official Secrets Act must often have been fractured by his hand. As for Maclean, he was secretary of the Combined Policy Committee on Atomic Development, which gave him no scientific information but much knowledge of a general kind, particularly relating to security and supply. He is said to have had a grave influence on the course followed by the Korean War. In October 1950 the American Central Intelligence Agency delivered a memorandum to President Truman reporting that the Chinese Communists would move in far enough to safeguard the Suiho electric plant and other installations along the Yalu River which provided them with power, and General MacArthur was told not to advance upon them, but to let them be, on that frontier. It is said that Maclean was in possession of this information and passed it to the Russians, who saw to it that the Chinese crossed the Yalu, with the result that the United Nations forces were scattered and a short war turned into a long one. That such material would ever be passed to the head of the

American Department has been doubted; but then the head of the American Department was in a very favourable position to receive information he never should have been given. We will never know the truth of this. On the other hand, we may draw comfort from the certainty that the bulk of the official papers which came into the hands of Burgess and Maclean could have been of interest to neither man nor beast.

But the damage done by these two on the hither side of the law has to be considered. Maclean served for some time under Lord Inverchapel, the eccentric diplomat whose presence as British ambassador at Moscow, Peking, and Washington made many an astonished traveller marvel at the Foreign Office system of promotion. His habit of having the bagpipes played by kilted pipers round the dining room at the British embassy at Washington caused many persons to calculate, often with fury, whether Stirling lies north of that city, since this Highland rite should not be performed in the Lowlands, which begin at Stirling. The question has probably never been raised before or since; and this was Lord Inverchapel's only respectable distinction. Not least among his disadvantages was a steady passion for the Soviet Union. This he did not conceal from the Foreign Office, giving a pro-Soviet lecture to the experts employed during the war in the Far Eastern section which none of them has ever forgotten. While it would be most unlikely that Lord Inverchapel ever committed an act of treachery, he certainly extended the hand of friendship to all who shared his passion, which sometimes caused him to commit official acts not treacherous but inconvenient. A German who had formed part of the extensive Soviet spy ring in the Pacific area, and who had no connection whatsoever with Great Britain, was not so many years ago expelled from France and made his way to England. To the surprise of the immigration authorities he produced a British passport, which he had been given by Lord Inverchapel when he was in China; and in Great Britain, a country towards which he had always professed the greatest hostility, this unattractive rascal lived until his death. There is no limit to what Maclean must have been able to do with such a chief.

Burgess must have had many achievements to his credit on the hither side of the law. He had two permanent lines of activity: he had close relations, before, during and after the war, with various French Communists who had infiltrated their own civil service and the Paris radio; and relations at least as close with certain Communist Germans of good family who were working in concert with the Left and a certain peer and peeress friendly to the Nazis. There was also much finding of jobs for the right boys; before the war the head of a provincial university made some broadcasts at the BBC and there was introduced to charming young Mr. Burgess, who made what seemed to the visitor a most intelligent suggestion about the advisability of having a course of lectures on certain phases of international affairs at his university. Mr. Burgess went on to recommend a writer named XY as the ideal lecturer on this subject, and presently he produced other friends, also charming, who were also enthusiastic about XY, who therefore was engaged to give the lectures. XY was indeed a man of some ability, but he was also a hireling who had just seen that the war was inevitable and had broken off a long flirtation with the Nazis to become a fellow traveller. Everybody who came within earshot of Burgess at that time was addressed on the subject of XY's virtues, in which he cannot have believed.

But perhaps the worst offence of the two men was the spreading and degrading cloud of doubt their flight engendered. Burgess and Maclean were employed together with a number of other men; they were acquainted with many through their clubs and through their ordinary social ties. Let us suppose that the ordinary Londoner was acquainted with three of their associates, AB, CD, and EF. He knew that AB was a homosexual, that CD joined the Communist Party at Cambridge but left it long ago, and that EF was a decent soul who knew Maclean and Burgess because he was at the same school or for some other neutral reason. Inevitably this scandal darkened and fused the Londoner's knowledge of these three men. Inevitably he suspected all these three men of communism, of which none was guilty, and of homosexuality, of which only one was guilty. Inevitably he smeared the organization to which Burgess and Maclean belonged, the society which they frequented, with a bigger and blacker smear than they deserved. This is a natural consequence of Communist activity. Once a secret society establishes itself within an open society, there is no end to the hideous mistrust it must cause. But there was not the slightest hope that this situation had not been made even uglier than it was bound to be. Burgess and Maclean would be under an obligation to lay a trail of bogus evidence behind them which would divert suspicion from the Communists who had really been their aides; and these Communists, and all others of their faith, had had to join in the game of misleading the authorities. It followed that suspicion often fell on people who were innocent.

There was a sowing of mistrust everywhere which could not be dispelled by complete candour on the part of the authorities. It must be noted that neither the Labour nor the Tory government, when either had to bear the responsibility for coping with this situation, found it possible to go ahead and blow the gaff. This did not proceed from a cowardly desire to whitewash their own parties, though they would not have been human had not this desire been in their minds. It proceeded from the fact that reticence was legally obligatory. It is unlikely that they had evidence in black and white that any colleague of Burgess and Maclean was on a level with them as a traitor. But there must have been mountains of evidence that a number of their colleagues had engaged in behaviour certainly indiscreet, possibly worse and sometimes possibly better, and never of a sort which provides subject matter for indictments under British law. What was done was all that could be done: the offending persons were slowly dribbled into positions where they could enjoy only the minimal opportunities of doing harm and acquiring dangerous knowledge, while deprived of the right to complain of termination of their employment. To give an example: in the housecleaning which followed the disappearance of the two diplomats, it was discovered that one of their associates had for thirty years been a fanatical Communist and had induced a certain celebrated British soldier of foreign origin to join the Communist Party not long before his death. This act was not an offence against the law; neither is it an offence to be a Communist. The authorities eased the suspected person out of the civil service into an academic post, where he taught and still teaches the young a subject on which he is an acknowledged authority; and it is unlikely he instructs them in anything else, for the head of the institution is a shrewd person of known loyalty, who was once in MI6 and is aware of all the implications of the arrangement.

It cannot be hoped that our government could do better than that, and yet how bad it is. An open society has been unable to defend itself against a secret society which has formed in its midst. That, when it happens to the cells of our body, is called a case of cancer, and the results were cancerous in their corrupting painfulness. The United States had reason to think ill of its ally, Great Britain, and, what was even worse, Great Britain had reason to think ill of itself. The West was tarnished in its own eyes. If one asks how Burgess and Maclean could bear to contrive such a disaster, there are several answers. There was the simple answer that to some people it is fun to deceive, and Burgess and Maclean and their associates had had endless opportunities to enjoy that particular sort of amusement. The statement which Maclean and Burgess made on February 11, 1956, when they were produced to satisfy the demands of Mr. Richard Hughes of the *Sunday Times* had made it plain that Mrs. Maclean had been prevented from accompanying her husband on his flight not by lack of knowledge of his plans or disapproval of them, but solely by the impending birth of her child. Month after month she had posed as a bewildered and heartbroken wife, taking advantage of such generous and trusting souls as Lady Violet Bonham-Carter, who attacked the press on her behalf. A deeper cause is the fear, recorded by Karl Marx, felt by the children of privileged parents lest the social changes happening so rapidly in our age should deprive them of enjoying such privileges in their time; hence, as Marx foresaw, they may cast their lot with the Communist Party in case that is the winning side. But there is a cause which lies deeper still.

It can be divined if one turns an eye on the Korean War, which was raging at this time. This had its interest for those who study treachery. Hostilities began in 1950, and, when they were over, twenty-three American prisoners of war refused repatriation because they had gone over to the enemy in camp. A number of American writers set themselves the task of finding out what manner of beings these were who had failed the Stars and Stripes. And what were they? Why, they were a transatlantic version of the poor old British Free Corps. Here were all the odd-come-shorts bobbing up again, poor little Herbert George, anxious to shine in the local Fascist Party, or, if the meeting fell on a more convenient day, the local Communist Party, Denis

John, the baker's son with the undesirable friends, the Byronic Alfred Vivian, the eccentric Mr. Putney; and in control of them were the white-collar men of the Concordia Bureau. But these were just the conspicuous failures. There was worse beneath the surface, in both American and British forces. In 1955 the Ministry of Defence published a pamphlet on *Treatment of British Prisoners of War in Korea,* which gave a hateful picture. The Nazis had tampered with British prisoners of war in an amateurish way, trying to subvert them but observing a certain restraint, a certain regard for their rights as human beings. The Communist Chinese and North Koreans had played the same game with no holds barred. The captured men had been faced with an alternative: either they submitted to an ingenious pedagogic treatment, called by some "brainwashing," which turned them into Communist believers and propagandists in the interests of the Soviet Union and Communist China and against the interests of their own country and the United Nations; or not only would they be deprived of the decent treatment recognized as their right by custom and the Geneva Convention; they would also be starved, shut up in filthy and insanitary quarters, refused medical treatment, and constantly exposed to physical maltreatment, as well as to the risk of solitary confinement and capital punishment for trifling offences. They were visited by some Britons: Mr. Allan Winnington and Mr. Shapiro, of the London *Daily Worker*; Mrs. Monica Felton, the daughter of a High Wycombe Nonconformist minister, a civil servant who in 1949 had been appointed by Mr. Silkin as the Chairman of the Development Committee of the new satellite town of Stevenage; a London solicitor named Mr. Jack Gaster; and an Australian journalist named Mr. Wilfred Burchett, now resident in Moscow. These visitations did not seem to cheer up the prisoners to any marked degree.

The captured officers and senior NCOs were virtually unaffected by their treatment; but of the junior NCOs and other ranks, one-third were found on their release to have "absorbed sufficient indoctrination to be classed as Communist sympathizers." Only one elected to remain with his captors. But this fact is not as reassuring as might appear. The junior NCOs and other ranks numbered less than seven hundred men, and it is quite true the community is not likely to be endangered by something like two hundred and twenty victims of indoctrination, though the damage done to them as human beings may be tragically intense. But it must be realized that, in the event of a peripheral war on a larger scale, or the simultaneous conduct of several peripheral wars, it would be deplorable if Great Britain were flooded on the cessation of hostilities by men who, speaking with apparent authority, would allege that their country's enemies had been in the right. It should be noted that this assault on the public confidence would be the more to be feared had the war been waged, not as the result of the country's unfettered action, but by the decision of the United Nations.

It does not seem that the Army authorities had taken the same precautions to arrange for adequate leadership of the prisoners of war within their camps by pre-elected and pretrained men of quality, as they did before the Second World War. But there were some men who took upon themselves the duties of doing what had to be done and without rehearsal played the hero's part. Amongst them was a young man named Terence Edward Waters, who is worth while considering because of his relation to his time. He was a lieutenant in the West Yorkshire Regiment, not long commissioned from Sandhurst. He was badly wounded in the Battle of the Imjin River, in April 1951, just about the time that, on the other side of the world, Burgess and Maclean were thinking of their move. Terence Waters was captured and sent with a detachment of wounded other ranks, whom he cared for with great devotion, on a journey of great hardship, ending in a camp known as "The Caves." This was a tunnel driven through a hill, and it had the peculiarity that a stream ran through it, flooding most of the floor. It was overcrowded with South Korean and European prisoners of war, ragged, filthy, and lousy, who were dying daily from wounds and sickness and underfeeding. There was no doctor, there were no drugs. When a North Korean political officer came to the cave and attempted to persuade the men to join a prisoner-of-war group known as "Peace Fighters" and do Communist propaganda of a treasonable nature in return for better food and medical treatment and dry quarters, the other ranks refused. But Lieutenant Waters saw that most of them would soon die if they stayed in this pest-hole, so he ordered them to join the Peace Fighters, and told them to march out. Because they were other ranks and he was an officer, he could take the guilt of treason off them by this order. But because he was an officer nobody could take guilt from him, so he stayed behind in the infected place and presently died of his wounds. It had been his opinion that it might serve his country if the Chinese and his men saw that he was not afraid to die.

For the comprehension of our age and the part treason has played in it, it is necessary to realize that there are many English people who would have felt acutely embarrassed if they had had to read aloud the story of this young man's death, or to listen to it, or comment on it in public. They would have admitted that he had shown an extreme capacity for courage and self-sacrifice, and that these are admirable qualities, likely to help humanity in the struggle for survival; but at the same time he would not please them. They would have felt more at ease with many of the traitors in this book. They would have conceded that on general principles it is better not to lie, not to cheat, not to betray; but they also feel that Waters' heroism has something dowdy about it, while treason has a certain style, a sort of elegance, or, as the vulgar would say, "sophistication." William Joyce would not have fallen within the scope of their preference, but the cause for that would be unconnected with his defence of the Nazi cause. The people who harbour such emotions find no difficulty in accepting French writers who collaborated with the Germans during the war. It would be Joyce's readiness to seal his faith with his life which they would have found crude and unappetizing. But Alan Nunn May and Fuchs, Burgess and Maclean would seem in better taste. And concerning taste there is indeed no argument. Those who cultivate this preference would not have been prepared to defend these men's actions if they were set down in black and white. They would have admitted that it is not right for a man to accept employment from the state on certain conditions and break that undertaking, when he could easily have obtained alternative employment in which he did not have to give any such undertaking; and that it is even worse for an alien to induce a country to accept him as a citizen when he is homeless, and then conspire against its safety by handing over the most lethal secret it possesses to a potential enemy of aggressive character. But, all the same, they would have felt that subtlety was on the side of the traitors, and even morality. They are of the same opinion as Monsieur André Gide, who

wrote: "To me the worst instinct has always seemed sincere."
To them the classic hero, like poor young Terence Waters, was
hamming it. People who practise the virtues are judged as if they
had struck the sort of false attitude which betrays an incapacity
for art, while the people who practise the vices are judged as if
they had shown the subtle rightness of gesture which is the sign
of the born artist. Burgess and Maclean were of the opinion, as
they worked out their long stint of treason, that they were proving themselves much better adapted to their time than any saint
or hero could have been.

⇥⇥ I I I ⇤⇤

Decline and Fall of Treason

1

In THE SUMMER of 1952 there was a spy trial which stands with the flight of Burgess and Maclean, because it too was not what it seemed. William Marshall, twenty-four years of age, radio telegraphist in the service of the Foreign Office, had committed breaches of the Official Secrets Act by handing over information to a Soviet diplomat, and no doubt these would have been detected by our security organizations in their own good time. But it looked as if the Soviet Union had settled the time and the place of the detection without the slightest regard for poor Mr. Marshall. For that reason he deserved a little more sympathy than anyone else ever charged with this kind of offence in Great Britain, and indeed he got much more; but that was for another and quite unsound reason.

This sympathy sprang from Mr. Marshall's social circumstances and a time-lag in public opinion. His home was in a street of little brick houses down in Wandsworth, the kind of street from which ability keeps pushing up, and occasionally misses its way, if it reads the wrong books and misunderstands what it reads. Round the corner from Marshall's home there lived a leader of the British Fascist Party as it reconstituted itself after the war, a man of great and wasted potentialities, coughing out Mosleyism through a haze of tuberculosis. Marshall's parents were people with strong and interesting personalities. His father had been a bus-driver until a V-1 wrecked him and his bus, and since then had drawn a disability pension for a painful back injury and had done odd jobs, being uncommonly gifted as a handyman; his mother, who was distinguished in appearance and manner, worked part-time for a news-agent. Their son had left school at sixteen to go to a nautical college and had there been trained as a radio telegraphist; but before he had succeeded in getting a ship he was called up to do his military service, which he did in the Royal Signals, first in Palestine and then in Egypt. He was then taken into the Diplomatic Wireless Service and as its employee was sent back to Egypt. There some of his Army companions detected signs of communism; and it seems probable that from boyhood he was a convinced and exalted Communist. Nevertheless, in 1950 he was given a post at the British Embassy in Moscow.

He stayed there a year, coming back, in December 1951, to work at Hanslope Park, the out-of-town establishment maintained by the Foreign Office fifty miles north of London. From January 1952 until June of that year he had meetings with a second secretary of the Soviet Embassy in London named Pavel Kuznetsov. On June 13 members of the Special Branch surrounded them as they were making their way out of King George's Park in Wandsworth and took them to the local police station. There they searched both men, and on Marshall they found a copy of a confidential document which he had been given for the purpose of his work. He was charged under the Official Secrets Act with having communicated to Mr. Kuznetsov information useful to an enemy, and with obtaining secret information, and twenty-five days later he appeared at the Old Bailey, with British public opinion feeling for him like a mother.

This was because of a passage in his statement which read:

> On December 31 I flew to Moscow. I was a misfit at the Embassy from the start. The people were not in my class and I led a solitary life. I kept to myself and spoke to as few people as possible. I did my work as well as I could and just waited for the time to go home. I was disgusted with the life at the Embassy and began to take an interest in the Russian way of life. I was impressed by the efforts of the Russian people and their ideals. They seemed to be building a society which gave the biggest scope to human endeavour. But they have a long way to go. When I came back from Moscow in December 1951 I was as friendless as when I arrived there.

It immediately became plain that if there was anything that the British public did not like it was the British diplomat. It thought as one man that Marshall's position, cooped up for a year with ambassadors and counsellors and attachés and the like, must have been quite horrible. This was not, as would have been the case had the public been as much influenced by the latest news as is often assumed, because overreading about Burgess and Maclean made them imagine Marshall as having been perpetually in danger of having a leg broken or his bathroom smashed up by intoxicated colleagues. It was because the diplomat seems to the man in the street the very essence of what used to be called a toff; and the toff was seen as a rude person, relentless in his insistence that his social inferiors were totally his inferiors. It is unprofitable to discuss how far this was a true picture. Regrettably enough, while everybody knows that Englishmen are sent to public schools because that is the only place where they can learn good manners, the manners they learn there are recognized as good only by people who have been to the same sort of school, and often appear very bad indeed to everybody else. This disharmony has had many results, and among them is to be counted the picture which Marshall's statement immediately conjured up in millions of British minds: of a huge room lit by chandeliers, where at a table surrounded by lackeys an insolence of diplomats (if that be the right noun of assembly) sits in a frozen silence, broken only by the snorts of the tiaraed females by their sides, because poor young Mr. Marshall has used the wrong fork.

In fact, nothing like that happened. At that time the community within the British embassy in Moscow numbered about a hundred, and of these only a small number were diplomats. The rest were clerical and technical employees, stenographers, cipher clerks, radio operators, pilots, and the like; one or two of the diplomats might have been scholarship boys from the sort of school that Marshall had been at, and certainly most of the clerical and technical employees would have been to that same sort of school. Marshall was thus one of quite a large group with which he could feel on equal terms; and it is to be noted that the standard of manners in his home was very high indeed, and that he should have been under no handicap at all in dealing with any of the staff.

These people were under an exceptional strain. The inmates of the British embassy at Moscow are apt to feel that they are in a mousetrap. The summer is short, the climate harsh, there are no playgrounds in the forest or on the mountains; there is a hostile society looking in through the embassy windows and seeming not to like what it sees, and a formidable language barrier to increase the tension. Commander Anthony Courtney, MP, an experienced security officer, who has been detained and questioned by security bodies behind the Iron Curtain, has spoken of this atmosphere very seriously in the House. In Moscow, he said, "We have an atmosphere which is very difficult to convey to Hon. Members, an atmosphere of overwhelming suspicion, a claustrophobic feeling of being inside a compound, or a ghetto as we sometimes call it in some Iron Curtain countries." Because this atmosphere is so strong, special means are taken to counter it. There is an abundance of social activities and efforts to make the lonely feel they have companions. The ambassador at that time was Sir David Kelly, an expansive Irishman with a gay, intelligent Belgian wife who could take anything that came her way. She had remarked that Marshall looked pale and over-serious and had seen to it that efforts were made to provide him with possibilities of friendship. She is a resourceful woman and had she learned that the young man was suffering from an un-gratifiable desire for a cannibal diet, she would have found some means of distracting him.

But that passage in Mr. Marshall's statement was a master stroke. It brought him sympathy which was undeserved; but his trial very soon showed that he deserved a great deal on other scores. He had not, in his dealings with Mr. Kuznetsov, had the slightest chance of getting away with them. Every security rule which the Soviet diplomat should have applied he had broken, one by one, although there was a special reason why he should have observed them. Marshall was very tall and thin and narrow-chested, and he was pale, with a chalky pallor intensified by the blackness of his hair. It was a very unusual and quite pleasant pallor, not due to ill health, for he shared it with his mother and his brother. His shoulders sloped as steeply as if he were a Gains-borough beauty, and his neck was long. He had furthermore a distinctive feature which did not amount to a deformity but which was instantly noticeable. There is an area beside the ear, below the cheekbone and above the jaw, which in thin people is flat or concave. In him it bulged in a slight protuberance, faintly pitted in the centre. He was the last person who could success-fully engage in espionage, since he could not have been more identifiable, more memorable, less able to melt into a crowd. If he were to be handled at all by a Soviet apparatus, it would surely be with the last refinements of caution.

There was, however, a wild disregard of precaution from the start. Spies usually choose as meeting places the haunts of the obscure, where it is taken for granted that nobody present is likely to get into the newspaper headlines and there is little inquisitiveness. Suburban parks and public houses are specially favoured. The fashionable restaurants, with their clients from all sorts of worlds, and their waiters with their own word-of-mouth "Who's Who," far meatier than the orthodox version, are the last places where one could expect to find an agent and his contact. From the time of Marshall's return from Moscow, however, Mr. Kuznetsov took him on a round of expense-account meals at restaurants varying in atmosphere but all presenting one common feature. The Berkeley, the Pigalle, the Criterion, Chez Auguste, the Royal Court Hotel—at all of these it was possible that someone might look up and say, "I wonder who that young man is who is lunching with the second secretary of the Soviet embassy," or "There's our young Marshall, I didn't know he was back from Moscow, I wonder who he's with."

These entertainments took them along to the end of April; and then they had a meeting unique in the history of espionage in its bid for the attention of any hostile security officer. It took place at the Normandie Restaurant in Kingston-on-Thames, a detached portion of a large department store, Bentall's, which though it is located in the suburbs has a metropolitan air and reputation. There are always crowds looking in at its windows, where a watcher could stand unobserved while he covered the single entrance to the Normandie Restaurant, which was then isolated between the entrance and the exit of a carpark. At one o'clock on Friday, April 25, Marshall and Mr. Kuznetsov arrived at this naked and unsheltered spot and went upstairs to the restaurant, where their party proceeded, though Marshall did not know it, to occupy one-seventh of the available accommodation. For there were twenty-one tables, and he and Kuznetsov had one table facing the door, visible from every part of the room, while officers from the Special Branch had another, and a third was taken by a party of police from the Soviet embassy who, though Marshall was not aware of it, were always in the offing at these meetings. This is a comic situation in itself, and there was another amusing overture. A member of the Bentall's staff had to go over to the restaurant while the party was there, looked at the men whom we now know to have been Russian police, and said: "Oh, there are the Russians who were walking round the store yesterday." According to her, these men had made a slow tour of Bentall's the previous afternoon, speaking their native language to each other and asking the staff questions in not very good English. She thought she knew they were Russians because they had been asked what they were and had said so, but it might have been that a customer had identified the language they were speaking.

This seems almost too good to be true. But it was no more improbable than what happened when the two men left the restaurant. They went down a narrow street called Water Lane, in which the most incompetent sleuth could not have lost his quarry, to a little public park called Canbury Gardens, a strip of greenery which runs along the river for less than a quarter of a mile, never more than a hundred and fifty yards in depth and sometimes as little as fifty. There is a line of plane trees on the garden side of the towpath, with benches between them. Mr. Marshall and Mr. Kuznetsov sat down on one of these benches, clearly silhouetted against the waters of the Thames, and, as the bank faces westward, against the afternoon light. When Marshall took papers out of his pockets and showed them to his companion, and when he drew maps for him, not a shade of his gestures could have been missed. The lot of a security officer who spies on spies is often uncomfortable, but here the suspects could be watched either from deck chairs on the lawn behind them, or from the windows of a teahouse.

On May 19 Mr. Kuznetsov and Marshall met in Wimbledon, following, according to the watchers, a curious conspiratorial ritual, meeting and passing without a sign of recognition, then turning back and going together into a doorway. All this was the more remarkable behaviour because it was in a heavy rainstorm. Ragov, the organizer of the Canadian spy ring, made a note on a contact's report of a meeting with the scientist Durnford-Smith, "Was a torrential downpour; but he nevertheless came. Give instructions not to come in the future in such weather, it is not natural." On June 14 the pair met again, for the last time, in King George's Park, Wandsworth. This is an open space beside the river Wandle, which up till the end of the war was one continuous stretch of grassland intersected by two roads and

some asphalted footpaths. After the war a colony of prefabri-
cated houses was planted in the middle, so that there are now
two separate King George's Parks. One gives a lot of cover, for it
contains a children's playground, a swimming pool, a restaurant,
several entrances, and a number of benches. But Marshall and
Kuznetsov chose to go to the southern park, which is a playing
field and nothing else: a rectangle of flat ground about eight
acres in extent, all grass, save for a cinder track, with ten trees
planted along this track, and three benches. On the last of these
Marshall sat himself down with his Soviet friend, while the
detectives settled on the bench which was farthest away. After
ten minutes they decided they would like to be nearer and
moved to the middle one. When the men rose to go the detectives closed in on them. At the police station Kuznetsov took
the oddest line. He complained that he had been arrested while
he was walking in a park, which, he rightly said, is not an
offence against the law. Then he amplified the complaint; he
had been arrested while he was walking in a park with a man
whom he did not know. He insisted that they had been strangers
until that day. But when his statement was read back to him he
withdrew the amplification. He could hardly have assisted more
ably at cooking poor Marshall's goose.

This was indeed cooked, but not so brown as it might have
been. He got five years at the Old Bailey, which meant, though
he earned his remission, that he had no life between the ages of
twenty-five and twenty-eight: a great, great loss, but not a severe
penalty considering the practical value of the information he
had given and his nagging determination to commit this breach
of trust. The jury had added a rider to their verdict, insisting on
it against the displeasure of the judge, who, like many before
him, disliked riders, feeling them to be encroachments on the
constitutional powers of the judge to pass sentence according to
his own unfettered discretion. "We ask," the foreman said,
"that the prisoner be shown the utmost mercy. . . . We feel that
he has been led astray." And so, poor boy, he had. He had the
nonsense, so to speak, strong on his breath. Asked what he and
Mr. Kuznetsov had been talking about on the bench beside the
river, he replied that they had "exchanged cultural information
about Moscow." And how easy it must have been to get him to
take the dose. He knew so little. Asked if he had anything to say

before sentence was passed on him, he replied, that "the learned jury in their wisdom have found me guilty of the offence with which I am charged, but I still say I am innocent." He did not even know that the whole point of a jury is that it is not learned as learned counsel are, or as learned judges, but chunks of laity, brought in for the special purpose of being unlearned. The poor boy, however, was resolutely thinking of things about which nothing can be usefully thought until one has grasped just such trifles.

It may be guessed that the judge needed no persuasion to give Marshall so much less than the maximum sentence of fourteen years which hung over him. He expressed his own certainty that Marshall had not committed treachery for the sake of gain, and this was true as it has not been true of any other of these offenders. All the rest accepted payment in some form of advantage. Nearly all of them took money, most of them on the curious plea that it was a token of their loyalty to the Communist cause, though they spent it as if it had been an ordinary bribe, which of course it was; others were guaranteed advancement in their professions or security in them when they might have been turned adrift. All were gratified by a promise of power they could not otherwise have attained, and this promise was sometimes fulfilled. But Marshall got nothing and would have refused anything he was offered. He said in evidence that when he and Kuznetsov had meals together Kuznetsov paid for the meal and he paid for the drinks, and if, as he said, they drank wine, this may have been the heavy end of the load. All the people who had known him spoke of a pleasant attitude to money. He was well paid; the special salary and allowance paid to Moscow employees had brought him a thousand pounds free of income tax in twelve months, and he had only fifteen pounds left in his savings-bank account when he was arrested. He had not flung it about, nor gone priggishly short on his record-buying or his other innocent pleasures, but he had been generous here and there, and especially generous in forcing it on his parents, who had characteristically not wished to accept it. His fellow employees at Moscow spoke of scrupulousness about the return of favours: if he ran out of cigarettes and had to borrow some, he replaced them at the first possible moment and with interest.

He was, surely, the best of all the offenders of his class, an upright young man who simply suffered from an inability to see through the *Daily Worker* as some other people suffer from colour-blindness. It is congruous with life as we know it that he was worse treated by his employers than any other of his kind. Amery was roughly dealt with: the way the Germans zestfully turned over to the British authorities all the information that had piled up against the poor wretch while he was serving them is in itself a masterpiece of treachery. But poor selfless William Marshall was put on a salver and served up to the Special Branch, with love from the Soviet Intelligence Service, and it was like robbing a child of its pennies on the way to the sweetshop. It simply cannot be believed that a Soviet diplomat could, at meetings with an agent supervised by his own embassy's police, break rule after rule of security practice without wishing that this agent should be detected and wishing it because his superiors wished it; and while other people might have suspected that such viperine entanglements can exist—Guy Burgess would have grasped the idea at once—it would never cross Marshall's candid mind. He would not have believed that he might be a sacrifice offered up in order that attention should be diverted from another and more valuable agent, possibly not British at all, who was working on so nearly the same field as Marshall that the British and American Intelligence authorities would think, having arrested Marshall, that they had stopped the leak which had been troubling them and could relax their vigilance. Capitalist countries might do such things, but not the New Jerusalem.

It is to be hoped that poor young Marshall made something of his life after he left prison. He must have found England and America almost insultingly indifferent, for by that time they had almost forgotten that there were spies. But in June 1957 a quiet and shabby man in his middle fifties was arrested in a small hotel on 28th Street, New York City, which knew him as Martin Collins. Elsewhere in the city a group of not immensely successful painters, also quiet and unspectacular and middle-aged, knew him as a fellow painter and a cosy companion, under the name of Emil Goldfus. Nine years before he had entered the United States from Canada under the name of Andrew Cayotis. After the war he had appeared under that name in a displaced-persons camp, posing as a Canadian who desired to be repatriated. To his employers, who were the KGB (the Soviet Commissariat of

State Security), he was Colonel Abel. The colonelcy was real, but the name was a John Doe of the Russian spy system and has been used in the past by more than one of their agents. His real name is not yet known.

In his room was more evidence of espionage than one would have expected an experienced spy to leave lying about: a cipher pad, a coded message, a transmitting radio, a hollow pencil containing a time schedule for his broadcasts to Moscow, a bankbook and a safe-deposit box key, which were to reveal an accumulation of dollars surprising for such a dim figure, and two birth certificates. One was made out for Emil Robert Goldfus, born in New York in 1902, and was a sample of a favourite Russian technique; for the real Emil Robert Goldfus had died when he was one year and two months old. The other birth certificate was made out for Martin Collins and was a forgery.

This man was one of the most important spies ever captured: he was what is known as the resident Soviet agent for New York, and it is suspected that he was more than that, that he was, so to speak, the secret-service ambassador in charge of North and Central America. Whatever his position, he had earned it by real merit. He was remarkably talented. He could pass as a painter because he could, in fact, paint. It does not seem likely that Sir Kenneth Clark would have become besotted with his work, but he had a professional command of technique. He was a fine linguist, and indeed that had once been his profession. As a young man in his native Russia he had been a teacher of languages in a secondary school. He was a skilled photographer, and he could do running repairs to any ordinary type of electrical equipment, even to elevators; and he was proficient both in carpentry and in the jeweller's craft to a degree which impressed those who did such work for a living. His musical knowledge was sufficient to get him on terms with the art of guitar-playing in middle life, to the extent of playing Bach and Villa-Lobos; and he was well enough acquainted with the sciences to regard books on mathematics and physics as light reading—not very advanced books, but not very easy ones either. The proof of his profes-sionalism as a spy was the use he made of these skills. He kept them going so that nobody suspected he could be doing anything else. He never would have been detected had not KGB in an aberrant moment sent him an aide named Hayhanen, who was a psychopath and alcoholic, who ultimately turned him in.

Nobody can estimate how much information Abel collected. We can be sure that almost all of it would be useless details, and we can be as sure that a fraction would be very useful indeed to the Russians as enemies of the West. An immense amount was coming in. His aide ran round New York collecting microfilms from caches such as a hidey-hole under a loose brick in a bridge spanning a bridle path near the Reservoir in Central Park, and a magnetic container nestling under a metal mailbox at a street corner; it all added up to something which earned Abel at his trial thirty years in jail and a fine of $3000. He was convicted on the evidence of Hayhanen and a fellow alcoholic, an American sergeant who had been washed into espionage on a flood of vodka when serving at the American embassy in Moscow; and the feeling in the courtroom was very strongly sympathetic with the accused man. He bore his ordeal with unresentful dignity and good sense. There had been difficulty about his legal representative, for the lawyer who usually handles such cases had pleaded previous commitments, and Abel had shrewdly used a provision of American law, for which there is no British equivalent, to get a lawyer of known talent and high reputation. He applied to the Brooklyn Bar Association to appoint a three-member panel to choose him counsel; and they gave him Mr. James Britt Donovan, a Harvard Law graduate, forty-one years old, just old enough to have been the last secretary to the great Mr. Justice Holmes, and brilliant enough to have stood out as a personality at the Nuremberg Trials, where he assisted the American prosecutor, Supreme Court Justice Robert Jackson. He was the last person to be suspected of communism, if only because he was a practising Roman Catholic. Abel's relations with Mr. Donovan were polite, balanced, and never showed any of the strain that might be expected from a man in peril of death. He was the perfect client, biddable and self-controlled. It was his lawyer's policy that he should plead not guilty but should not give evidence, and he sat quietly in court, quietly accepting sentence, thanked Mr. Donovan with quiet cordiality, and went quietly off to prison to qualify quietly as a model prisoner.

In fact, Abel was a professional spy, just as other people are professional singers or professional footballers, and being tried for his life was one of the risks of his profession which he had foreseen and was prepared to face, as professional singers are prepared to nurse troublesome larynxes and professional footballers to watch strained muscles. That was all there was to him and to his situation. He was not a member of the Communist Party in the Soviet Union, and from first to last no flicker of interest in Marxism, or indeed in any political issue at all, showed in his choice of reading matter in jail or in conversation. His only literary work was a pamphlet on the irrelevance of politics to art, which need not be taken as cover, for he was apparently really emotionally involved in a crusade against abstract art, which he appears to have envisaged as a rationalist but regressive interference with the instinctive pictorial processes. It is to be noted that he was not a traitor but a spy for his own country, a civil servant, part of the Establishment, and he had therefore never had to engage in the political arguments with himself which are a part of treachery. When we regard his encapsulated professionalism and hark back through the years to William Joyce, and hear again that impassioned twanging voice, vibrating in sympathy with what he believed to be the cosmic pulse, we realize that what we witnessed at the Old Bailey was the death agony of the amateur in a specialized age.

There, it seemed, we were going to leave Colonel Abel in 1957, as the triumphant specialist who had been brought low because of the human element, the human element which reaches out for a bottle of Bourbon whisky and throws knives at its wife at just the wrong moment. It was a pity that, instead of Mr. Hayhanen, Abel could not have had a robot courier; he would have known how to use him. But Abel had to be noted even then as a focus where many lines met. For example, he had known the unusually attractive Mr. and Mrs. Cohen who had been associated with the Rosenbergs. There was also a point of interest in certain microfilmed letters found inside his hollow pencil along with his broadcasting schedule. These purported to be from his wife and daughter, Helen and Lydia (Evelyn). In stilted terms they expressed great affection for him and regret at his continued absence, urging that he should terminate his employment and giving simple, heartrending details of their life in Russia. There is no doubt that they understood he was on espionage service. It is all very soap-opera; but there is some cultured cerebration at work. There are letters from his grown-up daughter, who turns out to be one of Freud's little girls and rather less self-conscious about it than one would have thought possible in this age, even in the Soviet Union. Her announcement of her engagement and her description of her marriage is a good clear posed photograph of a father fixation.

Daddy dear, I am missing you so much. You just cannot imagine how much I need you. It is about four months now since I have married and to me it seems like an eternity, so dull it sometimes is. In general, he is a good chap, but he isn't you. I have got a job. My boss is a bit like you though not so broad-minded and not a very great erudite. Though very clever. . . .

You say you want more particulars of my husband. I shall try to give you a better picture of him. He is short, green-eyed, rather handsome. He is rather gay and talkative when the conversation considers cars or football. He works as an engineer—he is capable though rather lazy. You ask me whether I am happy with him. As one of our greatest poets once said, there is no happiness in life but there is peace and free will. The only thing that worries me is that I find him boring sometimes. Now about my in-laws. They are awful. I do wish you were with us. Everything would be much easier for us then. I am missing you very much. I thought at first my husband could substitute you in some respects, but I now see that I am mistaken. Now about my work. I like it fine. I have a splendid boss. He is a very interesting man, clever, talented, tolerant, handsome. We like each other and spend much time talking about various things. He is forty-four, single and rather unhappy. I wish you could see him and talk to him.

The jury is said to have been much affected by this correspondence when it was read aloud, a process much facilitated because the daughter had, oddly enough, written to her father in English. But persons studying it at leisure may find themselves not so much moved as inquisitive. There is, for example, a dog who in late June 1956 is said by Mrs. Abel to be suffering from rupture of emotional ties with its master which must have been formed between July and November 1955. This report of canine fidelity may only be a piece of playfulness on the part of Abel's wife, but obstinately that dog looks like a stage-property dog; and about this picture of the spy's loving family, grieving while he bravely serves his country in a strange land, there is a haunting sense of unreality which was not dispelled, and was indeed to become more palpable, in the years to come.

Before Abel got settled in jail, in February 1958 there was a return of the amateur to the scene. Two Oxford undergraduates, one of Corpus Christi College, and the other of Lincoln College, both reading history, one twenty-three and the other twenty-four, contributed to the university magazine, *Isis*, an article based on their experience of National Service in the Royal Navy. It was a clear violation of the Official Secrets Act, it was committed from the highest motives, and it was quite frightening in its childishness. It related to the circumstances which arise out of the disadvantageous position in which the West finds itself as regards its opportunities for finding out for defence purposes what the military resources of the Soviet Union may be. The West cannot send spies into the Soviet Union, while the Soviet Union, and no blame to it, habitually sends spies into the West. A large part of the Soviet Union has, from time to time, been totally barred against the Western visitor, and in such parts as are open his freedom of movement is subjected to rigorous restrictions. In the very first years of the Soviet Union a certain number of Russian-speaking Englishmen penetrated its territory, and of these some, though not all, came back. But for the last thirty-five years no Western Colonel Abel has had a chance to snuggle in a Moscow apartment, or anywhere else where Russian is spoken, and the contacts with factory hands and research workers and civil servants which are so indispensable to his kind are impossible to achieve. For look-see spying the West has to rely on tourists and persons with some legitimate reason, probably commercial, for visiting the Soviet Union, and they can bring back very little. Hence the main source of the West's information about the resources of the Soviet Union is the defector, who is a Russian traitor. This is only sometimes satisfactory. The defector may be very useful indeed should he have left his country because he holds the idea of loyalty which is expressed in the English law of treason, and should he believe that if a state does not give protection to its citizens they do not owe it allegiance, and be of the opinion that the Soviet Union does not protect its citizens. Then he is a balanced person who knows what he is doing and has probably full command over useful information. But he may have left the Soviet Union because he was neurotic, drunken, in debt, a homosexual, or just a generally recognized and resented nuisance. He may, in any case, become any of these things after he has defected. As our material suggests, the traitor is not a happy man.

The Western skies are open to flight, and to aerial reconnaissance, which is about as harmless a form of spying as exists. It is indeed a prophylactic against war. For it enables the powers to learn exactly where bombing would hurt their neighbours most; and if all powers alike possessed in full measure this information, and knew it, no power would be very anxious to break the peace. But the Soviet Union has always kept its skies to itself, wishing to build up to the furthest possible limit its superior stockpile of information. Its legal position here is dubious. International law has not yet provided an aerial equivalent for the three-miles coastal limit at sea. The United States has had its own method of dealing with this prohibition. It sent the high-flying jet glider, the U-2, over Russian territory, without asking permission of the Soviet Union, just as the Soviet Union had not asked its permission to send Colonel Abel to New York. But the British dealt with the situation by means which involved no such appeal to the principle of tit for tat. They ran a line of listening stations down the eastern frontier of the Soviet Union from northern Europe to the Middle East, working in conjunction with an investigating fleet of planes, which record radio transmissions within the Soviet Union and thus acquire information about the character and disposition of all sorts of military installations and movements on the farther side of the fence.

This is perhaps the most innocuous form of spying imaginable. It involves no contacts between nationals of different states and no trespassing on territory. It is no more unfair than looking at the tanks in the Red Square when TV shows the May Day celebrations. If the British did not do it, then there might be a real danger of war, because the Russians would think they were daft and a fit prey for the sane and sensible. But to the two Oxford undergraduates it seemed utterly shocking. They must have known that the Soviet Union had happily accepted all the information it could get about Western military resources from Hiss, the Rosenbergs, Greenglass, Colonel Abel, Nunn May, Fuchs, Burgess, Maclean, and Harry Gold, but they thought it was morally wrong for a British soldier to monitor a radio transmission from a Soviet Union Army plane.

They had also an innocent idea that these purely mechanical proceedings were dangerously provocative. It sometimes happened that the British forces wished to gain more information about a Soviet plane than was coming over the air, and to pepper it into good revealing chatter they would send a plane to hug or even cross the frontier, sometimes so boldly that the Soviet planes forced it down. The undergraduates were of the opinion that some day some such incident might provoke the Russians to a sudden warlike act, and the Third World War would be upon us. This fear could have grounds only if the Russians did not understand why the British were acting as they were. But as the monitoring system had been in force for ten years the Russians perfectly understood both the system in general and the occasional forays in particular, and while their action was firm (which was right and proper), their verbal protests were purely conventional. No serious incident had occurred up to the time the young men wrote their article, nor has one wrecked our peace since then. They were sentenced to three months' imprisonment under the Official Secrets Act but served only four weeks.

Two other minor spies were in trouble about this time. The first was a sad man called Brian Frederick, an electronics engineer who was brought up for trial under the Official Secrets Act in June 1958, and who in 1955 was working at a Buckinghamshire aircraft factory on government work. At a party he met—by sheer chance, he thought and probably still thinks—the Czech military attaché, Colonel Pribyl. He invited him to go to a concert with him, and afterwards he and his wife became close friends of Mr. and Mrs. Frederick. For two years the colonel held his peace and never asked him about his work. This is Frederick's story, and it is confirmed by the MI5 men who, from the very first, were eavesdropping on the friendship.

In January 1957 Frederick moved to another aircraft firm at Shoreham and was accompanied by MI5 men, who warned the management that it might be all right, it might not. At any rate Frederick's work was compartmentalized; he saw thenceforward the part and not the whole. The MI5 men had perhaps noticed that things were going ill with Frederick's marriage. In April his wife left him, and then there was money trouble. He had to make an allowance to his wife just when he was trying to pay off debts on a new house. It was then that Colonel Pribyl offered to buy classified drawings and papers from him, and Frederick agreed. He went on giving Pribyl what he wanted for a year, except that it was not what he wanted. The documents were all faked by Frederick's superiors in order to mislead the Soviet Union's Intelligence men. For this the poor wretch got £500 from the Czechs and fourteen years from the judge at the Old Bailey.

It is not tolerable that human beings should do such things to each other. But the story of Mr. Anthony Maynard is more cheerful. It is indeed one of the few comic stories in the annals of espionage. He was a flying officer in training, who in January 1956, at twenty-two, went to the headquarters of the Society for Cultural Relations with the USSR and said that he wished to make inquiries about the art of photography as practised in the Soviet Union. Someone at the office suggested he should write to Mr. Soloviev at the Soviet embassy. He accepted this advice and went to see Mr. Soloviev, who was an active Intelligence officer and was just waiting for Mr. Maynard to come along. The young man confided that he was a serving officer in the RAF who wished to study at the State Institute of Photography in Moscow and would make arrangements to leave the RAF if this could be arranged. Mr. Soloviev was sympathetic and met him for a second time at the Odeon Cinema. After this meeting his commanding officer asked him to sign an order forbidding contact between RAF officers and members of the Soviet embassy, and ordered officers who had made such contacts to report them. He signed, but reported nothing.

In April the two met at the Odeon Cinema, at the National Film Theatre, at the Soviet Circus, and at the Soviet Film Festival at the Royal Festival Hall, and ended up with a visit to the Everyman Cinema in Hampstead in August.

In October, Maynard was interviewed by security officers and he explained that he wished to study photography in Moscow because he feared that he had no future in the RAF, as his eyesight was failing. This was a singular reason for wishing to become a photographer. He said he remembered signing no order which had any reference to contacts between RAF officers and Soviet embassy officials. There was a further interview, and general trouble, the painfulness of which may be judged from a letter he left behind and from other statements he made later. He was, he said, finding home life increasingly frustrating and his relations with his parents were "rapidly deteriorating." As for his oath of allegiance, he explained that that no longer bound him, as he had been a Christian when he took it but had since lost his faith, and were he asked to take it again would refuse, as he had ceased to believe that the Queen was of national or international importance. He explained also that he dreaded to be like his brother, who, it appeared, had no ambitions.

No defector ever found it easier to fly the coop. Maynard went from his flying school to London Airport and took a plane to Berlin on December 3. One could take a large bet that as the plane rose into the sky it was watched by a group of RAF personnel, all sighing deeply and then going off to have a drink. In Berlin he took the underground railway from the Western Sector to the East and was in no time broadcasting from East Germany. He told the population that his decision to defect had been formulated over a long period when he was becoming increasingly opposed to the colonial and foreign policy of Her Majesty's Government. He informed them that he had wished to work for the cinema but there was no opportunity to do that in Great Britain. (Had, perhaps, a studio proved unsympathetic, like the flying schools?) He also said that he had been forbidden to associate with Soviet officials, and "such interference in my personal affairs is intolerable to me."

In Moscow he trod on their faces. He lived a most enviable life. He got £1000 a year, free lodging, and much sightseeing, was instructed in Russian and constructive engineering, and given pleasant holidays, and he was allowed to telephone his family and receive letters. They tried to take his passport away, but he would have none of that. It is true that he drew maps of RAF installations for them and told them what he knew about Hawker Hunters, but it is clear that it was by sheer character he got them down. A letter survives in which he icily rebuked them about his terms of employment. "Indeed, regarding the financial assistance I am receiving by way of the Red Cross, I don't think it's unreasonable considering the small amount involved, and to bear in mind, as concerning information, what information I do possess."

Though, according to his account, he gave as little information as possible, much of the information he gave must have been faked for planting on the Russians by his superiors, or they would hardly have let him leave England. But the Russians continued to treat him well. He was allowed to go to Poland, a great privilege, and decided, though he had been entered in the School of Engineering Construction in Moscow, that it was in Poland he wanted to live. The Soviet Union could not take it any more. *Nyet,* it said, and it cannot possibly be blamed for saying it that time. Young Anthony was allowed to leave the Soviet Union without the slightest difficulty. As his Londonwards plane rose into the sky, surely it was watched by a group of Russian Security and Air Force personnel, all sighing deeply and then going off for a drink. Once back in England, he returned to his home at Eastbourne, to the parents with whom his relations had deteriorated, to the brother who had no ambition. No doubt they were glad to see him. At the Old Bailey he was sentenced to three years' imprisonment. One can be certain that he got the full remission and was seen off to liberty by a group of prison officials, all sighing deeply and then going off for a drink.

2

I N 1959 there was a striking demonstration that professionalism does not change its character in the sphere of espionage. The professional always wants the world to think well of his profession, and he does not abandon the attempt even though it might seem that the world had made up its mind against him. After Fuchs was convicted in 1950 he became aware that he would be deprived of his British citizenship, and he made a great fuss about it. At a sitting of the Deprivation of Citizenship Committee at the Law Courts on December 20, 1950, he submitted a very urgent petition that his certificate of naturalization should not be revoked. In a letter transmitted by Lord Shawcross, who was then Attorney-General, he pointed out that if deprival of citizenship was intended as punishment of his actions, there was little he could say except that he had already received the maximum sentence permissible by the law, and that the provisions of the British Nationality Act of 1948 excluded punishment as reason for revoking a certificate of naturalization. He assumed therefore that the question under consideration was his present and future loyalty, and though he modestly owned that he could not expect the Home Secretary to accept his own assurance of loyalty, he suggested that he should obtain the opinion of MI5 and the Director of Public Prosecutions. He had in fact convinced several security officers, one an American, that he was by this time heart and soul with the West.

Fuchs's statement went on to point out that his disloyal actions ceased early in 1949, before any suspicion had been voiced against him; that he had made a full statement and it was on this he was prosecuted; and that he had loyally cooperated with MI5 and the FBI, although no threat or promise had been made to him at any time before or after trial, and he submitted that in making his confession and in his subsequent actions he was guided by his convictions and his sentiments, and that that showed clearly enough where his loyalties now lay. Nevertheless the committee advised the Home Secretary to revoke Fuchs's certificate of naturalization under the Act of 1948 on the ground that "it was not conducive to the public good" that he should remain a citizen of the United Kingdom. Fuchs let it be understood that he was wounded to the heart.

When he was released from prison he could have remained in England, for he was now a stateless person and could not have been deported; and he could certainly have found work in some laboratory, for many of his scientific friends were loyal to him. Instead he followed a course of action entirely natural, and only discreditable by reason of his protestations of passion for the Western way of life. On June 24, 1959, he boarded a Polish plane and flew to East Germany, where he joined his father in the town of Schönefeld. He gave a press conference at which he announced that he was still a Marxist and intended to become an East German citizen and work for the new society. Shortly afterwards he became deputy director of the East German Central Institute for Nuclear Physics. It was the end of a polished performance; and if some credulous people had been deceived for some time into thinking him what he was not, it added nothing to the real injury he had done them.

But there was just over the hill a multiple exhibit of professional espionage which was more depressing. In March 1961 the trial of the Portland spy ring brought five people into the dock at the Old Bailey on charges, not of violating the Official Secrets Act, but of something more serious: of conspiring "together and with other persons unknown for purposes prejudicial to the safety or interest of the state to communicate to other persons information which might be directly or indirectly useful to an enemy." No person convicted under the Official Secrets Act can receive more than fourteen years' imprisonment. It is to be noted that persons who commit treacherous acts have not been charged under the treason laws since the wartime cases were finished with, because for treason there is no punishment but death. The Homicide Law has abolished capital punishment for most categories of murder, but treason it did not touch.

All of the five accused persons were professional spies, and the only two Britons among them represented the lowest grades of the profession. Harry Houghton was perhaps the most unattractive of all the betrayers of English trust, and Winifred Gee was hardly more winning, though both of them had the virtue of courage. Her bearing in court coerced a certain amount of respect, and in the Royal Navy Houghton had risen to the rank of master of arms by reason of creditable behaviour on the Malta and Russian convoys. They were in the dock together because they were fellow clerks in Portland Dock Yard, which was a sufficiently mysterious happening. In 1945 Houghton retired from the Royal Navy and became a civil servant, clerking in a minor naval establishment for six years, and then being posted to Warsaw on the staff of the British naval attaché. This appointment was very odd indeed, for he was already a noisy and conspicuous drunk. In Poland drinks were cheap, and he became very drunk indeed. He beat up his wife, formed friendships with some sinister English-speaking Poles, made a lot of money on the black market, and was finally encountered by his chief conspicuously drunk on a Warsaw street in broad daylight. He had been posted to Warsaw for three years, but after fifteen months he was sent home in disgrace.

The consequences were as odd as the appointment had been.

On arrival in England he was upgraded and made a permanent civil servant and posted to the Underwater Weapons Establishment at Portland. Even if it be admitted that the taxpayers' duty is to maintain drunks who beat their wives and are scandalously drunk on foreign streets, this was not the place to put an alcoholic extrovert. NATO had handed over to the British Navy the task of developing its underwater defence programme, and Portland was to be the centre of counter-submarine research. It was the nursery of numerous supersubtle devices, such as the sniffer apparatus (a device to detect submarines by tracing their Diesel fumes), which were an integral part of the West's armoury, and not then shared by the Soviet Union. Fortunately not all this work had been concentrated in Portland during the five years Houghton was employed in the Underwater Weapons Establishment, but much of it had. It is feared by some authorities that one of the most important among these devices, a method enabling low-flying helicopters to track submarines, was transfitted to Soviet agents during this period, though there is no evidence that Houghton was the transmitter.

Two years before Houghton left the Underwater Weapons Establishment, a clerk working in the same department, named Miss Gee, was moved from stores to the drawing-office records section, and they formed a close association. Miss Gee was in her early forties, short and plain, but not negligible as a personality. She lived with her aged mother and uncle and aunt, and the press and the lawyers regarded her as a starved spinster, drawn into the conspiracy only because Houghton gave her the love she had always lacked. It is true that Houghton's wife formed the darkest suspicions of their relations, that about that time she divorced him, and that afterwards Houghton and Miss Gee became engaged, and it is probable that when they went on pub crawls, a pastime to which they were addicted, the evening often terminated in embraces. But when Miss Gee met Houghton she was engaged to a carpenter in a fair way of business, a much more attractive man than Houghton, who was baldish and pallid. It is probable that what really drew Houghton and Miss Gee together was a shared enthusiasm for spying as a profession. In Houghton this was the simple product of greed for money and enjoyment of roguery. In Miss Gee it was perhaps a little more complicated. She loved money too, but she had her resentments. At the trial in the Old Bailey, after sentence had been passed, she wanted to attract the attention of her counsel, and she rapped her pencil on the ledge of the dock. The gesture was full of fierce, unexpended power, of the rage felt by people who think that society has given them no opportunities to use their ability or be honoured for it.

There was a great deal of money lying about to satisfy their greed. Houghton drew in pay about £750 a year and Miss Gee about £600. Houghton brought back £4000 from his fifteen-month stint in the British embassy in Warsaw, which he said was the product of black-market deals (including traffic in penicillin) and currency fiddling. Then he had a long run at Portland. In 1957 he was removed from the Underwater Weapons Establishment for incompetence; but as he had been made a permanent civil servant another job was found for him, this time in the Port Auxiliary Repair Unit. This gave him access to a good deal of all-round information, particularly after March 1960, when he was the only clerical officer in the department; and meanwhile Miss Gee was still at her useful post in charge of documents at the Underwater Weapons Establishment. It was Houghton's case that he did not begin to spy until 1957, when he was constrained to do so by threats of violence from Polish thugs. These thugs certainly existed; one was identified as second secretary of the Polish embassy in London. (In a moment of madness he gave his correct address to Houghton, who after his arrest handed it over to the police; it is not only the West that has its failures.) But we are under no obligation to take this story as pedantically accurate. Mr. Houghton was able to spend his salary on his drink bills, run a Renault Dauphine, buy a cottage for some thousands of pounds and furnish it well, with £650 of banknotes in a tin in the garden shed and £500 in a tin box under the stairs as fancy touches, and fit himself out with expensive clothes. Poor Miss Gee did not do so well: but she had over £300 in her home and £1300 of recently acquired securities. The couple were doing well for what they were, and they were lowly compared with the man who was alleged to act as their contact from the summer of 1960.

This was Gordon Arnold Lonsdale, or, to be exact, that was who it was not. In August 1924 a child had been born in Cobalt, Ontario, to a half-breed father and a Finnish immigrant, and given that name. Mr. and Mrs. Lonsdale separated, and the mother took her son back to Finland, and there he died, sometime after he attained the age of sixteen, perhaps in the Finno-Russian war; but some documentary proof of his identity as a Canadian citizen survived and fell into the hands of the Russians. This may have been a joint passport covering his mother and himself. Meanwhile the son of a Soviet scientist named Molody, born in 1922, was having a curious upbringing. His story is one of a number which suggests that clever children are dedicated by their parents to service in the Soviet Intelligence long before they can make such a decision for themselves, as we used to send our sons into the Navy, but at a still earlier age. Young Molody was sent by his mother at the age of eleven to live with her sister in California, who thereafter pretended he was her son. He stayed there for five years, attending a private school at Berkeley, and then was returned to the Soviet Union, where he was given a commission in the Red Navy and trained in espionage techniques. The Russians have always had a special interest in naval Intelligence since the days of Peter the Great, and the tradition was scarcely interrupted by the Revolution.

What young Molody was doing up till the age of thirty-two is not known; but he then assumed Lonsdale's identity. The persons responsible were not to know that among the few facts about young Lonsdale preserved in Canadian archives was a doctor's record of his circumcision, so the assumption was not as complete as, in a London prison years later, Molody must have wished. He made an illegal entry into Vancouver from a Soviet grain-freighter and spent three months converting himself into a Canadian with a present and a past. He brought plenty of money with him and was able to take his time, taking out first a driving license, then collecting such convincing documents as a membership card for the Young Men's Christian Association. Then, in January 1955, he acquired a Canadian passport, which was carelessly granted. The supporting affidavit was forged, and verification would have proved it. Once he had created his new identity, he took a bus to Niagara Falls and crossed the American border, obviously to contact one of the Soviet networks; and he was in London by March.

Again he had plenty of money, and he set about to build up at leisure the personality of a Canadian businessman with affairs which involved frequent travel. He enrolled himself as a student of Chinese at the London University School of Oriental and African Studies, and did pursue this study for two sessions, ending in 1957. He explained to the business friends he was cultivating that he hoped for a position with a large engineering firm trading with Communist China, which was to employ him on the sales staff. When he was asked what commission he was to be paid, he gave it as one-half per cent. This surprised his friends, for apparently the more probable figure would have been five to ten per cent, and hastily he explained that the orders would be so enormous that they would be most remunerative. As he would have had to sell a million pounds worth of machinery to make five thousand pounds, his friends still expressed surprise that he should put himself to the trouble of learning Chinese with no better prospect in view; Lonsdale was not unperceptive. He presently told them the plan had fallen through.

This shows that even a Soviet agent is not always up to concert pitch, and indeed Molody's impersonation of Lonsdale was far from perfect. He looked obstinately like a Russian, like the dark, thick-trunked, strong Russians Londoners can see any day walking down Kensington Palace Gardens or up in Highgate. Many people who encountered him remarked on this; and when he made his statement from the dock in the Old Bailey it became clear that he could not have been taken for a Canadian of Slav descent, because he had nothing like a Canadian accent. He did not even speak with the accent he might have been expected to have acquired in California when he was a child. He spoke a kind of English many of us have heard from refugees, the English of those who have learned our tongue in their own countries from American teachers. When he met Canadians, he put up a story that he had spent many years as a lumberjack, which would enable them to account for anything odd they might note in him, anything outside their own code, as due to a class difference. But his main cover was an active interest in the less stately kind of business enterprise and the kind of companions which it brought him. He rented out juke-boxes, financed the exploitation of a car security lock, and in 1956 bought a controlling interest in a firm which, God forgive it, made bubble-gum machines. He travelled abroad for the purpose, his unfortunate co-directors believed, of soliciting orders. They were surprised that he brought back so few.

Actually, the company, which had been prosperous until Lonsdale joined it, fell on evil days and was wound up in March 1960. Frequently before this and afterwards he gave signs that he was in financial difficulties. In 1958 he asked an acquaintance in the timber trade to lend him £400 so that he could pay off some hire-purchase debts. Another time he arranged for an overdraft at a branch of the Midland Bank. In August 1960 he bought a Studebaker from a garage in the Harrow Road, traded in a Standard for an allowance of £270, pled inability to pay the cash difference, and handed over instead a suite of furniture. Actually his regular allowance, which amounted to several thousand pounds a year, was still coming regularly from Canada. But he seemed to be wholly absorbed in starting up mediocre business deals, womanizing, and engaging in the minor social festivities, for which he had a great gift. He would have been the life and soul of a gala night at any Thames Valley hotel. His enjoyment of wine, women, and song seems to have been genuine enough, but his poverty was assumed. When his flat in the White House, Albany Street, was searched, large sums of money were found. He and the two other members of the espionage firm who had been planted in London by the Soviet Union had at their disposal vast resources.

These two others were the attractive Mr. and Mrs. Cohen, whom the FBI knew as associates of the Rosenbergs and Colonel Abel, but they were no longer Morris and Lona Cohen. They had become Peter John and Helen Joyce Kroger, and they lived in a comfortable bungalow with a neat garden in the suburb of Ruislip, which is ten or twelve miles from the centre of London, not far from the Third United States Air Force Headquarters. Morris Cohen was one of those American-born children of Russian immigrants, like Harry Gold, who turned against the country which had treated them and their parents not unhandsomely, and very readily served the Communist Party in its most subversive aspect. He had had a comfortable enough youth. His father kept a thriving vegetable store in the Bronx; he became a football star on the outstanding team of the James Monroe High School, got a football scholarship to the University of Mississippi, became a student trainer to the team when he injured his leg and could no longer be a player, graduated in science, and then went to take another degree, this time in social studies, at the University of Illinois. But in 1937 he enlisted in the Communist-dominated Abraham Lincoln Brigade which went out to fight in the Spanish Civil War, and thereafter communism was his faith, his bread-and-butter, his way of life.

On the victory of Franco he returned to America, worked as a security guard in the Soviet exhibition at the 1940 New York World's Fair, married Lona, the Communist daughter of Polish immigrants, and took a post in the New York office of Amtorg, the Soviet trading corporation. When America came into the war he went into the Army and cooked for the forces in Alaska, Canada, and England. He came back in 1945, and he and his wife were recruited into the Rosenberg spy ring, while he took advantage of the veterans' educational grant scheme to take a teacher's diploma while teaching in a New York Board of Education school. In 1950, after Harry Gold had been arrested and had led the FBI to Greenglass, the Rosenbergs gave the Cohens the signal to leave. They closed their bank accounts, cashed their saving bonds, and fled their apartment in such haste that Lona Cohen went off without her jewellery and cosmetics and with very few of her clothes. The FBI searched for the Cohens then, and again seven years later, when they found their photographs and dossiers in Abel's files, but in vain.

It is thought that they went to Australia and to New Zealand. At any rate they reappeared in 1954 in Austria, under the name of Kroger. They wrote to the New Zealand embassy in Paris and asked for passports, giving forged birth certificates and a marriage license in the name of New Zealand citizens who had died some time before. They then travelled to Hong Kong and Japan, returned to Paris, and then entered England to settle down in temporary quarters and look for a permanent home. A year later Kroger began to make appearances in the book auction rooms and to establish himself as an antiquarian bookseller. He must have spent the intervening year in acquiring the technique of the trade, for this was not a revival of any interest he had shown in earlier days. He set himself up in an office in the Strand, having meanwhile bought the Ruislip bungalow, which had been built by a retired official of the Indian police with more regard for comfort and solidity than most of its kind. Though there was to be ample evidence that they were not short of means, they did not buy the bungalow outright. It cost something under £5000 and £4000 of this was on mortgage, of which they had paid off £1000 five years later. There had to be no sign of easy funds.

In 1958 Peter Kroger had a small but healthy business with a stock worth several thousand pounds, but he gave up his office and used his home as headquarters. It may well have been that he and his wife wanted to keep a close watch on the bungalow, which was so stuffed with the tools of espionage that it was one of the most interestingly congested buildings in all history since the Ark. The place was protected like a prison with burglar-proof bolted locking devices which could, of course, be explained by the necessity of satisfying the insurance companies with whom Kroger had taken out policies for his books. Within there were many documents, some in cipher, some clear, some microfilms, and a microscope for reading microfilms, and inside a Bible a piece of do-it-yourself microfilm, made of cellophane coated with a chemical used in photography and easily obtainable. In a bedroom there was a flex fifty feet long with plug and bulb. There was a hip-flask with a concealed compartment containing iron oxide, which is used for sprinkling on magnetic tape to show up Morse code messages. There were flashlights which turned out to be hiding places for film. There was a Ronson lighter which contained two film negatives which were schedules for broadcasts to Moscow, with call-signs based on the names of Russian towns and rivers, as well as six rolls of the sort of cipher pad which had been found in Colonel Abel's room in the Hotel Latham in New York, these coated with a chemical which ignites at low temperature. There was a short-wave radio with peculiar arrangements for listening through headphones on high-frequency bands. In the bathroom there was another microdot reader, hidden in a box of face powder. In the attic there were apples and a seventy-five-foot-long aerial; there was a £200 camera. Dotted about the house were £200 in £5 notes, $2563 in cash, and another £120 in mixed traveller's checks.

In the kitchen floor, hidden by a refrigerator, was a trapdoor. It led down to what had been the last owner's unfinished effort to make himself a wine-cellar. Under a heap of rubble was a concrete slab four inches thick, and under that a board, and under that a hole with five bags in it. One contained a wireless transmitter, of no commercial brand, powerful enough to broadcast direct to Moscow. It had an automatic playing device which made possible high-speed transmission, and thus had the effect of baffling any detector beam. There were also a number of film rolls, a camera, chemicals, and $6000 in $20 bills. Later another $4000 were to turn up. In all there was about £7000 in the house.

The house also contained seven passports: one was British, dated 1951, bearing a serial number never issued; the two passports fraudulently obtained from the New Zealand embassy in Paris in 1954; two American passports; and two Canadian passports, issued in June and September 1956, to Thomas James Wilson, storekeeper, and Mary Jane Smith, secretary. Some of these were exquisitely forged. Attached to them were notes on the conveniently slovenly attitude of the British and the Canadians towards Canadian passport-holders.

In Lonsdale's flat in the White House there was the typewriter which had typed some of the documents in the Krogers' house, and there was another microdot reader in a powder box, and another dummy flashlight that held signal plans. He had, of course, a banking account, but in a secret pocket in a belt there were fifteen $20 bills and in the roller of a Chinese scroll hung above his bed there was $1800: in all, over £700. He had another £215 and $300 on him when he was arrested. It was put forward as an explanation of these last sums that he was about to use them as part payment for two tons of Spearmint chewing gum, but many of us, should we wish to acquire two tons of Spearmint chewing gum, would have a difficulty in finding that much money.

The cost of espionage is a vast tax laid upon the peoples of the world; and in this case more has to be allowed for than the cost of this equipment and the total amount of the cash. The Krogers may have made a fair profit out of their bookselling business, but their English friends and acquaintances, belonging to the same world and knowing how the ledgers run, assumed from the scale of their expenditure that they must have private means. There were at any rate five years between their flight from New York and their arrival in England when, wandering over the face of the earth, they cannot have followed any gainful employment. Lonsdale's picayune and ailing enterprises cannot at any time have covered a fraction of his outgoings. All these people had enormous travelling expenses. Money was being poured out like water and ran away like water poured on sand. For it was spent to steal defensive secrets with such cunning that the robbed felt more and more need for defence, and more and more need to be secretive, and the robbers felt more and more need to steal. But, as the Old Bailey showed, it was not money alone that was being wasted.

What brought the five spies into the dock is not known with any certainty, except that it was not the work of MI5. A story is told that it was the accidental result of a police inquiry of quite a different nature. It is said that a photographer at the Underwater Weapons Establishment reported to the local Admiralty police that he had received a scurrilous anonymous letter on dockyard notepaper and suggested that it might be from Houghton, who had sometimes seemed to bear him a grudge; and that the Admiralty constable in charge of the investigation found that Houghton had nothing to do with the letter but was struck by the rate at which he was spending money. But this is probably a legend, put into currency to hide the fact that the clue came from a defecting Soviet naval officer whose identity was then still being kept a secret. Whatever the mechanism may have been, the Special Branch, headed by Superintendent George Smith, watched Houghton and Miss Gee each time they came up to London to meet Lonsdale, with a shopping bag which was full of documents when they arrived and full of purchases when they left. On January 7 it showed its hand and arrested the three of them, and on the same day took Mr. and Mrs. Kroger from the house in Cranley Drive, which had been under surveillance for some time.

The five accused persons took the course, unusual in cases of such a nature in the English court, of pleading not guilty, and Houghton and Miss Gee chose to give evidence on their own behalf. It was evident that nothing would have stopped them. They may have stampeded the others into their pleas of not guilty, for they were very obstinate. Houghton obviously thought he was clever enough to get out of the charges and planned to use his evidence as proof of how willing he had been to assist the authorities. Miss Gee insisted on going into the witness box out of sheer combativeness; and indeed her testimony was oddly winning. This is how she described her arrest outside Waterloo:

We were absolutely swooped on. At that time, I could not imagine what it was. I thought they were Teddy boys. Mr. Smith stood out. I could not imagine how one gentleman came to be mixed up with a lot of Teddy boys. There was so much noise I could not hear a word. I did not know who they were.

This is how Dickens might have made a genteel spinster react to a brush with the constabulary; and there is grace in the invitation she extends to Superintendent Smith to share the shelter of her umbrella of gentility.

But Lonsdale and the Krogers elected not to give evidence; and they would have been better advised if they had not exercised the right of accused persons to make statements from the dock which are not under oath and cannot be cross-examined. Londsdale's statement was disillusioning. He had great physical distinction in his way, a bodily self-respect which survived difficult circumstances. After weeks in prison he looked as if he could have walked out of the Old Bailey to the nearest tennis court and played a good hard game. But he dropped much of his distinction as soon as he began his statement. His way of speaking was commonplace, even a little vulgar, and he was making too obvious a bid for the jury's sympathy. It was his claim that the Krogers had never understood the nature of the espionage equipment in their house and that he had asked them to keep it for him, because his service flat at the White House was entered by the domestic staff. As for the hole under the kitchen floor, he had made it himself, while the Krogers were away, and had put the radio transmitter there. Then it had occurred to him that the use he was making of the Krogers' house might get them into trouble, so he provided the false passports for them and hid them in the house. This preposterous story could have been told only in the hope that the jury was one of those assemblies of idiots which, in stern fulfilment of the law of probabilities, sometimes fills the jury box, or in the other hope that the judge and jury might think: what a nice, gallant man, of course he is not telling the truth, but he is trying to take on himself the blame of his comrades.

This, however, was simply professionalism. He had to give his side the opportunity of taking these two chances: of a jury who was imbecile, of a judge and jury who were susceptible. What the Krogers did was more wounding. They were an impressive couple, engaged in some ferocious struggle with reality, from which they were trying to extort an admission that it was at some point quite different from what was generally supposed. The man, with his white hair winding round his head like a gleaming bandage, was like a figure in one of Stanley Spencer's apocalyptic paintings; and his wife, a handsome, Rubensish woman, had the busy air developed by pious wives who have to cope with the problems arising out of their husbands' even greater piety. They might have belonged to the more puritanic type of nudist, who hold it positively wrong to wear clothes, or they might have believed the earth was flat, or they might have spoken with the dead at séances. Though by the luck of the draw communism was their chosen form of dissent, they held this secular faith so strongly that it gave them distinction of a religious sort.

When Mr. Kroger addressed the court he spoke like the dignified fanatic that he was. He claimed that he had been absorbed in his business to the exclusion of everything else, and indeed he talked about it at such length, in such detail, with such pride, that he sounded like a man obsessed. Such a man might well overlook anything that his young friend Lonsdale was doing about the house, for he was concentrating on his books all day, even late into the evenings. He added little touches to his story which lent conviction to the picture of a life voluntarily confined within certain limits and not less contented for that. When he said that his wife's hobby was photography he mentioned that she took pictures of the booksellers' cricket team, which was indeed a great interest of his. He ended his statement by saying:

We answered the police as truthfully and straightforwardly as humanly possible.

He had said earlier:

Neither my wife or I engaged in spying or any activities which may be considered or regarded as irregular.

Then Mrs. Kroger, in a clear and beautiful voice, made a statement less convincing because it was feminine to a degree attained more easily by women's magazines than by women. She stuck to the cozily concrete. She described Lonsdale as winning her friendship by carrying in the coals and helping her with the washing-up; she spoke of throwing on an apron and preparing a late lunch for her husband. She explained that she used the seventy-five-foot flex in the attic when she was lagging the roof and checking the apples she stored up there. As for the hole in the kitchen floor, she had only seen it once, when the plumber explored it. She ended up with the words:

> I took care of my home, helped my husband in business. I know nothing of spying and never had anything to do with such things.

These two people made their statements in the full knowledge that if the jury was unconvinced and found them guilty, their records would be read by a police officer before the judge passed sentence, and they would be proved liars. That is exactly what happened. The next day the court was told that they were the Cohens and had been Soviet agents for the best part of twenty years. This was quite horrible, for these people were committed to principle, and wished to be so. If they had to be defeated they should have borne themselves like classical martyrs, not with lies, and unavailing ones at that, on their lips. But it was impossible to feel indignant with the Krogers, because one cannot feel harsh emotions toward people who have been sentenced to what might be imprisonment for life, and because they were not free agents.

Had they wanted to stop being Soviet spies, they could hardly have done so. Had they wanted to walk out of that Ruislip bungalow, they would have had no place to go except a police station, which by this time in their careers might have been unwilling to receive them simply as defectors. They had to stay still and take their punishment, and they could not take it in the way that would have come natural to them, because they were not only fanatics but professional spies, like Lonsdale; and, like him, they had for professional reasons to act on the assumption that the jury might be imbecile and believe a lying story of their innocence. It would have protected the interests of their client, the Soviet Union, had they been acquitted and gone out of court with their records undisclosed. For that reason they had to betray their own worth and dignity.

The jury was not imbecile. All five prisoners were found guilty of the conspiracy charges, and Lonsdale was sentenced to twenty-five years of imprisonment; the Krogers got twenty years; Houghton and Miss Gee got fifteen years. Between them they had to contribute £4000 towards the court costs. The fraudulent pleas had been of no avail, and perhaps some other spuriousness had been wasted too. When Mrs. Kroger was arrested at her bungalow, she asked Superintendent Smith if she might stoke the boiler before she left, a simple-minded request for an experienced agent. Naturally it led to an immediate search of her handbag and the finding of several microfilms of letters to Lonsdale from his wife, and an ordinary longhand letter from him to her, which presumably Mrs. Kroger had been about to reduce to microdots. They were among some not very important code papers.

His wife, Galyusha, was full of complaints. She longed for her husband to return to her, telling him how his little boy, Trofim, said to her, "When is Daddy coming home? And why has he gone away? And what a *stupid* job Daddy has got." He also has a little girl of twelve, Liza, who is feeling his absence.

> For the first time in six years at school Liza brought home a school report with four "threes" for geometry, algebra, English, and party training, the rest are fours. You cannot imagine how this upset me, considering that the high school is not far in the offing. . . . Liza has got completely out of hand. Yesterday I was called to the school. She failed to attend the last two lessons, and was roaming about somewhere during these hours.

One has an uneasy feeling that one has read something very like this before, and so one has. This is a case history of a child becoming delinquent for want of her father's presence, as stark as the case history of a daughter with a father fixation in the letters from Colonel Abel's family found (also with some not very important code documents) in his hollow pencil. There is a curious resemblance in style throughout the letters; and there is one feature common to both which is surprising. It is true that the wives of Abel and Lonsdale must have lived in aching apprehension of the calamity which arose out of their employment and which eventually befell them. But would they constantly write to their husbands and candidly express their desire that they should leave the KGB, when all their letters were bound to be read by several other employees of the KGB? Supposing that the wife of a member of MI6 who was on a secret mission were sending him letters which she knew had to be opened and microfilmed by other MI6 agents, would she be likely to fill those letters with complaints of her loneliness and the inability of the family to get on without their father? Would he, answering, complain (as Lonsdale did in the letters found in Mrs. Kroger's handbag) of his loneliness?

It may seem far-fetched to suggest that both sets of letters were prepared in advance, to be discovered if and when the agent and his arsenal were discovered, to have just the effect that the Abel family letters had on the jury that was trying him: to make them regard the spy as a good patriot and a man like themselves, who is making the same sacrifices for his country as the soldier on a jungle post or the Navy man on an Arctic station, and should enjoy a like respect. Only at one point does it seem likely that the Lonsdale letters are what they seem; his letter to his wife makes an allusion to his mother's having sent him "to the nether regions" in 1932, which can be presumed to refer to her curious act of sending him to California as her sister's son. But on the other hand, in 1962, when President Kennedy exchanged Abel for Powers, the U-2 pilot who had been captured when he crashed on Soviet territory, Mrs. Abel took an important part in the preliminary negotiations, and the letters she then wrote seemed, as Mr. Donovan reveals in his illuminating book, *Strangers on a Bridge,* curiously unlike the letters she was writing to her husband in jail. Mr. Donovan's bewilderment increased when he went to East Berlin to negotiate the exchange and was introduced to Mrs. Helen Abel and her daughter Lydia (Evelyn) and a male cousin. The women's conversation baffled him, and the male cousin was under the impression that the wife's name was Lydia, the daughter's name was Helen, and that the daughter had never married.

There was to appear yet another parallel between the cases of Abel and Lonsdale. On February 10, 1962, Abel was exchanged for Powers, an exchange which, according to many Americans, was quite unfair and amounted to robbery. For the United States was giving back to the Soviet Union a brilliantly intelligent and highly trained agent whose mind must have been packed with knowledge of American conditions, and was receiving a man who could not be described in analogous terms. But obviously the

United States government regarded it as of paramount importance to know what had happened to the U-2 plane which had
crashed near the industrial centre Sverdlovsk in May 1960, and
had to swallow the Soviet Union's betrayal of its conviction that
it would be well worth its while to recover Abel.

On April 22, 1964, Lonsdale was exchanged for Greville
Wynne, an English businessman who in May 1963 had been
sentenced by a Moscow court to eight years' imprisonment for
espionage. He was alleged to have acted as a courier for Oleg
Penkovsky, a Soviet scientist who had been charged with acting
as a British agent and was found guilty and is said to have been
shot. As the facts of this case are not known, it is impossible to
describe it or discuss it. But it may be mentioned that a government often cannot, for security reasons, explain why it wishes to
recover an agent. The Soviet people would not expect to be told,
but a Western people would demand an explanation, and public
confidence would be shaken if it were not forthcoming. For that
reason it might be laid down that the exchange of persons convicted of espionage is undesirable in principle. But it would be
hard to adhere to that principle.

3

A F T E R the Portland spy trial a storm of indignation broke in Parliament and the press. The day after the trial
the *Daily Mail* printed these words on the front page, pointing
out the gravity of its revelations regarding Admiralty security,
and its consequences:

> [It] is regarded as the worst penetration of our security
> system since Klaus Fuchs gave the atom-bomb secrets to Rus-
> sia. . . . There will undoubtedly be serious repercussions on
> Anglo-American relations. It is only recently that the Ameri-
> cans have got over their mistrust of British security caused by
> the Fuchs case, the Pontecorvo case, and Burgess and Maclean.

The faults were blatant. Neither Houghton nor Miss Gee had
been screened by security when they went to work at the Under-

water Weapons Establishment. Not that that mattered in the case of Miss Gee. It is a proof of the limited value of all security precautions, which have to deal with human nature at its most mysterious, that she would have passed any such test like a bird. But Houghton would not, for he had been sent back from Warsaw because the naval attaché considered his Falstaffian habits made him a security risk. It emerged that when the Underwater Weapons Establishment, after five years, revolted against the continued presence of Houghton, it had taken them six months to get the Civil Service Commissioners to shift him. Meanwhile, his wife had over a long period remarked the number of confidential documents her husband was bringing home and had begged him not to do it. As a service wife she knew that she herself might have been implicated, had he been discovered, and indeed she might have found herself in the same position as Mrs. Kroger. She disclosed her anxiety to more than one official, and a security officer afterwards said that yes, he had disregarded certain rumours of Houghton's suspicious behaviour. But he added:

> These rumours came from his wife, who said Houghton was spying, and was reading Naval documents of a confidential nature at his home. But I did not pay too much attention to these rumours. They were based on allegations by Mrs. Houghton, who had no cause to love her husband.

In the course of this post-mortem a security officer made the astonishing remark that he had heard these rumours but had not passed them on to the Director of Naval Intelligence in London, because "it all sounded like a novel and I was afraid that the laws of slander would be invoked if I recommended an investigation into his activities." The speaker was a man with a long and distinguished record, and what he said meant that he had been made a security officer in the last years of his service and had not been properly trained. He was the only security officer at the base, and had appealed for assistants to the Admiralty, but his requests had been disregarded.

The Labour Opposition made much of this lamentable situation and demanded the resignation of the First Lord of the Admiralty, Lord Carrington, as required by the doctrine of ministerial responsibility. This doctrine is an interesting example of the self-creating power of the British Constitution. It means, according to the persons who invoke it in the Houses of Parliament and parts of the press, that the minister in charge of any department must take on himself the blame for any blunder committed by his subordinates, even if he had no part in making it and had known nothing about it. Strictly speaking, no such doctrine exists. The great Professor Dicey says that there is indeed a doctrine of ministerial responsibility, but quite a different one: it simply holds that every minister is legally responsible for every act of the Crown in which he takes part. But Members of Parliament and political journalists keep on using the term in the incorrect sense, and as this gives us a handy instrument for getting rid of an incompetent minister, it remains with us, like the stray cat who proves a good mouser and acquires hearthrug rights. Such are the benefits of an unwritten constitution. It adds to the graciousness of the persons who confer on us this particular benefit that most of them are quite unconscious of the good they are doing.

The attacks on Lord Carrington were very properly disregarded, for his record was immaculate. He had taken office in October 1959, and the security forces had started watching the Portland spy ring in February 1960, and nothing could be done to alter the security arrangements until the arrest of the spies. A committee of three was appointed to investigate the case, consisting of Sir Charles Romer, former Lord Justice of Appeal, Sir Harold Emmerson, a former permanent secretary to the Ministry of Labour, the recently retired Vice-Admiral Sir Geoffrey Thistleton Smith. These gave birth in due time to the Romer Report, a document of great importance, since it was the first official admission that history had taken a sudden turn, and instead of walking along the safe road which we had thought was the only road, we were crossing a rope bridge over an abyss, without having acquired the relevant technique.

The report pulled some of its punches. It seemed to take it for granted that Houghton should have been cherished in the bosom of our state; that the lion and the unicorn should have had to take responsibility for him in Warsaw. But it noted with appropriate severity that nobody had ever told the Portland authorities why Houghton had been thrown out of Poland; that when, four years later, an allegation was made to Houghton's immediate superior that Houghton was taking home secret papers, this officer told nobody but suggested that his informant should go to the security officer or to the police; that in 1956 Houghton had been twice reported to the authorities as a security risk, but the matter was blinked at rather than investigated, and an incomplete and misleading report was sent to the Admiralty, which should have detected at sight that someone was being silly and insisted on the matter being effectively pursued. True, it gave high praise to MI5 and the Special Branch for their slow and sure engorgement of the spy ring. But that was all it could say on the credit side. After all, it was admitted that neither the Special Branch nor MI5 had actually discovered the existence of that spy ring. For that we have to thank either the Dorset constabulary, for so productively pausing when in search of a poison pen, or a Soviet defector, according to which story one believes.

The fact is we were stumped by a new situation. Now the insignificant human being and the unimpressive material object could inflict crucial danger on Britain. Of course the bomb-throwing Fenians and Anarchists of the nineteenth century were dangerous; but they were aliens. The only way that Houghton, a homekeeping native mediocrity, could have been a menace in the past would have been for him to pretend to be someone else of greater importance, like Perkin Warbeck. He could not conceivably have been a peril to the English defences against the Armada, nor to Nelson's fleet. Nor could the bungalow in Cranley Drive have threatened an Armageddon. At most, a private conflict might have confided to the attic or the hole in the kitchen floor two or three corpses. But today there are millions of people as commonplace as Houghton who, by their employment in certain factories or offices, have access to documents which can deliver us over to death, with help provided from an arsenal concealed behind the most innocent piece of half-timbering in suburbia. It is not, of course, that only the small fry like Houghton can betray their people; Burgess and Maclean and their friends proved that. But what is new is that the small fry also have the power of betrayal, having now access to secrets which can be betrayed and are worth betraying. Science, adding to our armoury, continually demands more mechanics and more clerks, and with every demand makes the problem of security more difficult to solve.

It may be described as difficult, but need not be described as insoluble. The Portland spy ring could never have formed if certain simple rules had been observed. Houghton and Miss Gee would have had nothing to give Lonsdale if the "snap-check" system had been regularly carried out and the workers in the Underwater Weapons Establishment and the Repair Unit had been stopped at irregular intervals and been obliged to show what they had on them; and if there had been any check on the files during week-ends. Lonsdale would have been harder to frustrate, but there were two points at which he might have taken a fall. His application for a Canadian passport was not properly scrutinized, for it bore a forged name for reference. The existing Canadian law should have trapped him then, and there should be a law in Great Britain to have trapped him later, when a company of which he was a director went bankrupt.

In the spring of 1961 the quickening march past of spies must have caused in the British government some such emotions as the Eastern European states felt in the early Middle Ages when they found themselves helpless before Asiatic hordes making a new use of mounted men not as individuals but as cavalry. Espionage of this modern sort, the use of scientific method by the powers to steal each other's secrets, with each theft impairs the robbed state's defences as thoroughly as if it had fought and been defeated. It might be thought that such defeats make an agreeable substitute for the older type, since they are bloodless; but a succession of such bloodless defeats might lead to the total defencelessness of a state and a final eclipse in slaughter and enslavement. But this is not the only danger. The counterespionage in any state with secrets worth stealing is likely to be effective to a certain degree, but here, as in many other fields, attack is much easier than defence. This means that there is a theft here and a theft there, and then detection and a pause, during which the robbed state tries to recover lost ground by tightening up security measures and by readjustments and frenzied stepping up of the arms programme, while there is an unprofitable embitterment of feeling against the robber state, inimical to the establishment of world political peace, which is the only cure for this cancer.

Here it must be remembered that it is folly to feel any censoriousness against the Soviet Union for its espionage record. Like

Great Britain, like the United States, like all modern states, the Soviet Union has had this form of spying forced on it by history. On the other hand, after the discovery of a bad case of espionage a section of the public may cloak its defeatist attitude by the pretence that all these spies are really nice people, idealists serving a brave new state, which has its little difficulties, and what they are doing is a peccadillo, like stealing flowers from a park to give to the patients in a hospital. This is not a state of mind that promotes the public good. It would have gone ill with us had this view been strongly held in the days of Nazi Germany, which also impressed many as doing its best for its people.

George Blake, an important agent in MI6, was tried at the Old Bailey on May 3, 1961, and found guilty of such serious offences against the Official Secrets Act that he was sentenced to forty-two years of imprisonment (fourteen years on each of three counts), which is the longest term of imprisonment imposed in a British court for a hundred and fifty years. At first it looked as if the moral of this case was that we could trust nobody. For George Blake was an attractive man. An eminent lawyer present at the trial (which was held in camera) said sadly: "He looked the kind of man I would have been glad to have in my house." Blake had a story to account for his treachery which aroused some sympathy. It was told at length by his wife, the daughter of a retired Army officer, whom he had married in 1954, when she had been employed at the Foreign Office. After his conviction she sold an account of her married life to the *Sunday Telegraph*, and it began with a disarming passage:

> I had no idea my husband was acting as an agent for the Russians. But when they told me that he had betrayed the secrets of my country it never crossed my mind that they had made a mistake. I didn't say, "You must have got hold of the wrong man, it can't be true." As I thought back to George's background and to the 6½ years of our very happy life, it all fitted in somehow.

Nobody can doubt that Mrs. Blake believed the story she told, least of all her touching and proud account of how her husband had been converted to communism when he was a prisoner in the hands of the Chinese Communists. In 1948, as an established member of the Foreign Office, he had been given his first appointment as vice-consul at Seoul, South Korea, which was a cover for his real duties as MI6 representative. In 1950 he was arrested together with his chief, Sir Vivian Holt, and a mixed bag including among others the French minister and his staff, many ecclesiastics and missionaries, monks and nuns, a well-known journalist, Mr. Philip Deane of *The Observer,* a famous Jewish surgeon from Vienna, and a hotel manager. They spent the next three years mixed with Korean prisoners in a prison compound near the North Korean capital of Pyongyang, getting the roughest of treatment, housed in hovels, underfed, beaten, exposed to the heat in summer and the chill of winter in a country of climatic extremes, alive with vermin and untended in sickness. The prisoners were also exposed to some brainwashing, which oddly enough was administered by an official who afterwards defected to the United States, and they were given as their only reading matter magazines celebrating the fame and glory of the Red Dean of Canterbury and Mrs. Monica Felton, and the works of Marx, Engels, Lenin, and Stalin.

It was Blake's story that this instruction, and the study of these books, converted him to communism, for the reason (he told his wife) that his heart had always been wrung by the sorrows of the poor, and the sight of Asiatic poverty had been an agonizing revelation to him. He then came to the conclusion that communism promised to improve the lot of the masses and decided therefore that he would become a Communist. After about eighteen months he went to his captors and told them so and dedicated himself to the cause. But, according to him, he made three conditions: that he should receive no privileges as a prisoner, that he should receive no payment for the information he provided, and that he should be asked to give no report on his fellow prisoners. From that time onwards he was a Soviet spy.

This story was in outline given great publicity and the most impressive sanction, even before his wife's articles were published. At his trial the Lord Chief Justice, Lord Parker, said:

> To quote his own words, he resolved to join the Communist side in establishing what he believed on balance a more just society. What he did was to approach the Russians and volunteer to work for them.

When his appeal was heard, Mr. Justice Hilbery said:

> When he was a prisoner in Communist hands in Korea, the only works for him and his fellow-prisoners to read were those of Marx, Engels, Lenin and Stalin, so poisoning to him that he decided to remain in the pay and service of this country, and by every means in his power to betray it and by that method to help the cause he had secretly espoused.

In Parliament Mr. Harold Macmillan (who has rarely been properly briefed when he has addressed the House on matters concerning espionage) told Members of Parliament:

> Blake received no money for his services. He was never at any time a member of the Communist Party, or any of its affiliated organizations. What he did was done as the result of a conversion to a genuine belief in the Communist system. In these circumstances, suspicion would not easily be aroused in relation to a man who had served his country well for some eight years, who gave every appearance of leading a normal and respectable life, but who had decided to betray his country for ideological reasons. Indeed, having agreed to work for the Russians, he was careful not to arouse suspicion and to conceal his conversion to communism.

But there is no reason to believe George Blake's story of his conversion to communism in the Korean prison camp, and strong reason to disbelieve it.

It was extremely unlikely that an intelligent man would regard communism as likely to save the masses, when he daily saw how the Chinese Communists were treating such of the masses as were unlucky enough to find themselves in this prison camp. It was no rose garden. A large number of prisoners, including some elderly nuns, priests, and harmless peasants, some of them mothers with young babies, were subjected to prolonged hardship varied by physical ill treatment amounting often to torture, and there were not a few murders. It would be hard to take all this as a wholesome prescription for the sorrows of the poor. As for the enlightening works of Marx, Engels, Lenin, and Stalin, this was not the first time that Blake had been exposed to them. He had been prepared for service in Soviet and satellite countries by a proper Foreign Office course, which included studies in the sacred books of communism planned by that brilliant expositor the late Mr. Thomas Carew-Hunt. But even if he had been a humanitarian broken down by malnutrition and exhaustion to the point of accepting all the Communist claims he had learned to reject, his humanitarianism would hardly have consented to carry out the work which his Soviet employers then ordered him to do. For, after he was released from prison and returned to Europe, he was sent by MI6 to Berlin and there, for the benefit of the Soviet Union, he committed many acts which are alleged to have led to the imprisonment and in some cases to the death of German nationals who had trusted him and Great Britain. He is alleged to have given the Soviet Union the names of Germans working as agents for the West in East Germany, and he is alleged to have had a hand in the kidnapping of various prominent East German defectors who had sought refuge in the Western sector of Berlin. Such activities are an incredible result of such a high-minded conversion as his wife describes.

A quite different interpretation of Blake's treachery is suggested by his life story. He was the son of Albert Behar, who claimed to be a British subject. This man in 1922 married a Dutch lady called Catherine Beijderwellen, daughter of a good solid family, set up house with her in Holland, fathered George and two daughters, was always busy with some commercial venture which never went quite right, and died in 1936, leaving his family in straitened circumstances. Then Mrs. Behar, who had little knowledge of her husband's family, received a letter from a sister of his, the wife of a banker in Cairo, offering to take George into her home and give him a good education. The boy, who was just thirteen, was sent off to Egypt and once he got there sent home astounding news. His father had not been English; he was one of the fourteen children of a wealthy merchant who was one of the Sephardi, that is a descendant of the Jews who were driven out of Spain by Ferdinand and Isabella, and his family had been settled in Egypt for many generations. For some strange reason Albert Behar had left the parental roof and business to join the French Foreign Legion; later he joined the British Army during the First World War, and served as a French interpreter to the Royal Army Service Corps, being twice wounded and badly gassed. He certainly had a British passport, but this was either because of his war service or because his family had rendered services to the administration while Egypt was a British protectorate. All this was apparently as much news to the widowed Mrs. Behar as it was to the boy.

According to George, his new-found relatives treated him well, though he may have resented the discovery that they had severed all connection with his father because he had married a Christian. At the beginning of 1939 he returned from Egypt to finish his education at Rotterdam, where he lived with his grandmother. His mother and sisters went on living at the home they had occupied when the father was still alive, a villa near The Hague. Thus it happened that, when the Germans invaded the Low Countries during the spring of 1940, he immediately lost touch with them. Mrs. Behar and her daughters were told by a friend, Commander D. W. Child, who was an Intelligence officer at the British embassy at The Hague, to go to the Hook of Holland, and there they were put on one of the three British destroyers which went to fetch the Dutch royal family and government and British residents in Holland and take them to England. George was almost at once arrested and put in a civilian internment camp at Alkmuar, but after six months escaped, hid in his uncle's house for a short time, and then settled down on a farm where he could work with a resistance group. He took the name of Pieter de Vries. Presently he found that there was in the neighbouring town of Limburg a unit of what was known as the *Orde Dienst,* which was to become practically a secret militia, and he joined it.

Thus he became involved in a curious enterprise called "Operation North Pole," which was carried out by cooperation between the Dutch resistance groups, a secret-service section established in London by the Dutch government-in-exile, called "Military Preparation for the Return," and the British secret services, in particular an organization formed by Churchill "to set Europe ablaze," called the Special Operations Executive. SOE had some successes and some lamentable failures; and of these last, Operation North Pole was the most lamentable.

The cooperating bodies planned to send Dutch agents from London in planes by night, equipping each with his own radio transmitter, and drop them by parachute at prearranged spots, where they were to be met by members of the resistance groups and led to places of safety where they could radio back reports of

German movements to England. Should they be captured by the Germans and made to radio back false messages to England, they were to obey, but they were to make certain mistakes according to a code (for example, make an error of substituting one vowel for another in the second sentence from the beginning of the message and two in the next-but-one sentence). Thus London would know that the message was being sent under compulsion and would revise its plans for dropping the agents. There was no mistake about this arrangement. Every agent received instruction in these terms. But very soon after Operation North Pole began, some of the parachutists were captured by the Germans and made to send false messages to London. They made the agreed signals. But London disregarded them.

It kept on dispatching Dutch agents, who kept on being captured as soon as they were dropped. Out of fifty-four agents, brave and patriotic Dutchmen, fifty fell into German hands. One of them was George Louis Jambroes, a leader of the resistance, adored by his countrymen. They fell into the hands of unusually merciful German Army Intelligence officers who treated them quite well; but, as the end approached, the SS hustled them out of the Army jails, and forty-seven were put to death in the extermination camp at Mauthausen. This grim tragedy caused great feeling among the Dutch. After the war it was the subject of a Parliamentary inquiry in Holland which lasted for several years. Its investigation could hardly hope to recover the clear-cut truth about the proceedings of several organizations, all unrecorded for bad and for good reasons, particularly when of the fifty men who could have thrown light on what really happened only three survived. But the report ascribes much blame, very nearly all the blame, to the gross blunders of the SOE, caused, it alleges, "by lack of experience, utter inefficiency, and the disregard of elementary security rules."

At first sight the most likely explanation of this hideous misadventure seems to be German infiltration of one of the cooperating bodies in London. But the German Army Intelligence organizations knew nothing of any such success on their part. They were amazed at the phenomenon which was dropping these men into their laps. They had no contacts in London who could have been responsible for the failure to pick up the warning signals. German Intelligence officers gave evidence on this point with great candour, showing a professional desire to get at the bottom of the mystery and a professional sympathy for the men who were taken from their regulated professional care and butchered by those barbarian amateurs, the SS. We are left to consider the possibility that this was one of the cases where members of the resistance groups wished their movement to be wholly Communist, in order that it might become a revolutionary force at the end of the war and take over the government of all countries, as the partisans took over Yugoslavia. Such plotting for the future led on occasion in France to the murder of right-wing French parachutists who were sent over by the Free French in London. It was widespread enough to lead to the quasi-civil war following the liberation of France, which accounted for deaths estimated at anything between thirty thousand and one hundred thousand. There was also at that time an ugly situation in the Low Countries which the Allied commanders had to meet by the forcible disarming of the resistance groups.

The situation must be contemplated with full regard for its complexity. Some men in Holland and in England would have wished the collaboration between Holland and the West to be broken, and all Dutch anti-Nazi passion to be diverted to the support of the Soviet Union. They would therefore wish to frustrate the Dutchmen who had gone to England to work with the Allies, and they could hardly have had a more convenient way of doing it than by interfering with Operation North Pole. It must be understood that not all Communists would be party to this action. Many, it may be said most, would be horrified by it; some always, some only after the breach of the Stalin-Hitler pact by the invasion of Russia. It is certain that many officials of all and any Communist parties would never even hear of it. Some people who were strongly anti-Communist and pro-Nazi may have taken part in executing the plot. The fact is that it was executed, and that George Blake, as an adolescent, was in touch with the men who were capable of executing it. He may not have understood what was happening. It is improbable that at his age he would have been told the truth. We can never know. What we do know is that these were the people and the forces which had the power to make use of him during that period.

In 1942 Jambroes was dropped in Holland and immediately clapped into prison by the Germans, who then became alarmed lest the resistance movement should report back to London that it had not been able to establish contact with him. They therefore sent radio messages to London in Jambroes' name, alleging that he was dissatisfied with the Dutch resistance leaders and would not meet them. London ordered him to return, which raised an embarrassing situation for the Germans. The false Jambroes sent London a refusal, and an SOE officer named Dessing, working in Holland, was told to contact him and send him back by France, Spain, and Gibraltar. Among those whom Dessing asked to find Jambroes was George Behar, who had on occasion taken part in the arrangements for receiving the parachutists. Almost at once he was ordered by another SOE officer to go to England, and in July 1942 he set out on the established route, going by Brussels to Paris, where he hid for a month in a Dominican monastery, going out to collect false papers, then travelling south through unoccupied France for some months. Then he crossed the Pyrenees and reached the famous Miranda del Ebro camp where the escapees were interned. According to the usual drill, he wrote to the British embassy in Madrid; an official fetched him and sent him down to Gibraltar, where a British Intelligence officer scrutinized his credentials and put him aboard ship for England. He arrived in February 1943. He was twenty years old and this was the first time he had ever set foot on English soil. He was apparently a British subject, but not with finality. He was Dutch-born and under Dutch law could choose at twenty-one between British and Dutch nationality.

Like all such arrivals, he was sent to the Royal Patriotic School at Wandsworth, the clearing-station where fugitives from Nazi-occupied countries were screened lest they were spies sent over by the Germans. He passed with flying colours and joined up with his mother at Northwood near London, where she was earning her living as companion to an old lady while her daughters went to school. It is after this that George Behar's story becomes so very strange. He insisted that he and the whole family should change their name to Blake, for some reason hard to fathom. A number of people called Behar are soundly British subjects, like their ancestors before them, and the late Mr. Behar had been a quite respectable person. It would have seemed inevitable that Blake should have then gone to work for the Dutch government-in-exile. But he was allowed to enlist in the Royal

Navy, although his mother was an alien and he had been born and lived all his life in her native country and his father was not a British subject by birth. He was given a temporary commission in the RNVR and then put on parachute and submarine courses, but was physically unfit for either and ended up as an interpreter. Then he was abstracted by the SOE to work in their Dutch section. What work did he do? He handled Dutch agents who were to be dropped over Holland by parachute, briefing them and taking them down to the airfield from which their planes were dispatched. He had been in at the beginning of Operation North Pole, and he may have been in for the tail end. It must be realized that he may have known nothing of the exercise's consequences, and the man with whom he was in immediate contact may have been as ignorant. But he was moving in the magnetic field of the persons responsible.

In 1944 he was moved to SHAEF as an interpreter, then to ANCXF, the headquarters of the Allied Naval Expeditionary Force, with some stints at Norfolk House, the headquarters of the Allied invasion chiefs. He translated captured German documents and interrogated German prisoners, and did it well. Some weeks after D-day he went over to the Continent and was about during the struggle, long and difficult beyond expectation, for the liberation of the Low Countries. He was then, at the age of twenty-three, sent to Hamburg and put in charge of his own Naval Intelligence unit, with instructions to investigate all German naval matters, but especially those relating to submarine warfare. This meant that he personally interviewed the great aces of the German submarines and inquired into such technical matters as the Schnorkel system of submarine ventilation and the various new types of mine with which they had surprised us in the war.

It would have been surprising if this very young man, with almost no technological training and experience in only a limited area of Intelligence work, had discharged these duties successfully, and he did not. His German was perfect, and in that Alsatia of dishonesty which occupied Germany became, he remained an honest and unfiddling man. But he was rude, fussy, vain, and voluble, and he often struck his colleagues as a little mad. He was taken off his naval job and made a counterespionage officer against Soviet agents, but became more of a nuisance than ever, cloak-and-daggering the part to an embarrassing degree, and writing interminable reports on the slenderest material. Finally he demanded to be sent home to learn the Russian language, and one of his superiors gratefully took note of this desire and handed him on to the Intelligence Department of the War Office, then directed by Sir Gerald Templer. That department cannily fielded Blake to the Foreign Office, which accepted the strange gift with acclamation.

It had no right to do this. Blake did not satisfy the regulation that officials must be persons born in the United Kingdom or Northern Ireland or the Commonwealth, of parents similarly born. It was also unheard of that a candidate should be accepted with as low educational qualifications. Blake had left school at seventeen, without being able to take his last examinations. He had also become, since the end of the war, a case for severe screening. The Dutch government was now saying what it felt about Operation North Pole. He also had a record of unsuccessful performance in the British Zone of Germany. But he was accepted and was sent to Downing College, Cambridge, for a year's instruction in the language and literature and history of Russia and the theory of communism. He was then attached to the Far Eastern Division, shortly afterwards being appointed vice-consul at Seoul in South Korea, as representative of MI6. This was a responsible position, for it was already anticipated at the Foreign Office that South Korea would be the victim of Communist attack.

In 1950 these fears were realized, and George Blake went into prison camp; and it may be that the experience he was to endure there during the next three years included his conversion to communism. On the other hand, it looks uncommonly as if up to that date some force had been looking after him as a mother looks after her own, and, all things considered, it seems likely that this was the Communist Party. If it be objected that that could not be so, or the party would have seen that he did not endure the rigours of a Korean prison, further reflection will suggest that that was exactly what it had to do if he was to continue undetected as a Soviet agent working in the British Foreign Office. As it was, a curious piece of good luck befell him. He and a number of people all above suspicion, his chief, another legation official, an Anglican bishop, a Catholic priest, a Salvation

Army commissioner and Mr. Philip Deane were released from prison and sent back to England in April 1953, though it was two months before the Korean War came to an end, and many prisoners were not repatriated until months after that.

Back in London, Blake was given sick leave which he badly needed, then worked in Whitehall for a time, got married in October 1954, and a short time after that was posted to the MI6 headquarters in West Berlin. There the Blakes were given a top-floor flat at Charlottenburg in an apartment house reserved for British officers and officials, and they settled down there to live a life remarkable for its reserve. They did not make friends with their neighbours or accept the invitations which naturally came their way. No significance can be attached to this. It is possible, indeed probable, that Blake was, to the knowledge of his superiors, acting as a double agent. This is not, as might be supposed, a spy working for two powers, like a charwoman who obliges one householder in the morning and another in the afternoon. It is a spy who is working for his own country but pretends to go over to the side of the enemy by offering their secret service information which is either false and deliberately misleading or true but unimportant, in order to find out how the enemy system works, what information it is looking for, and what information leaves it indifferent. This is a dangerous game. The dyer's hand, as Shakespeare remarks, is subdued to what it works in. To pretend to be a traitor while practising an extreme from of loyalty is psychologically contortionist's work, and most people could no more do it than they can twist their legs round their necks.

To make life simpler, many double agents have in the end stopped pretending that they are traitors and become traitors in truth, and have found not much difficulty in doing so, since they have practised the technique till it has become second nature to them. Double agency has also a flaw that it enables a suspected traitor of this sort to put up defences hard to counter. "Yes, I told my Soviet contact that. Yes, I know we did not agree to it. You remember that we agreed that I should tell my contact this and that and that, and I did, but he was disappointed and suspicious, I had to think of something else. So I told him this other thing. At the time it seemed to be fairly unimportant, and I had to act then and there." Or: "I swear I did not give my

Soviet contact his information. We never mentioned the subject. Yes, I realize that I saw him that Wednesday and that by the end of the week the Soviet embassy knew all about it. But it was not I who was the leak." Some very nasty people have said that and kept themselves out of the dock, if not in the service. Nevertheless, we have in double agency one of the most rewarding professional tricks of espionage. A double agent can learn not only what the enemy is thinking, but how he thinks, and therefore can know what his thoughts are going to be tomorrow and the day after that.

George Blake, who had lived in the world of the professional spy all his life, would probably have felt some shame if he had had to admit that this or any other professional trick was not in his repertoire. What he gave the Soviet Union in the course of this trickery is not known. It may be guessed that it was very much more than the planted lie or the unimportant truth which is the stock-in-trade of the authentic double agent. At this time someone betrayed to the Russians the million-dollar tunnel which the Americans built to tap the telephone lines of the Soviet administrative offices and the East German and Polish communications. Blake had at least been nearer than one cares to think to the kidnapping of the defector Bialek, the former Inspector-General of the People's Police in East Germany. This unhappy man lived in great secrecy in the same block of flats as Blake, protected by steel shutters and a siren alarm, and never went out without a bodyguard, until the night when he ventured to take his dog out for a bedtime walk and was thrown into a car and driven to a Soviet prison, where he died. At this time there happened a grave tragedy, the arrest of four men belonging to an anti-Communist Russian group, the National Alliance of Solidarists, NTS, which has worked with the West for many years. Yakita and Novikov and Chlemnitsky and Kuravtsev had all been into Russia before, on several occasions, and had come back without trouble, but during Blake's stay in Berlin they went and, though the same precautions had been preserved, did not come back. These offences cannot be linked up with Blake, since his trial was held in camera and nothing specific was said about his offences save that the Lord Chief Justice mentioned that in Blake's confession he had admitted to having passed to his Soviet contact every important official document which had ever come into his hands. It is possible, to judge from a German spy trial held in 1960, that these included most of the defence and security plans of West Germany.

It is not necessary to look far to discover what George Blake and his Soviet contacts handed over to the British, for the look of the thing. There was a steady flow into the courts of oafs and drabs, weak brothers and weak sisters, who were trying to find their feet on the slippery surface of postwar Germany and had been spying for the Soviets, who had turned a cold eye on them and judged them expendable. What was happening to George Blake meanwhile seems horrible enough. He was directed by his British superiors to contact a German named Horst Eitner, who was working for them himself and handling a team of agents for them; but he was warned not to let Eitner know his real name and position. To establish a new identity for this purpose, he took a room round the corner from his own flat and called himself by the name he had used twenty years before when he was working in the Dutch resistance. He changed the Christian name, he was Max now and had been Pieter then, but he was again de Vries. Blake was a restrained man who lived for his wife and baby and his work, and Eitner was a jolly, vulgar little extrovert given to wenching and drinking, but the two men got on very well, and Blake visited the Eitners' apartment as a friend as well as a business partner. They appear to have had their disagreements, chiefly over the agents employed by Eitner, whom Blake criticized and tried to dismiss, with no success, for on this point Eitner developed an unexpected strength of character.

It is said that Blake suddenly discovered that Eitner too was an agent for both British and Soviet Intelligence, and this was indeed the case. It is also said that from then on Blake felt his position in Berlin to be untenable, and asked his British superiors to move him elsewhere, on the plea that his Soviet contacts had begun to see through him. This is unlikely. Nobody ever detected the light of candour on Eitner's brow, and, Berlin being full of double agents, the experienced Blake must surely have known from the first that here was one of them. If he was slow in realizing it, the discovery need not have alarmed him; so far as the British were concerned he had a perfectly good excuse for knowing Eitner, for his superiors had directed him to make the contact; and his experience would have prevented him from wondering why the Soviet Union had not informed him that Eitner also was one of theirs, for he would have known that he himself would not have been disclosed as a Soviet spy to a colleague in like circumstances. The real question that he ought to have asked himself, that we must ask ourselves again and again when contemplating the facts of espionage, is whether it is tolerable that a human being with only a few decades to live should spend them in playing this dirty form of cat's cradle.

Early in 1959 Blake, who had been informed by the Foreign Office that he was to be transferred to the Middle Eastern Division, left Berlin for London to get a preliminary grounding in Whitehall before he was sent to the Foreign Office Middle Eastern College for Arabic Studies at Beirut in Lebanon. He took a little house at Bickley, in South London, close to Chislehurst, and there his wife gave birth to her second son. It is said that when coming home by train from Victoria in the evening he used to meet his Soviet contact and hand him whatever he had found that seemed useful. In September 1960 he and his family settled down at Shemlan, the charming village twenty miles from Beirut where the Middle Eastern College for Arabic Studies is situated. Lebanon is almost as full of spies as Berlin, and much curiosity is shown in the doings at MECAS, which is attended by about fifty students, who include Foreign Office staff and trainees sent by commercial and industrial firms and the great oil companies, from all nations this side of the Iron Curtain. Among the interesting residents of Beirut was Mr. Harold Philby, whom the government had cleared of being "the third man" in the Burgess and Maclean case, now a correspondent representing *The Economist* and *The Observer*. George Blake seemed to take no notice of these complications of Lebanese life, enjoyed his linguistic studies, and manifested content in his family life and his pleasant new home.

But in the same month Eitner was arrested in Berlin by the German Federal secret service and charged with being a double agent working for the Russians. The German authorities had full knowledge that he had tape-recorded conversations he had had with British secret agents in his flat in Berlin, and had photographed them with a Minicamera, and handed over recordings and photographs to Soviet agents. Eitner was left in prison without trial for thirteen months, which stimulates reflections on the reality of progress. Under Hitler he would have been beheaded, but he would not have been held in custody so long without trial under the Weimar Republic or even under the last Kaisers. Eitner claimed to have acted for the Soviets under duress, and from his cell he wrote to Blake in London, appealing to him to help. He had always served him well, surely Blake would give testimony for him now, to say he had been an honest servant of the British. He was playing a professional trick, arising out of the professional trick of double agency. Blake did not answer, according to the well-known tradition that a professional spy, once discovered, is abandoned without pity by his employers: another professional trick arising out of the professional trick of double agency. In March 1961 Eitner asked to be brought before the judge who was preparing his case and then delivered a tirade, claiming that though he had spied for the Soviets it was only because he had become a double agent at the instigation of a British official who was a double agent himself, acting not for the British but for the Russians. He may or may not have known Blake's identity, but he certainly knew that he was a Dutchman who had had some connection with the Royal Navy. The deposition was sent to MI5 in Berlin, then to London. But it need not have been of great moment to Blake, for his colleagues would recognize that Eitner was resorting to a professional trick, had it not been that just at that time a Polish professional suddenly became an amateur.

An ancient force which had a title to this man's obedience called to this Pole and bade him cast away a disguise he had been wearing all his life. Colonel Alster, the Deputy Minister of the Interior in the Polish government, and head of the Polish Secret Police, was a Jew, and it came to his ears that the Soviet Union intended to promote various covertly anti-Semitic measures. He defected to the West and told all he knew of the spies who were working for the Soviet Union in Berlin; and one of them was Blake. The Foreign Office sent a telegram requesting Blake's return to London in as nonchalant terms as it could contrive, telling him that he could postpone the journey till after Easter if he cared. On Easter Monday, April 3, 1961, he went back to London, and almost as soon as he arrived the interrogations began. He answered hour after hour with such

skill and charm that the interrogators wondered if there had not
been some mistake. Then suddenly he confessed, and he was
charged at Bow Street ten days after his arrival. On May 3 he
was at the Old Bailey and received this prodigious sentence of
forty-two years, which amounts to a life sentence, as he was by
then thirty-eight years old.

There was a parallel between him and William Joyce. Neither
was English. Each had been drawn out of his native country and
into a perilous internationalism and treachery against the English people by a dead father's passion for England. Otherwise
they represented the antitheses of each other. William Joyce was
the personification of the amateur, inspired by a desire for self-
expression but with no technical tricks to help him express whatever that self might be. He was treason at its most naïve. He
crossed the North Sea and stood up at a microphone and bawled
his faith at us, take it or leave it. The world was the stage where
there was being performed a drama concerned with the transfer
of power. He had his Perkin Warbeck ambitions, but in fact the
only part he could play in such a drama was the noble whom we
have often seen in Shakespearean plays, who in long speeches
backs either the crowned king or the usurper on religious and
legalistic grounds, with certain allusions to troops. These peers
were of such use to the crowned kings and usurpers that they
were rewarded with good broad acres, useful alliances, and offices
at court, or the promises of these. But that was a long time ago.

George Blake was the personification of the professional. He
must have been inspired by a desire for self-expression when, as a
boy of seventeen, he joined the Dutch resistance movement,
being also involved in another drama concerning a transfer of
power. But in the drama now holding the stage the crowned
king and usurpers have not the same need for advocates to cele-
brate their religious and legalistic advantages. Long ago they
polished off that side of the conflict. The pro-Western and the
pro-Soviet propaganda machines are so well established by this
time that they run by inertia. The typical middle-class father of
a family today was in his twenties after the First World War;
and he considered the issue between the West and the new
Bolshevik Revolution as most human beings consider political
issues, with an eye apiece on ethical and material aspects. In
some cases, if he was an intellectual, his judgment may have

been influenced by strokes of what kindly myopia might see as good luck: jobs rather better than might have been expected, rather hard to explain by market conditions, or enthusiastic press notices coming out of the blue. But after the Second World War the pattern started to harden, and now the conflicting powers need take only a little trouble to maintain it. The log-rolling of Communist writers, actors, and painters is now largely automatic. Occasionally the help from the Soviet Union steps up the process and as a brilliant personality comes along is ready with the bribe, but the small fry can now be trusted to do the work for nothing. Today a young man or woman forming definite left-wing political convictions at Oxford or Cambridge but of no very great distinction is not nearly so likely to step into a lifelong comfort-able job, as he or she would have forty years ago. All that such a person gets now is the chance to sit down in the streets in a Tra-falgar Square demonstration. Propaganda is still a career, but not the glittering career it was.

But there are Shakespearean characters which the conflicting powers of our age urgently require: the First, Second, and Third Murderers. They need traitors and spies to steal the political and scientific and technological secrets which their enemies mean to use against them in warfare. If it be objected that one or other of the great powers means to use these secrets only for the purpose of defence and not for aggression, and that it is unfair to call these traitors and spies murderers, let us concede the point. There are wars and preventive wars, and, no doubt, had Shake-speare had a good working crystal ball, he might have written of First, Second, and Third Preventive Murderers. Leaving aside their ultimate moral status, these Tudor catalysts, like their con-temporary descendants, must have studied a great many technical tricks unknown to the orating noble, who had need only to cultivate his mind at leisure and keep his ears open to what was said in Westminster Hall. The Murderers must have known all about ambushes and dagger-play, listening for whispers round the castle kitchens and stables and shaking information out of ostlers at wayside inns, the quick getaway and the hiding place, the flight out of Britain. Their descendants shed less blood, not that this has been a bloodless battle. Krivitsky, the high official of the Russian secret service who defected in the late thirties, gave the authorities much information about his agents, including a description of Donald Maclean lacking only his name; he was assassinated in a Washington hotel in 1941. There are many such among the dead. But for the main part the quarry is not human life but information, often in the form of documents kept under lock and key in forbidden territory. The technique has therefore advanced as much since Tudor days as the technique of burglary; and the practitioner of value to the contending forces is the professional such as George Blake.

There was therefore little relevance to the situation in Mr. Macmillan's statement in the House of Commons that Blake was "never at any time a member of the Communist Party or any of its affiliated organizations." To begin with, this is not a statement which can be made about anybody with any definite significance. The Communist Party has long refused to grant applications for membership to people who can work for them better if they are clear of any such formalized adherence. Nor, if precise information be acquired, is it of any value. For it is not formal membership or conviction which makes the spy and the traitor. William Joyce was moved by a desire to change the social system, and was tied to an organization, and so were Alan Nunn May and Fuchs. But Harry Gold had only the vaguest sympathy with communism and an active dislike for such members of the Communist Party as he knew, with only one exception. The Rosenbergs were convinced Communists. Greenglass was too simple a soul for the issue to have much meaning for him. Burgess and Maclean were convinced Communists. It cannot be doubted that Marshall admired the Soviet Union. Houghton was apolitical; it is comic to think of him as believing it sweet and decorous to die for either communism or capitalism. Miss Gee may have felt some social discontent, but it would be hazy. The Krogers were convinced Communists, but Abel seems to have been indifferent, and it would be a fair bet that to Lonsdale the political system under which he had grown up was something he took for granted as much as the hearty friends to whom he sold bubble-gum machines took capitalism for granted. Pontecorvo (though he should not properly be included in this inquiry, for he was convicted of no illegal act) probably fell into the same category, considering the members of his family who had found a niche in the Italian Communist Party. As for George Blake, given the peculiar cops-and-robbers world he had lived in in his adolescence, and the peculiar events which had followed, it is to be wondered if the battle between the West and the Soviet Union would have any more meaning to him than, say, the battle between Coca-Cola and Pepsi-Cola would mean to an energetic salesman belonging to one firm or another.

Mr. Macmillan's other statement, that Blake "received no money for his services," is as little worth making. This again is something which nobody can know, and which would be of little significance if it were known. The acceptance of pay is not inconsistent with sincerity in this field. To begin with, the labourer is worthy of his hire; the most self-sacrificing medical missionaries in tropical plague-spots are usually paid by the missionary societies, and nobody would cast this up against them. We cannot tell the missionary from the mercenary; they are both found in the infected ranks. William Joyce gained little advantage from being a Fascist traitor; he could have satisfied all his wants by continuing as an university coach. It can never be known whether Nunn May or Fuchs obtained any professional advantage by their Communist activities, but their scientific rating would have guaranteed them a pleasant and comfortable livelihood. Pontecorvo certainly was admitted, when he went to Paris, to a laboratory where few but Communists were welcomed, but he could have found a niche anywhere. Harry Gold received great advantages from his service to the Soviet Union, if only in the way of education. The Rosenbergs at one time made much more money through their service to the Soviet than they would otherwise have earned, but they were later abandoned by the party, and remained loyal to it. It would be absurd to think that the prospect of reward played a decisive part in determining the allegiance of these people who so gladly offered themselves up as martyrs to their faith. But Greenglass would certainly never have handled anything like the sum of money he got as a Communist spy for any other reason. Burgess and Maclean would certainly have been dismissed from the Civil Service if they had not enjoyed special protection; they would have been unlikely to find other employers who would have tolerated their misbehaviour. But that special protection was a compound of the different sorts of tenderness felt for them by their Soviet employers, fellow homosexuals, and friends who felt genuine affection for them. Marshall, on the contrary, had not a drop of mercenary blood in him. Houghton was purely mercenary and Miss Gee to a lesser degree. The Krogers could have earned good livings in any circumstances and probably had plenty of the true believers' blood in them, but the fact remains that spying was their profession and it gave them a very enjoyable living indeed, with thousands of pounds coming their way annually over many years. This too is true of Lonsdale. We cannot speak with certainty of George Blake. But some influence had been caring for him over a long period, and it may well be that he had communism to thank for a comfortable home and a good income.

A traitor may or may not be a Communist; he may or may not be working for gain, and there is a third uncertainty. He may or may not be able to bring his treachery to an end. William Joyce could not have refused to go on playing the role for which he had cast himself, once he had made his broadcasts aimed at destroying British morale. Both Nunn May and Fuchs could quite well have stopped their dissimulation at any time, for they were surrounded by very silly and richly sentimental colleagues, who would (as indeed they did in the case of Fuchs) have heard out their confessions and burst into tears and begged the Special Branch to remember that more true joy shall be in Heaven over one sinner that repenteth than over ninety and nine just persons which need no repentance. Harry Gold, the Rosenbergs, and Greenglass could not have got away, had they stopped spying and confessed. Even if the authorities had forgiven them, they would have been the victims of ferocious assaults on their honesty made by crypto-Communists who would have professed not to believe them. Their lives would not have been worth living. Burgess and Maclean would never have had much reason for fear if they had stopped spying, but they were so temperamentally suited to the niche in which the Soviet Union secret service had placed them that they would never have wished to step out of it until the last possible moment. We may doubt if Houghton ever wanted innocence as much as he wanted money; and he could not have got himself clear by going to the police as an informer unless he had acted very soon after he began his crimes at Portland, and he would certainly have hesitated to stop these crimes without going to the police, for fear of his Soviet employers. Miss Gee probably saw the situation through his eyes. The Krogers and Lonsdale were committed to going on doing what they did as long as possible. The Soviet Union had spent so much time and money on all three of them that it would not have taken their voluntary retirement kindly, and they had done much that the British and American authorities would have been unlikely to overlook on any terms. It is strange that the Krogers and Lonsdale should have been in the same position as regards defection, considering the differences in their moral and intellectual fibre; and strange that Blake also should be locked inside espionage, being quite different from the other three, so much less coarse than Lonsdale, so much less individual than the Krogers.

No court and neither House of Parliament should ever bother to inquire whether a traitor or spy be moved by ideological considerations, or is instigated by a desire for gain, or has been obstinate in his ill-doing. One might as well ask whether a lawyer took up his profession out of a passion for justice or on the rumour of QC's fees, and, should his clients be disreputable, if he could manage to get a more respectable practice: or whether a doctor took up medicine out of a desire to heal or for the opportunities for a steady income given by the National Health Service, and, should he send the death rate up rather than down, why he does not retire. The professions exist because men want to do certain things for motives which are mixed (like all motives), and they cannot abandon their professional lives easily because the training is too long and expensive, and the longer they refrain from cutting their losses the more difficult does it become to pass over into another occupation. It is exactly the same with opera-singing, tennis-playing, political life, show-jumping, and treason, which, however, is different from these, since, like burglary, embezzlement, forgery, and all the other crimes which are the result of the premeditated use of technique, it is illegal in all its manifestations. Once a traitor comes before a court or under the notice of Parliament, all that should interest the lawyers or the ministers concerned is whether he has been exercising his profession or not, and who has been helping him. If inquiry is made into his politics and his morality much will be said, probably untrue, which will divert the attention of the community from the real threat offered by the new traitor. This is the threat inherent in the professional type itself, if that be not restrained by some body like the Law Society, the Bar Council, or the British Medical Association. Professionalism is not necessarily a vice, but, as we will see demonstrated more and more clearly, it gives opportunity for the vicious.

4

GEORGE BLAKE was convicted in the summer of 1961. In the autumn of 1962 another professional spy passed from Bow Street to the Old Bailey, different in kind but equal in magnitude. Though William John Christopher Vassall, Admiralty clerk, aged thirty-eight, was doe-eyed, soft-voiced, hesitant, and ephebic, he had the historic quality of Lonsdale, Fuchs, and Blake. He had been as little suspected as these men and he had no early training in street-fighting with the Nazis or in Russian naval warfare or in the Dutch resistance movement to teach him toughness and secrecy. He belonged to a well-bred and well-educated family, which had produced some good schoolmasters and athletes and, in the person of his father, an admirable clergyman. But no branch of the stock had made much money, and his father had suffered a misfortune which affected Vassall himself disadvantageously. The Reverent William Vassall had married a gay and charming and temperamental hospital nurse who, when her husband had been vicar for fifteen years of Christ Church, Hendon, suddenly became a fervent and proselytizing Roman Catholic. The parish took it ill. It was 1940, and doubtless it was exasperating in the middle of the Battle of Britain to be pressed by the vicar's wife to go over to Rome. The unlucky Mr. Vassall resigned his living and was found a chaplaincy in the RAF, which meant that his income declined and he was obliged to withdraw his son from Monmouth Grammar School, though he was only sixteen. After a brief period at a bank young Vassall went to the Admiralty as a temporary Grade II clerk and then did four years in the RAF as a photographer. By then, though he probably did not know it, he had laid the foundation of his life as a spy. He was an expert photographer. He had also got his foot in the door of one of the defence ministries. In 1946, when he was demobbed, the Admiralty accepted him for establishment as a clerical officer.

Thus he was employed in the lowest of the three main divisions in the civil service, the other two rising steps being the executive and the administrative. He first worked in the Air Equipment Department and was moved to Naval Law and then to War Registry, the Admiralty's chief communication centre. By this time he was twenty-eight, with a deprecating manner and a tendency to nervous dandyism; but he had made a world for himself, or even several worlds. He was a devoted son. He enjoyed social life and was welcome in several quite different milieus. He had a genuine liking for the society of old ladies, and as some of them were rich he was suspected by the malicious of legacy-hunting, but in fact he was as attentive to old ladies who were very poor indeed. (There is no question but that he liked to do kindnesses; it was one of his dominant traits.) He was an excellent bridge-player and was often asked out for that reason. He was religious, and oddly enough went into the Catholic Church but never told his parents, not even his Catholic mother; and he spent much time with many Catholic friends who thought him genuinely interested in liturgical matters. He was drawn into another circle by his passion for model railways, and to yet another by his intelligent interest in music. But, most important of all, he was a homosexual, and not just that. He was no tortured bearer of a cross, flinching under philistine scorn. He was a much-sought-after "queen," playful and girlish, who loved being courted and appreciated. The homosexual section of society has itself many subsections, and he was unknown to many of its more conspicuous groups; but the circle to which he belonged included some rich, important, and intelligent men. They made his life amusing in London, and when he went abroad, even so far as Egypt and Mexico, he was passed from host to host. He was very successful in this sphere, which meant that he was not merely playful and girlish, but could hold his own in an outlaw world where tact, toughness, and vigilance had to be constantly on the draw.

When Vassall was working in War Registry, he saw an Admiralty circular inviting applications for the post of clerk to the naval attaché in Moscow. It is impossible to say why he was moved to apply. The report on his misdoings issued by a tribunal which sat under the chairmanship of Lord Radcliffe alleges that "at no time" did he show any interest in alien ideologies, but this is something which cannot be said of any living creature who can read or talk. Understanding of communism was not beyond a man as well versed in religious controversy as Vassall showed himself often enough, even in the company of priests and churchmen. But it is true that the motive impelling Vassall to leave London at the height of his attractiveness must have been strong, and it is not easy to imagine his becoming quite such an ardent Communist. It is, however, very easy to imagine him feeling mild enthusiasm for communism combined with an ardent passion for a Communist. There is no evidence of this, but it could have happened. Other winds to fill out his sail on the voyage towards Muscovy would have been his love of travel, the pleasure he would have felt at being any kind of a diplomat *en poste,* and his delight in any new thing. Anyway he got his wish and was sent off to Moscow in March 1954.

Whatever motives drew Vassall to the British embassy at Moscow, the motives of at least one of its inmates who welcomed him were sinister. Only three years had passed since William Marshall had left it, and it was still a compound in the jungle: a prison where people served out their terms with a hostile climate, an alien culture, and an incomprehensible language as their jailers. The junior members of the staff sought distraction with something rather discreditably like hysteria, and for that reason they regarded with grateful affection one Sigmund Mikhailsky, a junior interpreter and administrative officer of the embassy, who got them theatre and travel tickets, bought specially good food for them in the markets, and was an amusing guest at parties. He said he was a Pole and did not like Russians, and, having thus economically engaged the trust of these simple-minded souls, he went on to facilitate the conduct of black-market operations for such of the staff as wished to turn a dishonest penny, and to offer heterosexual and homosexual attentions to those who seemed likely to respond. It is obvious that the British embassy in Moscow has always to recruit part of its domestic and administrative staff locally, for it would be impossible to find English volunteers for such service, and even if that could be done it would be very expensive and a quite inefficient way of keeping house, in view of the language difficulty. But this neces-

sarily means that the British embassy is full of spies and informers, since all this local staff can be engaged only through a
bureau which is a branch of the Soviet Union's Foreign Office.

This risk is fully realized by the British authorities, and good
sense should make the situation just tolerable. It could not,
however, have made the continued employment of Mr. Mikhailsky anything but deplorable. He was not only a Soviet agent, but
a Soviet agent actually engaged in the corruption of the staff.
This is not hindsight. One of the staff, never named, repeatedly
urged the head of Chancery to warn the junior staff against the
serpent in their midst. Meanwhile Vassall was settling down
cosily in the embassy. His chief, Captain Bennett, at first disliked
him, writing in a report to London of "his handicap of an
irritating, effeminate personality," but Vassall worked hard on
him, and finally Captain Bennett and his wife became his
friends. He was asked to many parties and enjoyed them all, and
he established himself as a personality by his talent as an
amateur actor. In the meantime he had had an affair with the
versatile Mikhailsky, and possibly another with a diplomat at
another embassy in Moscow. By the autumn he was regularly
abstracting documents from the naval attaché's office in the
embassy, taking them off the premises and giving them to Russian agents who photographed them, and then returning them to
the files.

This little citadel of happiness he had constructed for himself
in the midst of officialdom did not go unassailed. The anonymous member of the staff who thought Mr. Mikhailsky no better
than he should have been plugged away at the head of Chancery
until, in 1955, that gentleman reluctantly took the step not of
dismissing Mikhailsky, but of issuing two circulars addressed to
all members of the staff, warning them to report all Russian
contacts and making a special reference to Mr. Mikhailsky.
There was some talk among the senior members of the staff
whether this was sufficiently drastic action, but it was decided,
with the approval of the Ambassador, Sir William Hayter, to
retain him, on the ground that if they got rid of him he would
only be followed by someone who would be as bad or worse. The
Radcliffe Report describes them in an oddly humourless passage
as considering that they would be unlikely to get another man
"as useful and obliging as he had been in serving the needs of

the staff," and it adds that "this was a matter of some importance having the desirability of making local conditions as pleasant as possible."

The warning circular produced results. A typist in the office of the military attaché named Miss Wynne, who appears to have been unique in her common sense, reported to her chief that Mr. Mikhailsky was making great efforts to make local conditions as pleasant as possible so far as she was concerned, and had indicated to her that he was under Russian control. He had, furthermore, mentioned as special "targets" on whom he was concentrating Vassall and three other officials. The military attaché wrote a minute on these remarkable confidences, ending with the remark, "I have no evidence, however, that the friendly approaches have been other than innocent," and sent it to a Mr. O'Regan, who was acting as head of Chancery while his chief was on leave. On this minute Mr. O'Regan wrote, "HMM has informed HE." That meant that Mr. Parrott, the Minister, had informed the Ambassador, Sir William Hayter.

But that was untrue. Sir William Hayter told the tribunal that he thought he must have seen the minute; but this seems unlikely, for Mr. Parrott is certain that he never saw the minute and never spoke to the ambassador about it. Mr. O'Regan is now dead. The air attaché and his assistants never heard of the minute, nor the naval attaché or either of his two assistants. The military attaché seems to be the only person in authority who heard of this minute, and this nobody had been able to prevent, as he himself had written it; hence he warned one of the three targets, who was working in his office. No steps were taken to warn the other two targets, who had gone home, or to raise the matter with Vassall. It is true that the naval attaché ordered his staff to avoid all contact with Mikhailsky after office hours, but that was on his own initiative and not because he had ever heard of the minute. Mr. Mikhailsky remained at the embassy for another nine months, until he was reported by a clerk whom he started to blackmail after he had persuaded him to engage in black-market operations.

In July 1956 Vassall returned to London by an extremely circuitous route, visiting Sweden, Norway, the United States, and Canada, and then returning to London by way of Stockholm. He told nobody in the Admiralty of this, and nobody in the Admiralty found it out. Before he left Moscow he had been posted to the Naval Intelligence Division, and there he worked for nearly a year. It is essentially a repository of secret matter. Then he went for two and a half years to the private office of the Civil Lord of the Admiralty, Mr. T. G. D. Galbraith, MP for the Hillhead Division of Glasgow. There he had little access to material which could have interested the Soviet Union, for his chief duties were collecting newspaper cuttings, making travel arrangements, meeting distinguished guests at the airport, and bringing in the tea. But in October 1959 he was posted to the fleet section of Military Branch 11, the secretariat serving the naval staff, and there he stayed till he was arrested in September 1962, up to his elbows in material such as his Soviet employers loved to have. He dealt with documents concerning radar, communications, torpedo and submarine, gunnery trials, Allied tactical publications, Allied exercise publications, fleet operational and tactical instructions, and general matters concerning naval liaison with Commonwealth countries. In Moscow he had taken the documents to the Russians for them to photograph, but now the Russians had given him his own camera, and he was photographing the documents he borrowed, using the professional competence he had acquired in the RAF. That he was an industrious and accomplished spy is proven, for the Soviet Union gave him a great deal of money, and the British judge who tried him sentenced him to eighteen years' imprisonment.

The trial was exasperating. Once again the prosecution believed the statement made by the person accused of treachery, disregarding the reasons a traitor would have to put up a smokescreen to conceal what he had been doing, and disregarding too the probability that a person who had chosen to be a traitor might have a talent for lying and certainly had a need to lie. Vassall told the authorities after his arrest that, when he was in Moscow, Mikhailsky had invited him to a dinner party, made him drunk, and photographed him while he was engaged in homosexual gambols, and that some time afterwards officials belonging to the Soviet secret service summoned him to a meeting and told him that if he did not spy for them they would show the photographs to senior members of the British embassy staff and would "make an international incident of the matter," bringing down on him the rigours of Soviet Union law.

The drunken party may have taken place. But it was probably engineered so that Vassall might refer to it, should his treachery ever be discovered. It is unlikely that this sort of blackmail can still be practised with any ease on embassy staff in Moscow, for they meet it with open eyes. They are supposed to be warned against it before they leave England, and once they set foot in the embassy they will hear their colleagues constantly gossiping of this local dragon. Constantly were employees reporting such attempts on their integrity, constantly were they being sent home. Only a very stupid and helpless man or woman would have succumbed, and Vassall was not stupid, was extremely resourceful and, as an additional defence, accustomed for years to the idea of blackmail. His friends had a special liability to be blackmailed, as skiers have a special liability to break their legs. There was no need to teach them, of all people, anything about the wisdom of going to the police. If Vassall really had been blackmailed by Mikhailsky and he had really wished to free himself and put Mikhailsky out of business, he would have known the drill. He would have gone to the right member of the embassy to make his report, and made it in terms likely to bleach the embarrassment out of the blushing occasion; he would have made the journey home with just the right, slightly "camping" humour; he would have dined out on the story at home, telling it in two different ways to please the two different sorts of people; and if he had found the atmosphere chilly in Whitehall he would have found some shelter in an art gallery or interior decorator's shop where the air was balmier. He was dexterous in many fields, and in this field his dexterity would have risen to a challenge and given a dazzling demonstration.

But at Vassall's trial the prosecution repeated this story of the drunken party, and so did the judge; and as he pleaded guilty no evidence was given at his trial. So the House of Parliament imprinted it more deeply on the public mind when it debated the case, and the press accepted it, and it got a fresh lease of life at the tribunal which Parliament appointed to investigate the wilder implications of the case. The effect of this legend was to beget another: that Vassall was a weak and silly little man, poor in intellect and indecisive in character. This was unlikely to be the correct view of a man who for seven years had carried on an occupation demanding unremitting industry in a skilled craft in clandestine conditions, an endless capacity for dissimulation, and sustained contempt for personal danger. The error was regrettable. There was need for society to contemplate the drama in which Vassall had played a part, and its members could get no clear idea of its theme if they had a wrong conception of the principal actor.

It was indeed disturbing that we should be unable to keep our national secrets to ourselves. There are those who feel that candour is all and that the international situation would be ideal if only we invited the neighbours to come in and look in our cupboards, but they should reflect that had we been as steadily robbed by Hitler's spies we could not have won the Second World War and those of our fellow citizens who are Jewish would not be with us today. If any generation should be cautious about staking our lives on human innocence, it is ours. It was therefore natural enough that there should be a public outcry at the procession of spies which had been brought through our courts and which had not come to an end, although the government had set up some quite imposing machinery. The Romer Report had soundly smacked the Admiralty security organization, and it would have seemed inevitable that there must have been an improvement in that quarter. After the Blake case the government had set up a committee to report on Security Procedures in the Public Service, with Lord Radcliffe as its chairman; Sir Gerald Templer, Director of Military Intelligence at the War Office before he became famous in Malaya; Sir David Milne, an eminent Scottish civil servant; and the Right Honourable Mr. Kenneth Younger, formerly of the House of Commons and now of the Royal Institute of International Affairs. It had issued a workmanlike report, making unexciting but practical suggestions, such as, for example, urging the intensive application of what is known as "the need to know" principle, under which information classified as secret is disseminated only in the area required for the efficient discharge of the business in hand, by subjecting personnel within this area to formal indoctrination relating to security; in other words, if only Smith and Jones have to know about the new G-pipe gotcher, never let Brown and Robinson come near it, and let Smith and Jones know that their whole future careers depend on the premise that no whisper of what they are doing reaches Brown, Robinson, or anyone else in the world.

This was obviously sensible talk, of an unexciting nature which aroused confidence. All the same, here was Vassall, who had gone on year after year neatly weaving his way every evening down Whitehall to his flat in Dolphin Square, with an envelope in his overcoat full of secret documents, spending fussy and capable evenings photographing them nicely for the Soviet government, and every morning neatly weaving his way up Whitehall to the Admiralty again, to spend five minutes fussily and capably replacing the documents in the files. This was more than flesh and blood could bear, particularly as Vassall had been represented as a perfect idiot who should have been detected in five minutes by any security officer worth his salt. Contempt for the security organizations flared up, followed by resentment against the government, which was half an Opposition manœuvre and half sincere disgust at what looked like administrative incompetence. Out of this grew suspicion not so much political as moral. It was felt that if this worthless little homosexual had been earning his living in Whitehall it must be because he was protected by some person or persons of power who were themselves homosexual.

The criticism of the security organizations was only partly justified. The Vassall case was not nearly as black a mark against them as the Blake case. At no time should Blake ever have been in the employment of the British government. But there was no reason why Vassall should not have become an Admiralty employee in the first place, and the degree of culpability afterwards shown by the security organizations in their dealings with him varies from black to nearly white. In the British embassy at Moscow security had obviously gone down the drain. The set-up would have been difficult in any case, with Soviet spies coming and going because they alone could fetch the groceries and get tickets for the ballet, but there was evidently an element within the embassy which was determined that this difficulty should become an impossibility. That Miss Wynne's report concerning the sinister intention of Mr. Mikhailsky regarding his various "targets" should be ignored might have been due to extreme negligence, but the statement inscribed on the military attaché's minute, alleging that the Minister had told the Ambassador of Miss Wynne's report, speaks of something worse. Whoever had informed Mr. O'Regan of this had lied. There must have been someone in the embassy who was extremely anxious that the activities of Mr. Mikhailsky and Vassall should continue unchecked.

This is a shocking state of affairs; and it is shocking too that when Vassall left Moscow he should have gone on a trip to Scandinavia, the United States, Mexico, and back to London via Stockholm, without the Admiralty's learning about this. He got handsome extra pay and allowances over his normal salary of £700 a year for Moscow service, but this extensive tour would have gone far to wiping them out; and the authorities considered Moscow service as a strain on the toughest character. To deplore this lack of vigilance by officers of the state is not to range oneself on the side of the man-hunting bloodhound, for the immediate victim of Vassall's treachery was Vassall himself. We may all be blown to bits in a future war because he betrayed our defensive secrets, but this is a hypothetical danger. Vassall, however, is actually in prison, and will be there for many years. As for his return to Whitehall, far too little was done to save him then. Since he was posted to Naval Intelligence, he should have undergone the intensive form of security screening known as "positive vetting," but there was what the Radcliffe Report described as a "heavy backlog" in this clearance department, and he went through to work in Naval Intelligence without being vetted until he had been there for nearly a year.

After that he was given clearance, and this was not as much to the discredit of those who cleared him as might appear. He looked mild as milk; he lived with his father (who was by now curate at a famous West End Church, his wife having become less zealous) in the family home in St. John's Wood and appeared to fill every moment of his spare time with the practice of such hobbies as listening to classical music, playing bridge, and going to the theatre. Only two things strike one as faulty about the positive vetting. One was that the examiner never made inquiries of Captain Bennett, who had been Vassall's chief in Moscow, because he was informed that he had left the embassy and was now on his way to the Far East. This was an error, as Captain Bennett was stationed at Portsmouth. It can have been no more than an error, for Vassall would have been sure of getting a good report from Captain Bennett. What was disturbing was the implication that the Admiralty knew no way by which communication could be established between a civil servant in Whitehall and a naval officer travelling in the Far East. As disturbing was the disregard of an obvious hint given by one of the references Vassall gave his examiner. Like many homosexuals, he liked elderly ladies, and when asked to name responsible persons who could vouch for his character he gave Dr. Agnes Francklyn, an old family friend, and Miss Elizabeth Roberts, a retired civil servant who was his neighbour. Miss Roberts gave him a good character but was careful to point out that he took little interest in the opposite sex. The Royal Navy was, however, too innocent to take the old lady's point.

This was, however, not unnatural. Unconsciously a security officer might take the point and decide to disregard it. There is great good sense in the rule which excludes homosexual civil servants from employment in departments considered sensitive from a security point of view. It is possible that a civil servant might be blackmailed by persons wishing him to engage in espionage, which was what Vassall was afterwards to say had happened to him. But the official would know that few people are traitors, whether they be heterosexual or homosexual, and he would know too that most people of either sort in this age would resist blackmail, and that the rule was far out on the side of cautiousness. It is possible that the very natural disinclination to obey an injunction when one has the knowledge that almost never is it worth obeying, accounted for the failure of the security organization to note Vassall's homosexuality as the years went by, and act on it. But it is of course the duty of a security officer to disregard the laws of probability and arm us against the one-in-a-million chance, but that is a hard thing to remember.

However, once Vassall got into the Admiralty, means could have been taken to circumvent him, though again not so simply as might be supposed. Espionage is, like almost all our contemporary troubles, an aspect of the population problem. Our fruitfulness is the real foe of security. The more people there are, and the higher their standard of living, the more civil servants there have to be and the more cluttered the world they live in, for many persons engage in scientific and technological research, and many more engage in development of the researchers' discoveries and thus cause material objects to increase and multiply even faster than the human beings around them, and that without the checks of birth control and infant mortality. The process is visible on our roads. They are choked with motor-cars; for we cannot stop a single motor-car coming into the world, since it is essential that the people who make them remain employed, and few motor-cars suffer serious accidents on their way from the factory. Documents, though their prolific habit is not so overt, are almost as incontinent. Scientific and technological researches produce millions of papers which have to be read, copied, discussed (on paper chiefly), and filed. Thus it happens that nine thousand people go in and out of the Admiralty every morning and evening and burrow in large accumulations of papers. Many of them looked not unlike Vassall, just as many people at Portland Naval Base looked like Houghton, and as these people who looked like them were loyal and innocent, the presumption was that Vassall and Houghton were too; and it is staggering to think how many security officers would be needed to check on these nine thousand people, if we really started to turn them inside out. It would be an appalling addition to the burden of taxation, and one hard to make the taxpayer accept, for it would appear not to be justified by results. We would be paying highly trained men to spend their lives on the unproductive work of looking for a needle in a huge haystack, and unproductive it would seem, since for years together it would be proved that there was no needle in that haystack, until, after all those years, another needle turned up.

It is true that not so much was being done as could be done without making such heavy weather of it. The Radcliffe Report's account of Military Branch, where Vassall was working like a happy little beaver for three years before his arrest, is alarming.

. . . The security arrangements in Military Branch were such that if he had been a more adventurous spy, he could readily have gained access to a great deal of secret material. Many, if not the majority of the security cupboards in the Branch were suite cupboards, operated by common keys; and as the user of one of these cupboards Vassall had his own suite key. It was not the practice to segregate the more highly classified documents and store these in the more secure cupboards fitted with detector or combination locks, and to use the less secure suite cupboards to house only the less sensitive material. Staff used whichever cupboards were available to them in their rooms for storing all their material, regardless of its classification, and regardless of the type of cupboard. Key control was also less than adequate.

There is really no excuse for this sluttishness, except that here too there is a problem of numbers. Even the supervisors are so numerous that it would take a huge and expensive increase in security officers to keep them in order. It is said that the situation is worse in the Admiralty than in other defence ministries, because of a peculiarity in its organization. "Methods and Routine" is in the same hands as its security organizations, though these are separate elsewhere, and this leads to psychological conflict. In the Foreign Office, or the Air Ministry, or the War Office, one set of people says, "It will be convenient if Brown, Jones, and Robinson work in the three separate rooms at the end of the corridor so that the Under-Secretary can have them along in a second or two if he wants them," and another set says, "No, for the sake of security they must all work in the same room, with the clerks of all three coming in and out, and all six being under each other's eyes throughout the working day." But in the Admiralty the same set of people has to put these two contradictory views to itself, and it can be believed that the security considerations too often go to the wall. We all of us tend to believe that life is more like the novels of Angela Thirkell than like the novels of Eric Ambler, even when we ourselves are living out an Eric Ambler plot.

It might be hard to alter this questionable arrangement, for it is never convenient to knock about the structure of defence institutions, which cannot shut up shop for a day. But it should not be impossible to introduce the technique which was mentioned at the time of the Portland spy-ring trial. This is the snap-check, the stopping and search of so many employees, chosen at random at irregular intervals, as they make their way out of their offices. This would have stopped Houghton, and it would have stopped Vassall. The trouble is that there is a resistance to this technique which is based on class feeling. It might be thought that nobody would object to a routine instituted for the purpose of lessening our common risk of being blown up, but such snap-checks are imposed in certain industries and for that reason are resented by some white-collar workers.

But the public did not want to be bothered with such considerations, which was natural enough; who wants to realize that any inconvenience he is suffering is due to that quite irrepressible phenomenon the birth rate, acting in conjunction with human intelligence, which we cannot afford to repress? It would be much more agreeable to throw the blame on some human being in a position of power, who could be removed from that position; and that would satisfy a desire felt constantly by persons temporarily out of power or not likely ever to be in power, which is to humiliate the powerful. There was therefore a fierce campaign waged against Lord Carrington, the First Lord of the Admiralty. The Labour Party in Parliament and certain sections of the press (Tory as well as Labour) called for the resignation of Lord Carrington, on the ground that Vassall's case was the second serious breach of security while he had been at the Admiralty. In point of fact, Lord Carrington's record regarding security was impeccable. He had gone to the Admiralty in October 1959; the security forces had started looking for Lonsdale and Houghton and Winifred Gee in February 1960 and had found them at the beginning of the next year, after which there could be no more spy-catching, because the Soviet Union told all its spies in Britain to lie low for a time. Vassall had only started work again in the spring of 1962, and by August he was walking into a trap. Nowhere in the world are modern spies caught quickly and easily, and Lord Carrington's time-table was to his credit.

But there was the other popular campaign, which was even more fervently conducted: to track down the powerful homosexual who had enabled this wretched little pansy-boy to get into the Admiralty and had protected him and promoted him when he was there. The objects of this campaign were unfortunate, for Vassall could not fairly be described in such terms. He was, so far as birth, appearance, manners, and education are concerned, much like many other people in the civil service. There was no reason at all why he should not have been accepted by the Admiralty when he presented himself with quite usual qualifications for a clerk, at the age of seventeen; and it was per-

fectly obvious that nobody had been nursing his career, for it
had not been nursed. He had never succeeded in getting promotion, and he was once put in a department (Naval Intelligence)
which he actively disliked. As for the influences being Communist and not homosexual, he was put for two years into the office
of the Civil Lord, where he could get no documents for his
Soviet employers. It is just possible that he chose not to be
promoted, for the reason that in the lower echelon he had a freer
range among documents than would have been his had he been
given superior and therefore more specialist duties; but there
was no need for a patron to secure this result. To dodge promotion he simply had to go on playing the dumb gazelle.

But the public was determined that they had Vassall on their
backs and, looking round, they found a candidate who had every
qualification except probability. Vassall, as we know, had served
for two years in the office of the Civil Lord of the Admiralty,
who was then the Honourable Mr. Thomas Galbraith, the eldest
of the seven children of the first Baron Strathclyde, and since
1948, when he was thirty-one, MP for the Hillhead Division of
Glasgow. It is as well to state at once that Mr. Galbraith's
relationship with Vassall was entirely blameless, and that his
only fault had been to treat his clerk with a certain unworldly
kindness. This is proved beyond doubt by Mr. Galbraith's good-
natured and trivial letters to Vassall, which were obviously written out of conscientiousness rather than with zest, and by a
poignant incident which occurred in the spring of 1962. In late
1960 or early 1961 Vassall had been told by his Soviet contacts to
stop spying because Lonsdale and his associates had been detected, and a year later he was told to start again. There was no
doubt that he felt a strong affection for Mr. Galbraith, and,
though he realized that this was not returned, he still felt sure that
Mr. Galbraith would do his best for him. He evidently did not
want to start spying again, as who would, in view of the long
sentences given the Portland spy ring, and he wrote to Mr.
Galbraith (who by this time was Under-Secretary of State for
Scotland), asking him to see him as he wished for his advice, and
in return got an invitation to lunch at Mr. Galbraith's house in
Westminster. A year before Vassall had come to him as clerk,
Mr. Galbraith had married a young and beautiful Belgian lady,

and in the six years since then she had had two children and was then about to have a third.

When Vassall arrived at the house in Westminster, Mr. Galbraith had not come home yet, and Mrs. Galbraith gave him sherry and talked of this and that. She happened to mention the Portland spy ring, and her remarks had a curious effect on Vassall. He stopped talking, and when Mr. Galbraith arrived he found his guest in a disturbed and almost incoherent state—"in a maze," was his expression. He could not explain what his trouble was, and shortly afterwards wrote to Mr. Galbraith to say that he was resigned to staying at the Admiralty. It is likely that Vassall had wanted to consult Mr. Galbraith about his career, and had possibly the idea of asking if Mr. Galbraith could get him transferred to some other branch of the civil service unconnected with defence, which would have meant his escape from the espionage net. Or he may have wondered if he might not throw himself on the mercy of a man who was sympathetic and friendly, and make a full confession. All that we know is that he was in such a state of apprehension that Mrs. Galbraith's expressions of disgust regarding the Portland spy ring were enough to make him, for the one and only time on record, lose his self-possession. "He was never ruffled," Captain Bennett said of him at Moscow, at a time when, whether he was blackmailed or not, he was making his first steps as a traitor. But now he was. It is significant that, though he was so greatly distressed by his involvement, he was not able to insist on seeing Mr. Galbraith alone. Had there been any substance in the charges against the two men, Vassall could surely have demanded to see him without his wife, and Mr. Galbraith would hardly have dared to refuse. The link between them must have been innocent.

But the public would not have it so, and curiously enough they got what they wanted not from the popular press, as might have been imagined, but from the House of Commons. Here and there the press gave some help, but the real crusaders were at Westminster. In the debate on the Queen's address in November, Mr. George Brown uttered these extraordinary words:

> We cannot leave the Vassall case where it is. There are other letters in existence, copies of which I and, no doubt, others have seen, the originals of which are in the hands of what are

called the "authorities" which indicate a degree of Ministerial responsibility, which goes far beyond the ordinary business of a Minister in charge, being responsible for everything which goes on in his Department. The Lynsky Tribunal was set up to deal with a junior Minister for far less than is involved in this.

The Lynsky Tribunal, of which no sensible Labour politician would wish to remind the country, since the persons involved were Labour members of the Labour government of 1945–1950, dealt with charges of "receiving payments or rewards in return for the granting of licenses and permission and the withdrawal of any prosecutions." The matters involved, in fact, were bribery and corruption. But the letters Mr. Brown had seen consisted of this sort of thing:

My dear Vassall,
Goodness knows what you will think of me for having taken so long to write. We were both delighted to receive your charming card of congratulation and I would have thanked you ages ago except for the fact that the Scottish Office, when Parliament is sitting, keeps me more busy than the Admiralty. . . .

We will never know what Mr. Brown meant, except perhaps in the hereafter, and unfortunately this wild statement was not isolated, which makes the debates on this subject painful reading. The pages of *Hansard* often record speeches so feeble that they would not be delivered or listened to in public were it not for the charity inherent in the conception of democratic government; but there is a marked difference between the charity offered at a hospital and the promiscuous hospitality of a disorderly house which alone would have welcomed this debate. The Labour Party behaved far below its real intellectual and moral level, and it angrily attacked the committee of three appointed by Mr. Macmillan, which consisted of Sir Charles Cunningham, the Permanent Under-Secretary at the Home Office; Sir Harold Kent, Procurator-General and Treasury solicitor; and Sir Burke Trend, Second Secretary at the Treasury, and it demanded that a tribunal be set up under the Tribunal of Inquiries Act, a much more expensive and complicated form of court, requiring skilled legal handling.

It showed some sense in calling for such a tribunal, but only because it was an inquiry with special powers of investigation, which might be able to find out why the Labour members themselves were talking such nonsense. The Prime Minister took advantage of the opportunity they had given him by publishing Mr. Galbraith's letters in all their blamelessness and setting up the tribunal they had been so eagerly demanding. The Labour Party then lost its sense of humour. It happened that Mr. Galbraith, who must have thought that the world was going mad, resigned his office in a letter which showed a real desire to crawl away and lick his wounds, and that Mr. Macmillan very properly accepted it. The Opposition immediately set up a cry that Mr. Macmillan was being very unkind to Mr. Galbraith, for whom they were showing a tender concern which was surprising, and they attacked the tribunal as a very cruel form of inquiry. It seemed that people's names were mentioned at tribunals, reputations were shattered, people were smeared. Of this, it now seemed, they could not bear to think. Mr. Michael Foot remarked:

> The Prime Minister, with matchless insolence, talked of McCarthy, but he is the man who is asking the House to institute the McCarthy procedure. He is the most brazen McCarthy of the lot. The Prime Minister's capacity for hypocrisy staggers even me.

The candour of this last sentence is magnificent.

Never in Victorian days was a Parliamentary debate so redolent of humbug, so cruelly irresponsible, so silly. But the public showed no repugnance whatsoever. On the contrary, they followed its example, and, even after the Galbraith letters had been published, the lying gossip spread. The press joined in fitfully, having been in some quarters misled by an informant posing as having inside information, who has never been named, and who was lucky in the credulity with which his story was received. But it was the amateurs, the man and woman in the street, who really kept the hysteria going at its height.

In 1962 a charge was brought under the Official Secrets Act which was far less sinister, and lamentable in the old decorous way to which we had formerly been accustomed. This concerned Barbara Fell, a woman of fifty-four, member of a family distinguished for its services to the state, herself a civil servant of gratifying eminence, a senior official at the Central Office of Information, drawing a salary of nearly £4000 a year. She was a reserved character, something of an enigma to other eminent women civil servants, but she had her own friends, and these included people regarded with respect and affection in the world of letters. She was charged with having shown papers she had taken from her office to Mr. Peciak, press counsellor of the Yugoslav embassy, between May 1959 and October 1961. These papers were admitted by the prosecution to be in no way related to national defence, but it was maintained that they were classified as confidential, and as they included memoranda sent home by the British ambassador at Belgrade on such subjects as "The effect of Yugoslav foreign policy on a policy of the United Kingdom," confidential they certainly should have remained. The representatives of all nations think of the representatives of other nations as lesser breeds without the law. It is an occupational disease, and these documents were probably symptomatic.

It was admitted that Miss Fell had been the mistress of Mr. Peciak, and this was not at all difficult to credit, for she was an attractive woman, looking far younger than her years, and quite as attractive as Mr. Peciak. Nevertheless the story surprised. Miss Fell's claim was that she found Mr. Peciak to be anti-Russian and to some extent anti-German, and, as she put it, "eventually I began to select certain papers for him which I thought would influence him in a pro-Western direction." This could easily be translated into amorous tones. In emollient circumstances, an infatuated voice might murmur, "But you're wrong, darling, Sir Oliver adores all your people, I'll bring his last memo for you on Wednesday and you'll see for yourself." But it was Miss Fell's habit not merely to show Mr. Peciak the documents, but to let him take them away with him in the evening and return them to her in the morning by dropping them into her letterbox. This procedure was an odd manifestation of *Vénus toute entière a sa proie attachée* and it worked out as the systematic provision of light night work for the Yugoslav embassy photographer in his darkroom. Miss Fell was sentenced to two years' imprisonment on December 7, 1962, after a brief trial which was painful without being interesting. This was treachery below the historic plane, the purloining of mediocre documents which has gone on ever since there were embassies, and it was tragic that it had meant ruin for a human being considered far from mediocre by her friends.

5

WE are guilty of such hysteria as visited England during the Vassall case only when the emotions we normally repress burst their barriers and we try to force them back into captivity. We all fear death, and the agitation against atomic weapons has obsessed us with fear of death at the hands of the Soviet Union, and for that reason a detected Soviet spy makes us expect that we will die as a result of his theft. Most of us repress such homosexuality as we have, and when Vassall avowed that he was homosexual, that repressed part of us envied his audacious choice of gratification. When he avowed that he was a spy, and that he had been forced into espionage because he had been blackmailed as a homosexual, then our sense of guilt was aroused. The thing was lethal after all.

Vassall had a peculiar power to raise such disturbance, because he evoked the image of homosexuality as it appears to all interested inhabitants of a great city, fascinating and repellent. It can be taken that Vassall was never mercenary, that he could have claimed that he was petted rather than paid, and that his alliances were in fact always conducted with a certain fastidiousness and were justified by affection. But in the public imagination he was the slender figure in sweater and tight jeans who lurks in the shadow by the wall, just outside the circle of the lamplight, whisks down the steps of the tube-station lavatory and, with backward glances under the long lashes, offers pleasure and danger.

There is a charm inherent in the idea of prostitution which is more complex and in one sense less sordid than is commonly admitted today. It is not a question of simply going off with a tart for mechanical sexual reasons. Its innocent part is the dream of love not as a slow-growing plant, requiring attention lest it perish, but as a shooting star, which, so much more miraculously, flashes out of the night where an instant before there was nothing. This coexists with a thriftier fantasy: of a shooting star flashing back into the night without presenting much of a bill. The mean man likes to think of supreme sexual pleasure (as it might be, now and then, since the young and the beautiful are sometimes tempted into prostitution) which can be paid for in cash and calls for no settlement in the way of gratitude or the sharing of responsibility. Moreover, the transaction offers a double moral triumph. The prostitute's client can at the moment of union feel that he is a splendid rebel defying religious and social prohibitions, but later he can get back on the safe side, and that through two sorts of pleasure, the masochistic pleasure of repentance and the sadistic pleasure of hating the prostitute.

The prostitutes' technique of self-adornment also offers the ego two sorts of refreshment. The client's common sense knows that such enhancements of the human aspect are bought over the counter, but why do the buyers make their purchases? In the hope of attracting me, the client smugly thinks. How potent the prostitute must judge me. If common sense intervenes with the reminder that the prostitute must eat, the ego goes off on a new tack. How rich the prostitute must judge me, how recognizably a man of substance I must be. There, of course, he is quite right. But even so, he gets some value for his money, perhaps in laughter. Without doubt Pan and the satyrette and Venus in her more popular manifestations pulled off more good things in conversation than were ever ascribed to Juno. But, on the other side, prostitution is the irrigating system by which the venereal diseases are spread through society. True, antibiotics have done much to control them, but they have not exterminated them, and in the mind of man the dread is hardly diminished at all. But against this is the seduction of the secret society, the locked door, the drawn curtain, behind which is plenty, the free flow of sex, the amassing of fortunes. Many persons starved of sex and money feel for this reason a wolfish jealousy of the prostitute.

Therefore forces normally held in comfortable suspension within our society, sensuality, sadism, panic fear, and a jealousy surpassing any class jealousy, were precipitated by the legend of Vassall. But the power of that legend affected only the overt and latent homosexuals in our society. These may fairly be judged to be still in a minority. (Otherwise, unless the birth rate were higher than it is, the population would go down instead of up.)

In the early part of 1963 a girl named Christine Keeler appeared in the news as certainly involved in prostitution and possibly in espionage. She was at once desired and hated more than her deserts.

It was not unreasonable that she should have excited desire, for she was beautiful in a nostalgically unfashionable style. She was not at all unlike the Virgin Mary in Dante Gabriel Rossetti's "Annunciation." She had a remote distinction of bearing and manner unexpected in one who had been brought up on a riverbank near the Slough desert (a district comparable in charm to the New Jersey flats) in a converted railway carriage. As for hatred, she might have been spared the full blast of what she got, for she had hardly had the benefit of the protection we profess to give the young. Admittedly by the time she got into the news, at the age of twenty, it would have been difficult to protect her save by some such drastic technique as bricking her up in a wall, according to the practice which the cruder kind of Protestant used to believe prevalent in convents. But earlier she had had bad luck. She had been seduced by an American sergeant at a tender age and went off to earn a living in London in her middle teens. Eventually she found herself in the cabaret show of a famous London night-club, and there she might have found a way out of the dust, for this club looks after its girls well and a fair number make good marriages or break into the entertainment world. But she was committed to a less fortunate destiny when she met a man thirty years older than herself, named Stephen Ward, and went to live with him. They apparently remained throughout their association on brother-and-sister terms, but she joined the long line of girls who had lived under his control during the years since the end of the war, most of whom he handed over to various rich men of his acquaintance, most commonly as mistresses though sometimes as wives.

Attempts have been made to represent Stephen Ward as a glamorous rebel and sexual deviate. But to the experienced eye he was a not unfamiliar type of daffy. He struck some people as mildly insane, and indeed he had the shining eyes and effusiveness of a manic-depressive on the upswing, and something of the single-minded mindlessness which Harpo Marx used to affect. Other people who met him at the houses of his wealthy patrons regarded him as a quite gifted court jester, with a flow of amusing gossip. Other people again regarded him as brilliant, but it must be admitted that they were themselves not so much brilliant as loyal and affectionate. They were apparently much impressed by a kind of diluted Nietzscheanism which had filtered into his brains through smoky night sessions with his more literate (but still not very literate) friends. As a witness at his own trial and as an interviewee on television he seemed ingenious rather than intelligent, and curiously blind to the effect he was creating on his audience. His memoirs were poorly written and trivial.

But he was a man of many and marked gifts. He was a born professional: he was capable of acquiring all the skills necessary to the successful pursuit of an exacting occupation, and using them continuously at a high level. It was not for him to claim much originality or individuality; he joined the ranks of those who find it enjoyable and profitable to march along the paths traced out by original individuals of the past. His first profession was osteopathy. It is not clear how he came to adopt it. His father, a clergyman, a handsome man, only slightly handicapped by a malformation of the spine which just stopped short of making him a hunchback, was a noted preacher and ended his days as a Canon of Rochester Cathedral. The Wards were certainly prosperous and by all accounts were a united and affectionate family, and one would have expected all the sons to have an orthodox education. But after a number of experiments (which included a term or two at the Sorbonne) Ward went to America at the age of twenty-two and took a degree at a well-known osteopathic college in Missouri. It is beyond question that he became a master of his craft. Other osteopaths, even those who thought him mad and bad, admired him for both his manipulative powers and his acuteness in diagnosis.

But he also played bridge like a professional and could hardly have encumbered his time more heavily with fixtures had he been a bridge-player by profession; and there was nothing amateurish about the portrait drawings he was ceaselessly producing. They were of limited artistic value. Some of the faithful (whose devotion recalls the spaniel) compared them to the work of Michelangelo, but a juster comparison would have referred to Miss Olive Snell and Miss Molly Bishop, the charming and industrious chroniclers of English society beauties in this and the last generation. Stephen Ward was less gifted than either of these ladies and not nearly so well schooled, but he possessed something of their expertise, the power to pick out the sweeter aspects of an image and put them down on the right part of the paper with just the right weight of line to make looking at the thing as easy as swallowing cream. As time went on he marketed to advantage the products of his emollient art, and when his career came to an end he was drawing £1500 a year from a contract with an illustrated weekly.

His three professions worked in well together. If a prominent man came to him in his capacity as an osteopath, he would offer to draw him or her and would then ask for introductions to other prominent people in the same field, on the plea that he wished to draw them too. He would then, if the signs were favourable, invite them to his bridge parties or to his country cottage, and familiarity would be established. This process sometimes developed so far as to land the prominent person in the field of Ward's fourth profession, which was pimping.

The general public hesitated to believe that Ward was a pimp. He was tried and found guilty of living on the immoral earnings of Christine Keeler and another and still younger girl, Mandy Rice-Davies, but the average man was inclined to think him the victim of a technicality, for the reason that there was little evidence of money having passed from them to him. He could hardly have been convicted had it not been that a man who is habitually in the company of prostitutes is presumed by the law to be living on their earnings, though it accepts a disproof. But his innocence cannot be established by criticism of that presumption, which is in fact a realistic recognition of the shyness of pimps to confide their financial affairs to paper. The situation is discussed in a curious passage in Lord Denning's report on Ward's affairs and their consequences. "In money matters," Lord Denning oddly states, "he was improvident." He goes on to explain:

> He did not keep a banking account. He got a firm of solicitors to keep a sort of banking account for him, paying in cheques occasionally to them and getting them to pay his rent. More often he cashed his incoming cheques through other people; or paid his bills with the incoming cheques. He had many cash transactions which left no trace.

But these practices do not indicate improvidence. On the contrary, as the Inland Revenue would testify, they are devices practised by persons so excessively provident that they grudge wasting money on the payment of income tax. Here in England the improvident have no aversion from banking accounts, which they open optimistically and which offer them their own peculiar food in the English conception of the overdraft. Neither is there any special feature attractive to improvidence in the act of paying in cheques to a firm of solicitors rather than to a bank manager; the excessively provident might find the solicitors preferable, particularly if they did not tell them absolutely everything. Moreover, we must dismiss any picture of Stephen Ward running across the road to ask his greengrocer to cash a patient's cheque for five guineas. An organization which was sued for libel by Stephen Ward made its own inquiries and discovered that he was in the habit of cashing cheques for both small and large amounts at gambling-houses which performed this service for their clients and charged quite a heavy commission.

There is much evidence that Stephen Ward was capable of great generosity. True, he was close-fisted with his girls. When they lived under his roof the housekeeping was frugal, and they had to pay their share of the overheads. But he gave free treatment to many needy patients and on some hard cases he bestowed not only his skill and his time but considerable sums of money. Yet there is much evidence that he loved money and that he pimped for gain. There was really, from his point of view, no reason why he should not be a procurer. He liked, as some people like teaching and others like nursing, to bring together two human beings in order that they might have sexual relations on a mercenary basis. This conception existed in his mind in a strange, diagrammatic isolation. The public in its daydreams saw him as surrounded by beautiful girls, and so he often was, but some of his chosen companions were ill-favoured in face and in figure, and were repellent or pitiful in personality. It was as if he wished his women to incarnate the idea of prostitution in its impure purity, without making allusion to the agreeable in any form. Pimping was thus to him a mission, and many missionaries accept payment for their labours. It would take unusual credulity to hold, on the evidence given at the trial, that Ward did not do that very thing. The only thing it did not show was where the money went.

The pattern had been glaring enough before the trial. In the late fifties the wife of an MP called on Ward to arrange for osteopathic treatment and never went back to have it. She saw enough to make her certain that some sort of call-girl racket was being conducted from his house. Again, he treated as friends and colleagues various well-known vice-racketeers, including the two most celebrated disseminators of pornography in our day, and an internationally known organizer of flagellationist orgies. Again, Ward was careful to profess great hatred for Peter Rachman, the slum-landlord and club-owner, but two of his girls, one of them being Mandy Rice-Davies, became Rachman's mistresses, and he himself was Rachman's tenant. Again, it was his habit to give frequent bridge parties, and some of these were that and nothing more; but others ended in the sudden incursion of a troupe of young women, lightly clad and brandishing whips, who performed a bizarre cabaret turn. Our story has now strayed so far from normal territory that the pattern may be so surprising as to be vitually unacceptable. It appears to be true, but could never be credible, that many of these young women were quite respectable, and amongst themselves alluded to the elderly gentlemen who formed the larger part of the audience in derisive and even hostile terms. Nevertheless, even if allowance is made for these singular facts, it appears unlikely that such a party should be given, not now and again, but again and again, by a man far from lavish in his expenditure, from motives of hospitable altruism.

Ward's four professions worked together to give him yet a fifth, which is hard to define. He was not a traitor and not a spy. Let us say he mucked about with security in the shadow of the Soviet Union. This, like his pimping, would not strike him as morally wrong. A highly intelligent woman, who was his patient and was also involved with him through her husband's association with one of his close friends, asserts that he had been a convinced Communist for about seven years, from about 1955 or 1956. This was not at all rare in his social ambiance. On the more slippery slopes of the entertainment world, where it shelves abruptly to the vice racket and the unorthodox financial complexity, there is a great deal of revolutionary enthusiasm. Some of this wells up from deep sources. A man who wants to destroy sexual taboos or to make money in socially forbidden ways may be moved to take these particular actions by a general desire to overturn all existing institutions. But the motive may be more naïve and less ferocious; there may be a belief that under communism everything is divided up and everybody is equal, so social prohibitions will be less stringent; and if one got on the right side of the machine, one might have the benefit of all this new simplicity while fiddling a bit on the side for oneself in the good old way. Among Stephen Ward's friends were several men and women who had made large sums out of various bizarre enterprises and were closely connected with Communist underground activities.

Round about the end of 1960 Ward told a patient of his, the editor of a newspaper, that he wished to go to Moscow and draw various people there, including Khrushchev, and would like to get in touch with some Soviet officials in London who could help him to realize this ambition. The editor knew an assistant naval attaché at the Soviet embassy, called Captain Eugene Ivanov, and introduced the two men at a large luncheon-party he was giving at a London club on January 20, 1961. At this early stage the story is already odd. Ward had for a long time known a number of people, some highly respectable and some not so greatly that, who could have helped him to contact the Soviet embassy.

The two men immediately struck up a warm friendship. Ivanov was a Soviet Intelligence officer, and he was very much the same sort of operator as Gordon Lonsdale. He was superficially expansive, vulgar, jolly, sociable, a cheerful womanizer, and good-natured. He spoke English fluently and was allowed by his embassy to go here, there, and everywhere, wherever he was invited, which is not the case with Soviet diplomats as a general rule. He ingratiated himself with his hosts by playing a good game of bridge, eating and drinking with naïve enjoyment, telling funny stories, and chattering and laughing in the character of a simple child of nature. He shared with Lonsdale a curious readiness to be photographed when engaged in amorous horseplay. It was as if both men were looking for certificates of frivolity.

Meanwhile Ward was acting as if he meant to be to Ivanov what Houghton was to Lonsdale. How completely he had moved into the classic role of the agent is shown by an unpleasing episode concerning Madame Furtseva, the Soviet Minister of Culture, who paid a visit to London in 1961. He asked if he might draw her and through Ivanov this was arranged. The sitting took place in a drawing-room at the chief Soviet embassy building in Kensington Palace Gardens and lasted for an hour. Madame Furtseva sat on the sofa under the huge picture of a Soviet peasant woman and in excellent English chatted away on such subjects as Pasternak, the Hungarian rising, the hopes and fears of her country, and the problem of the Russian immigrant groups. She talked with unusual candour, and Ward thought the conversation so interesting that when he went home he wrote down what he could remember of it. Then it struck him, he said, that the editor who had introduced him to Ivanov might like to publish it. He realized that he could not publish the notes without permission, so he sent them, not to Madame Furtseva, but to the Soviet embassy officials.

They were, he reported afterwards, horrified. Madame Furtseva had spoken so very openly. They refused him permission to publish the notes, and he thought this a great pity. That is his account of it. But it can hardly be doubted that he was performing with professional skill a well-known technique of a profession he had only just adopted. It could be objected that Madame Furtseva may have left London by the time his notes were finished and that he could not send them to her to be passed, so he had sent them to the Soviet embassy officials as the next best thing. But he could, on learning of her departure, have decided to drop the whole idea of publication, lest he should find himself informing on her to her own security system.

The most conspicuous service Ward rendered to Ivanov, however, was of a far less chaste nature, and it was also complex. It showed Ward performing another professional trick, indeed two of them. His association with Ivanov did not go unremarked. On June 8, 1961, a representative of security met Stephen Ward at a restaurant in Marylebone in order to question him about this involvement, and was taken by him to his mews flat, where he met a girl who was living there, possibly Christine Keeler. At the end of the interview Ward asked the security officer whether it was all right for him to continue his friendship with Ivanov, was told that it was, said that he was very ready to help in any way he could, and was instructed to get in touch with security should Ivanov make any propositions to him. To his superiors the security officer reported that he thought Ward's political ideas were probably exploitable by the Russians, but that he himself was not a "security risk," and that the appearance of the young woman in the mews could be considered "corroborative evidence that he had been involved in the call-girl racket." He also added that "he is obviously not a person we can use."

The result of such a visit would be, in most cases, the visited person's instant resolve to break off the association which had been the subject of inquiry. It was not so with Ward. Exactly a month later, in the evening of Saturday, July 8, Ward was bathing with some of his girls at the swimming pool at Lord Astor's house, Cliveden. Lord Astor had been a patient of Ward's for thirteen years and was on familiar terms with him, often treating his needier friends to courses of Ward's osteopathic ministrations; and Ward's country cottage was on the Cliveden estate. One of the girls was Christine Keeler, who had been separated from her bathing dress and was swimming naked when Lord Astor came down with his guests from a dinner party. They included Mr. Profumo, the Minister of War. For Ward there can have been no element of surprise in the situation. He knew very well at what time Lord Astor was accustomed to bring down his guests to the swimming pool, and he knew what guests were staying at the house. He also knew Mr. Profumo. Miss Keeler dressed herself, Ward and his girls spent some time with the Astor party round the pool, and they went up to the house for a short time. The next day, Sunday, July 9, the Ward party joined the Astor party down at the pool again, and this time Ward brought with him Ivanov, who thus made the acquaintance of Mr. Profumo. Ivanov took Christine Keeler back with him to Ward's house in the early evening, where they were reported to have drunk a great deal of whisky and to have had sexual relations. Whether these relations actually occurred we can never know for certain, and it is an aspect of truth we can well suffer to elude us.

On the day after that, Monday, July 10, Ward telephoned to the security officer who had visited him and asked if he might see him; and when the security officer arrived two days later, he told him that he had summoned him in obedience to the instructions he had been given to report any propositions Ivanov might make to him. Ivanov had, he said, asked him to find out why the Americans were going to arm Western Germany with atomic weapons. He also made a peculiar communication regarding Christine. It is obvious that during the week-end she was making a play for Mr. Profumo, and by the time Ward saw the security officer there had probably been a telephone call from Mr. Profumo which showed that the play had succeeded. Ward, however, told the security officer that Ivanov "was undoubtedly attracted by Christine." It is very doubtful if he ever was. Lord Denning thinks he was not. All that is certain is that for a time Christine seems to have felt it obligatory to say that he was, and presumably she was coached to say this by Ward.

The security officer reported the matter to his superiors in terms which inspired them to follow two lines. First, they asked the Special Branch to make inquiries about Ward's character, which they thought might be not all it should be, and to identify Miss Keeler. It must make us all blush to learn that the Special Branch could not trace Christine Keeler, who could have been found by some simple inquiries at certain photographers', coffee bars, and shops in the Marylebone district; and we must blush again to hear that the Special Branch was of the opinion that nothing was known to Ward's discredit. His address, it claimed, "was in a respectable neighbourhood where any openly unseemly conduct would come to police notice." The security organizations' second line was to explore the possibilities of getting at Ivanov, possibly through Mr. Profumo, and persuading him to be a defector. These deliberations were simplified by the failure of any of them to notice that Mr. Profumo was spending hours alone with Miss Keeler in Ward's flat and other places and driving her round London.

The head of the security service then suggested to Sir Norman Brook (now Lord Normanbrook), the Secretary of the Cabinet, that he should speak to Mr. Profumo on the subject, which he did on August 9. Sir Norman then put it to him that he should be careful in his dealings with Ward, since any information he might drop would be passed on to Ivanov by this master of indiscretion, and asked him if he thought that Ivanov could be persuaded to defect. Mr. Profumo said he felt no enthusiasm for the project and went away, sweating at every pore. As Lord Denning was afterwards to learn, he thought that the security service had discovered his relations with Miss Keeler and that Sir Norman's conversation was a tactful way of warning him. He had an assignation with Miss Keeler the very next night, but wrote a letter to her calling it off. Lord Denning cautiously says, "I am satisfied that the letter, if not the end, was the beginning of the end of the association between Mr. Profumo and Christine Keeler." In March 1963, Mr. Profumo told the House of Commons that he had gone on seeing her till December. But he afterwards explained that this was only because Sir Norman had said, "I thought I should see you before we go away for the recess," and when he recollected this he thought it was the December recess, but realized later it was the August recess. In other words, he could not, in March 1963, remember whether an affair he had had in 1961 with an exceptionally beautiful girl had lasted one month or six. This fact should be put before all young girls over the age of twelve as an important part of their education.

The longer the affair lasted, the better for Stephen Ward in his capacity of Soviet dogsbody. It was not that there was much hope, or any at all, of Christine Keeler's getting from Mr. Profumo the date of the American delivery of atom bombs to West Germany, and imparting it to Ivanov. Not only would Mr. Profumo never have told her; she would never have asked him. The girl had a vigorous if sombre and joyless intelligence. But there was another purpose served by her relationship with the Minister of War. Lord Denning states:

> It has been suggested to me that Ivanov filled a new role in Russian technique. It was to divide the United Kingdom from the United States by these devious means. If Ministers or prominent people can be placed in compromising situations, or made the subject of damaging rumour, or the Security Service can be made to appear incompetent, it may weaken the confidence of the United States in our integrity and reliability. So a man like Captain Ivanov may take every opportunity of getting to know Ministers or prominent people—not so much to obtain information from them (though this would be a useful by-product) but so as to work towards destroying confidence. If this were the object of Captain Ivanov, with Stephen Ward as his tool he succeeded only too well.

Unfortunately, Lord Denning is wrong in thinking the technique new. It has been in use for many years and practice has brought it to the pitch of perfection. It is to be noted that during the next two years the story was plugged throughout London that Christine Keeler was having an affair with both Mr. Profumo and Ivanov. In late July 1962 a glossy magazine published an allusion to it. Yet by that time Mr. Profumo had not seen Miss Keeler for at least six months, and Lord Denning is of the opinion that she had never had a love affair with Ivanov at all. The story must have been circulated by Ward. People might have remembered seeing Mr. Profumo with Miss Keeler in compromising circumstances, but they could not have had a glimpse of an affair with Ivanov which had never happened.

Ward would naturally have liked to satisfy his Soviet masters; but perhaps he felt this a special urgency just then, for it looks as if he was attempting to perform an operation only possible to agents who are valued employees. Throughout 1961 and 1962 he advertised himself more and more blatantly as a Communist sympathizer, particularly to his patients. A number of reports were made to the security services, and again the same officer was sent to interview him and made a mildly unfavourable report. He described Ward as "basically a quite decent fellow," whose only fault was that he "accepted as true much of the propaganda Ivanov has pumped into him." Again he did not think him a security risk. Significantly he wrote: "More than once Ward assured me that if Ivanov ever attempted to make use of him for any illegal purpose, or *if he showed any inclination to defect* he would get in touch with me immediately."

Meanwhile Ward and Ivanov carried on a campaign of ingratiation with the official world of London. As soon as Mr. Profumo had begun his process of disengagement from Miss Keeler, Ward, as if trying a new tack, offered his services to the Foreign Office as an intermediary with the Soviet embassy through Ivanov and got a chilly dismissal. He got a credulous MP to involve the Foreign Office in some twitterings about the Berlin problem and the Oder-Neisse line, and he succeeded in introducing Ivanov to Sir Harold Caccia, permanent Under-Secretary of State at the Foreign Office, who recoiled vigorously. When the Cuban crisis blew up in October 1962, the activities of the pair became frenetic. On October 24 Ward telephoned to the Foreign Office

and alleged that Lord Astor had recommended him to contact
Sir Harold Caccia, as Ivanov wished to tell him that the Soviet
government was looking to the United Kingdom as the only
hope of mediation in this crisis, and that the United Kingdom
should call a summit conference immediately. The Foreign Office
remained impassive, and the next day Ward got the credulous
MP to meet Ivanov and go to the Foreign Office with this proposal, about which Ward telephoned to it himself later. On the
same day he got Lord Astor to speak to Lord Arran, a newspaper
director, and tell him, as Lord Denning puts it, that there was a
Russian official who was trying to pass information of an urgent
nature to the British government. Two days later, on October
27, 1962, Ward took Ivanov to Lord Arran's house, where he
repeated the suggestion of the summit conference, adding that
Khrushchev would accept the invitation with alacrity. Lord Arran
suspected that this was an attempt to drive a wedge between the
United Kingdom and the Americans and reported it in an unfavourable light to the Foreign Office and the Admiralty. Lord
Arran has a notorious sense of humour, and these proceedings
must be thought of as punctuated by his robust laughter.

The next day, Sunday, October 28, Ward and Ivanov went up
to Cliveden, where there was the usual week-end party, and
while they were there it was announced on the radio that the
Russian ships had turned back from Cuba. Ivanov gave way to
his surprise and rage, and all the guests noticed it. But three
days later they were at it again. Ward accidentally picked up an
MP in a restaurant and took him back to his house, where they
found Ivanov and Christine Keeler and Mandy Rice-Davies.
This peculiar assemblage discussed the Cuban crisis with passion,
the two young ladies occasionally breaking in with support of
Ivanov. This must have been an entrancing spectacle. In appearance they were like the strange women against whom King Solomon warned us, but the voices were those of good readers of the
left-wing weeklies. When the Tory MP got up to go Ward said,
referring to Ivanov and himself, "that they too must go, for they
had to dine with Mr. Iain Macleod." This statement froze the
blood of the Tory MP, Mr. Macleod being then Minister for
Commonwealth Affairs, and in view of the company present this
can well be understood. In fact they did not know Mr. Macleod.
Ward had persuaded a young man to ask Mrs. Macleod if he

might bring him and Ivanov to a party the Macleods were giving for their young son and daughter and their friends. On finding that Mr. Macleod was not there, the pair stayed only a few minutes and left.

The MP who had been inveigled into this astonishing visit compared notes with Mr. Macleod, who reported the matter to the Foreign Office, with the result that on November 2 that body entered into further exasperated correspondence with the security service about Ward. It is to be noted that by now the security service had very strong suspicions indeed that Ward was (the security officer put it in a letter to the Foreign Office) "providing some of his influential friends with highly satisfactory mistresses," or (as he put it more tersely in his report to his own department) was "a provider of popsies for rich people." This knowledge undoubtedly lowered the temperature in which Ivanov and Ward were working.

But they were indefatigable. On November 7 Ward wrote to Mr. Harold Wilson about his activities, telling him that the Russians had made an offer to the Foreign Office for a summit conference. "I can vouch for the authenticity of this," he declared, "since I was the intermediary." But Mr. Wilson was unimpressed. A veil then drops but is lifted for a moment on Boxing Night to show us a dinner party given by a peer and his wife, who had been a close friend of Ward before her marriage, to which Ward and Ivanov had been invited to meet a highly placed Foreign Office official and his wife. It seems that they brought up in conversation the Nassau Conference and the American delivery of nuclear weapons to the Germans, but the Foreign Office official preserved silence. It is to be doubted, however, that Ward and Ivanov hoped to extract any information. It is much more likely that they came to give rather than to receive. That had certainly been the role Ward had been trying to play for the previous eighteen months. If we trace the story from the beginning, we find something which looks very like the attempt of an agent, who was perhaps not quite an agent, to become a double agent. Ward showed himself very obliging to the British security service. A security officer had only to tell him that his friendship with Ivanov had been remarked upon, and instruct him to report any propositions made to him by Ivanov, for him to come back within a month with the story that Ivanov had indeed made him a proposition, and the further (and false) story that Ivanov had taken a mistress who was under his own control. From then on, in the communications of the security service, there are references to the possibility of Ivanov's defecting: a possibility which must have been conjured up by Ward. During the Cuban crisis Ivanov was presented to Lord Arran as "a Russian official seeking to pass information of an urgent nature to the British government" behind the back of his ambassador: that is, as next door to a defector.

In fact, Ward was trying to insinuate himself into the British security service with the high prestige of a double agent who brings to his second employer a valuable agent recruited from the security service which was his first employer. He may have been inspired by genuine patriotism of a cracked sort; he may have been, knowingly or unknowingly, acting at the instigation of the Soviet authorities who wanted to plant Ivanov on the British in order to supply them with misleading information; or he may simply have been gratifying an unassuageable appetite for complications. Which motive impelled him we shall never now learn, but we do know that Ivanov had no intention of becoming a defector, straight or crooked. Some time late in January, Ward had to tell Ivanov that their joint effort had been wrecked by a disregarded human element, and the whole story of their connection might be published at any moment. Then was the moment when, had Ivanov desired to forsake his own people, and had his proceedings not been known and approved by his own superiors throughout, he would have applied to the British for political asylum. Instead, he returned to his country on January 29.

It was Christine Keeler who, for reasons partly to her credit and partly to her discredit, had wrecked Ward's venture into the field of security. She and Mandy Rice-Davies were growing resentful of the control Ward exercised on their lives. Both had had some taste of luxury, but not much. Though Peter Rachman was still living with Mandy at the time of his death in 1962, he had made no provision for her in his will. There was no ill feeling. He merely suffered from the same testamentary difficulties which must have vexed King Solomon if he had a grateful disposition. After that, times had gone badly with them. Neither of them was really framed for success in the terms Ward could provide it.

The courtesan who satisfies the rich and great must have a woman's body and a yes-man's soul; and Christine had an uneasy, donnish intelligence, while Mandy's wit and humour were untamed and formidable. Under Ward's direction they were frittering away their lives on prostitution only occasionally mitigated by affection and friendship, and they were most meagrely rewarded in money or comfort. They wanted to get away from him, and it was a sign of character that they did.

But Christine had gone downhill rapidly in the last few months. About the time of her parting from Mr. Profumo, Ward had introduced her to the use of marijuana cigarettes, which he smoked himself. This had involved her with two West Indians, Lucky Gordon and John Edgecombe, both convicted criminals. She lived with both of them in turn and left them, and they engaged in a barbaric fight for possession of her. When she sought refuge with Ward, Lucky Gordon perpetually raised riot round the house, banging on the door and shouting, at all hours of the day and night; Edgecombe was even more to be feared. On October 27, 1962, he inflicted serious wounds on Lucky Gordon in a brawl over Christine, but he eluded arrest. Discontented with Ward's regime as she was, she was forced by this sort of mishap to take refuge with him, but he received her with some acrimony. He could not approve of one of his girls' abandoning her appointed duties and going off on her own; and it is possible that his conscience told him he had led her too far away from the normal. It must be admitted also that, at a time when he was trying to impose himself on the Foreign Office and the security service as a discreet and responsible person, it was awkward to have his home besieged by West Indians whose conduct might well attract the attention of the police and who, if questioned, would declare themselves in search of a young prostitute, under his roof for reasons hard for him to explain.

On December 14, 1962, the crisis broke. Edgecombe came to Ward's house when Christine was paying a visit to Mandy, and on being refused admission shot the place up, whereupon he was arrested. Christine was badly shaken. She had had reason to fear for her life. At all times she suffered from a neurotic garrulity, but now she became a cascade of reminiscence. She talked to everybody she met, about everything which had ever happened to her, whether it concerned Edgecombe or not. Nine days later she happened to meet a former Labour Member of Parliament, a technologist and inventor of some note in his younger days and more recently a financier. He encouraged Christine to talk, and soon he heard the whole story of Mr. Profumo and Ivanov and the request for information about the American delivery of nuclear weapons to Germany. He did in fact give the distraught waif some good advice, telling her that to protect her own interests in these matters she must go to a solicitor. But he also passed on the Profumo story to the Labour Party security expert, Mr. George Wigg, a soldier who had risen from ranker to colonel. He was appalled by it. The campaign Mr. Wigg then started was to his party's advantage, but he is a man of integrity, and it is fair to say that in all his reactions he was moved by honest disgust at the twilit world which the story revealed. He has that peculiarly intense primness which is found in that rare breed, a prim soldier.

But Christine's loquacity had found another outlet. She was in a deplorable state. Edgecombe's shooting affray had led to a bitter quarrel between her and Ward, and she could no longer find a room in his house. She had no money. At a time when prostitutes are prosperous as never before, she had no banking account; a curious fact. It was not surprising that Ward had none; but the same considerations did not apply to her. She was unlikely to earn more money at the moment, for she was ill and overwrought and cannot have been any real recreation for the warrior. Some friends suggested that she should sell her story to the press, and she immediately started hawking it round Fleet Street, presently concluding an arrangement with a newspaper, the first of a series, which, among other benefits, set her up in a comfortable apartment of her own. It is hard to see any other way by which this poor little waif could have got a home at that moment. What is strange, in a girl who appeared to her friends as scatterbrained and inconsiderate but not ill-natured, is the ruthlessness with which she pursued a course certain to bring ruin on Mr. Profumo. But it is the case against prostitution that it puts people in the power of others who have no affection for them, and Mr. Profumo had taken the risk with his eyes open.

But Christine continued to talk, involving him in another sphere. On January 26 a police sergeant called on her to serve her notice to attend the trial of John Edgecombe, and she gave him a reward which must have been far beyond his expectations with a statement in which she told once again the whole Profumo-Ivanov-nuclear-arms story. Meanwhile there were repercussions from her disclosures in Fleet Street. They had come to Stephen Ward's ears, and on January 28 his counsel brought her proposal to publish memoirs involving Mr. Profumo to the attention of the law officers of the Crown. They had already heard the rumours, possibly much earlier. They sent for Mr. Profumo and questioned him on the matter, and he denied having committed any sexual impropriety with Christine. On February 1, a senior executive of a newspaper telephoned Admiralty House and, as the Prime Minister was abroad, was given an appointment with a secretary, to whom he reported the sale of Christine Keeler's memoirs to a certain newspaper (which in the event never published them) and indicated the extent to which they compromised the Minister of War. Therefore the security services were immediately alerted, though not, it proved, to any very good purpose.

On February 4, Ward tried one last professional trick. He reported to Marylebone police court that two photographs had been stolen from him. They were taken at the Cliveden swimming pool and one showed Ward and three of his girls and bore a quite innocuous inscription by Mr. Profumo on the back, and the other showed Mr. Profumo with two girls, one of whom was Christine. Later Ward made a statement alleging that the photographs had been stolen by a friend of Christine's who meant to sell them. Then, to quote the police officer's note as given by Lord Denning:

> Dr. Ward said that if this matter, including the association between Mr. Profumo and Miss Keeler, became public, it might very well "bring down" the Government. He also added that he had no personal liking for this Government but would not like to see it go out of office in this way.

He then indicated quite clearly that Miss Keeler's memoirs would mention many well-known names, and that he himself had connections with MI5 and was involved with a Soviet diplomat. This was blackmail, quite unpunishable as such, since it was made in the course of a complaint about a theft made to the police, but also quite certain to reach its mark. This should be remembered when attempts are made to present Ward as an artless and sincere deviate.

It would be pleasant to report that this nefarious effort was unsuccessful, but in point of fact it attained its ends, though indirectly, through a grotesque official decision. The security service, and also the Special Branch, and the Criminal Investigation Department alike came to the conclusion that Ward and Christine Keeler were low persons and they wanted to have nothing to do with them. This fastidiousness, which seems peculiarly misplaced in the police, was not the result of political pressure. On the contrary, the government was clamouring for all possible assistance in getting at the truth. The action of these organizations was entirely spontaneous, and it was responsible for all the subsequent scandal which makes 1963 a black date in Parliamentary history. If Christine Keeler had been questioned by the police then, she could have furnished many proofs (as she did some weeks later) that her story of an affair with Mr. Profumo was true. He would thus have had no temptation to deny his relationship with her.

Ward had only six months to live, and he spent them trying to repeat this success. He was inspired by an intense anxiety regarding his association with Ivanov. He explained his own innocence of espionage on television; and after Mr. Wigg had appeared on "Panorama" and spoken of Ivanov as a slick and competent Intelligence officer, Ward called on Mr. Wigg at the House of Commons in a dithering condition and for three hours protested that he and Ivanov had been just friends, that Ivanov had nothing to do with Intelligence, and that there had been nothing whatsoever between Miss Keeler and Mr. Profumo which Ivanov could have exploited. He seems to have spent much of the twenty-four hours in making such confidences to anyone who would listen to him. When Mr. Profumo had untruthfully denied his guilt to the House of Commons and an uneasy hush had fallen, Ward seemed to be relieved and to grow more confident.

But almost at once there were threats of another sort of trouble. The CID received a number of communications alleging that Ward was living on the immoral earnings of his girls, and that he was being protected from prosecution by his influential friends, and in April it started taking statements from a number of persons connected with him, including some of his patients.

When this reached his ears in May, he tried to defend himself
again by blackmail. For this purpose he had deliberately to
assume again the contacts he had taken such pains to abandon:
he had to become again a security risk. Making use of Mr.
Profumo quite as ruthlessly as Christine, he sent a letter confessing the truth of the Profumo-Ivanov-nuclear-arms story to the
Prime Minister, Mr. Harold Wilson, his Member of Parliament,
the national newspapers (which did not publish it), and the
Home Secretary. There could be no mistaking the purport of
this last letter: unless the police stopped their inquiries, the
truth about Mr. Profumo would be published. He took the
opportunity to involve his friend and patient Lord Astor, who
had lent him £500 three months before and had consented to
guarantee his overdraft up to £1500 a few days before. "It was by
accident," Ward wrote of Christine, "that she met Mr. Profumo
and through Lord Astor that she met him again. I intend to take
the blame no longer."

The blackmail failed. The government made up its mind to
set up an inquiry, and when Mr. Profumo realized this he confessed the truth. Ward found himself adrift in a world which
had become much more dangerous for him in the last few weeks.
Christine Keeler had suffered a complete collapse. On the tide of
her own hysteria she had been swept up and down Fleet Street,
out to Spain and back again, in and out of solicitors' offices, on a
continual merry-go-round swinging between Marylebone police
court and the Old Bailey, in and out of the witness box, in and
out of expensive flats rented by eccentrics with no visible means
of support, into motor crashes, back and forth through booing,
jeering, leering crowds. She was a pitiful sight. She remained
beautiful, but her beauty was now a thin veil worn by a sick and
grubby child. Her one salient characteristic was the desire for
respect; she would have enjoyed being the head of a women's
college. But external circumstances and her own will, which
seemed as indifferent to her well-being as if it too were external
to her, conspired without end to annul any possibility that she
should be respected. The same enmity between the will and the
self was visible in Ward. Considered as a sexual being, he was
the incarnation of a chemist's window in the Charing Cross
Road. Not merely did he offend the god of love; he insulted
Silenus. The bare catalogue of his efforts to degrade sensuality

below the level of charm would have been enough to alienate the court. Yet though he bore himself as if he were born on the side of authority, unalterably among those who passed judgment rather than among the judged, the unfortunate man kept on strengthening the case for his exclusion from honour. He actually handed himself over to his prosecutors. Yes, he had had relations with one of the prostitutes who had given evidence, a poor puny little waif who looked like a photograph of an Indian famine-relief poster. But that was natural, indeed it was inevitable. He had gone out late at night to buy cigarettes, and there, beside a cigarette machine, this waif had been standing. Well, that was enough, wasn't it? The two machines had been standing side by side, waiting for custom; of course he had taken the mobile one home. *Of course* he had, he insisted, though the judge, as a flash of gold had reminded us from time to time, was one of the few Englishmen who wear a wedding ring. It was no use for Ward to try to disguise what he was. The poor demented man, in spite of all his kindness, all his gifts, had committed himself to be a pimp. In him disloyalty had gone on the streets.

A little less than a quarter of a century had passed since Joyce had sat where Ward was sitting in the Old Bailey dock. The only similar quality in the men was their willingness to deal too obediently with another country, to their country's danger; otherwise the differences were extreme. Joyce was the apotheosis of the amateur, who was sustained only by his ideals and unsupported by any technique. He had broken out of England and fled to Germany as artlessly as a boy breaking out of an approved school; he had forced himself on the insufficiently organized propaganda system in Berlin as he might have joined the gipsies; when the end came he had to go out alone to flee the armies. Ward was the apotheosis of the professional: since there was a technique for helping foreign powers, he had acquired it, and when there had been a technical hitch he had met the technique of the police with the technique of legality. Joyce would never have been a pimp, nor would most of the traitors of World War II who had followed him into the dock; the nineteenth-century political dissenter practised innocence as a defence from conformist criticism. Ward was so much of a pimp that the charges which got him into the dock related to pimping, and when he died by his own hand after the sixth day of his trial, his death shocked into protest everyone who in his heart of hearts would have liked to be a pander.

Supposing, a surprisingly large number of people asked, that Ward had been procuring young women for rich men, was there anything so shocking about that? Surely it was archaic to regard with disfavour any action which promoted sexual intercourse? That was loudly asked, but in the overtones of the inquiry could be heard a rider: "particularly if there is money in it." Through the memory of those who had attended the Joyce trials there range the voice of the Scotsman who had raised a disturbance in the lobby of the House of Lords when the last appeal was lost, urging that when Joyce had left England to broadcast for the Nazis he had simply gone abroad to better himself, and there could be nothing wrong about that. "He had a fine position waiting for him, and he just took it." In 1945 this had been the cry of a lone eccentric. In 1963 he could have spoken for a considerable and not undistinguished part of England.

The Ward case had many ugly consequences. The crowds round the courts were uncommonly nasty. The witnesses had to walk through a vast leer, a huge concupiscent exposure of cheap dentures. The children were grown up who had been brought by their mothers to wait outside Wandsworth Jail while Joyce was being hanged; they were now bringing their own children to see these poor sluts on their way to humiliation. The show was perhaps at its grimmest in the Dickensian streets round the Marylebone police court. Christine Keeler was every afternoon led out by the police and put in her car, which was covered by a tent of photographers, who climbed on the footboards, the bonnet, and the roof. Then they fell away and their place was taken by a mob of women, mostly old or middle-aged, without exception illfavoured and unkempt, and shabby elderly men. Inside the car Christine Keeler sat in terrified dignity, her face covered with the pancake make-up which levels the natural toning of the skin, and her determination not to show her fear ironing out her features to the flatness of a mask. The cries and boos of the crowd expressed the purest envy. It was disagreeable to see a number of women candidly confessing that at the end of their days they bitterly resented not having enjoyed the happiness of being prostitutes, and a number of men in the same situation wishing they had been able to afford the company of prostitutes.

The passion of the mob was rushing in to fill a vacuum. It is natural for a community to think and feel and express itself when anything threatens its accustomed habit, so that it can explain the significance of the threat and take appropriate action. But the community did not know what to think or feel about the Ward-Profumo affair; it could not understand its significance and it most certainly could not promise itself that it could guard against the recurrence of just such a scandal. Obviously the ordinary penal mechanism did not work in this case. Mr. Profumo had had an affair with a young woman deeply involved in the disreputable; he had thus involved himself in the sphere of security; he had lied to the House of Commons, which is indeed a comprehensive insult to the English present and the English past. But none of these are punishable offences. The public would probably have felt better if the Foreign Office had been able to ask for the withdrawal of Ivanov from the Soviet embassy as a *persona non grata*. But, alerted by Ward, he had already gone back to Russia. Ward himself had been pursued by the law, but not for the offences which the community was so bitterly resenting, which led to the suspicion (fanned by the special character of the law under which he was charged) that he was being prosecuted out of revenge by an Establishment jealous of its own. Even Peter Rachman, the slum-landlord and club-owner who had kept Christine Keeler and Mandy Rice-Davies, could not be prosecuted, for the good reason that he was dead.

The fear caused by recognition that the law was not able to prevent or punish such gross misbehaviour was transmuted, for the sake of the community's self-respect, into a fear that the law was doing too much. Miss Keeler had had a series of long legal involvements with the West Indians, John Edgecombe and Lucky Gordon, who had both been sent to prison. Lucky Gordon appealed, and the Court of Criminal Appeal quashed his conviction in nine minutes. But it did not disclose the evidence which led it to this decision. There were three reasons which made this reticence inevitable. The Court of Appeal had received the evidence in a form difficult to discuss within its own limitations, which are crippling. The evidence must have referred to matters alluded to at the trial of Ward, which was still progressing. And as the Director of Public Prosecutions was not resisting the appeal, there was no case to be disproved by the judgment. But the public, by now thoroughly confused, misinterpreted the action of the court as an attempt to cover the derelictions of other branches of the law. The men in high places who had assumed the burden of responsibility became suspect, and so did their brothers whose irresponsibility had caused this crisis. It was felt that Ward's rich patrons had shown shocking disloyalty by not giving evidence at his trial. This was unjust; the defence would have called these men, and they could not have resisted the summons, if their evidence would have disproved the charges against Ward instead of confirming it. These public attitudes were absurd, yet they were founded on a vigilance of which England had need. Scepticism was necessary. The administration of the law had grown slipshod; there were to be several police scandals to prove it. It was true too that if Ward had gone too far out of the course prescribed by society, he had been paid to run the extra distance, and his wealthy paymasters were worse than he was, not being as daft as he was and capable enough to exercise considerable responsibility in other fields. But all the same, circumstances had intensified the natural reactions of the public to a paranoiac extreme.

The public's state of mind in England in 1963 was itself a historic event; and there was a resemblance to other historic events not too cheering. As Ward gave evidence, he summoned up from the past a shadow who has been no more than that for nearly fifty years: Prince Andronnikov. He was called as a witness before the tribunal convened by Kerensky in 1917 to inquire into the conduct of the war by the imperial government, and his evidence sticks in the mind because of its comic disreputability and a certain moral pretentiousness which Ward recalled. The tribunal could not find out what he really did and got a little peevish.

PRESIDENT: Let me put to you a straightforward question, what do you do? Who are you?

ANDRONNIKOV: I can only answer that I'm a man, a citizen, and I hope to be of some use in the world.

PRESIDENT: That is too abstract an answer. Speaking in concrete terms, who are you? What is your business?

ANDRONNIKOV: I find that question quite hard to answer. I've often asked myself the same thing, and I've said, "Well, thank God, I'm a human being who is interested in society as a whole, takes everything seriously, and wants to help, so far as he can."

Like Ward, he never seemed to have any money. But he was quite an active person, a man of good family, who had been in his youth one of the Corps des Pages at the Tsar's court and then became a well-known homosexual and pimp, finding acquiescent adolescents for his rich friends, and also acted as a paid contact man for a financial group controlling certain Russian transport and electricity corporations, largely owned by German stockholders. He not only pushed their claims with ministers and civil servants, he was able to establish a direct line with the court, where he established friendly relations with the personal secretary of the Tsar and the lady-in-waiting Anna Vyroubova, the hysterical simpleton who lived in Rasputin's pocket. He not only used these connections to safeguard the interest of German investors in his companies, but worked for German war aims with sufficient diligence to be described as a traitor, though it was probably more just to put it lower and say that, like Ward, he mucked about in the field of security. It is of relevance to Stephen Ward's case that the Kerensky government, though it had access to the tsarist archives and examined a number of hostile witnesses, could not discover exactly what he had been doing or how he had been paid. Later the bolsheviks resolved its uncertainties by shooting him. This is not one of the saddest episodes in history. But unfortunately they shot a large number of other people too.

If one wants to look further back for an analogy, there is the Affair of the Diamond Necklace, where an alliance between the criminal de la Mottes and a deluded cardinal, who was also a great aristocrat, led to unfounded suspicions of Marie Antoinette and inflamed an existing distrust of all existing social institutions. Nearer our own time, the Weimar Republic weltered in a succession of small scandals which made the German people feel that they were not being told what was going on and that the government was unable to punish the guilty and protect the innocent citizens from their depredations. That is apparently what a modern community cannot bear to feel, and it is to be remembered that such dynamic feelings can be engendered by such apparently powerless persons as the de la Mottes, Andronnikov, and Stephen Ward.

Conclusion

THERE is a case for the traitor. He is a sport from a necessary type. The relationship between a man and his fatherland is always disturbed if either man or fatherland be highly developed. A man's demands for liberty must at some point challenge the limitations the state imposes on the individual for the sake of the masses; and if he is to carry on the national tradition he must wrestle with those who, claiming to be traditionalists, desire to crystallize it at the point reached by the previous generation. It is our duty to readjust constantly the balance between public and private liberties. Men must be capable of imagining and executing and insisting on social change, if they are to reform or even maintain civilization, and capable too of furnishing the rebellion which is sometimes necessary if society is not to perish of immobility. Therefore all men should have a drop of treason in their veins, if the nations are not to go soft like so many sleepy pears.

But, all the same, there is a case against the traitor. The law states it with simple logic: if a state gives a citizen protection it has a claim to his allegiance, and if he gives it his allegiance it is bound to give him protection. But there are now other reasons for regarding treachery with disfavour, which grow stronger every year.

We are not yet within sight of disarmament. Our total population increases, and with it our population of scientists and industrialists, who continue to present the state with more and more intricate and terrible weapons, each arousing the curiosity of our neighbours. This curiosity can be satisfied partially by such devices as the monitoring which gives confirmation of the discharge of nuclear weapons on alien territories, and these are fair enough uses of scientific technique. But the other forms of espionage, such as are grouped under the title of "cloak and dagger," are becoming more and more objectionable.

361

The stories told in these pages have behind them a second story of huge unproductive expenditure, of lifelong labours which do not add one single grain to the world's resources. Lonsdale and the Krogers, Abel and Hayhanen, the grimy small fry which circulated round George Blake, these were maintained by the honest people who teach, doctor the sick, till the soil, work in factories, and are scholars and poets and scientists. Only one-eighth of an iceberg, they say, appears above the water; the proportion of detected espionage to the whole is probably considerably less. Facing the spies are the security officers, probably as numerous, unproductively engaged in catching the unproductive. The size of the bill is the more lamentable when it is considered that when a spy expensively succeeds in stealing a secret document and security officers expensively succeed in catching him, the document is probably obsolete by the time he has served half his term in prison; and that probably both spy and security officers are sufficiently gifted to have been capable of much sound productive work.

In this situation, as Vassall showed us, we are threatened by collaboration between the primary form of overpopulation and its secondary form: the excessive production of objects by an excessive number of people. The vast population excretes a number of documents so vast that a vast number of people have to be employed to work on them, so vast that it becomes impossible to buy their honesty by high wages and impossible to employ enough security officers to see that they keep their filing cupboards locked and take nothing secret home. The existence of a huge accumulation of unguarded secret documents extends the same invitation to thievery as the huge number of automobiles which have to be left in the street because their owners cannot buy garage-space. Treachery and allied misdemeanours thus cease to have the connection with idealism of which they could boast when the Fascists and the first Communist offenders stood in the dock against the Official Secrets Act. That idealism was never not disputable. But such men were all certainly interested in ideas, and that is to be interested in ideals at one remove. The kind of offences for which they were sentenced are, however, now committed by people who have no ideological interests at all but who have rejected all moral taboos and will pursue any prohibited activity, provided it brings them sufficient reward in money, power, or security.

This alters the whole character of the security field, partly because these purloiners of secrets have now to satisfy technical demands which make it possible to class the traitors of the past as amateurs and traitors of the present as professionals. Andronnikov could play his part by chattering to ministers and Rasputin, and Joyce could utter generalizations over the radio, but Vassall had to practise the advanced technique of photography as he learned it in the RAF. But there is a difference which goes deeper than that. When the spy becomes a man who has made a sweeping rejection of taboos and pursues other prohibited activities as well as espionage, his detection opens the door to a general suspicion of society. He will of necessity have found the paymasters for his illegal activities among the wealthy, and some of them are likely to be identified with one or other of our social institutions. It will also be difficult for the public not to believe that he was aided in his attack on national safety by the influence of these powerful persons for whose unsanctioned tastes he had catered. It can never be easy to prove or disprove these suspicions, for the reason that when such connivance exists it functions in secrecy, and that very often no such connivance exists, and it is still impossible to prove a negative. The public therefore suffers a sense of impotence, and in despair engages in the devaluation of values at a moment peculiarly unfavourable to the creation of new ones. The march towards civilization is interrupted, and on that journey, though we have eternity before us, we are always short of time.

At least we have large and able security organizations to protect us from our spies; and it is impossible not to applaud the courageous, shrewd, and patient men who work to preserve our national safety. Yet they too are a source of danger to the state The essential conditions of their being work out badly for themselves and everybody else. They can find the infinitesimally small proportion of the population which takes to spying only by subjecting large numbers of persons to restrictions on their freedom against which it is a good citizen's duty to protest, unless he is told the reason for them; and such explanation is often inadvisable from a security point of view. The officers are obliged to

work in the strictest secrecy, and this is unhealthy. No organization working under cover can remain fully efficient, least of all
one which is perpetually in danger of infiltration by the forces
which it is fighting. Yet it is necessary for the security organizations to work behind a veil, so necessary that the habit of secrecy
has to be cultivated until it becomes a monomania. The Denning Report tells us that the head of the Special Branch decided
not to interview Christine Keeler, for fear she might inform the
press that she had been interviewed by the Special Branch. This
was a calamity, for the whole Profumo scandal would have been
short-circuited by what she had to say; and it is impossible to
imagine that that highly desirable state of affairs would have been
discounted by any disadvantage arising out of the fact that the
public knew the interview had taken place.

This is but one example of the conflict between the secrecy
practised by the security organizations and the public good. A
more striking example, indeed, happened later in the summer of
1963. In March 1963, Harold Philby, who had been named "the
third man" in the Burgess and Maclean case, disappeared from
Lebonon, where he had been representing *The Observer* and
The Economist, and in July it was known that he had gone
behind the Iron Curtain. There was perhaps no immediate political implication in his flight at all. He was a close friend of Guy
Burgess, who had fallen ill with a mortal sickness, and was to die
later in the year. Mr. Heath, Lord Privy Seal, was obliged to admit to the House of Commons that at the time of the disappearance of Burgess and Maclean it had become known that Mr.
Philby had had Communistic associations and that he had been
asked to resign from the Foreign Service in July 1951, which he
did; but that now, twelve years later, he had admitted that he had
worked for the Soviet authorities before 1946 and that he had in
fact warned Maclean through Burgess that the security services
were about to take action against him. Again it must be noted
that this is an incomprehensible statement. It does not explain
why a Soviet agent in England, certainly in touch with local
agents, could be warned that he was being watched by English
security agents only by another Soviet agent in America who sent
a third all the way to England to tell him so. Soviet intelligence
has better communications than that. This cannot be the story.

But let that rest. Mr. Philby was now officially recognized as part of a Soviet apparatus, which had long been known to many persons on both sides of the Atlantic. This exasperated Mr. Marcus Lipton, the MP for Brixton, who in the year 1955 had said the very same things about Mr. Philby that Mr. Heath was now saying, had received no end of a dressing-down from government spokesmen, and had made a very handsome apology to Mr. Philby. It shows the moral degradation of the Soviet agent's life that Mr. Philby could accept that apology. This revelation of Mr. Lipton's wrong exasperated the public, and their rage mounted when the editors of *The Observer* and *The Economist* disclosed that they had employed Mr. Philby as their correspondent at the direct suggestion of an official of the Foreign Office. It was then stated, and generally believed, that even in the Middle East Mr. Philby had continued to have connections with British Intelligence. This was not a helpful contribution to our national well-being in the summer of 1963.

The government would have been well advised to specify the reasons which had made the security organizations so long nourish this viper in their bosoms, and to announce the resignation of some of the bosoms. But this was not done, and the Philby affair is an unhealed sore in the public mind. Doubtless there were sound reasons for this failure to solve the mystery, but all the same the sore did not heal. If we try to solve the mystery by speculation, we are forced to recall that persons who work in a self-contained unit are apt to develop theories which develop none the better for never being subjected to open discussion. The security organizations have shown a disposition to believe that by skilful manipulation they can persuade Communists that communism is not incompatible with patriotism, and they will be drawing the Soviet Union and the West closer together if they act as British agents. This is a preposterous theory. A Communist might collaborate with an England which had gone Fascist, because Fascists and Communists share the doctrine of totalitarianism, and what Stalin and Hitler once did, men could do again. But a Communist could not collaborate with a democratic England because he is in love with its opposite. Failure to recognize this truth led the security organizations to load themselves up with some terrible material in the Second World War; and it is possible that for the same reason they acquired Mr. Philby. If they had to air their theories they would have been laughed out of this one; but obviously security organizations can air neither their theories not their practice.

This situation is not static. It will develop, and a melodramatic pessimism might envisage its development as hideous. The world might be dotted with huge weapon-making installations and huge bureaucratic office buildings in which all the workers would be degraded by inhibiting controls, and distracted by suspicion of their fellows, owing to the operations of espionage coldly organized by professional criminals. These would be found in mass, with their talents highly trained, and their powers of expenditure a menace to society, since such espionage would go on the budgets of foreign powers who could pay them highly because they would buy secrets as a cheaper alternative to researches and experimental constructions on the monstrous scale necessitated by modern scientific discovery. In such a vicious world a government could not form a respectable image of itself or its functions. It would toil on, perhaps sustained only by memories of our age (which might look quite agreeable, seen from the angle of such a future), nervously cultivating distrustful and joyless alliances, and giving up any hope of not being a police state. The security organizations would be no help. They would have to operate in more stringent secrecy than ever. They would be therefore even more subject to infiltration, which would reinforce the endemic distrust and might even lead to conquest by alien powers. If they resisted that temptation, they might form peculiar and too simple political theories which would lead them to perpetrate those nasty events known as "palace revolutions" or exercise a tyranny by threatening such uprisings, in the tiresome manner of the Praetorian Guard.

This will not happen. Though men draw many straight lines, they are not, except in fantasy, prolonged into infinity. Here and there our kind has gone on doing what it ought not to do till it nearly died of it, but there would not be so many of us alive today if our forefathers had not obeyed a deep-seated instinct to stop before it was too late. But we may go a very long way to that nightmare future if we do not regard espionage with a realistic eye. If nuclear weapons were used they would inflict the most hideous damage on the human kind; such as would survive might find survival not worth while. But nuclear weapons have not been used since the error born of ignorance which was committed in Japan eighteen years ago, and it is to be doubted whether they will ever be used again. But in modern espionage there is being used, day in and day out, a weapon which inflicts on society considerable spiritual and material devastation. Let anyone who does not consider the life of George Blake as horrible consider the poor rats who, fawning, brought him titbits of lethal gossip out of the maimed city of Berlin. It makes civilization impossible if the government has to suspect the governed of participation in such squalor and tease them with constricting routines, which the governed cannot accept with a sense of necessity because they know that the government is itself involved in that squalor. The expenditure of wealth on munitions has many times been denounced; but it is not less disgusting to pour it out on the promotion of theft and deceit.

There is no immediate remedy. The unilateral abandonment of espionage is the only real remedy, and this is as unpractical as unilateral disarmament; and obviously multilateral disarmament must precede the multilateral abandonment of espionage. Nevertheless there are some holes which can be stopped up. The cutting down of our embassies behind the Iron Curtain to a skeleton staff is obviously advisable; and in the opinion of experts such as Commander Anthony Courtney, MP, it is feasible. If it is not, the modern development of communication is a mockery. There is also the proposal, espoused by the Tory government and apparently favoured by the Labour Party, to set up a standing commission on security. This would have a judicial chairman and be composed of retired civil servants and officers of the armed services experienced in security matters, and the Prime Minister would decide when it was to be brought into use, having consulted the leader of the Opposition. If ever the commission found it desirable to have powers to compel evidence, then it would be converted into a tribunal of inquiry under the 1921 act; and again before this could be done there would have to be consultation between the Prime Minister and the leader of the Opposition, though the Labour Party seems more likely to have recourse to the appointment of select committees of the House on such occasions.

The intention behind the creation of this new body is to lift security matters out of party politics, and this is indeed necessary. Security is literally concerned with security: with safety:

with the survival of this country and, indeed, this globe. It is disgusting that at least a third of any Parliamentary debate on security consists of partisan jabber. The commission would also for the first time give security a voice of its own. The public knows nothing of treachery and espionage except what it hears from the lips of ministers in the Houses of Parliament, or from counsel and judges at the trials of persons charged with offences against the Treason or Official Secrets Acts, or from the press. Of these three sources the last has been much the most reliable. The press is often vulgar, because, like all commercial enterprises, it tends to adapt itself to the tastes of its customers, and large numbers of these demand vulgarity. But, vulgar or not, it has brought striking ability and courage to this particular duty of telling the public what is happening to national security in our times. The work done on the Burgess and Maclean case by the *Daily Express,* for example, informed the community of a series of gross administrative blunders indicative of a degree of eccentricity in the standards of permanent officials which required correction. But the press works under severe handicaps. One of these may be its own sensationalism; but that there are others, and those not to its discredit, will be realized if it be considered just how a conscientious editor could have discharged his duty of telling his readers the truth about Mr. Harold Philby. It is to be hoped that the standing commission would prevent such unfortunate happenings.

But once security is given a public voice, that is to say a public identity, it is certain to become the object of a Communist assault such as has not been previously experienced in Great Britain. If the United States had been the venue of the achievements of Fuchs, Nunn May, the Portland spy ring, Vassall, or Blake, or Barbara Fell, their innocence would have been maintained day in day out from the moment of their arrest till long after their trial, and attacks would have been made on all persons concerned with their trials. The probity of the prosecuting counsel, magistrates, and judges alike would be attacked, and every witness giving evidence against them would be denounced as a Titus Oates. Hence a large number of Americans form the opinion that there is no such thing as a Communist spy and never has been, and against this another large section of the population reacts by coming to believe that everybody is a Communist spy and always will be. An American who considers an espionage case with the same balance and detachment that he would bring to a case of robbery with violence or grave larceny has to exercise unusual independence of judgment. In Great Britain the public is protected from a like situation because of our laws, which prevent comment on cases *sub judice* and protect the bench from criticism. But it can hardly be doubted that, if British security were given a public personality in the standing committee, this would become a target for dishonest attack in the Communist interests. This will face the public with a new challenge.

Treachery is a problem we will have to live with for a long time, and the nearest we can come to a solution is to recognize the problem for what it is. The man tempted to become a traitor will be helped if public opinion keeps it clear before him that treachery is a sordid and undignified form of crime. It is not necessary to hate him. Few of us spend much time hating burglars, but the community has established that burglary is not in its opinion an honourable or humanitarian profession, and this ill repute, coupled with our penal laws, constitutes a useful deterrent. Even so we should abandon all sentimentality in our views of the traitor, and recognize him as a thief and a liar. He may be other things; a criminal is very rarely simply a criminal. But to a marked degree the traitor is also a thief and a liar.

But beyond that we must be quick to detect and frustrate the effect of treachery. The traitor can change the community into a desert haunted by fear, and it is our business to realize what force is at work and change it back again. Loyalty has always had its undramatic but effective answer to treason, insisting on its preference for truth instead of deceit, and good faith instead of bad. But on occasion the answer has to be framed more cleverly than at other times, and ours is a period when it becomes no answer at all, but a pact with treachery, if it be not dictated by caution and fastidiousness. We must keep our clear sight; we must not, for example, blind ourselves to the knowledge that the Rosenbergs faced death with magnificent courage. We must reject evil and dispel suspicion without falling into the error of confusing unpopular forms of virtue with evil. We must remember that quite noble attempts to defeat evil may, in sufficiently perverse circumstances, be mistaken for evil; and unfounded suspicions may be engendered. Since the traitor's offence is that he conspires against the liberty of his fellow countrymen to choose their way of life, we ally ourselves with him if we try to circumvent him by imposing restrictions on the liberty of the individual which interfere with the legitimate business of his soul. It is true that such issues do not often arise. The story told in these pages shows that we would have been spared a great deal of trouble if we had simply kept our cupboards locked and had removed from our public service officials who were habitually blind drunk. But if we do not keep before us the necessity for uniting care for security with determination to preserve our liberties, we may lose our cause because we have fought too hard. Our task is equivalent to walking on a tightrope over an abyss, but the continued survival of our species through the ages shows that, if we human beings have a talent, it is for tightrope-walking.

Index

371